SOUTH AFRICA'S
BORDER
1966 WAR 1989

WILLIAM STEENKAMP

Photographs by Al J. Venter

SOUTH AFRICA'S
BORDER
1966 WAR 1989

Helion & Company

Helion & Company Limited
26 Willow Road
Solihull
West Midlands
B91 1UE
England
Tel. 0121 705 3393
Fax 0121 711 4075
Email: info@helion.co.uk
Website: www.helion.co.uk
Twitter: @helionbooks
Visit our blog http://blog.helion.co.uk/

Originally published by Ashanti Publishing (Pty) Ltd 1989.
This edition published by Helion & Company Limited.
Original edition – design and layout by Axel Adelbert and Dieter Mandlmeier;
typeset by Pointset, Randburg; final proofs by Leona Labuschagne. This edition
managed by Bookcraft Limited, Stroud, Gloucestershire.
Cover designed by Bruce Gonneau, email beeatbyrne@gmail.com
Printed by Henry Ling Limited, Dorchester, Dorset

Text © Willem Steenkamp
Cover photograph © Al J. Venter

The unique collection of photographs assembled for this
book comes from many sources. Most of the photographs
were taken by Al J. Venter. Others were taken by professional photographers or photo-
journalists, some by people – soldiers, policemen or civilians – who happened to be on the
spot with (usually) an unauthorised camera. Because they come from so many sources, some
obscure, the original publishers of this book decided not to provide the usual list of credits.
However, they would like to thank the *Cape Times* newspaper of Cape Town for making
available a number of file photographs of the various personalities who featured in the border
war at one time or another.

ISBN 978 1 909982 01 7

British Library Cataloguing-in-Publication Data.
A catalogue record for this book is available from the British Library.

For details of other military history titles published
by Helion & Company Limited contact the above
address, or visit our website: http://www.helion.co.uk.

We always welcome receiving book proposals from
prospective authors.

CONTENTS
SOUTH AFRICA'S BORDER WAR 1966-1989

PART I How the war began – and how it ended

PART II The war in close-up

FOREWORD
A GENERATION OF WAR

Southern Africa's longest war effectively ended on November 1 of 1988, when South Africa and the South West African People's Organisation finally called it quits, 23 long years after the first shot had been fired. It had gone on for so long that for several generations of people of all races it was hard to believe that peace had come; that (on the South African side at least) a father and son could be wearing the same campaign medal for fighting on the same front but 15 years apart. In the latter stages, in fact, the brunt of the war was borne on both sides by young men who had not even been conceived when it had started.

This book is not a detailed history of what is popularly known as "the border war", but an attempt to paint its broad extent in words and show some of its detail in close-up by way of pictures. The definitive histories on both sides will come later, when the dust of battle has settled enough for most of the facts to be released. Till then, a book like this will serve to give some sort of profile to a struggle which was so protracted and of such low intensity generally that it has acquired a curious shapelessness, even to those who spent years of their lives fighting in it.

There is a good deal of politics in this book, but this is unavoidable because the border conflict was a highly political war at all times. The full political background would be enough to fill several volumes; because just enough has been included to place the narrative in perspective, very little has been said about the other ventures in which South Africa was involved up to 1989, such as the raids it launched into other neighbouring territories.

By the nature of things this book views the war mainly from the South African side because that is where most of the statistical and other published material, both official and non-official, was available. An effort (largely successful, we hope) has been made to verify most of the facts used, either by comparison or by deduction, and public statements by both sides are, of course, a matter of record. Our overall conclusions appear in the Epilogue, so that the reader will have ample opportunity to study the unvarnished narrative of the war before turning his thoughts towards formulating his own final judgement.

It is inevitable that some readers will suspect the provenance of this book. To them let us say that it is not an official or "authorised" work, except in the sense that the South African Defence Force agreed to place at my disposal certain material, such as statistics and photographs, which had not previously been released for publication (although most of the book is based on readily accessible published material). The SADF has not censored it for opinions or conclusions.

Efforts have been made to ensure that the book is as accurate as possible. However, there are probably some errors of fact and deduction, because the book was put together from many different sources, published and unpublished, and there is no other accurate narrative to compare it with. In fact, this is the first time that an alpha-to-omega narrative of the border war has been written. How it will stand up to the standard histories that are still to appear is for posterity to judge.

The reader will notice that at various stages of the book I refer to the territory north of the Orange River as "South West Africa" and "South West Africa/Namibia" and never as "Namibia". This is simply a matter of historical accuracy; in order to avoid becoming embroiled in the argument about who was responsible for the territory in its latter years I use the name by which it was officially known by the power in actual control (South Africa) at the time in question. Strictly speaking, "Namibia" is the territory's post-independence name, and the period covered by this book stops well short of that date. To talk about "Namibia" when dealing with 1964, therefore, would be as historically incorrect as to refer to the Rhodesia of 1975 as "Zimbabwe" or the 1979 Zimbabwe-Rhodesia as "Rhodesia".

Left
This was the reality of what it was like to be a fighting soldier in the bush war: Grime and a stubbled chin, clothing stripped to the basic T-shirt and trousers, foam-rubber to soften the endless chafing of your webbing, a dirty cloth band around your forehead to keep away the abundant sweat that might fog your eyes for those crucial

PROLOGUE
THE LAND BEYOND THE ORANGE

To understand the border war it is necessary also to know something about the territory which, in the past 200 years, has been called by various names, most recently South West Africa/ Namibia and now Namibia.

Physically it is immense, particularly by the cramped standards of many nations in Europe and elsewhere: 823 000 square kilometres, bounded in the west by the Atlantic Ocean, in the east by Botswana, in the south by South Africa and in the north by Angola. Most of it is an elevated plateau between 900 and 1 200 metres above sea-level, with mountain ranges running north to south for most of its length.

It is, to use a worn-out phrase, a land of contrasts. It has an almost infinite variety of terrain; often the landscape varies so abruptly and dramatically that the traveller can scarcely believe that he is still inside the same set of borders. It has the Namib, one of the oldest deserts in the world, that runs down its western side and forms the bleak, harshly beautiful littoral that is known as the "Skeleton Coast" because it is a centuries-old killer of men and ships, although it is redeemed by the diamonds and other minerals found under its deadly sands. The south and east vary from dry bushveld to semi-desert, while north of the central high-grass plains one finds typical African savannah country, flat bushveld which is well-watered in the summer by torrential rains.

The seeker can find soft beauty within its borders, or towering sand-dunes, or rock formations so strange that his heart quakes. Often he will hate it at first sight - and then, after a while, find that it has quietly stolen his affections. It has been said of many a place that "it only makes you weep twice - when you see it the first time and when you leave". That is true of many territories … but it is probably truest of the land that the travel-writer Lawrence Green once described as "the last frontier".

For thousands of years the land between the Orange and Cunene Rivers lay almost unknown to anyone except its inhabitants, protected from the outside world by the barrier of the ferocious Namib desert, which runs along the entire coast-line and up into neighbouring Angola. Foreigners did not take serious notice of it before the late 18th Century, and till about 130 years ago it had no name or corporate entity.

The first inhabitants of the south were probably the nomadic hunter-forager Bushmen (this name is now going out of favour in academic and liberal circles, who prefer "San", even though it translates literally as "robbers"), but they were gradually displaced by the Namas (more properly "Namaqua"), ethnic Hottentots who had lived on either side of the Orange River before gradually expanding north-wards.

At approximately the same time the negroid people now known as the Bergdamara ('Mountain Damara') also moved into the territory and were promptly enslaved by the Namas, although many eventually escaped from their bondage and found refuge in the remote mountains of the north-west.

In the north, the oldest inhabitants were seven tribes of blacks, now commonly known collectively as the Ovambos, agriculturists who had trekked down from the lakes district of East Africa around the middle of the 16th Century and settled on either side of the Cunene River (it is commonly accepted by most people that the Ovambos constitute one people composed of seven sub-tribes, but Andreas Shipanga - of whom more later - says that this is a misconception resulting from an early missionary's wrong understanding of his Herero guide's exclamation of "Ovombo! Ovombo" (There they are, the people you are looking for), and that "in fact there is no such thing as an Ovambo nation, an Ovambo language or an Ovambo culture. The seven tribes are quite distinct".

East of the seven tribes lived the Kavangos, a related group which had also originated in the East African lakes area, moved down through what is now south-eastern Angola and settled south of the great Kavango River between 1750 and 1800. At some stage, too, the warlike cattle-owning Hereros drifted down from Northern and Central Africa and settled for some considerable time in the inhospitable Kaokoland before all but two tribes - the Ovahimba and Ovatjimba - moved on to the greener pastures of the territory's midlands region towards the end of the 18th Century.

In the early 19th Century five tribes of "Oorlams" Hottentots from the Cape entered the territory and settled in the south. The Oorlams (the word is said to derive from the Malayan "Orang Lama", meaning people who are wide-awake) were technologically advanced by local standards, having absorbed not only some of the Cape colonists' social and organizational structures but also their knowledge of firearms, and they were to change

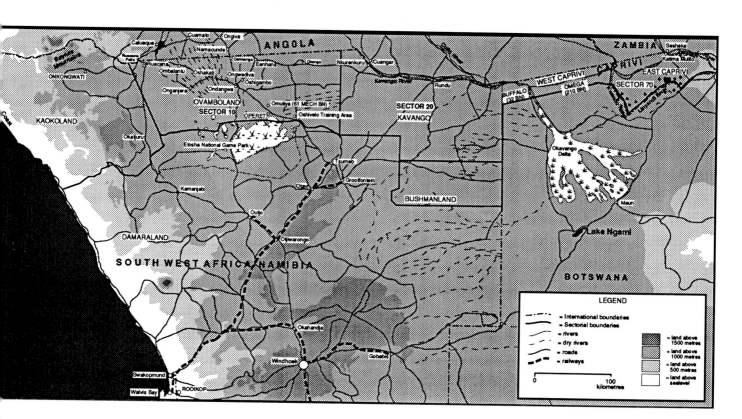

Above

Chief Hendrik Witbooi, hereditary leader of the Witbooi Hottentots, with his Mauser carbine at the age of 80, shortly before he died of wounds while fighting the Germans during the 1904 rebellion. His hat is covered with the white cloth that was the trademark of the Witboois

the face of the territory and give it the nearest thing it has ever had to a common language, Afrikaans.

Barring the downtrodden Bergdamara and the elusive Bushmen, all these groups were typical frontiersmen, aggressive and land-hungry; and the 19th Century was a time of almost continual warfare, particularly between the two great cattle-owning nations, the Namas and the Hereros, both of whom expanded relentlessly northwards and southwards in search of more water and grazing for their herds.

This expansion resulted directly in the rise of one of the territory's greatest war-leaders, an Oorlams chief named Jonker Afrikaner. Asked by the non-Oorlams Nama tribes to help against the Hereros, he attacked them in the late 1830s and drove them out of Namaland, settling his tribe at a pleasant location in the midlands which he named Windhoek.

Jonker then proceeded to make his name as the most fearsome robber-baron in the territory's history, impoverishing the Hereros by constant pillaging – an example many of the other Namas followed, albeit with less success.

When Jonker died in 1860 and was replaced by his weakling son, Christiaan, it signalled a resurgence for the Hereros. Led by the great Paramount Chief Maherero, they mauled the Afrikaner tribe at the Battle of Otjimbingue in 1863, among the dead being Christiaan himself. His successor, Jan Jonker Afrikaner, concluded an alliance with another Oorlams tribe, the Swartboois, and counter-attacked, only to be utterly defeated in a fierce battle south of Rehoboth, which in the meantime had been settled by the Basters, a people of mixed racial ancestry who had come up from the Cape.

Soon afterwards, in 1864, the Hereros enlisted the help of the famed explorer Charles John Andersson and attacked the Namas to the south-east of Windhoek, putting them to flight. This was

the start of years of intermittent warfare, occasional massacres and shifting alliances involving not only the Hereros and Namas but white missionaries and traders, trekking Boers from south of the Orange River and an assortment of explorers, hunters and naturalists. In the meantime the Cape Colony, a self-governing British possession, annexed Walvis Bay – an action which was to have important consequences in later years, since it was the territory's only really viable port.

Up to this time the territory had been popularly known as "Great Namaland" in the south and "Damaraland" in the north. Then Andersson coined the name "South-Western Africa" to cover both areas, although this was not the beginning of a national identity; for several decades more the territory was to remain what it always had been, a cockpit of sporadically warring clans and tribes.

In 1884 occurred an event which was to lead directly to the present situation. The Germans, who had set out on a belated search for an overseas empire, obtained a foothold at what was to become Luderitz on the inhospitable southern coast, agreed to the hard-pressed Hereros' request for a protectorate (a favour the latter were to regret) and proceeded to expand inland. Soon the process was complete, and for the first time the territory between the Orange and Cunene acquired a corporate identity (at least as far as the outside world was concerned) under the name "German South West Africa".

For 30 years the imperial flag waved over German South West. The Germans were energetic developers who provided the territory with its first roads, railways, health services and structure of civil government. At the same time they ruled it sternly and, as with all colonial powers, frequently without much concern for their subjects' property and other rights.

Thanks partly to this and partly to the local inhabitants' reluctance to part with either their

independence or their former way of life, the Germans were involved in a long series of tribal wars in which they fought alone at times and in concert with various factions of the local inhabitants at others.

The last major wars of colonial times occurred just before and just after the turn of the century. In 1891 the Oorlams Witbooi tribe under its famous chief, Hendrik Witbooi, rose in rebellion and fought a three-year guerrilla war against the Germans which ended in Witbooi's defeat and the proclamation of a German protectorate. In 1904 the 80 000-odd Hereros, angered by German encroachment on their land, turned their backs on their 1885 treaty of protection against the Namas and took up arms under their revered chief Samuel Maherero; they were soon joined by the aged Hendrik Witbooi, while elements of another Nama tribe, the Bondelswarts, fought their own war against the Germans under the soon-to-be-famed bushveld general Jakob Morenga, a man of mixed Nama and Damara ancestry.

The result was the bitterest and most sanguinary war in the territory's history. The Germans soon recovered from their initial reverses; reinforced by large numbers of well-trained soldiers and marines (a total of 14 000 by the end of hostilities) they went on the offensive, and by 1905 had gained the upper hand.

By the time the war petered out in 1907, both sides had paid a terrible price. No fewer than 2 000 Germans had died, while the Nama rebels had been defeated and Hendrik Witbooi had died of wounds, but the proud, warlike Hereros suffered most of all. The Germans had crushed them with the utmost

Above
A typical traditional Ovambo Kraal — surrounded by a log palisade, its entrance cunningly devised to confuse and delay anyone seeking entrance with malicious intent. It is a design dating back to the days when enemies came armed with assegais and bows instead of automatic weapons and rocket-launchers

Left Top
The Ongwediva teachers' training college near Oshakati a strange architectural blend of tribalism and futurism, a hotbed of political activity during the border war and sporadically the target of Swapo bomb attacks

Left Below
The war brought the army to Kaokoland — and the army brought food and money. Here a soldier hands out bucketsful of mealie meal to Kaokolanders during a drought

Above
General Von Trotha, who broke the Hereros with the utmost ferocity

Opposite Top
The Zambesi near the tip of Caprivi, a common border for no fewer than four Southern African countries. *Inset:* A Masubia fisherman in his tree-trunk "makoro" canoe. The Zambesi's fish feed thousands of Caprivians

Opposite Below
Cruelly beautiful, the sharp-toothed ridges march into Kaokoland from the equally inhospitable Skeleton Coast

Below
Herero warriors after being captured by General Von Trotha. Thousands of others — men, women and children — had died, and thousands more had fled

ferocity; as a result, two-thirds of them were dead or had fled to what is now Botswana, where about 40 000 of their descendants live to this day, and for many years scientists feared that those remaining in South West Africa had dwindled below the point of recovery. Only the northern tribes such as the Ovambos and Kavangos had not suffered, and but for the Herero War the territory's ethnic (and therefore political) composition would have been very different today.

One tribal war the Germans did not win involved the Ovambos, a peaceable enough people unless provoked, when – as combatants on both sides of the border war later proved – they were liable to fight fiercely. The Germans had left the Ovambos more or less alone during most of their tenure in South West Africa, but when it seemed in 1905 that they intended taking firmer control of Ovamboland, King Nehale of the major Ondonga tribe raised an army of about 1 000 men and attacked the northernmost military post of Namutoni. After some fighting the garrison fled southwards; the Ondongas sacked the little fort and returned home in triumph with a herd of pedigreed dairy cattle. The Germans left them alone after that and the industrious Ondongas proceeded to upgrade their own herds by means of their looted animals.

Then in 1915 the South Africans invaded on behalf of Britain and conquered the Germans. After World War I the League of Nations entrusted South West Africa to South Africa as a Class C mandate, to be governed as a virtual extra province for the betterment of its inhabitants. The mandate laid down certain requirements and required the South African government to report annually to the League of Nations.

It is interesting to note that Class C mandates were created to provide for territories which, the League of Nations had concluded, were not capable of being turned into viable independent states, and in fact the mandate did not have any provision for the granting of eventual self-government, or impose any legal restriction on the way in which the mandatory power was to apply its laws to the territory.

When the moribund League of Nations officially died immediately after World War II South Africa undertook to continue administering South West Africa in the spirit of the old mandate, although

denying that ultimate responsibility had passed from the League of Nations to the United Nations. The UN, however, maintained unsuccessfully that South West Africa should be placed under its trusteeship.

South West Africa's northern border, which had always been a vague one, was finally settled in the early 1920s, mainly at the insistence of the Portuguese. The result can be seen from the map: a typical colonial boundary, running die-straight from west to east without account being taken of the local circumstances. As a result, parts of the seven tribes found themselves living north of the border; they did not take kindly to this and Mandume, king of the largest, the Kwanyama, died when he resisted a joint South African-Portuguese force in 1924. In the main, however, the South Africans left the seven tribes alone, and apart from some missionaries and a few government officials, white faces were few and far between in Ovamboland. But the seven tribes never regarded the border as anything except a transient and unnatural thing, and this was to have a distinct effect on the course of the border war which broke out decades later.

During the 1920s and 1930s there had been considerable pressure from inhabitants, mainly the whites, that South West Africa should be incorporated into South Africa, but matters did not come to a head till 1946, when the government of Field Marshal Jan Smuts (ironically enough, one of the founders of the UN) sought approval from the world body to do so.

The UN refused on the grounds that the inhabitants had not yet attained self-government and therefore could not give their opinion on the matter. Smuts accepted this ruling and undertook to submit reports for the information (but not action) of the UN; but this practice stopped almost immediately when the UN used a 1947 report as the basis of criticising South African policies and practices in South West Africa.

In 1949 the government of Smuts's successor, Dr D F Malan, granted South West Africa a greater measure of autonomy. The all-white Legislative Assembly which had been founded after World War I became a fully elected body and substantial numbers of governmental functions were transferred to it, so that it enjoyed greater autonomy than any of South Africa's own provinces. At the same time South Africa remained in overall control and South West Africa was represented in the South African Parliament by six MPs and four senators.

In 1949 the first of several World Court cases on South West Africa started when the UN requested a ruling on South West Africa's status. The World Court deliberated about this till 1950, when it ruled that the UN had inherited the League's supervisory functions, but that South Africa had no legal obligation to transfer South West Africa to UN trusteeship, and could modify the territory's international status with the UN's consent.

The UN accepted this ruling, but South Africa disputed the contention that the mandate lived on under UN trusteeship. Thus were laid the foundations of the long wrangle over South West Africa.

In 1953 the UN appointed a committee to report on conditions in South West Africa because South Africa had refused to do so, and in 1955 and 1956 the issue of who should control South West Africa twice more ended up in the World Court.

At this stage the seeds of the eventual South West African insurgency were sown, 1 400km away

from the territory itself, when a 33-year-old former railway policeman and World War II veteran called Herman Toivo ja Toivo living in Cape Town founded a political movement called the Ovambo People's Congress.

Before embarking on the story of the border war, we should say something about the population of what is soon to be Namibia. The territory lacks many things, but most of all it lacks people. In its entire vast extent - three times the size of West Germany - there live just over a million people; in November of 1986 the then General Officer Commanding South West Africa, Major-General Georg Meiring, put it even more aptly when he described SWA/Namibia as being four-fifths the size of South Africa ... but with the same population as the Transvaal city of Germiston.

The last census, taken at the height of the border war in 1981, gave the population total as 1 033 200 (expected to rise to 1 252 000 by 1988) and the mix as follows: 506 000 (623 000 by 1988) Ovambos; 95 000 Kavangos (117 000); 76 400 whites (80 000), mainly of Afrikaans, English and German ancestry; 76 300 Hereros (94 000); 76 200 Damara (94 000); 48 500 Namas (60 000); 42 300 coloured (51 000); 38 600 Caprivians (47 000); 29 400 Bushmen (36 000); 25 200 Rehoboth Basters (31 000); 6 700 Batswana, mainly drifted over from neighbouring Botswana (7 000); and 12 000 "others" (12 000).

There has been a considerable amount of urbanisation, but most of these groups are still closely linked to their traditional stamping-grounds. The Kaokolanders, Ovambos, Kavangos and Caprivians have traditional tribal homelands in the far north, immediately below the border with Angola. The whites, Hereros and coloureds mainly inhabit the central part of the country and the Namas the dry south. The demographic distribution largely determined the battle zone in the border war: it is no accident that most of the infiltration and fighting took place in Central Ovamboland, for that is where about 25 percent of all SWA/Namibians live, including the Kwanyama and Ondonga tribes.

It is an indication of the low intensity of the border war that during its course the population increased rather than declined, and no part of the territory was laid waste. It is remarkable, in fact, how little the struggle impinged on daily life in SWA/Namibia.

South of the black tribal areas it was always barely noticeable except for the occasional urban bomb blast and a couple of small-scale Swapo raids on white-owned farms in the midlands, and in places such as Ovamboland the regional economies actually benefited from the conflict; ironically, probably the greatest consequence of the war was the accelerated abolition of most segregation laws and the inclusion of blacks in the previously all-white administration, so that by 1988 the territory's internal government was mainly non-white.

Above
The Ovahimba and Ovatjimba clans — left behind in Kaokoland when the other Hereros moved south centuries ago — still remain locked into the ancient rhythm of their traditional folkway

Above Left
Windhoek in 1960, at the time of the Old Location shootings

Opposite Top
A motorcycle patrol takes time out to visit a cuca shop — and perhaps buy a couple of bottles of the soft drinks it advertises. About 12 000 little Ovambo shops like this did a roaring trade with soldiers and civilians alike ... even though the Cuca beer which gave them their generic name stopped coming down from Angola when the border slammed shut in 1976

Opposite Below
A long-disused border post, its bullet-pocked walls testifying to the fact that the thud of rubber stamps had long since given way to the metallic chatter of assault rifles

Left
An Ovambo child, aping his elders. Many who were this age when the war started were adults by the time it ended ... and many others were dead

Following Page
Battered and streaked with rust, this sign says it all. Till well into the 1970s, much of the border was even less formal than this

PART I

HOW IT BEGAN –
AND HOW IT ENDED

1957–1973

The beginning of the South West African/Namibian insurgency can be traced back to the day in 1957 when a group of expatriate Ovambos working in Cape Town decided to found a political movement called the Ovambo People's Organisation, later the Ovambo People's Congress.

One of the leading figures in the new-born OPO was a 33-year-old former railway policeman and World War II veteran called Andimba or Herman Toivo ja Toivo who belonged to the Modern Youth Society, a multi-racial organisation strongly linked to the South African Communist Party, which aimed at supporting "national liberation movements".

Two of the other early members were men whose names, like Toivo's, were destined to stalk the South West African military and political scene for the next three decades: Andreas Shipanga and Sam Daniel Nujoma.

It is commonly believed that the OPO was a black nationalist political movement from its inception. By Andreas Shipanga's account this was not so. The OPO started, he says, mainly as a labour organisation, aimed primarily at destroying the migrant-labour system by which thousands of Ovambos and Kavangos were hired on two-year contracts to go and work in other parts of South West Africa. It was a much-hated system, run without much compassion or interest in the workers' welfare, and was the target for condemnation by many organisations (including, although this is not generally known, the Dutch Reformed Church). The body responsible for running the system, the South West African Native Labour Association, also owned all the substantial shops in Ovamboland (although not the thousands of little "Cuca shops"), and, says Shipanga, the OPO also aimed "to break the SWANLA monopoly" (both of these things came to pass long before the border war ended).

Nevertheless, it must have been obvious to the founder-members that at some stage the OPO would enter the broader political arena. The OPO was a child of its times; independence was in the African air, and in many countries political movements had started as labour organisations. Why not in South West Africa as well? Shipanga himself says that when Ghana became the first black African state to achieve independence, "it was an inspiration to us. Kwame Nkrumah had been imprisoned by the British and had subsequently won freedom for his country: why shouldn't we?"

South West Africa, a land riven by its history of ethnic warfare, did not have a clear vision of itself as a nation, but a national identity was developing slowly, and no doubt the men who founded the OPC were well aware of the fact that their tribal group had a built-in advantage because it made up nearly half of the sparse population.

Shipanga, however, claims there was a different reason: "If the name of the party seems at odds with its membership – after all, its leaders and membership were drawn from the different tribes of Namibia – there was a purpose behind it. Although SWANLA recruited its contract labourers only from among the Ovambos and Kavangos, people from other tribes were also badly affected by the system because the abundance of cheap labour from the north depressed wages generally and made jobs hard to find. Thus all black Namibians were equally eager to be rid of the system. But the founders, casting about for a name for their new party, considered that the Ovambos, particularly, needed a personal symbol of their resistance, since they would be at the forefront of the action against SWANLA."

The OPC was a typical 1950s "liberation organisation" in another way as well. A number of its early members were also unashamed adherents of the South African Communist Party, and the OPC, like the African National Congress and other similar movements, saw no harm in this.

The result was that the organisation enjoyed a link with Moscow which was never to wither away, and there is indisputable documentary evidence that during the border war its military trainees received heavy doses of straight Marxist indoctrination. But it would be simplistic to describe the OPC and its successors as communist organisations (at his trial in 1967-8, answering accusations that many Swapo documents contained typical communist jargon, Toivo replied that many others "finish with an appeal to the Almighty to guide us in our struggle for freedom").

Toivo's activities were soon curtailed in a general crack-down on "liberation movements" in both South Africa and South West Africa. In 1958 he was arrested on a charge of agitation and exiled to northern Ovamboland, where he proceeded to further his war on SWANLA by establishing the first Ovambo-owned formal store. In 1959 Nujoma took over the presidency and soon fell foul of the security police as well when, in December of that year, he was arrested for his activities in Windhoek.

The authorities had decided to evacuate the population of a long-standing black-occupied area known as the "Old Location" to a new township they had built further away, named Katatura. The Old Location's inhabitants declined to be moved, and the OPO took full advantage of their disgruntlement to foment a mass civil-disobedience campaign, boycotting all municipal and government-supplied services and amenities. Tension grew. Then, on December 10, there occurred what Shipanga calls "one of the bitterest incidents in our history". A large group of residents marched, as he puts it, "to confront the authorities". Police tried to disperse the marchers, failed, and opened fire, killing 11 and wounding 54.

It was a watershed event. Shipanga says: "The time for a movement limited to labour questions was over. Workers needed a broader message. We realised that everything, including labour matters, would fall into line behind a political movement, and so, in 1960, the OPO became the South West African People's Organisation."

No doubt the new name helped to broaden Swapo's popular support, but (given the absence of any impartial survey of its popular support) it does not appear to have turned it into a truly representative organisation – possibly a reflection of the territory's history of internal conflict and ethnic division. Although its political wing recruited sympathisers from members of all or most other ethno-cultural groups, it still remained strongly Ovambo-based in the years to come, particularly as regards its soon-to-be-established military wing.

This can be seen from the fact that about 95 percent of all Swapo insurgents killed or captured in the decades-long border war which was soon to break out were Ovambos, most of them from the two main Kwanyama and Ondonga tribes, and several non-Ovambo members who gave themselves up in later years complained of racial discrimination. It is also a fact that except for some activity in Caprivi in the early years, the insurgency rarely moved beyond the main operational area of Ovamboland, although there were several outbreaks of activity in Kavango and Kaokoland at times in the early and mid-1980s.

Top
The "father" of Swapo, Andimba (Herman) Toivo ja Toivo, after his release from prison in the 1980s

Below
Sam Nujoma, who became president of Swapo after Toivo ja Toivo

Opposite page
The Freedom Memorial in Lusaka, depicting a "freedom fighter" breaking the fetters of colonialism. Although Zambia did not have to fight for its independence, it provided help for various insurgent organisations

FREEDOM

MONUMENT DEDICATED TO
— FREEDOM FIGHTERS —

The world campaign against South African control really began in 1960, although the UN had been disappointingly passive about the Old Location shooting – "We had believed that the shooting of unarmed demonstrators would be the signal for our friends to come to our aid", Shipanga later recalled, "but it did not happen. The UN simply denounced South Africa and life continued as before". But Liberia and Ethiopia, the only black members of the old League of Nations, went to the World Court to charge South Africa with breaching her mandate obligations. Nujoma fled abroad and continued his political activities, among other things testifying to the UN's Committee on South West Africa.

A provisional Swapo headquarters was set up in Dar es Salaam, Tanzania, in March of 1961. Nujoma then returned to South West Africa. He was promptly arrested, and subsequently left the country and set himself up in Lusaka, which was to be the main headquarters of Swapo's external wing for the next quarter-century. (Oddly, considering the South African government's willingness to ban political movements it regarded as subversive, Swapo's internal wing was never proscribed, and was allowed to remain active to various degrees throughout the course of the war, although it was careful about making public statements that would enable the authorities to take direct action against it.)

Swapo's move towards a violent solution was set in motion soon after the Old Location shooting. There is an enduring myth that Swapo did not contemplate an "armed struggle" till 1966, following the World Court's decision on the Ethiopian-Liberian case. The court did not rule on the merits of the case but decided, in a narrow decision settled by the chairman's casting vote, that Ethiopia and Liberia had no legal right nor interest in the matter. Various African states, infuriated because they had expected a ruling in their favour, took the matter to the United Nations General Assembly.

The General Assembly resolved that South Africa's mandate should be terminated because it had failed to carry out its obligation and was exploiting and oppressing the inhabitants, and that South West Africa should be taken under its wing.

Like so many General Assembly resolutions of the next 25 years it served no purpose except to aggravate the general situation, and South Africa promptly rejected the resolution as unlawful.

In point of fact, however, it would appear that Swapo – born into the era of the "freedom fighter" as it was – began entertaining the option of using violence within three years of its founding. According to Shipanga, the Old Location shooting "also sowed the seeds of the armed struggle against the South African occupation of our country … Many of us concluded that we could not push our people into the muzzles of machine-guns. We would have to confront guns with guns".

Then again, during his 1967-1968 trial on terrorism charges, Toivo stated: "It is not really a question of whether South Africa treats us well or badly but that South West Africa is our country and we wish to be our masters … Violence is truly fearsome. But who would not defend his property and himself against a robber? And we believe that South Africa has robbed us of our country."

A more exact dating, however, is to be found in the fact that in 1962, soon after Swapo had set up its headquarters in Lusaka, it founded a military wing called Plan (the "People's Liberation Army of Namibia". Given the South African government's complete disinclination, then or later, to yield to Swapo or any other "liberation organisation", this effectively set the stage for a shooting war.

That year also brought the first chapter in the United Nations General Assembly's long squabble with South Africa. The newly-formed UN Special Committee for South West Africa sent its chairmen, Victorio Carpio of the Philippines and Dr Salvador Martinez de Alva of Mexico, to the territory to investigate various complaints. The South African government welcomed them, and after talks at Pretoria they and their entourage arrived in South West Africa in May.

The UN party spent some time touring the remote northern territories and talking to representatives of various racial groups and organisations. On May 26 they issued a joint communique stating that they had been well received and had not found any threat to international peace or signs of militarisation or genocide. The South

Top
Victorio Carpio, Chairman of the United Nations Special Committee for South West Africa

Right
While the countdown to the border war begins along the faraway northern border of South West Africa, Prime Minister Hendrik Verwoerd speaks at a 1964 meeting commemorating the 50th birthday of the National Party. Ironically, the NP's founder-members were utterly opposed to the invasion of the German-held territory beyond the Orange River at the beginning of World War I

African Prime Minister, Dr Hendrik Verwoerd, had undertaken to intensify efforts to uplift the black population and to investigate allegations that certain persons had been "repatriated" (exiled to their home areas) because of their political activities.

Soon afterwards, however, the entire visit collapsed into farce when Carpio denied he was a party to the communique (all evidence to the contrary notwithstanding) and said that he did not agree with its findings, particularly as regarded the allegations of militarisation. De Alva hotly denied Carpio's claims that he had been pressured or had not been consulted, but the Special Committee subsequently repudiated the communique.

On July 27 Carpio and De Alva submitted a report to the committee which amounted to a complete about-face on the communique. The report accused Pretoria of oppressing the inhabitants of South West Africa, failing to prepare them for independence and noting no evidence that the South African government planned any reforms or intended to scrap its policies, which conflicted with the UN charter.

Therefore, the report concluded, since the indigenous population had expressed an "overwhelming desire" for independence, the General Assembly should give South Africa a short period of grace and then revoke the mandate if Pretoria did not respond.

All this time Swapo had been recruiting fighters for its embryonic military wing. Progress was slow at first, but eventually some 900 recruits were gathered by a variety of means, ranging from signing up genuine volunteers to offering in-country youths bogus scholarships for overseas study and then diverting them to Plan.

The recruits were given basic training in Tanzania, and those selected for advanced and/or specialised courses were then sent to countries such as Algeria, Cuba, Egypt, China, the Soviet Union, North Korea and Red China. At the same time Swapo forged links with the anti-Portuguese Unita insurgents starting to operate in southern Angola, a handy and advantageous relationship because the southern Angolans and the Ovambos are part of the same broad ethnic group and such a friendship would give Plan easy access to its main target, Ovamboland. The links were so close, in fact, that when the later-to-be-famous Dr Jonas Savimbi slipped back into Angola for the first time in eight years in late 1966 he was carrying a Tokarev pistol given him by Nujoma.

Swapo did not put all its strategic eggs in one basket, however, and also forged a close working relationship with the Caprivian African National Union (Canu), an insurgent movement which was recruited from inhabitants of the Caprivi Strip. Canu enjoyed an important advantage: it would be able to operate from neighbouring Zambia with the official sanction of the government in Zambia, which bordered on the northern and north-eastern side of Caprivi, whereas Swapo's activities in southern Angola were still restricted by the fact that Portugal was friendly to South Africa.

In the peaceful 1960s, when international boundaries were still regarded as virtually inviolate and the principle of hot pursuit and pre-emptive "external operations" was virtually unheard-of, this was a tremendously important factor in the coming insurgency.

The intended *modus operandi* was a simple one, well suited to the geographic and demographic circumstances. While Zambia was less than ideal as a jumping-off point for operations for Swapo's

main effort, the link with Canu meant that Plan insurgents would be able to move westwards from Zambian territory into sparsely populated southern Angola and then swing southwards to enter central Ovamboland. At the same time Canu insurgents could cross directly into Caprivi to harass the South African administration there.

By September of 1965 Plan was ready to launch its first infiltration, and that month six trained insurgents slipped over the border from southern Angola into Ovamboland - an easy process, the international border existing more in name than in fact, with no-one to guard it except a handful of South West Africa's small 600-man police force.

The insurgents busied themselves with basic political activation and also gave about 30 young Ovambos some elementary military training before sending them home to await a call to arms. By this time suspicious tribal elders had passed word of their activities to the police, but except for surveillance no immediate action was taken.

In February of 1966 a second small group set out to infiltrate southwards, only to become the authors of a total fiasco when they murdered two Angolan shopkeepers and an itinerant Ovambo in the apparent - and mistaken - belief by its members that they had crossed the border. The group then dispersed, only to have three of its members arrested by police in the neighbouring tribal territory of Kavango, where local inhabitants had wasted no time in informing the authorities about the presence of foreign tribesmen.

In July of 1966 a third group of insurgents crossed the border. They were an unimpressive group, trained in half-a-dozen different countries and armed in some cases with assagais and bows and arrows - a far cry from the uniformed, well-equipped and trained insurgents of later years. In spite of this they launched the "armed struggle" in no uncertain terms by attacking a number of Ovambo tribal chiefs, firing at a white farmer's house in the Grootfontein district just south of Ovamboland, and shooting up the South West African border post at Oshikango.

Top
A raggle-taggle mob of Plan recruits — a far cry from the well-uniformed, well-armed insurgents of later years — undergoing light machine-gun training at the beginning of the border war, probably in Tanzania

This opening phase of the struggle was short-lived, however: the following month helicopter-borne policemen attacked their camp at Ongulumbashe, killing two insurgents and capturing nine others. Later, acting on information passed on by the local inhabitants, they arrested many more, bringing the total number of captures to 45. This effectively strangled the infiltration and, incidentally, knocked out the only permanent base Plan ever managed to establish anywhere in the operational area during the entire 23-year course of the war.

The then Minister of Justice, Police and Prisons, John Vorster, announced the incident in Parliament the same day, the first public inkling that there was trouble in the border regions.

"I want to make it clear that we have to deal here with an advance guard and that it cannot be excluded that more of such groups will try to cross our borders," he added. "I say this because I want to be realistic and not because I want to create panic."

Vorster's prediction was accurate. In late September the homes of two white officials were set alight at Oshikango, but no infiltration as such took place till December, when another group of insurgents crossed the border and launched an intensive activation and recruiting campaign in both Ovamboland and Caprivi. A number of armed attacks were carried out on tribal headmen and a white farmer named P J Breedt in a remote area of the Grootfontein district was wounded.

As before, police reacted immediately. By the end of the year the insurgency was over in Ovamboland. Eight insurgents had died, 59 had been captured and, in September of 1967, the first Plan members to appear in court - 37 of them - had gone on trial in Pretoria, charged under the Terrorism Act and Suppression of Communism Act.

By this time the UN had appointed a "Council for South West Africa" which was intended to administer the territory till independence, which it hoped would be achieved in 1968. It was a vain hope, and what actually happened in 1968 was that early in the new year Plan started new infiltrations, this time into East Caprivi from bases in Zambia.

The local population was disappointingly apathetic - due probably to their general remoteness from mainstream politics in South West Africa and the fact that Caprivi had never been colonised - and the insurgents were forced to concentrate on killing or breaking down the authority of traditional tribal leaders in preparation for activating the people.

The police struck back in greater force than ever before, and as a result the distant and beautiful bushland became the scene of the most ferocious fighting seen so far. Many insurgents were shot dead or captured and a top field commander in Caprivi named Tobias Hanyeko was killed in a fire-fight on a barge in the Zambesi River; by March of 1968 a total of 160 insurgents were behind bars. Later that year Herman Toivo ja Toivo was sentenced to life imprisonment (he was released in the 1980s).

Following the crushing of this latest infiltration, Ovamboland and Caprivi were now so quiet that the police withdrew their counter-insurgency unit, but the border war was far from over. In October of 1968 two large groups of insurgents slipped in from Angola and restarted the Caprivian end of the moribund insurgency. Police retaliation was swift. Within a week no fewer than 56 insurgents had been arrested. At year's end a total of 178 Plan members had either been killed or captured, and the infiltration ended with the remaining operatives withdrawing over the border into Zambia.

South West Africa had now changed its name, at least in the eyes of the UN General Assembly, which had unilaterally conferred on it the historically baseless but attractive appellation of "Namibia" and called on the Security Council to eject South Africa and obtain independence. It was a significant move in the history of modern South West Africa for, unlike the General Assembly, the Security Council enjoyed powers of enforcement, and it can be seen as the foundation for the future sanctions campaign against South Africa.

In 1969 the Security Council duly endorsed the termination of the mandate and called on South Africa to withdraw from the territory by October. The South Africans paid no heed to either the termination or the demand, but no immediate consequences followed; the border remained quiet for all of 1969 and 1970, although in the latter year the Security Council condemned South Africa's refusal, declared its occupation illegal and invalid, and asked the World Court for a confirmatory ruling.

In 1971 the World Court obliged with a verdict that South Africa's continued presence was indeed illegal and called on all states to recognise that illegality. The Vorster government took no more notice of this ruling than it had of any of the previous ones on South West Africa, and concentrated on fighting a new Plan infiltration into Caprivi, not only from Angola but also from Zambia.

The local population still declined to rise en masse, and the insurgents concentrated on harrying the security forces. In April a Russian-made mine blew up a police vehicle near Katima Mulilo, heralding a new and terrifying dimension, and during 1971 and 1972 five policemen were killed and 35 wounded by landmine explosions. For the

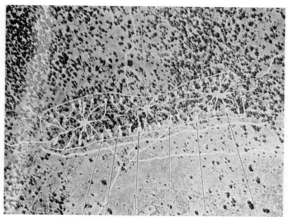

next few years the landmine was to become a prime weapon against the South Africans (as it was against the Portuguese in Angola and Mozambique), although in due course its threat lessened and eventually became a minor one as the South Africans learnt from their experiences and developed a series of the most effective mine-protected vehicles in the world. But, right to the end of the border war, it continued to claim the lives of civilians, almost all of them Ovambos.

In March of 1972 Andreas Shipanga conceived and carried out a disinformation stunt which was so successful that the South Africans have never managed to shake it off. Tobias Hanyeko's successor, Dimo Hamaambo, who had just returned from an incursion into Caprivi, told Shipanga that en route he had come across a village 16km inside Angola which had been totally wiped out by the Portuguese. Now it happened that just previously Shipanga had met an old man named Haingula who had come to him with a rather vague story about having been shot and wounded by un-specified South Africans. Shipanga arranged for a Swedish television cameraman named Per Sanden to visit "a Namibian village where there's been a massacre".

In due course Sanden and his crew were taken into Angola, blissfully ignorant of the fact that they had crossed the border, shot reels of film showing the ghastly remains and interviewed a well-primed Haingula, who displayed his wounds and explained that he was the sole survivor of the massacre. Shipanga then showed the film to foreign journalists and produced Haingula, who repeated his bravura performance as sole survivor. It caused an enormous international storm which drowned out the South Africans' genuine protestations of inno-cence: 15 years later Shipanga gleefully related the story to Foreign Minister Pik Botha. It was one of the first Swapo disinformation stunts, and one of the most successful; later ones were mostly less subtle, possibly because the highly intelligent Shipanga had fallen from influence.

In the meantime the UN General Assembly invited the Secretary-General, Dr Kurt Waldheim, to initiate new settlement talks with South Africa. Waldheim visited South Africa; given assurances that South Africa's aim for the territory was self-determination, he appointed Dr Alfred Escher of Switzerland as his personal representative for negotiations and sent him to visit Pretoria.

By the beginning of 1973 Plan had recovered from its earlier losses and launched an intensified campaign of political activation, intimidation and terrorism; occasionally police patrols were ambushed and in one instance a police camp was

briefly shot up with recoilless guns, although the only casualties were suffered by the attackers before they withdrew over the border into Zambia. The activation and intimidation proved so successful that a poll of only 2,7 percent was recorded in that year's regional election. For the South Africans it was the lowest point yet in the border war.

By the end of 1973 it was becoming patently obvious to the government - although not to the South African general public, which was still looking towards Rhodesia, where a police contingent had been campaigning for several years in support of the Ian Smith government - that the SAP simply did not have the manpower or other resources simultaneously to keep the peace in South Africa itself, secure the South West African borders and provide a Rhodesian contingent. The SAP had never been a large force, but it had always managed to carry out its tasks with reasonable efficiency; this burden, however, was more than it could handle.

This being the case, it was decided that the South African Defence Force would take over re-sponsibility for counter-insurgency operations in the border operational area, leaving the police to concentrate on their normal duties, although still maintaining their small anti-terrorist unit.

By now the long struggle between South Africa and the United Nations had gone a stage further: Waldheim had reported back that there was still no common ground between the UN and Pretoria, and the Security Council had retaliated by severing further contacts. All the same, some progress had been made.

While unable to reach agreement with the UN, South Africa had committed itself to free elections and unitary independence, possibly within 10 years. Another important principle which was established in this period was the government's insistence that agreement on a future scheme of things had to be reached by Swapo and the other internal parties and not by Swapo and South Africa. The gov-ernment stubbornly adhered to this view in the ensuing years, while Swapo just as stubbornly insisted that it would not deal with "puppets" and "traitors".

1974

The date for the SADF's assumption of responsibility was set at April 1 of 1974, and in the second half of 1973 increasing numbers of military personnel and quantities of equipment started to arrive in the operational area. All these preparations took place in great secrecy, so that news of the insurgency's escalation leaked out in fits and starts.

The first public intimation of the move came in mid-March of 1974, at a political meeting in Glencoe, Natal Province, which was addressed by the Minister of Defence, P W Botha.

Answering questions put to him by a member of the audience, Botha explained that South Africa had not sent military forces to Rhodesia in support of the Ian Smith government there because "our police are stationed in Rhodesia – as the Prime Minister has explained – to protect, or help to protect, Rhodesia against the infiltration of terrorists on their way to South Africa. At this stage it is police action, as we intended".

This was a straight-forward reiteration of government policy, but Botha's next remarks were slightly more ambiguous:

"But right through the world, where revolutionary wars are being conducted, you have the problem that you don't always know exactly when to change over from police action to military action … at a certain stage in terrorist warfare one must still use police. It is always a difficult question to know when to switch over from police to military action … (Terrorism in Southern Africa) is becoming more and more a war of low intensity, but gradually escalating with the bringing in of sophisticated weapons and the development of the TanZam Railway."

Asked whether a "better trained force" was needed on the border, Botha said: "Yes, that is so." He reminded the questioner that legislation had been laid before Parliament which would allow national servicemen to voluntarily extend their training period from 12 to 18 or 24 months, adding: "The idea is to bring about a force under arms to be ready on all occasions to act as a deterrent."

In view of the escalating wars in Southern Africa, he added, the SADF was being prepared "not to attack anybody, or to be aggressive against other countries, but to be able – with the most modern weapons and the best training – to defend the borders of our country … If you really want to be prepared against the better-trained men on the terrorist side, I think your answer lies in a better-trained Defence Force".

A Natal newspaper immediately interpreted these remarks as meaning that the despatch of the military to the border was now on the cards – which was promptly denied by the SADF's chief of public relations, Brigadier Cyrus Smith.

A few days later Botha, addressing another rally at The Strand, near Cape Town, said it would be "irresponsible" of him to say at that stage whether the SAP contingent in Rhodesia would be replaced by troops, adding that South Africa did not practise an aggressive policy but wanted to build up a defence force that would be able to hold her borders.

He added that he doubted the Portuguese would pull out of Mozambique and Angola, since they had been there for 300 years and had done much to develop the two territories: it was an aside he must have rued in the near future, since in fact Portugal was within a month of a military coup which would lead to her withdrawal from Africa and an entirely new politico-military ball game in the southern part of the continent.

Just three days later, on March 17, the Sunday Express newspaper in Johannesburg published a now-it-can-be-revealed story in which reporter Tim Clarke stated that the question of deploying troops on the border had been "debated between Army and Police chiefs and at Cabinet level".

However, Clarke added, "so far no decision has been made on this delicate matter. A decision to commit the South African Army could only be taken at Cabinet level".

On March 18 the Rapport Sunday newspaper of Johannesburg quoted Botha as saying that there was only one answer to the long-term war being waged on the borders (although he did not specify exactly which borders) and that was "a military solution with highly trained people and effective weapons. It is something I have been saying for six years, since I became Minister of Defence".

The primary task of the SADF, he added, was to guard the country's borders on land, at sea and in the air, and "it is an accepted principle in South Africa – by previous governments as well as this one – that our defence cannot take place only on one side of the Limpopo". But he would not commit himself on the possibility of involving the SADF because "this is a matter of international relations. The Prime Minister has often said that when we are asked to combat terrorists we shall do so. This is a matter between governments. It must not be anticipated".

None of these portents of things to come received the attention they merited: the news story that dominated the headlines at this time concerned the deaths of four South African policemen in a contact in Rhodesia, which brought the SAP's losses in the Rhodesian and South West African fighting to 19 dead and 37 wounded. To the average South African, what was happening in Rhodesia was a great deal more real and immediate than events in the faraway bushlands of Ovamboland and Caprivi.

Top
Prime Minister John Vorster and Minister of Defence P W Botha, in the pre-1974 days, when the police were still in charge of the borders. Flanking them are then Chief of the Air Force, Lieutenant-General J P Verster, and the then Chief of the SADF, General R C Hiemstra

The same incomprehension applied to the important distinction Botha had drawn in his concluding remarks in the Rapport interview. There were immense diplomatic and political implications involved in sending troops into Rhodesia or Mozambique, ranging from questions of face-saving by the recipient countries to the existence of a long-established clause in South Africa's Defence Act which specified that SADF members could not be deployed beyond the country's borders except if they volunteered to do so.

At the same time the possibility could not be ignored. Even as clear-sighted a body as the International Institute for Strategic Studies believed at this stage that there was a possibility of South African "pre-emptive intervention" in Mozambique for reasons such as the imminent success of the Frelimo insurgents (which was assured just the following month when Portugal's Marcelo Caetano government was overthrown by a coup d'état).

But to deploy military servicemen along the borders of South West Africa would require no more than a stroke of the ministerial pen - and by this time, in fact, the process was already in full swing, as a party of journalists discovered in June, just two months later, when they were flown to the Caprivi Strip for the revelation of the decade: SADF soldiers and airmen were in position along the 1 680km border that started at the Cunene River mouth and ended at Eastern Caprivi's "fist".

Above
Admiral H H Biermann, Chief of the SADF at the time that the armed forces became involved on the border and in Angola

Above Right
Visiting a fortified bushveld base, these journalists returned from Caprivi in early 1974 to reveal that the SADF had taken over. With them are Brigadier M A C Kotze (in beret, sixth from left in the front); Admiral H H Biermann; P W Botha; Army Chief Lieutenant-General Magnus Malan; and Minister of Law and Order Louis le Grange

Below
Lieutenant Freddy Zeelie. This is the first photograph to be published of the SADF's earliest border fatility

National servicemen officered by professionals of the Permanent Force and assisted by local black and Bushmen trackers were roaming the wild, beautiful Caprivian bushland. Some of these excursions were normal fighting patrols; others were "contact patrols" that visited the scattered kraals and villages, giving agricultural and medical help, listening to grievances and generally helping out. At the same time government officials were spending hundreds of thousands of rands on "hearts-and-minds" (later renamed "civic action") operations.

The journalists noted with some amusement that the Army seemed to have done its homework, so that veteran regulars were spouting the jargon and intentions of seasoned counter-insurgents: "It's a political struggle," as one earnestly explained. "It's important to concentrate on the population; I personally believe that the only solution for South Africa is for us to trust the black man."

Another officer accurately described the situation as "a terrorist campaign of extremely low intensity", although he dismissed as "sheer propaganda" various Swapo claims of successful contacts, stating bluntly: "The furthest Swapo has been in since we came is one-and-a-half miles."

The host at this visit was none other than P W Botha himself, and strangely enough he announced what turned out to be one of the first fruits of border war when he said the SADF had a place for people of all races, including blacks.

It was an important statement, as blacks had not been used as combatants in the South African forces since the 19th Century. As a result, observers assumed he meant citizens of the black "home-lands", the former tribal reserves which were being groomed for independence. But a week later it was announced in Pretoria that the Army had started recruiting blacks, who would be given full infantry training and be used for unspecified guard duties.

Within the first month more than 300 blacks had volunteered; at the same time the first coloured officers in the country's history went into training, and the integration of the South African armed forces had begun.

On June 21 a news report dateline Pretoria said that about 100 Ovambos, including Swapo leaders, had crossed into Angola "this week", adding that the SADF was "ready to counter any intensification of the terrorist threat". According to the authorities, the report said, this move was motivated by the likelihood of an independent government in Angola within a year "and the probability that it would have a sufficient representation of blacks to support terrorist action against Ovamboland".

The concluding paragraphs of the report were remarkably percipient, although it is to be doubted if even the author realised just how percipient they were:

"Senior SADF officers have stated the main objective of the Swapo terrorists is Ovamboland and not the Caprivi – an area which has been virtually free of terrorist activity for the past 18 months.

"Those fleeing into Angola, it is being speculated, are doing so in the hope of getting encouragement and aid from a sympathetic independent Angolan government to mount a terrorist offensive against Ovamboland.

"Earlier this week the Chief of the SADF, Admiral (Hugo) Biermann, said South Africa would never commit its forces to internal struggles in Mozambique and Angola. But there is no doubt that the government is watching the developments in Mozambique and Angola with the closest interest."

Although it must have known about the militarisation of the border for some time, the Zambian government waited till June 25 of 1974 to react to the stationing of South African soldiers in Caprivi. On that date a Zambian Foreign Ministry spokesman condemned South Africa's "uncalled-for, wanton aggression", adding: "The Zambian government reiterates its condemnation of the Pretoria regime, and calls on her to respect law and world opinion by withdrawing forthwith South African military units and handing over power to the Namibian people."

South Africans were still digesting this early salvo in what was to be a drawn-out war of words between Pretoria and Lusaka when, on June 29, Admiral Biermann announced the death of Lieutenant Freddie Zeelie, saying the young officer had died the previous week "in a skirmish with a group of terrorists which attempted to cross the South

African border … a unit of the Permanent Force killed and wounded a number of terrorists."

As far as is known, 22-year-old Zeelie was the first South African soldier to be killed in action on the border. The circumstances of his death were shrouded in secrecy – not even his parents were told exactly when and where he died – and remain so to this day. At the time it was not even known what unit he belonged to, although a green infantry beret lay with his sword on his coffin when he was buried with full military honours at his home town of Alberton, near Johannesburg (it later transpired that he had been a member of the super-elite Reconnaissance Commando, the forerunner of today's Reconnaissance Regiments). About six months later his parents received his posthumous Louw Wepener Decoration for gallantry, but even this was done in such a subfusc way that the first public intimation was a photograph of them which appeared in the armed forces magazine Paratus weeks after the event.

This period also saw the first signs of what was to become a vigorous, if never very widely supported, South African conscientious objection movement: the generally anti-government South African Council of Churches sent a petition to the SADF's Chaplain-General on the subject. Soon afterwards, the staff of the Federal Theological Seminary at Alice in the Eastern Province – the only one in Southern Africa where black students of various denominations were trained for the ministry – strongly supporting the SACC resolution, said: "The Christian Church has the right to ask its members to consider whether they can conscientiously bear arms or not in any particular situation. What is beyond dispute is that the right

Top
Mpalela Island, about 180km along the river from Wenela, was more or less the outer limit of SADF patrols. It was an important lookout, particularly in the 1980s, because it was within eyeshot of the border between Zambia and Zimbabwe

Left
"Hearts and minds" work – later called "civic action" was the big buzzword in Caprivi in the early days. In addition to fighting patrols, the Army made as much contact with the local population as possible, providing medical services and agricultural advice, and generally helping out. It was to prove an effective formula in time. Some patrollers also acquired a liking for the indigenous maize beer, which was not to everyone's taste but was routinely consumed all the same as a matter of good manners

of Christians to fight any war, or to refuse to fight this particular war, ought to be recognised."

Meanwhile, after an inevitable slow start the SADF's combination of heavy patrolling and hearts-and-minds started having its effect, and by late 1974 some recovery was being seen, although not without cost: on October 3, for example, a regular soldier, Staff-Sergeant W J Burger of 2 South African Infantry Battalion was killed in a shooting incident east of Katima Mulilo. Swapo did not lose heart, however – on December 16 its London representative, Peter Katjavivi, said the Caprivi insurgency would continue till Vorster made "a genuine gesture of goodwill" towards Swapo and the people of South West Africa, such as calling off the elections for an Ovambo ethnic authority scheduled for January of 1975, and halting the trial of its national chairman, David Meroror.

Needless to say, the South African government did not respond to these suggestions, and the year closed with the melancholy announcement that since July of 1968 at least 31 policemen had died on border duty from operational or accidental causes.

Although most South Africans did not realise it, a new phase of the war was about to start, one which would have a radical effect on the border and would force Admiral Biermann to eat his assurances about South African non-intervention across its borders.

Above
Professor Marcelo Caetano,
dictator of Portugal from
1968 to 1974, when he was
overthrown in a coup
that signalled the start of
Angola's long agony

Right
Luanda in its salad days
just before the civil war.
The ultimate prize, it was
never captured by the
MPLA's opponents

Opposite Top
Dr Jonas Savimbi (second from
right, with stick), then still the
most obscure of the Angolan
insurgent leaders, at Nova
Lisboa in central Angola at
the start of the civil war

Opposite Below
By December of 1975 the
MPLA was already organising
the youth into "Pioneer"
units like this one, seen at
the north-eastern town
of Andrada, even though
the battle for Angola was
far from over

Above
MPLA chief Dr Agostinho Neto,
initially written off as a
drunken psychotic Marxist
by the Americans, soon after
seizing power in Angola

Till the first quarter of 1974 the support of Prime Minister Marcelo Caetano's regime in Portugal had been of great value to Pretoria in its counter-insurgency campaign in South West Africa, principally because it had meant that Plan could not freely use southern Angola as a sanctuary, training-ground and jumping-off place for infiltrations into Ovamboland.

But by 1974 years of fighting simultaneous insurgencies in its three African provinces of Angola, Mozambique and Guinea-Bissau had brought Portugal, the poorest country in Europe, to the brink of financial and spiritual collapse.

The colonial wars were absorbing 50 percent of the national budget, the country was deeply in debt and the populace was discontented, while draft-dodging and anti-war sabotage had become a way of life. In addition, sections of the armed forces had become disaffected and a group of young professional officers had formed themselves into a clandestine left-wing organisation called the Movement of the Armed Forces (MFA).

A staggering blow to the Caetano regime's credibility came in February of 1974 with the publication of a book entitled "Portugal and the Future". The writer was General Antonio de Spinola, an officer of impeccable conservative military credentials who was not only deputy commander of the army but a revered hero of the wars in Mozambique and Guinea.

Spinola called for a return to parliamentary democracy in Portugal and warned that the country faced certain defeat if it tried to win the insurgencies by purely military means. In the eyes of Portugal's rulers it was an act of amazing heresy and Spinola was instantly cashiered, along with his chief of staff, General Francisco da Costa Gomes.

The government banned the book, but by then it had sold 50 000 copies and played a major role in creating the optimum conditions for the MFA coup which took place in April and replaced Caetano's government with a Junta of National Salvation, led by Spinola as president.

Spinola soon found that the MFA's dominant leftist element (most people did not realise at the time just how far left it was) did not favour his original idea of a "Lusitanian Federation" linking the colonies, Portugal itself and Brazil. The MFA preferred to grant independence to the Portuguese possessions, and took steps to make sure that the ultimate winners would be ideologically compatible with it. This was to present no problems in Guinea-Bissau and Mozambique, but in Angola it was an entirely different story.

No fewer than three Angolan insurgent movements were in direct opposition to one another in spite of various attempts at reconciliation, differing in almost every important way.

The MPLA (Popular Movement for the Liberation of Angola) under the politician-intellectual Dr Agostinho Neto was an out-and-out Marxist organisation with strong ties to Moscow. It was said to have at least 4 500 reasonably well-trained guerrillas drawn from some country areas and also Luanda and other urban areas.

In the north and east of the country there operated the FNLA (National Front for the Liberation of Angola), an allegedly 7 000-strong black nationalist movement based on the far northern Bakongo tribal group and led by the avowedly anti-communist (but not necessarily pro-Western, as many outside observers assumed) Holden Roberto, the brother-in-law of President Mobuto Sese Seko of Zaire.

The third was the vaguely socialist but essentially pragmatic Unita (National Union for the Total Independence of Angola) under Dr Jonas Savimbi, a former member of the FNLA, which was based in the south and south-east and was drawn mainly but not exclusively from the Ovimbundu tribal group, blood-brothers of the Ovambo in South West Africa and the largest ethno-cultural bloc in Angola.

All three had friends of one sort or another in the outside world. The MPLA was armed by the Russians and their allies, while the FNLA and, to

some extent, Unita, received some support from African and Western sources, and also from the People's Republic of China, which was always willing to counteract the interests of its bitter ideological enemy, Russia.

The irony of the situation was that at the time of Caetano's ouster none of the three insurgent organisations had managed to achieve significant success in spite of nearly a decade of activity, the result not only of their own deficiencies as fighting organisations but also the personal bad blood that existed between the leaders, particularly Neto and Roberto.

The FNLA's army had fought more engagements against the Portuguese than either of the others, but the little success it had achieved had been due more to Portugal's decline and the advantage of sanctuary in Zaire than the prowess of its horde of partly trained, badly led men. In addition, Roberto had spent as much time making life difficult for the MPLA as harassing the Portuguese.

The MPLA had withdrawn to Zaire and Congo-Brazzaville after mounting two unsuccessful and bloodily suppressed insurrections against the Portuguese, after which it had achieved little in the military sense: thanks to the personal animosity that existed between Neto and Roberto, its fighters had great difficulty in infiltrating into Angola because the FNLA controlled the north. So intense was the hatred between the organisations that such MPLA members as managed to enter Angola usually squandered their resources on harrying the FNLA in the north and Unita in the east.

The MPLA's military effectiveness had been further reduced by a chronic leadership struggle between Neto and his able chief military commander, Daniel Chipenda, who was to play an important role in the tragedy which was engulfing Angola.

Unita at that stage was primarily a political organisation, its main support-base isolated in the south and east and its forces seriously short of arms and trained men.

An even greater irony was that Angola itself was on the verge of an economic boom which would have made it even more difficult for the insurgents to achieve their aims if the Portuguese coup had come a year or two later. But it had not, and the fall of the Caetano government gave all three a new lease of life.

What happened then is a long, amply documented (and sometimes misdocumented) story, but the essence of it was that the Portuguese army in Angola assumed a passive stance under control of the new Governor-General, Vice-Admiral Rosa Coutinho, a man of such leftist sympathies that he was known as "Red Rosa".

As Coutinho confessed in a 1984 television interview – the first time he had broken silence over Angola, "I was first of all the commander-in-chief of all military forces. Second, I was the executive, I was the head of the administrative branch … I directed the government. Certainly, certainly I had influence – and I exerted it."

With Angola under Coutinho's control, the MPLA began to enjoy a favoured status, and with his approval clandestinely set about building itself for the day when it would assume power.

In late 1974 alone, for example, an estimated six million US dollars' worth of heavy Russian weaponry – including 122mm BM-21 multiple rocket-launchers, obsolescent weapons but highly effective against unsophisticated African troops – was shipped to remote rural MPLA depots from Dar es Salaam and later Congo-Brazzaville, and large numbers of MPLA officers were flown to Russia for training (although in fairness this happened only after Red China had sent the FNLA some instructors and 450 tons of light arms through Zaire in June of that year, followed by another shipment from Roumania in August).

In addition, more Cuban military advisors and instructors were quietly slipping into Luanda. For years Swapo and MPLA sympathisers inside and outside South Africa have claimed that Cubans started arriving in Angola only in late 1975 to combat South African aggression, but in fact there was an old relationship between Neto and President Fidel Castro, and Cuba had been providing Neto with instructors and a personal bodyguard since 1966.

Top
FNLA boss Holden Roberto — traditional northern tribal chief, wilful autocrat and leader of the "good guys" in American eyes (at first, anyway)

Above
Dr Julius Nyerere of Tanzania, self-proclaimed humanist, and long-time supporter of both Swapo and the MPLA

Right
Supremely over-confident FNLA soldiers in the early stages of the Angolan civil war

Opposite Top
Unable to develop protected vehicles of their own, Portuguese patrols in the dense bush that covered so much of Angola rode soft-skinned lorries that offered no protection against either landmines or ambushes

Opposite Below
Portuguese troops drive into the jungle to relieve an isolated outpost north of Luanda

1975

Top
The MPLA flag — a gear-wheel to represent the workers, a machete for the peasants, and a star to symbolise the fusion of both elements into an harmonious force under socialism

Above
Unita's black cockerel crows over a call for the construction of a new Angola

Right
As Angola slid into chaos in mid-1975, attempts were made to bring the disputants together. They did not work

Below
An FNLA banner. "Liberty and Land" — a straightforward appeal to Roberto's mainly rural power-base in the north

In the meantime, the Portuguese government proceeded with its plans for Angolan independence. Supported by politically moderate African nations such as Zaire, Kenya and Zambia, it pressured the leaders of the three movements into attending a conference at the Portuguese seaside resort of Alvor, and on January 15 of 1975 joined them in signing the so-called Alvor Agreement.

The agreement specified the formation of an Angolan transitional government under a Portuguese High Commissioner, in which each of the three movements would hold three ministerial portfolios and the Portuguese another three, and the founding of an 8 000-man defence force recruited from soldiers of all three movements. All but 24 000 of the Portuguese soldiers in Angola would be sent home in April, and the remainder would stay on in progressively diminishing strength to support the new defence force. In October there would be nation-wide elections for a constituent assembly, and on November 11 Angola would become independent.

On paper it all looked very grand, but in fact the Alvor Agreement was a dead letter from the moment it was concluded because neither the MPLA nor the Portuguese regime had any intention of going through with it.

As Rosa Coutinho, who was in charge of the Alvor negotiations, confessed in the 1984 television interview: "I knew very well that elections could not be held in the territory ... because Angola was still in a kind of turmoil. And if elections would be held it would be a fantasy. I said it at that time: the only solution was to recognise (that) the MPLA was the only force capable of directing the government, and the Portuguese should make a separate agreement with the MPLA (to) transfer power to the MPLA on the date of the 11th of November."

That was basically what happened, and after Alvor there was never any doubt in the minds of either the Portuguese or the MPLA about who was going to take power in Angola. The bottom line was that the MPLA, although the best-organised and most politically sophisticated, did not intend to fight the agreed-upon election because it simply did not have enough popular support in largely rural Angola to have any chance of winning.

At the same time, Roberto's personal dislike of Neto and his objective of gaining sole power for himself - the reason why he and Savimbi had parted company originally - meant that losing the election was literally a matter of life and death for the MPLA. It was a textbook case of African politics at its most basic: a simple struggle for power, unencumbered by the democratic trappings that had developed over centuries in the faraway countries of the West.

At this distance it would appear that only Savimbi, who was neither caught up in super-power manoeuvring like Neto nor interested in simple military victory like Roberto, was genuinely interested in fashioning some sort of national unity. His efforts to do so were fruitless, however, and the FNLA-MPLA struggle for supremacy began almost immediately after the birth of the transitional government.

No time was wasted in implementing the Alvor Agreement. The transitional government was inaugurated on January 31, to great public acclamation, and the movements set their election campaigns in motion. There was an early hitch for the MPLA when a climactic leadership struggle broke out between Neto and Chipenda, which

UNITA   FNLA

UNIDADE
FRATERNIDADE
PODER
PAZ
PROGRESSO

became so heated that at one stage Chipenda warned that if Neto became president he would be an even greater dictator than the deposed Marcelo Caetano had ever been.

Moscow had earlier thrown its weight behind Chipenda but now supported Neto because he obviously commanded more support within the MPLA, and in late February of 1975 he was formally expelled from the movement. Chipenda promptly went over to Roberto, accompanied by about 2 000 of the MPLA's best troops who were personally loyal to him. It was a move which was to have long-lasting consequences for both Angola and South West Africa.

The struggle centred on control of Luanda, which was not only the MPLA's central power-base but also the largest city, the best harbour and the seat of national government. By mid-May many weeks of fighting and unrest had laid large parts of Luanda in ruins; food had begun to run short and law and order had commenced to crumble in various parts of Angola as the rigidly centralised bureaucracy's chain of command to the capital progressively broke down.

The MPLA soon began to prevail in the struggle. With the aid of the increasing numbers of Cuban instructors and advisers who had been arriving since the previous month - 250 by the end of May, according to various observers - its military wing, Fapla, was being turned into an ever stronger conventional-warfare force which was bound to prevail in any toe-to-toe confrontation with the FNLA and Unita, which were still basically guerrilla movements equipped with a crazy assortment of light weapons and no heavy firepower at all.

Nominally the Portuguese adopted a neutral role in all this, but reports from usually reliable sources stated in mid-May that some of Coutinho's officers were openly siding with the MPLA, and on

May 30 the High Commissioner, General Antonio Silva Cardoso, openly blamed the MPLA for launching what he described as a clearly planned and premeditated campaign of violence.

To military observers, Cardoso's accusation made sense. Since the MPLA had no hope of winning the election, it was logical for Neto to take advantage of the virtual immunity conferred on him by Coutinho to deal first with the FNLA and then attend to the militarily much weaker Unita.

With dismaying rapidity Angola began to slide into full-scale chaos as the three contenders fought – for survival in the case of Savimbi and for supremacy in the case of Neto and Roberto. In July the MPLA won the first round by throwing both the FNLA and the small Unita presence out of Luanda and establishing itself in almost every sizeable population centre between the capital and the South West African border.

Roberto holed up at Ambriz, a stone's-throw from the capital, and started hatching plans to retake Luanda at the head of his FNLA troops, with which he still controlled everything up to the Zairean border. Savimbi made his headquarters in the central Angolan town of Silva Porto and proceeded to consolidate his grip on the south and south-eastern rural areas while appealing vainly for help from various African countries, the United States and even South Africa. For a nominal but much-disliked ally he had Daniel Chipenda, who had been despatched southwards to support him and was now lying up at the central-southern town of Serpa Pinto (according to one observer the wily Roberto did this in the hope that Chipenda and Savimbi would neutralise one another enough to allow him to concentrate on the MPLA).

South of the border, the breakdown in public order in Angola had brought a temporary benefit to the South West African administration because it resulted in South African troops being deployed in relatively large numbers in Ovamboland for the first time. But the insurgents benefited from the chaotic situation reigning in southern Angola and their old ties with Unita.

Virtually every day insurgent groups would slip over the border into Ovamboland, commit various acts of activation and intimidation which included murder, and then vanish into southern Angola again. For the Swapo high command it was the realisation of a cherished dream: at last the main thrust of the insurgency could be aimed directly at Ovamboland instead of being virtually confined to remote Caprivi, and with any sort of luck they would end up with being able to operate from behind a safe border. Now, at last, all the ingredients for a successful insurgency were coming together.

To the South Africans it was obvious that an extremely serious situation was building up. Refugees, who were now streaming over the border in thousands, had started bringing word of the close Cuban involvement with the MPLA, and independent proof of this involvement – and possible future plans – was obtained when one of the numerous small hot pursuits launched by the South Africans over the ever more irrelevant border turned up Cuban-origin ammunitions and weapons dumps which, as one official spokesman later said, "placed the security situation of southern Angola and the (Ruacana) water scheme in a completely different light".

Above
Daniel Chipenda, the MPLA's foremost military commander, after defecting to Holden Roberto's FNLA with 2 000 of his best troops when he lost his leadership struggle with Dr Agostinho Neto and was expelled from the movement

Below
At the start of the civil war the MPLA's troops were lightly armed, lightly equipped guerrillas like their equivalents in Unita and the FNLA. That soon changed from mid-1975 onwards as Cuban and Russian instructors turned them into semi-conventional soldiers, armed with enormous quantities of heavy weapons

The South Africans were much concerned about the Ruacana scheme, an ambitious hydro-electric joint project which they had been building in co-operation with Portugal for some years. An enormous generating plant had been erected on the South West African side of Ruacana, and at Calueque, about 25km inside Angola, a barrage and pumping station. The Calueque barrage not only regulated the flow to the Ruacana turbines but also pumped large quantities of water directly to Ovamboland through a 300km-long network of canals, so that it was an integral part of the South African hearts-and-minds effort in the homeland.

It is hardly surprising, therefore, that Swapo regarded Calueque and Ruacana as prime targets – particularly Calueque, which was vulnerable and on Angolan soil, while Ruacana was on the South West African side of the border and was, moreover, mostly underground.

The real pressure on Calueque started in late July, when the protective element of Portuguese soldiers stationed there in terms of the co-operative treaty was withdrawn; the immediate result was so much intimidation of the workers that by early August most of them had fled. At this stage one part of Calueque was held by Unita and another by the Chipenda-FNLA, while the MPLA was said to be approaching and Swapo was preparing to settle in.

The last straw came when the last three remaining pump technicians fled as well, raising the spectre of a summary halt to the vitally important flow of water to mainly agricultural Ovamboland.

Brigadier (later Major-General) Wally Black, an experienced World War II airman turned staff officer, was hastily flown to Ruacana to assess the situation. He discussed matters with the OC 1 Military Area, Brigadier Dawie Schoeman, and they concluded that the only possible course of action was to occupy Calueque. On the morning of Friday, August 8, Black returned to lay this recommendation before the SADF Chief of Staff, Major-General R F Armstrong.

Armstrong immediately held a staff conference and suggested to Admiral Biermann that aircraft be placed on stand-by to transport detachments of 2 South African Infantry Battalion from Walvis Bay to the border. Biermann in turn forwarded the recommendations to P W Botha, who approved them, and Schoeman was told to stand by for immediate action.

On August 8 an SADF officer, Commandant Gert van Niekerk, tried some last-minute negotiations with the local Unita commander but was arrogantly brushed off. Next morning a South African civilian intending to visit Calueque tried to cross the river at Beacon 5½, just beyond Ruacana, but was summarily turned back by Unita soldiers. It was an ominous development, for a total of 10 South African nationals were still in Calueque.

Van Niekerk assembled a small force consisting of a platoon of infantry and two armoured cars and headed for the crossing. Attempts to open negotiations drew fire from the Unita side, and Van Niekerk waited no longer. He fired back, scattering the Unita soldiers, then crossed the river and barrelled down the dusty road with his tiny force. A little later he burst into Calueque to find its former occupiers had almost all decamped. Van Niekerk settled in and in due course a combat team from 2 SAI arrived from Walvis Bay to occupy the village.

In Pretoria the Portuguese ambassador protested feebly. The South African government replied that it would not leave till Portugal had guaranteed the safety of the pumping station and its workers, not only *pro tempore* but also after Angolan independence on November 11. Needless to say, neither of these assurances could be given and the South Africans stayed put at Calueque.

In the meantime the anti-MPLA movements' military situation was worsening. The MPLA held Luanda, all the other important harbours and a swathe of territory extending across north-central Angola and encompassing the Benguela railway line and all the important population centres except Nova Lisboa, the country's second-largest city.

At the same time weapons and people who knew how to use them were still streaming into the MPLA's hands: more rocket-launchers, anti-aircraft guns, T-54/55 battle tanks, amphibious PT-76 reconnaissance tanks and other conventional-warfare items, as well as instructors and other experts. The FNLA was also receiving help, but on a much smaller scale - rocket-launchers, anti-aircraft missiles, small arms and other items, as well as a handful of mercenary soldiers recruited in several countries - all channelled in through Zaire by a hastily established Central Intelligence Agency organisation.

The Americans' grasp of the issues involved does not seem to have been very strong, if one is to believe John Stockwell, who came almost straight from the disaster in Saigon to be made

Above
South African troops fortify themselves at Calueque after the little town had been occupied by a minute force of infantrymen and armoured cars in the first "action" of Operation Savannah. No more action was seen at Calueque for the rest of the operation or even for the rest of the border war, but it always remained a source of friction, and in fact the last action in the 1987-1988 confrontation in Angola was fought near and in it

Previous Page
Holden Roberto's FNLA troops before the military disasters of late 1975. Originally thought to be the best soldiers in any of the three competing movements, the FNLA turned out to be good basic human material but badly trained, badly led and armed with a crazy assortment of Western and East Bloc weapons

head of the operation the CIA hastily set up in Angola in 1975. In the 1984 television documentary, Stockwell – who by then had severed his ties with the organisation and become one of its strongest critics – described the first briefing on Angola to be delivered by the CIA director to the National Security Council, US President Gerald Ford's inner cabinet:

The CIA director (said): "Gentlemen, this is a map of Africa, and here is Angola. In Angola there are three liberation movements. There is the FNLA, headed by Holden Roberto, they're the good guys. There is the MPLA, headed by Agostinho Neto, who's a drunken psychotic poet with a Marxist background. They're the bad guys" – and they used exactly that terminology, the "good guys" and the "bad guys", so that those people on the National Security Council could get it straight what the game was.

The reason why Savimbi did not get a mention at this stage was undoubtedly the fact that (as Stockwell noted) "nobody knew much about Savimbi. Savimbi didn't hit the international cocktail circuit the way FNLA and MPLA activists and leaders did. Savimbi stayed in Angola, tending to his business".

The fact is that throughout the crucial first six months of 1975 the US government was virtually inert as far as Angola was concerned. No doubt the Americans' deeply ingrained parochialism was

partly to blame, and in addition the US was not only still too deeply mired in its post-Vietnam nervous breakdown to take positive action but was entering its traditional pre-presidential election paralysis.

According to a former US civil servant stationed in Luanda at the time, warnings that the MPLA was not intending to take part in the election agreed to at Alvor were rejected by the State Department on the grounds that the MPLA leaders were stating the opposite in one African capital after another – although at grass-roots level the MPLA made no secret of its intentions:

We had a minor (administrative) problem with the MPLA ... and we said: "Well, all of these problems will be solved when we have elections and the elections are over and we have a national government," and the MPLA military leader said: "You don't really believe there's going to be an election, do you?" Now this was at the time when the MPLA and everybody else was saying there were going to be elections, and we looked at him and said: "Well, yes, why shouldn't we believe it?" He said: "Well, because we'd lose." It was just that simple.

Acting without authority from either President Ford or Congress, the CIA set up an operation to supply arms to the FNLA and Unita. Due to its clandestine nature it did not operate very satis-factorily. By the nature of things shipments were sporadic; the agency could not send state-of-the-art weapons like the Redeye anti-aircraft missile, or its own advisers.

It was a feeble attempt, but at least it was made; other Western countries did even less than the Americans to avert the approaching tragedy. Britain steered clear of the entire Angolan affair, as did West Germany, and the French did not provide much material help till months later, in November, by which time it was far too late. No help could be expected from sympathetic states like the Ivory Coast and Zambia; the only exception was Zaire, who had sent Roberto some armoured cars and two battalions of smartly uniformed but distinctly unenthusiastic troops.

And so South Africa was sucked into the burgeoning war.

Pretoria's involvement in Angola has been put down to everything from blatant racism to out-and-out neo-imperialist expansion, and Stockwell's theory is that the South Africans' main reason for giving in to the American urgings was because they scented a lever which they could use to force the US to support their policies.

Be that as it may, such evidence as is available indicates that the South Africans - particularly Vorster and his closest confidant, former policeman Lieutenant-General Hendrik van den Bergh, head of the Bureau for State Security - were reluctant participants who would have been satisfied, in the early stages anyway, with merely providing weapons and advice to anti-Swapo elements and protecting the water supply to Ovamboland, where the struggle with Plan was growing worse almost by the day. On August 16, for example, Swapo assassinated Chief Filemon Elifas, a widely respected senior traditional tribal leader and also Chief Minister of the newly-elected Ovambo internal government: a staggering blow, not only because it represented a distinct propaganda victory for Swapo but also because he was a leading figure in the multi-racial Turnhalle constitutional talks which were about to start.

There is a common misconception that Operation Savannah was a carefully planned military adventure, orchestrated by Botha and Vorster. One of the few behind-the-scenes sources available - "PW", the 1984 Botha biography by Dirk and Johanna de Villiers - tells a different story.

On the one hand there was Vorster, strongly influenced by his henchman Van den Bergh's open contempt for the military's viewpoint. On the other was the more pugnacious Botha, totally supportive of his generals' argument that it was necessary to reach beyond the borders in order to contain the insurgency.

It was a fundamental difference of strategic approach. The De Villierses quote an entry that one of the soldiers involved, Major-General Constand Viljoen, made in his notebook just after a stormy meeting in the early days of the Angolan incursion: "It is clear that General Van den Bergh sees this matter as solely a political objective. He dismisses the entire Swapo threat as meaningless and something which is not a great problem. He says there are no Swapo terrorists in Angola. That differs from our view. The reason why we tackled this business was because we had in mind the short-term aim of giving Swapo a coup de grace so that the SWA strategy could unfold."

In the eyes of Botha and the generals, the De Villierses say, it boiled down to the fact that "he was a policeman ... and a policeman's training and approach differed from that of the soldier".

The question of personalities entered into the matter as well. Van den Bergh was a hard-nosed career policeman who had won Vorster's respect and affection while chief of the security branch and later as one of his top aides in the detente exercise, and Vorster - essentially a cautious man in spite of his bellicose public persona, and understandably fearful of destroying his arduously constructed detente policy with black Africa - pretty much gave him his head. As a result, the De Villierses say, "some of the military men regarded the presence of General Hendrik van den Bergh as a nuisance. It looked as if he was Vorster's personal representative and intermediary in Angola, as it were."

The consequence was two distinct and conflicting schools of thought, with Vorster in the middle, and the generals felt aggrieved by what they perceived as his inability to keep Van den Bergh in check. The De Villierses quote an unnamed senior officer as saying, "when there was a clash of opinions ... Vorster did not act as enough of an arbiter and depended too much on Van den Bergh's standpoint". One has sympathy for Vorster. If the gamble failed, he would bear the blame (which was how it turned out). Then, too, it could have been no easy task to keep the peace between the tough-minded Van den Bergh and strong personalities like those of Botha (who deeply disliked Van den Bergh

Above Left
Two chief ministers of Ovamboland, both destined to die at Swapo's hands. Chief Filemon Elifas, left, a believer in separate development and an outspoken foe of the insurgents, was gunned down outside a beerhall in August of 1975. Pastor Cornelius Ndjoba, his successor, was killed in a landmine blast less than four years later

Above
Major-General Constand Viljoen, artilleryman and paratrooper, who played a key liaison and advisory role with the South African allies during Operation Savannah. He later became Chief of the Army and Chief of the SADF

Left
The Angolan civil war was never a simple conflict of white against black. Men of all races, impelled by various motives, fought on all sides. This Portuguese mercenary soldier was serving with the Chipenda-faction FNLA force at Nova Lisboa in July or August of 1975, just before the South Africans launched Operation Savannah. He is carrying the standard Portuguese G-3 service rifle, with two magazines taped together for more firepower

Above
Lieutenant-General H J van den Bergh

Below
Lieutenant-General Magnus Malan, Chief of the Army when the military first moved into the border areas. He saw the war through to its end 15 years later, having become Chief of the SADF and Minister of Defence in the meantime

because the latter had opened a BSS dossier on him a few years earlier), Admiral Biermann and Lieutenant-General Magnus Malan, Chief of the Army and Botha's confidant.

These basic differences were never totally ironed out. Consequently, as the De Villierses say, during the months that were to follow "the political leadership of the government hesitated, struck fast, got going and then halted again. There were reasons for this: among them uncertainty and unpreparedness and the danger of too large a loss of life. Not the least of them was the role of the Americans.

"Nevertheless, the unavoidable impression after the passage of years is that the government's hesitation and its uncertainty about aims and priorities was a major reason why South Africa was dragged further and further into a war for which, in any case, it had not planned. It was as if there were no helmsman, such as Britain enjoyed in the person of Margaret Thatcher during the Falklands War. The helmsman's art of reconciling political and military aims was lacking".

But this is to anticipate. In mid-1975 a variety of pressures was bearing down on the South African government. There were the urgings of US Secretary of State Dr Henry Kissinger and anguished appeals for help from both Roberto and Savimbi, while the strategists and planners in Pretoria were coming to the conclusion that it was imperative to provide the FNLA and Unita with substantial help. Otherwise the MPLA seemed likely to end up running Angola. If that happened the border war would escalate dramatically because for the first time Swapo would have a safe border directly opposite its main area of operations, central Ovamboland.

It was also obvious to both Botha and Vorster that if they stood by and let the MPLA's opponents go under it would cost them the hard-won credibility Pretoria's detente policy had built up among various nations in Africa, a continent where excesses of power may be excused, but never weakness.

Botha had suggested to Vorster as early as April of 1975 that South Africa should give help to the anti-MPLA movements. Prompted by Van den Bergh, Vorster hesitated at first, but on July 14 - a month after Rosa Coutinho had visited Havana to settle the details of large-scale Cuban help to the MPLA - he agreed to supply FNLA and Unita with weapons, and it was not till August 28 that Brigadier Schoeman was told to start providing clandestine help to the two movements. On September 15 Savimbi was visited in Kinshasa by Viljoen and Van den Bergh. Both men were frankly sceptical of Savimbi, but he won them over by delivering a masterful and highly professional appreciation of the military situation. They left Kinshasa with Savimbi's message to Pretoria: that he had plenty of soldiers but no weapons, boots, instructors or anti-tank weapons.

The result was that on September 24 Savimbi received an SADF liaison officer named Commandant Kaas van der Waals, an old Angola hand who had been a military attache in Luanda in the pre-coup days and had also spent time with the Portuguese forces fighting Unita. Van der Waals was under orders to advise Savimbi on the training and reorganisation of his forces and generally ensure that Nova Lisboa was held at all costs - no small task, seeing that three different approach-routes had to be secured.

Van der Waals was soon reinforced by a team of 19 instructors under Major Louis Holtzhausen, armed with a variety of light machine-guns and mortars and four Entac anti-tank guided-missile launchers (one of the Entacs turned out to be unserviceable on arrival, and Holtzhausen promptly turned its vehicle into his personal command car). At the disused Calombo airfield near Silva Porto, Holtzhausen's team began putting the Unita soldiers through basic and leader training, all in such strict secrecy that the South Africans wore Unita uniforms and were ordered to speak only English so as to create the impression that they were mercenaries. The secrecy extended all the way back to South Africa, where a complete blackout on news of SADF participation was to be enforced for many months to come.

Holtzhausen's was a daunting task, for his 1 000-odd recruits were keen but raw, and so short of weapons that they reportedly had to drill with sticks. However, the tough, crop-headed little ex-sergeant-major set to work with the skill and ingenuity acquired during a lifetime of professional soldiering, and his men also began to repair the four old World War II-vintage Panhard armoured cars that constituted Savimbi's entire armoured force. Three of the Panhards were in running order by the time six South African Armoured Corps soldiers were flown in to teach the Unita crews how to use the armoured cars, but they were able to give only three days' instruction before both cars and crews had to be committed to battle early in October.

This came about after Van der Waals was informed that three Fapla columns were converging on Nova Lisboa from Benguela and Lobito in the west and Cela in the north. Holtzhausen personally reconnoitred in his Entac vehicle-turned-command car, discovered that the columns were approaching even faster than suspected and recommended that they be attacked before they had had a chance to link up and throw their combined weight at Nova Lisboa.

Van der Waals had placed the responsibility for defending Nova Lisboa in the hands of Commandant Eddie Webb, an experienced infantryman, but the situation had suddenly become so critical that he realised there was no option but to fight immediately, even though he was ill-equipped and unprepared and Webb was temporarily at Rundu. On October 2 he formed what was to become Battle-Group Foxbat out of a company of Unita troops and his handful of instructors, placed it under Holtzhausen's command and sent the grandly-named pocket force off to battle.

On October 5 Foxbat clashed head-on with the Lobito column at Norton de Matos, half-way between Lobito and Nova Lisboa. The battle got off to a bad start when the Fapla column's leading armoured car fired the first shot and disabled Holtzhausen's makeshift command vehicle with a strike in the chassis. Most of the raw Unita troops wasted no time in fleeing, but Holtzhausen contrived to rally his small force, and in heavy exchanges of fire it killed more than 100 Fapla troops and knocked out one of the Lobito column's five armoured cars.

This action, South Africa's first of the war, temporarily halted all three Fapla columns. The Unita forces went into defensive positions west and north of Nova Lisboa and Van der Waals requested a squadron of armoured cars. The request was granted (in fact it had already been decided that he should have them) and in mid-October the stubby little Eland-90s, heavily modified local versions of the French Panhard AML-90s, were flown in by C-130 transports and unloaded at Silva

Above left
All sorts of people from many countries found themselves involved in the Angolan civil war and Operation Savannah. These Rhodesia-based pilots of Air Trans Africa — Adrian Charlton, left, and American Ed Davis, right, a veteran of the Belgian Congo and Biafran airlifts, flew many loads of refugees out of Nova Lisboa as the military situation in Angola started to collapse. Other, more clandestine, flights to the north brought planeloads of Central Intelligence Agency weapons and munitions to the FNLA

Above
Dr Henry Kissinger of the United States, one of the prime movers in getting South Africa to move into Angola in late 1975. Later he blandly denied all complicity in the controversial incursion

Left
The old order changeth … a memorial honouring the Portuguese era is defaced by the slogans and colours of the new power in the land. All of these statues were later destroyed

Porto - the first of many such flights which were to be a backbone of the South African effort in the Angolan war. The Elands were a formidable addition to Webb's scanty armoury of 81mm mortars, machine-guns, Entacs and CIA-supplied 106mm recoilless guns, and in the days to come these and other South African armoured cars built a fearsome fighting reputation among all the Angolan fighting forces.

Foxbat was the first of several South African battle-groups which were destined to dominate the Angolan war for months to come; the second, Task Force Zulu, had in fact already been formed as Operation Savannah began escalating into a second and more ambitious phase, which envisaged the expulsion of the MPLA from as much of south-western Angola as possible by November 11.

Specifically, this meant the recapture of the harbours of Lobito, Benguela and Mossamedes, the securing of the economically and strategically important railway line from Benguela to Zambia and Zaire and the seizing of such towns as Sa Da Bandeira.

If this could be accomplished, it was hoped, the FNLA and Unita between them would be able to lay claim to leadership of Angola when independence came - a hopeless pipe-dream, it might seem, except that the situation was still extremely fluid; so much so that the Organisation for African Unity was hopelessly split down the middle about which side to support. In the opinion of some observers the OAU's indecision when one would have expected an automatic vote against Unita and the FNLA because they were receiving South African help can be attributed partly to

moderate states' strong qualms about non-African (specifically Russian and Cuban) involvement and partly to Vorster's detente policy.

This expanded aim required a larger force level, and no time was wasted in setting it up. On October 9 Colonel Koos van Heerden, OC 72 Motorised Brigade, was summoned from his headquarters at Vereeniging in the Transvaal and hastily flown to Rundu base in Kavango.

There Brigadier Schoeman gave him a raggle-taggle force consisting of Battle-Group Alpha, a battalion of Angolan and Caprivian Bushmen under Commandant Delville Linford of the South African Army; Battle-Group Bravo, three companies of partly trained Chipenda-faction soldiers, commanded by an Angolan named Comandante Businha, advised by the renowned SADF special-forces soldier, Commandant Jan Breytenbach; and a handful of 81mm mortars and Vickers medium machine-guns.

With this motley and polyglot crew, all dressed in FNLA uniforms and mounted in a tatterdemalion collection of former vegetable lorries, Van Heerden was expected to capture as many towns in the south-west as he could by November 11.

Considering the size of the task and the means available it was a classic forlorn-hope mission, but Van Heerden, a wily character, accepted the challenge and set off on a headlong dash which was to make military history.

Van Heerden crossed the border at Cuangar on October 14 and overran Pereira D'Eca in a surprise attack on October 19. Vila Rocades fell the following day, before Van Heerden's arrival, to a squadron of armoured cars, infantry and a mortar

Below
Eland-90 armoured cars are made ready at a forward base during Operation Savannah. The tough little vehicles played a leading role in the incursion, carving out a fearsome reputation for themselves and being used for everything from reconnaissance to tank-killing and direct fire support

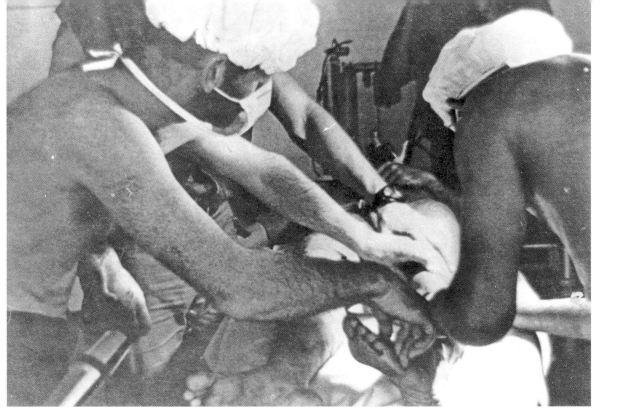

group under Commandant Boy du Toit which had been sent from Ruacana to join hands with Zulu. On October 23 he captured Joao de Almeida, an important communications centre and MPLA local headquarters, after fierce but brief fighting.

On October 24 he took Sa da Bandeira, a district civil capital and MPLA regional headquarters. Three days later he took the port of Mocamedes after chasing away its Portuguese garrison and a frigate by means of a blood-curdling but totally fraudulent threat.

Van Heerden then headed for Benguela, the terminal of the copper railway. Before he got there he ran into a well-prepared Cuban/MPLA position at Caporolo, but the defenders withdrew when they realised Van Heerden was outflanking them. On November 4 Van Heerden finally reached Benguela, captured it after a two-day battle and went on to Lobito, which he occupied on November 7 and then linked up with Eddie Webb.

Foxbat had seen considerable fighting by now, starting in late October. Informed that very strong Fapla columns from both the north and the west were concentrating at the Quibala crossroads, Webb took up defensive positions in and around the town of Luimbala; the advancing MPLA northern force unexpectedly bumped into Webb's forward elements south of Cela and then laid down a softening-up bombardment (which failed to achieve its purpose). The Fapla reconnaissance element advanced, led by a Cuban brigadier in a black Citroen car which was promptly destroyed by a shot from one of the 106mm recoilless guns.

Webb took Foxbat down the western route, capturing Luimbala on October 27, Cubal on November 1 and Norton de Matos (after heavy fighting) on November 3. It was then ordered to the coast, the idea being that it would cut off the Cuban/MPLA forces' withdrawal route north of Zulu so that they would be caught in a hammer-and-anvil situation. Several running fights later, Webb was holding a crossroads near the coast after cutting off several Fapla vehicles' retreat when he heard that Van Heerden had reached Lobito, and on November 8 they finally joined hands.

After discussing the situation the two commanders decided to go their separate ways; Foxbat returned to the central front and Van Heerden

continued up the coast. He was near the important sea-town of Novo Redondo when independence day dawned on November 11.

In Luanda the High Commissioner, Commodore Leonel Cardoso (who had earlier replaced General Silva Cardoso), ignominiously ended five centuries of Portuguese rule with a short proclamation of independence in which he expressed regret that he had not been able to join in any celebrations "since in the present circumstances this could be taken to signify Portuguese interference in the sacred right of any people, that of deciding its own destiny". Having said that, Cardoso boarded a warship lying in Luanda harbour and sailed for Portugal, leaving Angola to its fate.

According to Pretoria's original game-plan the South Africans should have been out of Angola by now, but the progression of the war - not to mention the sheer distances involved - had made this impossible. So, as an official spokesman later delicately put it, "after mediation by go-betweens, the South African forces, which comprised at that

Above
All was grist to the medical officers' mill: their battle was not to take territory but to win the battle for a wounded man's life. Here army surgeons, stripped to the waist in the killing heat and humidity, operate on a Cuban wounded and captured during the fighting at Cela, where Battle-Group Foxbat mauled a Marxist column

Below
Government House, Luanda. In this gracious old building the Portuguese High Commissioner, Commodore Leonel Cardoso, ignominiously ended five centuries of Portuguese rule with a short proclamation, then boarded a warship in the harbour and sailed away

stage about 300 advisers/instructors and personnel as well as a limited number of armoured cars, mortars and anti-tank weapons, remained in anticipation of a political solution which was the prospect held out by the mediators".

The prospect did not materialise, and the jury-rigged armistice lasted only till November 13. On that date Zulu's forward elements started coming under heavy 122mm rocket fire. By now Van Heerden had acquired three 25-pounder artillery pieces and with their help seized Novo Redondo on November 14 after a brisk fight along the way in which he lost the first South African soldier in the entire unlikely episode - Captain George Schoeman, who was severely wounded in a mine explosion and later died of his wounds at 1 Military Hospital, Pretoria.

At this stage Zulu's advance bogged down. To advance northwards to the next target, Porto Amboim, was likely to prove a grim task, because all the bridges over the large and flooded Queve River had been blown and a strong enemy force occupied the northern bank. A push north-eastwards towards Gabela was equally unfavourable.

In 1977, when the military went public about Operation Savannah for the first time, a spokesman opined that "the allied FNLA/Unita forces, supported by South African forces, could have conquered the whole of Angola, but Dr Savimbi insisted he was only interested in controlling his traditional area because he was determined to reach a settlement with the MPLA to the advantage of Angola". There was more to it than that, however: specifically, the final defeat of the FNLA's Holden Roberto in the north.

At his headquarters at Ambriz - so tantalisingly close to the capital that he could see the great city's lights at night - Roberto had spent three months engaging in some local skirmishing and polishing his plans for a triumphal return to Luanda on the eve of the November 11 independence date.

He had achieved some local successes in the second week of October, but their effect had been negated by logistical problems, irregular and insufficient supplies of weapons and, most of all, his wilfulness. Unlike Savimbi, who accepted that he lacked expertise as a field commander and relied on his South African advisers' professional knowledge, Roberto insisted on going his own way.

In the end his stubbornness sabotaged not only his own future but, to a large extent, that of Operation Savannah as well.

Nevertheless, Van Heerden drew up a plan involving a simultaneous parachute assault and river-crossing. The plan was rejected by his higher headquarters, however, and Zulu pulled back to Novo Redondo for a few days before Van Heerden was summoned to Cela, where Brigadier Schoeman had set up his headquarters. Leaving Alpha behind at Novo Redondo, Van Heerden took the rest of his ragged force to receive his new orders.

But for both Van Heerden and Webb it was the end of the war; they were recalled and their forces reorganised into a new Task Force Zulu, commanded by Colonel C J Swart and consisting of most of Van Heerden's Zulu men (renamed "Battle-Group Bravo") under Commandant Breytenbach, and Battle-Group Foxbat, now under Commandant George Kruys.

Van Heerden's and Webb's departure more or less coincided with the start of an irreversible decline in the fortunes of the anti-MPLA forces, although this might not have been obvious at the time.

In practical military terms Roberto's ambition to retake Luanda made no sense at all. His troops were inexperienced, his leader group lacked expertise; the MPLA was much more heavily equipped and enjoyed the services of the Cubans. In addition he lacked heavy weapons. The FNLA was equipped with an assortment of Western and communist-bloc arms that turned his logistics into a nightmare, possessed no hard-skinned vehicles except a few old Panhard armoured cars and disposed of exactly one piece of reasonably long-ranged artillery. Roberto certainly had no answer to the MPLA's prime terror weapon, the Russian BM-21 multiple rocket-launcher.

The obsolescent BM-21's unguided 122mm rockets were not particularly accurate or extraordinarily lethal for troops who were well-trained and properly dug in (in one theatre of the war South African troops actually took to playing "chicken" with the rockets, the winner in the game being the last man to jump into his slit-trench before the "red-eyes" landed), but they played havoc with the morale of Roberto's mainly unsophisticated troops, some of whom came from such remote areas that they had never even heard a rifle being fired before joining the FNLA.

Roberto's appeals to the CIA were answered by periodical shipments of arms, but because of the CIA's need to conceal its operation from the US Congress the shipments tended to be irregular and did not include the artillery he needed so badly. The South African connection, thanks to the assiduous work of Brigadier Ben Roos, the SADF liaison officer at Ambriz, worked better. The De Villierses quote an exasperated Roberto as saying: "I go to the South Africans and ask for help, and they react within 24 hours. What happens when I speak to the Americans? Sometimes it takes weeks, and sometimes I don't get even that."

To highly trained and experienced officers like Ben Roos and the visiting Major-General Constand Viljoen it was obvious that an advance on Luanda was a formidably difficult project. Roberto's forces were hardly top-of-the line. In addition to his horde of partly trained and mostly completely unsophisticated Bakongo tribesmen he had about 120 white Portuguese mercenaries, his contingent of faint-hearted Zaireans and a few resident advisers, among them Roos and a small CIA contingent. His

Below
Captured BM-21 missiles, unguided artillery rockets, commonly known as "Red-Eyes" by South African troops and used in quantity by the MPLA and its allies. The South Africans soon discovered the Red-Eye's weak points — inaccuracy, high visibility and heavy blast but poor fragmentation — and learnt to respect rather than fear it. But the Red-Eye was a potent psychological weapon when used against their Unita and FNLA allies' mostly unsophisticated rank and file

armour and artillery assets, as mentioned earlier, were virtually non-existent.

The nature of the terrain was also distinctly unfavourable. The approach to Luanda was bounded on the west by the Atlantic Ocean and on the east by enormous stretches of marshy areas, this being the rainy season. Since Roberto's FNLA troops were convinced the marshy areas were infested by man-eating snakes, this meant that his advance would effectively be restricted to the road, which in turn was sure to be covered by the other side's abundant artillery assets (the Cubans had proved to be unskilful at South African-style bush warfare, but adept at preparing defensive positions).

In Viljoen's and Roos's considered opinion a large enough force of well-trained and well-equipped South African soldiers could have broken through to Luanda (although a conquest of the capital was not part of South Africa's game-plan), but Roberto's force stood no chance at all. Both officers earnestly and repeatedly counselled him to give up his dream of taking Luanda and concentrate instead on holding on to the territory he controlled; by doing so, they pointed out, he would be in a position of strength when independence came.

It was sound advice. Luanda was militarily strong but crumbling from within, thanks to the fighting of the past few months. Its people were beginning to go hungry because Unita now controlled many of the agricultural areas, while power and water cuts were a frequent occurrence because of the sporadic fighting around the hydro-electric scheme at Dondo to the south-east. It was obvious that if independence came with Roberto and Unita in position in their traditional area the MPLA would be forced to negotiate. But Roberto spurned their advice and decreed that the attack on Luanda would take place on November 10, the eve of independence.

This was the message Magnus Malan and Viljoen brought back to Pretoria after a lightning visit to Ambriz on November 4 to consult with Roos. Dismayed though they were by Roberto's insistence on adhering to his suicidal plans, P W Botha and his senior officers nevertheless decided to continue supporting him; no doubt they cherished a faint hope that Angola, the land of surprises, might spring another one and allow him to succeed.

Accordingly the South Africans co-operated to the best of their ability while a supremely over-confident Roberto made his final preparations for his knock-out blow at Agostinho Neto. For example, on November 7 Roberto asked for artillery pieces; Botha agreed and by 9.30 the next morning aircraft

Above
South African soldiers inspect two captured vehicles, a BRDM armoured scout car and, in the background, a BM-21 multiple rocket launcher. The BRDM was a feeble thing, lightly armoured and lightly armed, but the BM-21 had a catastrophic effect on the South African's allies ... and, which was just as serious, it outranged the SADF's artillery

took off from Air Force Base Waterkloof in Pretoria, carrying a troop of three 5.5-inch medium guns under Major J C D F Bosch. It was also decided that the SAAF would provide offensive air support, in the form of three Canberra light bombers under Commandant A P Steenkamp, which would fly from Rundu, 1 200 km away, and soften up the opposition prior to the attack. The news that some air support would be forthcoming was welcomed by an increasingly perturbed Roos, who was deeply involved in planning the attack.

In its final form the design of the attack was as follows: Steenkamp's aircraft would make a first-light bombing attack on the morning of October 9 and Bosch's guns would fire a barrage of airburst shells to soften up the enemy. Roberto's trusted senior commander, a former Portuguese secret service agent called Colonel Santos e Castro, would seize the bridge over the Bengo River and the main force under Roberto would roll down the road towards Luanda. In the meantime the guns would move forward and be placed on a high point south of the Bengo River from where they could fire on enemy positions defending Luanda.

What actually happened was rather different. At 5.40am on November 9 Bosch's guns fired a 19-minute barrage; then, precisely on time, Steenkamp's aircraft arrived from Rundu. Unfortunately the requirements of secrecy had forced Steenkamp's aircraft to fly high and maintain radio silence, so that only one of the bombs dropped hit its target; even so, it transpired later, the off-target explosions had persuaded the MPLA troops to evacuate some of their positions.

After that fortuitous success, however, nothing went right. Much might still have been made of the attack if the infantry had assailed the Bengo River bridge immediately after the bombing attack, but the FNLA force could not move without Roberto being at its head, and he did not arrive with his entourage till long after H-Hour, having enjoyed a good night's sleep and a leisurely breakfast. As a result the attack began 40 minutes late, and walked straight into a force of 800 Cubans and MPLA awaiting it on the other side of the river.

The Cubans and MPLA were armed with a variety of heavy weapons ranging from vehicle-mounted recoilless guns to BM-21 MRLs, their defensive positions were well-sited and properly constructed and their artillery was ranged in on the road; and the inevitable was not long delayed. In vain Roberto's Portuguese officers suggested a flanking attack through the swamps, while Roos mooted a wide swing around in the east. The FNLA soldiers refused point-blank to wade through the marshy areas and Roberto shrugged off all such subterfuges in favour of an advance straight down what later became known as "Death Road".

Death Road it was. Artillery fire rained down on the attackers as they approached the Bengo River, and one by one the armoured cars were knocked out. The attackers hit back as best they could, out-ranged and outgunned.

It is possible there were more sinister overtones, although at this distance it is impossible to prove or disprove anything. The De Villierses claim that "when the allies wanted to fire back with their mortars, they found the firing-pins were missing. It is at times like these that soldiers begin speaking in tongues ... Suffice it to say that the word 'sabotage' was in the air; also that the previous day the black mortar men had been instructed by two Americans".

Then again, in a series of in-depth articles on the war written in 1977, Robert Moss of The Economist claims that on the eve of the attack on Luanda the CIA hurriedly shipped in a load of weapons which included 10 heavy mortars and some 106mm recoilless guns, but they arrived without handling instructions or sighting equipment, and the instructors themselves did not appear till after the battle (in fairness, Moss notes that according to American sources the sights and instructions had been included, but must have been lost somewhere after delivery).

Be all that as it may, the fact of the matter was that the FNLA troops and Zaireans along Death Road began taking casualties; as John Stockwell writes somewhat dramatically in his book "In Search of Enemies", the FNLA soldiers' "hearts burst with clutching terror as they dived to the ground or stood helplessly mesmerised, watching the next salvo landing in their midst".

Soon soldiers began trickling away, including all those detailed to help the South African artillerymen and elements which had not yet been committed to battle. When the trickle turned into a flood Roos ordered the artillerymen to fall back and take up new positions some distance north, then returned to Ambriz to transmit his doleful tidings to Rundu.

According to the De Villierses the disastrous import of Roberto's victory was not fully grasped by the South African Cabinet as its members sat in Pretoria and grappled with the problem of whether to withdraw from Angola or stay on, now that November 11 had come and gone. In some ways the situation looked relatively favourable. As the De Villierses point out, the MPLA regime had not yet been recognised by either Portugal or the OAU, and there was still a chance of conquering Luanda and the few remaining MPLA-held regions. Failing that, it might be possible to secure the Benguela railway and fortify the FNLA and Unita in their respective areas. In addition, the American government was still urging the South Africans to stay on, and Savimbi had urgently requested that the railway be made safe.

What Pretoria did not yet know, as the De Villierses remark, was that the FNLA was crumbling after the defeat at Death Road (in fact it had collapsed altogether and its members and the Zaireans were to be chased all the way to the Angola's northern border in the next two months); that CIA aid to the anti-MPLA movements was fading away; that the remaining Portuguese population was getting out as quickly as possible; and that Luanda was still receiving both Russian weapons and Cuban troops - according to W Martin James III, assistant professor of political science at Henderson State University, Arkansas, 4 000 Cubans were in Angola by November 11.

Above
Captain Sam Davis

Below
Locomotives of the CFR — the "Caminho de Ferro de Benguela" — at a marshalling yard. The economically vital railway line became an early casualty of the civil war and never again operated along its full length, thanks to constant sabotage by Unita insurgents

By late November it was obvious that there was nothing more to be done in the north, and Ben Roos began making preparations to evacuate from Ambriz. The FNLA collapse had left him in a decidedly ticklish situation. Marooned in Ambriz with no direct land access to "own forces" and no airfield at his disposal any more, he was effectively cut off behind enemy lines and landed with the massive headache of evacuating his staff of 26 men and communications and cryptographic equipment worth something like R500 000. In addition there was himself. He knew far too much to even contemplate the thought of allowing himself to be captured. It is said that he resolved to take his own life if the evacuation went sour and capture was imminent.

One of his first actions was to make contact with the nearby CIA element, which had promised to help him to get out. To his anger and dismay he learnt that sometime after November 24 the Americans had quietly decamped without any prior warning. The next most feasible avenue of escape was the sea, and so a shipborne rescue operation was organised which is unique in South African military history.

The South African Navy had been actively, although extremely unobtrusively, involved in Operation Savannah for some time. In this particular case the anti-submarine frigate SAS President Kruger (Captain R D Kingon) had spent almost three weeks quietly loafing about, under strict radar and radio silence, in the vicinity of the Cunene River mouth. Ostensibly Kingon was on a routine fisheries-protection patrol, but in fact he had been ordered to stand by in case of an evacuation and to this end was equipped with a Puma helicopter, extra automatic weapons, a cutter and several Gemini inflatables.

Towards the end of the month the Kruger's sister ship, SAS President Steyn (Captain A S Davis) was despatched to relieve her. Davis was also supposed to be going on a fisheries-protection patrol, but unlike Kingon he was given very specific orders. He was to maintain station at a suitable position along the Angolan coast, avoiding contact with other ships as far as possible, so that if necessary he could evacuate SADF personnel from Ambriz, Ambrizete, Benguela or Lobito at short notice; as a sideline he was also to monitor and record ground forces' radio transmissions for later analysis. Strict radio silence was to be maintained from the time of departure from Cape Town, and was not to be broken except in dire emergencies.

Davis duly rendezvoused with Kingon, took over the Gemini boats and a special map, and was on station on November 27 when Roos contacted him to request evacuation. Davis radioed back that Ambriz was unsuitable for such an operation; Roos must proceed to the nearby harbour of Ambrizete, 70km to the north, and he would start lifting them off from 11 pm on November 27. Davis then broke his long-maintained radio silence to inform Naval Headquarters in Pretoria of the proposed evacuation. Naval Headquarters replied approving the operation. If it succeeded, Davis would send one word, SUPER. Failure would be indicated by the word DUCK (the Steyn was jocularly known in the service as "Super Duck" because several of the birds appeared on its crest).

Somehow the two code-words were very appropriate to those who knew Sam Davis. He was a familiar figure in naval circles: large, plummy, a bit of a character who spoke fluent French but not much Afrikaans and was in the habit of riding

around Simon's Town on a motor-scooter (the best antidote, he claimed, for the narrow-gutted town's traffic-clogged streets); a competent seaman whose service afloat dated back to the last days of World War II and was now nearing retirement after a long and varied career.

Just how competent he was as a seaman was soon to be demonstrated, for the evacuation was bedevilled by extraneous factors from the start.

By late afternoon on November 27 the Steyn was in place near Ambrizete, her normally spick-and-span appearance sadly marred by the need for secrecy: she flew a tattered, very dirty ensign, her glittering brass name-plate had been removed and all her identification numbers had been painted out.

But now things began to go wrong. Roos radioed to ask for a postponement of the evacuation till 5 am on November 28 because the rains had left the road to Ambrizete in such atrocious condition that he was making very slow progress.

Davis agreed to hold back, but he was a sadly worried man as the Steyn rose and fell on the

grey Atlantic swells. Earlier, while proceeding towards the rendezvous, he had intercepted considerable radio traffic from numbers of Russian ships and also from aircraft flying between Luanda and Cabinda, some of which he had also picked up on his radar screens; was he being lured into a trap? If the Steyn were to be sunk, it would be both a great propaganda victory for the Marxists and also an irreparable loss to the South African Navy, starved of large fighting ships by the arms embargo. In addition there was the time factor. Moonrise was as early as 2.30 am, but he would lose a couple of hours due to Roos's late arrival, and it would be perilous if the evacuation of the shore party could not be complete by the time the sun rose at 7.10 am.

There was nothing for it, however, and Davis crept closer and closer to the coast. He was quite close to Ambrizete at 4 am on November 28, when Roos signalled that he and his men were in position, adding that the little harbour had no pier and the evacuation would have to take place from the beach. Unable to make use of his sophisticated navigational aids, Davis began feeling his way closer to the shore in classic fashion, hampered by the lack of landmarks and a heavy overcast which obscured the moon, so that the land was totally invisible.

However, he made good progress after handily avoiding the most hazardous known navigation obstacle - an underwater sandbank - and at 4.24 am, when the Steyn was three and a half nautical miles from the coast, two vehicles' headlights were spotted on land, giving the agreed-on recognition signal of flashes at 10-second intervals. Davis flashed a reply, and Roos came on the air to report that there were no enemy forces in the vicinity.

At 4.40 am Davis sent off his three Gemini inflatables under command of Lieutenant R N Erleigh, followed soon afterwards by the ship's cutter. No doubt Erleigh was acutely aware of the fact, as he fought swells up to three metres high, that he was faced with anything but an easy task. In spite of Roos's assurance, there was no disguising the fact that he was heading for a potentially hostile shore, and moreover, one that he still could not see at all.

About a quarter of a nautical mile from shore Erleigh signalled to Roos's party with a lamp whose lens was covered with red masking tape. There was an immediate response; Erleigh ordered the two other Geminis to stay where they were and closed in by himself. Soon he could see the harbour's sea-wall to starboard, and also the surf breaking on the beach. To his delight he saw, too, that thanks to the sea-wall the swells had diminished so much that an evacuation was entirely feasible.

Erleigh came on shore quite near the town square and was soon being heartily welcomed by Roos's party; he then summoned the other Geminis, and soon afterwards the cutter arrived and took up position near the sea-wall.

While the inhabitants of Ambrizete slept on in happy ignorance of what was happening in their town, the South Africans began to prepare for the evacuation. The troops had already been divided into groups of five by Captain Malcolm Kinghorn, whom Roos had put in charge of the evacuation, but it was immediately evident that Erleigh's boats would not be able to evacuate both men and equipment by sunrise.

Roos then informed Davis that it would be safe to use the ship's helicopter to lift out the

communications and cryptographic gear; Davis gave permission, and at 5.54 am Captain Ben van der Westhuizen (South African Air Force) and his flight engineer, Sergeant B B Smit, took off. A few minutes later they landed at Ambrizete, guided in by vehicle headlights and torch-flashes. Its first cargo consisted not of equipment but of the brigadier and two of his men, Kinghorn pulling rank as evacuation officer and insisting that Roos be flown out first.

Van der Westhuizen made four more trips, lifting out the equipment and some of the personnel. At 6.43 the boats arrived at the ship and seven minutes later Van der Westhuizen made his last landing on the dark, pitching flight deck. Then, with seemly haste, Davis took the President Steyn out to sea.

At Cape Town's Silvermine maritime communications centre, meanwhile, ever more anxious senior officers had been waiting since 5 am for word of failure or success. But it was not till 9 am that Davis broke silence with a cryptic message reading "super successful duck". It was later determined that this supremely cryptic response had resulted from an incorrect interpretation of the original order, and the tension did not diminish till it had been sorted out.

Two days later, on November 30, Roos and his party were landed at Walvis Bay. Then, in the best tradition of the "Silent Service", the President Steyn headed out to sea again, but this time to make for her home-base of Simon's Town.

It is only now that observers are beginning to realise what a pivotal event the Battle of Death Road was; in the opinion of some it might well have been the turning-point of Operation Savannah. It will remain a moot point till the political histories are written and the incursion can be seen in full perspective, but it is certain that after Roberto's defeat the anti-MPLA forces' chances of holding Angola evaporated.

With Savimbi holding the south and Roberto the north, the MPLA might well have been forced to reach some sort of modus vivendi with its opponents, since the alternative would have been to form a virtually powerless rump state around Luanda, cut off from all food supplies and deprived of income from at least two of Angola's main sources of revenue, the Benguela railway line (the most economical route between the Zairean and Zambian copperfields and the sea) and the diamond fields in the north-east. In addition, the isolated oil-rich enclave of Cabinda would have been in constant peril.

But it was not to be. Thanks to the collapse of the FNLA, the MPLA was no longer engaged in a war on two fronts and Savimbi was out on a limb, his forces totally unequipped to fight off Luanda's forces and his support from friendly nations fast drying up.

At this stage the South African government was still keeping the lid clamped on events in Angola, although on November 20 the Minister of Foreign Affairs, Dr Hilgard Muller, had come close to being driven into a corner when he was interviewed on the BBC programme "Focus on Africa".

Asked if South African mercenaries were operating in Angola, Muller replied: "In the case of the independence of Mozambique the recruiting of mercenaries was prohibited in South Africa, and that is still our policy. You will appreciate that it is very difficult to control the activities of citizens once they are outside the country."

Above
"Civic action" meant a variety of things. One skilled carpenter-national serviceman ended up running a furniture factory in Kavango, this one, 19-year-old Justin Pierce, was teaching elementary English to Ovambo schoolgoers in December 1975, less than 12 months after he had left school himself

Muller ducked the question of which party in the Angolan war received South Africa's support by saying that to answer this would expose him to "the accusation that I am very undiplomatic and trying to interfere. We in South Africa sincerely hope that whatever government is in charge in Angola should not be dominated by communists from outside".

The presence of South African troops in Angola was no secret, he said. They were there to defend the northern borders of South West Africa and the Cunene project, into which "we've put millions, and not only for our advantage, and I hope the situation will be normalised as soon as there is a representative government in Angola".

It was obvious, however, that official assurances were no longer enough to lull the South African public's unease about the Angolan incursion. The public was still unaware of the precise extent of the fighting north of the border, but since South Africa was part of the "global village" disquieting items of news emanating from abroad could not be kept out of the newspapers by mere censorship, particularly since many South Africans habitually listened to BBC and other foreign news broadcasts anyway.

On December 1 the government finally yielded to the clamouring of the South African press. Senior executives of all the mainstream newspapers were invited to Pretoria for a strictly off-the-record briefing by the Chief of the SADF, Admiral Biermann. Biermann made no bones about the situation in Angola as he sketched a stark and alarming picture:

● The MPLA had pushed Unita out of Luso and was mounting offensives out of Luanda against the FNLA-held towns of Carmona and Ambriz in the north.

● SADF troops were now 700km inside Angola.

● Most of the South African troops killed to date had been fighting well inside Angola.

● To date 47 South Africans had been wounded (this helped to quash disquieting rumours about Cuban secret weapons that had left hundreds of troops so seriously wounded that they had been segregated under guard in one wing of 1 Military Hospital at Voortrekkerhoogte, Pretoria).

● FNLA morale was low, and there were continual arguments between Roberto's black and Portuguese soldiers.

● The MPLA had about 23 000 soldiers, said to be the best of the troops in any of the movements. The FNLA had about 27 000 now that the Zairean troops had returned after showing hopeless form and proving to be of generally poor quality. Unita had about 12 000, mostly trained and reasonably efficient (all these figures are now regarded as far too high).

● It was not possible to see the end of the struggle. Even if the FNLA and Unita managed to capture Luanda, which now seemed unlikely, the indications were that battle for supremacy would continue. Without large-scale Western intervention the MPLA was well-placed to win.

● Plan was operating from a few bases inside Angola and Zambia; its men had discarded their uniforms and taken to carrying out attacks in civilian clothes. They carried both MPLA and Unita membership cards, but where possible made it their business to link up with MPLA troops.

This last marked yet another important watershed in the border war. Savimbi had broken his ties with Swapo as early as September, no doubt

partly as a result of his burgeoning relationship with the South Africans; in December the MPLA and Swapo had forged a link for equally valid strategic and ideological reasons. It was an inconvenient and painful turn-around, bearing in mind that Swapo had strong ethno-cultural links with Unita, and one that was to aid and hinder Plan in more or less equal measures, because large tracts of the south remained Savimbi's fief in the years to come, regardless of the fact that the MPLA reigned in Luanda.

Tactically speaking, however, Swapo had no option. By this time it was fairly obvious that the MPLA would emerge the overall winner, and for Swapo it was vital to enjoy the patronage of the new regime if it was to achieve its greater aim - victory in South West Africa.

None of Biermann's briefing could be released to the general public, however, and disquiet continued to grow. In early December 1975 the opposition United Party MP for Simon's Town, John Wiley, appealed to the government to take the country into its confidence and "tell us exactly where we stand". By now (as the pro-government newspapers Beeld and Rapport pointed out) even staunch government supporters were showing signs of deep worry.

During all this time the insurgency continued apace, even though Swapo's staging areas just north of the border had been disrupted by the general confusion; Angolan refugees arriving in Ovamboland in mid-October described how they had been searched by Afrikaans-speaking blacks wearing the olive-green uniforms favoured by Plan.

In mid-October, for example, eight Ovambo civilians had been killed by Plan raiders and a South African soldier had died in Caprivi. Swapo claimed responsibility for the soldier's death, but denied its operatives had killed the Ovambos.

Soon afterwards the SADF destroyed two Plan bases and killed seven insurgents in what it described as a "follow-up action", the spokesman adding somewhat cryptically that the action had been "in line" with the principle of hot pursuit. By now various civilian observers were earnestly discussing the likelihood of hot-pursuit actions if the raids continued, not realising that they had been in progress for some time.

On November 20 an army patrol wiped out a 10-man insurgent gang after a mortar attack in which one soldier had been fatally wounded, and on November 26, four South African soldiers - two members of the Permanent Force and two national servicemen - were killed in a hot-pursuit operation, bringing the year's total of SADF operational deaths to 11.

The following day newspapers in Cape Town and Johannesburg published a sensational story that "terrorist suicide squads based in Zambia and Angola" were responsible for the sudden escalation in border skirmishes. This was totally incorrect, since Plan never carried out any kamikaze missions, but the reporter concerned was nearer the mark when he wrote that the alleged suicide squads "number between 25 and 35 men - bigger combat units than have been thrown against South African armed forces in the past, and better equipped".

By now the authorities were making cautious efforts to prepare the public for something the planners knew only too well: that counter-insurgency campaigns are not quick-fix affairs, that time itself was a weapon which could be used by whoever was willing to use it. On December 5, for example, the OC Western Province Command, a seasoned World War II veteran named Brigadier

Above
Brigadier Ben Roos, Holden Roberto's SADF liaison officer

L H Robertson, warned in a speech that South African soldiers would have to realise that in future "border service is going to be the rule and not the exception".

As if to underscore his words, mid-December brought news of a "skirmish", as it was officially described, in which 61 insurgents and three South African soldiers were killed.

By this time the South African Cabinet had already decided to withdraw from Angola, and in fact in mid-November a formation known as 101 Task Force had been formed at Rundu and placed under the able Lieutenant-General Andre van Deventer to prepare for an orderly pull-out. There was nothing else to be done. Luanda could still be taken, but a force of 1 500 South African infantry would be needed and casualties could run as high as 40 percent, which was totally unacceptable. In addition, Van Deventer had expressed serious reservations about the ability of the SADF's logistical system - withered by 37 years of peace - to sustain any further escalation of the war, and in any case American support was fading fast.

By now, too, the fighting had resumed in Operation Savannah. The principle of a total withdrawal had been accepted, but South African forces in the field were ordered to move out as aggressively as they could in order to leave Unita with the greatest possible advantage for the lean days which undoubtedly were on the way.

On December 9 Battle Group Foxbat, now under Commandant George Kruys, fought its last major engagement, which later became known as the "Battle of Bridge 14".

Faced with a substantial Cuban/MPLA force at Catofe, Kruys's sappers built a log bridge across the Nhia River while under heavy enemy fire. Then, under cover of fire from 5.5-inch guns, the infantry and armoured cars went bald-headed for their opponents, losing four dead but killing an estimated 400 Cuban and MPLA soldiers (the exact number will never be known because the bush was so thick that enemy dead and wounded were being found for days afterwards, while the British Broadcasting Corporation reported at the time that loads of corpses and wounded men had been ferried away by the MPLA).

The victory was so complete that Kruys had difficulty in restraining some of his more junior armoured car commanders from chasing after the fleeing enemy. One or two of them hold a grudge

about the restriction to this day, but there can be no doubt that Kruys was right. Here, as was to be the case in several future operations, the South African force was so small that it simply could not maintain the initiative and turn a retreat into a rout.

At Silva Porto, meanwhile, the South Africans had formed another battle-group, commanded by Commandant A P R Carstens and nicknamed "Orange". Made up of a Unita infantry battalion and a South African infantry company, armoured car squadron and artillery element, it was tasked to watch over the northern marches of Unita territory by sweeping around to the west and linking up with Task Force Zulu, which was in the vicinity of Quibala but unable to make further progress because it was faced by one demolished bridge after another.

Carstens left Silva Porto on December 8 and passed through Mussende, his intention being to wrest the town of Malanje from the MPLA. He got as far as the Cuanza River - Unita's northern border - only to find that he could not cross it because the large Salazar Bridge had been blown. This left him with no option but to make his way back to Mussende and turn westwards towards Quibala. By mid-December he had reached the Unita-held town of Cariango, which he defended against a Cuban force in a sharp action which involved Carstens being attacked by jet fighters and tanks (one of which was knocked out). The defence succeeded, but Carstens's further advance was blocked by yet another demolished bridge. Highly frustrated, since he had come within a hair of joining hands with Zulu, Carstens pulled back to Mussende again, stayed there till the general SADF withdrawal started and then headed southwards towards the border.

A fourth battle-group, commanded by Commandant S W J Kotze and nicknamed "X-Ray", was formed in early December at Savimbi's express request to ensure the security of the entire Benguela railway line. Structured very similarly to Orange, Battle-Group X-Ray cleared up various pockets of Fapla resistance and then, Kotze having handed over to Commandant Hans Moller, embarked on a three-day battle for the important town of Luso on the eastern section of the railway. The battle ended on December 11 with the seizing of Luso at a cost to the MPLA of about 250 dead and the capture of a substantial amount of equipment and heavy weapons. In the meantime yet another force

Left
Harassed by intermittent enemy fire, South African sappers hastily construct the later-to-be-renowned "Bridge 14" over the Nhia River in December of 1975

Right
Commandant C P van der Westhuizen stands in front of the completed Bridge 14, which enabled armoured cars and infantry to cross the rain-swollen Nhia River and inflict a shattering defeat on the Angolan/Cuban forces in the last big action of Operation Savannah

called Battle-Group Beaver, under Commandant Yvo de Bruyn, was formed and deployed as a mobile reserve at Lobito.

Savimbi was very eager that X-Ray should occupy the railway town of Texeira da Sousa, which was virtually on the Zairean border, so Moller sent a strong element eastwards. The force captured Bucaco on December 14 and seized the bridge over the Luchia River. When it got to the Lumege River on December 20, however, it found that the MPLA had destroyed the great rail bridge there with such thoroughness that it would have taken at least two months to rebuild it. As a result there was nothing for it but to return to Luso.

X-Ray's failed attempt to reach Texeira da Sousa was overshadowed by a series of events, all of which took place on December 17 and 18.

First there was an announcement on December 17 from Defence Headquarters which tore a huge rent in the veil of secrecy that had been thrown over Savannah by the South Africans and had remained remarkably intact, all things considered.

Up to this time the extent of South African operations in Angola had remained so obscure that correspondent Larry Heinzerling of United Press International had noted in one despatch published in mid-December that "the possibility of direct South African involvement in the Angolan conflict has been raised but not proved by journalists on the scene. Newsmen in southern Angola have recently reported the presence of what appeared to be white mercenaries with South African accents, but could not establish whether they were army regulars".

The DHQ statement ended all that. It stated baldly that four South African soldiers - Corporal Hannes Terblanche and Privates R H Wiehahn, G Danney and R Wilson - were missing and were believed to have been captured while recovering a disabled vehicle "in the operational area" (in fact the four men, all members of the Technical Services Corps attached to Battle-Group Foxbat, had been captured between Cela and Quibala, about 700km inside Angola).

It was the first of several shocks in rapid succession for the South African public and the government.

That same day P W Botha announced that due to "the exingency of the circumstances" the mem-

bers of the 1975 national service intake would have their term extended by a month, to February 6 of 1976. In addition, a number of Citizen Force units would be called up for operational service during 1976, the period to be three months because of the long distances and travelling times involved. This, he added, was "not a panic measure but is intended to increase effectiveness".

What had happened was that the SADF had been caught in a manpower squeeze. Although it was obvious that withdrawal from Angola was now the only option, it was equally obvious that this could not be carried out in such a precipitate fashion that all the gains of Savannah would be lost. However, the national servicemen's term had less than a fortnight to go. So the extra month would provide time to mobilise the trained reserves.

Various Citizen Force units were placed on a six-hour stand-by. The command cadres at each realised that a three-month call-up was inevitable and began making as many preparations as possible. Other than checking out that call-up procedures were ready to go, there was not a great deal they could do. The SADF was not prepared for any sizeable sort of mobilisation: it was short of everything, from maps of Angola to wheel-spanners for its vehicles.

Meanwhile, the MPLA's "ambassador at large" in the United States, Elisio de Figueiredo, announced that there were no less than 6 500 South African

Above
Jonas Savimbi and his South African liaison officer, Commandant P Lombaard, with Commandant A P R Carstens, OC Battle-Group Orange (far left) and his successor, Commandant A J Snyman (far right)

Below
Jonas Savimbi at his Silva Porto headquarters in December of 1975 with Commandant S W J Kotze, OC Battle-Group X-Ray and a veteran of Task Force Zulu during Koos van Heerden's dash up the coast

"regulars" in Angola, 4 000 of them involved in the civil war and the rest patrolling the border. He added that up to 50 South African prisoners of war would be put on display in Luanda in the next three or four days. Both statements were gross exaggerations, since there were never more than 2 900 South Africans in Angola at any stage in 1975, and the only other SADF soldiers captured during Operation Savannah were three members of Battle-Group Orange.

De Figueiredo scoffed at Western claims that 3 000 to 4 000 Cuban soldiers were in Angola as being vastly overstated. "I wish we had them," he said, "then we would be in complete control of the country." At that stage, in fact, there were already about 12 000 Cubans in Angola and more were arriving all the time.

On December 18 two of the four captured soldiers, Terblanche and Wiehahn, were shown off at a press conference in Lagos, Nigeria, which was chaired by the MPLA Prime Minister, Lopo di Nascimento. Terblanche and Wiehahn were handcuffed and weary but obviously in good health. The more rabidly anti-communistic South Africans had feared the worst, but the Angolans treated them reasonably well, both then and later.

That same day Wiehahn and Danney were interviewed on Radio Luanda. They gave little away, claiming to know nothing, but that did not detract from the enormity of the Angolans' propaganda coup - one that the South Africans could not counter, although they had a number of Cuban prisoners by now.

At the Lagos press conference Di Nascimento's statements were nearer the truth. South Africa, he said, now had about 1 000 regular troops in Angola (although in fact most of them were national servicemen and only "regular" in the sense of being full-time) and the number was rising. The fighting in Angola was not a tribal, racial or regional struggle but a "struggle against foreign aggression perpetrated by Zaire, South Africa and other agents of international imperialism". He pointed out that Nigeria had recognised the MPLA government and had offered all possible help in restoring territorial integrity.

Nigeria's early recognition of the MPLA was a crucially important indicator of the way things were to go. Nigeria, which had recognised the MPLA as early as December 6 (followed soon after by

Tanzania), was the heavyweight of the Organisation for African Unity. Up to now the OAU had done little except wring its hands. But intense politicking was going on, and many states were likely to follow Nigeria's lead.

On December 19 there were tidings from the United States which added to the South Africans' worries - the US Senate, responding to a campaign led by Democratic Party Senators Dick Clark, Frank Church and John Tunney, voted 54 to 22, with 144 abstentions, to cut off aid to the anti-MPLA movements.

If the campaign proved one thing, it was that Clark was not primarily concerned with majority rule in Angola: on June 16 of 1975, while serving on the Senate Foreign Relations Sub-Committee on African Affairs, he had asked Angola experts John Marcum and Douglas Wheeler who would win if genuine free elections were to be held in that country. Marcum had replied that Unita would win, with the MPLA coming second. Wheeler said: "It is possible Unita would win (with) perhaps even a slight edge on plurality or majority."

The vote still had to be matched in the House of Representatives, but no-one in Pretoria had much doubt about how that round would go. Dirk and Johanna de Villiers describe the Senate vote as "a knockout blow … for the anti-communist forces".

On December 20 South African journalists were allowed to visit the troops who had been guarding Ruacana and Calueque since August. Their reports had hardly hit the newspapers before, on December 24, Citizen Force units of Cape Town-based 71 Motorised Brigade were warned that they could expect to be called up for three months early in January 1976.

Christmas passed tensely, overshadowed by the war in Angola. On December 29 news came that three more soldiers had been killed in the operational area. Angola? The border? No-one knew. The long news black-out was having a malign effect now. Rumours, each one worse than the last, were flying freely about. Most of them centred on the allegedly enormous numbers of Cubans in Angola and the ghastly secret Russian weapons they were deploying and using.

P W Botha, in an evident attempt to cool the situation, said in a widely reprinted interview with political correspondent Tom Copeland of the Cape Times that the government would almost certainly

Above
Senator Dick Clark

Top Right
Armoured Corps troops of Battle-Group X-Ray maintain their Eland-90s during a halt on the way to fight at Luso late in the war

reconsider involvement if its interests in southern Angola were guaranteed and Swapo stopped its attacks across the border. South Africa wanted only "an orderly and free Angola". However, he declined to comment on speculation that the government was ready to withdraw its forces as part of the newly launched OAU peace initiative.

The actual situation was that Savimbi had requested that the SADF stay on in Angola till after an Organisation for African Unity emergency meeting which had been scheduled for December 9, then re-scheduled for the first week in January – an indication, when one considers the urgency of the agenda, of the serious divisions among the African states on the Angolan issue. It would appear that the South Africans had no great hopes of the OAU meeting achieving anything, for on Christmas Day Constand Viljoen had arrived at Cela to tell Savimbi, Roberto and Chipenda that the SADF was about to withdraw. All three pleaded with the South Africans to stay on, protesting that they would be left with nothing but bad names as a result of their association with Pretoria. Viljoen explained that

there could be no change of plan: in a few days' time the South Africans would begin their withdrawal (in fact the first elements were scheduled to start pulling out on January 3).

In his book "Jonas Savimbi: A Key to Africa", Fred Bridgland quotes Savimbi's description of what happened:

Chipenda began crying in front of the South Africans. I said no, it is just that: they came in, they want to go out, so let them go.

Then when we went outside Roberto asked me what made me so confident that I had troops who could replace the South Africans. I said I didn't have any, but I wasn't going to cry in front of the South Africans. If they want to leave us, they leave. If we have to die, let us die; this is our country; what can we do? We were not part of the arrangement when they came here, so we have no power to persuade them to stay.

The one who sent them in is sending them out, so we have to accept it.

Below
One hard lesson the South Africans learnt during Operation Savannah was that their artillery, all of World War II vintage, was badly outranged by the MPLA's more modern Russian guns. They compensated for this technology gap by using their guns far further forward and with much greater mobility than was laid down in the book. Here an old 5,5-inch medium gun hurls a 140mm shell at an MPLA position: the troops — either from necessity or to satisfy one of those instant bushveld fashions — are all wearing captured East German steel helmets

The SADF withdrawal was put on ice at the last moment when the OAU re-scheduled its meeting once again, to January 18. This time there was no further postponement, and the heads of state met in the Ethiopian capital of Addis Ababa under the chairmanship of President Idi Amin of Uganda. Furious debate followed, with accusations of collaboration being hurled back and forth. By this stage several nations were wavering and some, including Zambia, had bowed to what they considered the inevitable outcome of the Angolan intervention and turned against Unita.

President Leopold Senghor of Senegal proposed an immediate ceasefire, the withdrawal of all foreign forces and the formation of a government of unity. Nigeria replied with a proposal that the MPLA be formally recognised as the legitimate government of Angola. Put to the vote, the result was a well-nigh incredible tie, with 22 nations voting for each proposal, and two abstentions - Uganda because its leader was OAU chairman, and Ethiopia because it was the host country.

In fact it was a victory for the MPLA. Soon after the summit Ethiopia and Uganda recognised the MPLA, and immediately one African country after the other began to follow suit.

If there had been any doubt about the paucity of South Africa's options, it was dispelled by the OAU vote. Hard reality dictated an immediate withdrawal. South Africa now stood alone in the world, condemned by its enemies and shunned by the countries which had urged it to intervene in Angola. Its lonely status was driven home on January 27, when the US House of Representatives voted 323 to 99 to support the Clark amendment passed earlier by the Senate.

"Savimbi has no illusions about how swiftly the end is coming," Senator Tunney told reporters afterwards. "The war in Angola, beyond guerrilla fighting, is almost over." For historically-minded South Africans, Tunney's words now have a strangely familiar ring: during the Second Anglo-Boer War, too, the end of the "conventional" fighting had seemed to most people a signal that the war was virtually at an end, whereas the guerrilla phase that had followed had been far longer and more arduous. So it was to prove in Angola, where Savimbi not only survived his initial reverse but enmeshed the MPLA in a drawn-out civil war which by 1988 had reduced its economy to tatters and caused great suffering among its population.

On January 23, guided by General Van Deventer's expert hand, the South Africans began to withdraw in a deliberate, orderly fashion, northernmost forces first. Shaggy-haired troops dressed in oddments of South African, FNLA, Unita and MPLA uniforms drove southwards in a heterogenous collection of vehicles ranging from Unimog lorries to former fruit and vegetable trucks and civilian cars, the muzzles of their 25-pounder and 5.5.-inch guns still blackened and blistered from the fighting. They passed through a screen of Citizen Force units dug in well north of the border, then congregated at reception centres where they were able to clean up and don new uniforms before heading for home at last.

Streaming after them were long convoys of refugees of all colours (as Lopo di Nascimento had said, this had not been a racial war) who had either held out hope to the last or had been trapped by the fighting.

Most of the refugees went to the camps at Pereira d'Eca before being shipped back to Portugal or settling in South Africa, but not all. The Chipenda-faction FNLA troops were brought out at dead of night, and the South Africans who saw them pass could not have foreseen that they were later to resurface as the most feared and controversial soldiers of the border war (see THE FIGHTING MEN in PART II).

Then the units which had been holding the line started leapfrogging back themselves. By February 4 the SADF rearguard was within 50km of the border - between 4 000 and 5 000, P W Botha told newsmen, who were patrolling the area "for the security of the growing refugee problem".

In the meantime the Cubans and MPLA had begun filling the vacuum left by the South Africans. In the first week of February they occupied San Salvador in the far north, the last town still held by the FNLA. Their movement southwards started when a force of several thousand, backed by artillery and aircraft, pushed Unita out of its administrative capital of Huambo, the former Nova Lisboa. On February 10 the Cubans and MPLA reoccupied Lobito and Benguela, and on February 11 Sa Da Bandeira. Later there were boasts that they had driven the South Africans out of Angola, but the dates tell a different story.

Only two more important events occurred before Operation Savannah became history.

On February 23 Angola, having been recognised by the vast majority of African countries, became the 47th member of the OAU, more or less at the same time as Dr Henry Kissinger was blandly telling a Senate committee that when Unita had appealed for help in warding off the MPLA advance into its tribal areas "South Africa responded by sending military equipment and some personnel, without consulting with the USA".

And finally, on March 27, P W Botha and some of the men most intimately involved in Savannah - including Magnus Malan, Constand Viljoen and Ben Roos - stood on a makeshift dais at Ruacana

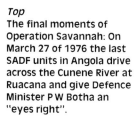

Top
The final moments of
Operation Savannah: On
March 27 of 1976 the last
SADF units in Angola drive
across the Cunene River at
Ruacana and give Defence
Minister P W Botha an
"eyes right".

Above
Andreas Shipanga,
years after he and many
other dissenting insurgents
were imprisoned in 1976
by Sam Nujoma

Far Right
Shattered by their
misfortunes, this family
waits at Chitado for
repatriation. Like so many
of the refugee families,
this one mirrored Angola's
agony: the father was white,
the mother black. All of
them were Angolans, not
Portuguese

Right
In Nova Lisboa and
elsewhere the last of
the refugees prepared to
pack up their remaining
belongings and move
southwards with the
withdrawing South Africans

and took the salute as the last South African troops, including those who had been holding Calueque, rumbled out of Angola.

On March 29 a total of 3 000 refugees of all races, virtually the last of the hordes who had quit Angola in the past months, fled over the border.

Several days into April the first MPLA troops arrived at the border, and on April 5 officials of both sides met at Calueque; Foreign Minister Hilgard Muller later reported that they had agreed that the power would be switched on, that pumping of water to Ovamboland would soon resume, that the barrage would not be damaged and that workers there would not be harmed.

So the great gamble ended in a cloud of recrimination, its opponents pointing bitterly at the cost: 29 South Africans killed in action and about 100 wounded, another 20 dead from non-operational causes, the seeming destruction of Vorster's detente policy and the ire of much of the world.

Yet Operation Savannah had come very close to being a total or partial victory for Vorster's government. Looking back now, it is obvious that if Holden Roberto had not squandered his advantages with his attack on Luanda, and if the Americans had stood firm and thereby kept the Russians from intervening too enthusiastically, the result might well have been some sort of neutral government in Angola. There is no doubt that this would have satisfied the South Africans, whose primary concern all along had been not to fight the advance of Marxism but to prevent Swapo from using the Angolan "shallow area" as a jumping-off point to further the insurgency.

When it was all over, the main emotion among the prime movers on the anti-communist side was regret - not at having taken part, but at having lost the game through extraneous circumstances. Koos van Heerden of Task Force Zulu called it "a

war of lost opportunities". Henry Kissinger testified at a hearing: "Friend and foe alike cannot fail to contrast the sending of a large Cuban expedition force with our apparent inability to provide even indirect financial assistance ... We are told that by providing money and arms in Angola we are duplicating the mistakes we made in Vietnam. If we accept such a gross distortion of history ... the tragedy of Vietnam will be monumental."

P W Botha opined: "If America had shown her teeth the Russians might have capitulated, because they don't like to fight away from their fatherland. It is true the Cubans were there, but when they came up against us they ran away. The Americans' poor showing resulted in the majority of the OAU joining the strongman. In the future Angola will be remembered as the Free World's great lost opportunity."

Whether Savannah did, in fact, destroy South Africa's detente policy remains a moot point. Military historian Sophia du Preez, who has spent years compiling facts about Savannah, is adamant that the 22-22 tie at the OAU meeting in January of 1976 proved that the Angolan intervention had not killed detente; and it is a fact that 14 years later South Africa still enjoys cordial relations with the Ivory Coast, Zaire, Senegal and various other African states who had been involved in Vorster's original outreach in the early 1970s.

From Pretoria's point of view all had not been lost. The SADF had gained valuable battle experience which had enabled it to re-evaluate its equipment and systems, it had given notice of its fighting ability and it had managed to save Savimbi from destruction so that he could occupy at least some of the MPLA's - and Swapo's - attention in the future.

On the other hand, the losses were as great as the gains, particularly as regards the border war, and in fact many military observers regard March 27 of 1976 as the date when the insurgency started in earnest. Swapo was now in a stronger military position than ever before. For the first time it had what is virtually a *sine qua non* for a successful insurgency, namely, a safe border behind which it could withdraw. It could set up an open training, administrative and logistics structure inside Angola and launch its insurgents southwards as it chose. It was all a vast change from the hole-in-the-corner days of Portuguese rule.

In addition, Zambia had faced the facts, abandoned its anti-MPLA stand and not only allowed Plan members to re-establish themselves on its soil for forays into Caprivi but actually supplied them with food and other requirements (it co-operated in other ways, too - when Swapo dissidents under Andreas Shipanga began agitating for a long-overdue leadership election, Kaunda

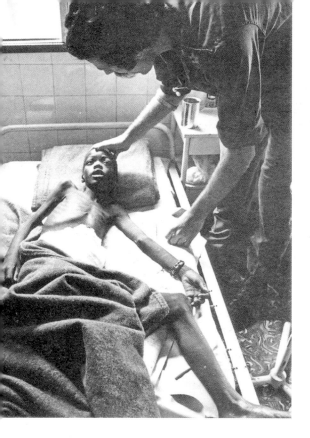

threw them in jail at Nujoma's request. When another 1 800-odd Swapo members protested against Shipanga's arrest, he put them behind bars as well). Of the neighbouring countries only Botswana maintained its strictly neutral stance towards South Africa, and Zaire's President Mobuto Sese Seko did not alter his implacable hostility to the Neto regime.

From Swapo's point of view there were some disadvantages in the new state of affairs. Nujoma's former ally, Jonas Savimbi, was now his bitter enemy, which presented certain problems because both men's organisations were operating in the south of Angola. In addition, Swapo was expected to divert some of its manpower into the MPLA's campaign to finish off Savimbi. Still, Savimbi was retreating into the remote vastnesses of the south-east and was fighting for his organisation's very existence: no doubt his days were numbered. And meanwhile Swapo had achieved its aim of direct and untrammelled access to central Ovamboland.

Now the worst fears of the military planners – the fears that had led in such large measure to Operation Savannah being launched – started coming true. Plan set up an extensive network of permanent training camps and permanent bases in southern Angola, and the insurgency escalated significantly.

For the South Africans – short of men, short of equipment, their defence force still struggling to wrench itself free of the decades of neglect that had followed World War II – the situation was immensely worrying. It was obvious that three-month mobilisations of reservists were going to become a fact of life for the foreseeable future, and in fact as early as January 27 Major-General Neil Webster, the SADF's highest ranking citizen-soldier and its Director-General (Resources), had warned that "the security commitment on our borders is likely to get bigger, not smaller, and this country must stand prepared". He added that it was unrealistic to hope "that the threat to our borders will melt away".

A series of permanent battalion bases was set up along the border, their location determined by local circumstances and known or suspected crossing-places, their inhabitants carrying out endless patrols and occasionally skirmishing with Plan insurgents, and carrying out as many hearts-and-minds tasks as possible.

Citizen Force and Commando Force battalions were now being called up regularly to man the bases and carry out other tasks such as escorting convoys. It was basically an inefficient system: travel and refresher training cut the actual operational service to something over two months, Plan could calculate pretty carefully when units would be rotated and no-one stayed long enough in an area to build up a comprehensive knowledge of people and places, although great stress was laid on passing intelligence and operational knowledge from one unit to the next. But at this stage there was no alternative. South West Africa possessed no uniformed forces of its own except the police, small patrols of whom came and went about their business in the top-heavy but effective "Hippo" mine-protected vehicles which were the envy of the soldiers, who mostly had to make do with open Unimog lorries packed with old conveyor-belting and sandbags.

And so, as they had done so many times in the past, the part-time forces provided an instant reservoir of trained men which enabled the small standing army to instantly expand its operational capacity three- or fourfold. If the early part of the border war proved anything, it was that for South Africa the citizen-army was as valid a concept in the nuclear age as it had been a hundred years earlier.

By now the SADF had adapted to this war, the strangest it had ever fought. Black tribesmen had been recruited as soldiers, trackers, guards and tribal policemen; more and more Bushmen, renowned for their superlative tracking, were signing up and adapting their ancient know-how to such tasks as smelling out landmines; mounted and foot-mobile units specialised in following up insurgent trails with humans or dogs, or both; the horse soldier was back – an anachronistic but effective fighting man in Ovamboland because he could travel far and quietly. Techniques for hunting insurgents were constantly being refined, so that eventually there would be units mounted on

Above Left
A South African doctor tends a desperately ill child at Pereira D'Eca as the withdrawal gains momentum. There were many heart-wrenching scenes like this

Above Right
South Africans visiting the former Chipenda-faction FNLA troops brought down to Chitado found that some were forlorn but others were surprisingly full of fight, considering what had happened to them. Thanks to the SADF, they soon had the opportunity of putting their deeds into words

scrambler motorcycles for following up and cutting off infiltrators. Mine-sniffing dogs were pressed into service.

New roles were found for established weapons and units. Armoured cars were used for base defence as well as patrolling, and paratroopers were used as quick-reaction forces, riding in helicopters. The Chipenda-FNLA soldiers evacuated from Angola in the dying days of Operation Savannah were formed into a regiment known as 32 Battalion and deployed along the border, where they saw constant action. Clandestine help began filtering across the border to Savimbi's Unita, although years were to pass before the South African government admitted it.

The border war was still of very low intensity, but an intermittent dribble of contacts, mine explosions and shoot-and-scoot rocket and mortar bombardments inexorably pushed up the casualty rate. For the Plan insurgents, operating on their home ground against relatively inexperienced enemies, the environment was still comparatively favourable; the SADF's immediate reaction was to mount intensive counter-insurgency operations in May and June, employing white and Bushmen trackers, mounted infantry and dogs. On June 29 Brigadier Ben Roos, who was now the Army's Director of Operations, announced that 70 Plan insurgents had been killed, wounded or captured since the beginning of May, the security force suffering 17 wounded in the actions. The Army had scattered the insurgents to north and south, he said, sealing off the area and closing down escape and infiltration routes; 22 had been killed in northern Ovamboland while trying to cross the border into Angola.

Angola subsequently accused South African troops of crossing the border early in July and razing three villages, which was flatly denied by the SADF. On July 12, the day after this accusation had been made, Zambia claimed South African troops on a hot-pursuit operation had violated its border and attacked the village of Sialola, killing 24 civilians and wounding another 45. This, too, was denied by Pretoria, but the Zambians were not satisfied and took the matter to the United Nations.

The South Africans were now enjoying considerable success in Ovamboland, thanks partly to their increased efforts and partly to the fact that the dry season had arrived, making it difficult for the insurgents to operate. On July 18 a military spokesman, Brigadier W J Matthews, announced that 26 insurgents had been killed and large quantities of weapons had been captured since the beginning of the month, security force casualties being one dead and five wounded.

A breakdown of the various contacts given by Matthews makes illuminating reading at this distance and illustrates the type of action being fought in Ovamboland at that time:
- On July 1 five security force members were wounded when they drove into an ambush and insurgents raked their three vehicles with fire.
- On July 2 security forces killed two insurgents in a contact just south of Ovamboland.
- Also on July 2, insurgents killed a tribal policeman, a woman and child, evaded pursuing security forces and escaped over the border into Angola.
- On July 4 security forces made contact with an insurgent group near the border and killed six of them.
- On July 7 security forces killed one insurgent in a "skirmish" (type unspecified).

- On July 8 security forces killed one insurgent in a firefight at the border.
- On July 10 insurgents sprang an ambush from the Angolan side of the border, but inflicted no casualties and suffered none.
- On July 10 eight insurgents died in two separate contacts along the border.
- On July 11 a police vehicle - presumably a mine-protected one - detonated a landmine near the border but its occupants were unscathed. A follow-up action resulted in the deaths of two insurgents who were believed to have been responsible for the mine.
- On July 13, in an action of unspecified type, one insurgent was wounded and taken prisoner and a large number of Russian weapons were captured.
- On July 14 six insurgents were shot dead in a contact along the border.

Even more revealing was a description of the action which cost the life of the lone security forces fatality, Rifleman Andries Blaauw of Aroab, South West Africa.

Blaauw's twin brother, Pieter, who fought alongside him in the action, said that their patrol had made contact with a group of insurgents and forced them to scatter. A little later the patrol came to a kraal where it was thought insurgents might be hiding. The patrol members dumped their excess kit and went off to sweep through the kraal, leaving the twins to guard their possessions.

"We were lying just outside the kraal," Pieter Blaauw said later, "when a group of terrorists apparently came across our footprints and started following us. When we first saw them they were quite close. Andries took up position on the right-hand side of a tree and I was on the left."

The brothers then opened up on the insurgents. The ensuing firefight lasted just five minutes; when it was over, Andries Blaauw had been mortally wounded by a ricochetting bullet.

On July 27 the matter of the alleged Sialola massacre came up at the United Nations, with Zambia's Foreign Minister, Siteke Mwale, supplying more details of the attack - the culmination, he said, of 14 "provocative acts" by South Africa during 1976.

It now transpired Sialola was not a civilian village but a Swapo transit camp about 30km from the border with Caprivi. According to Mwale South African helicopters had dropped armed men who had planted mines around the camp, then attacked and shelled it. Some of the inhabitants were killed inside the camp and others by the mines when they tried to escape.

Mwale's South African opposite number, Pik Botha, flatly denied the government had given authorisation for any Zambian villages to be attacked and denied all knowledge of the Sialola incident. In addition, violence was being committed by "hostile elements which enjoy refuge in Zambia", he said, giving 10 dates in the previous 18 months on which South Africa had made representations to Zambia about border violations; Pretoria had tried to obtain more details about Sialola from Zambia but had not received a reply, and South Africa did not instigate or support the guerrilla attacks of the factions, private armies and marauding bands that had plagued the Sialola region for many years.

Liberia then made an unexpected suggestion that a Security Council fact-finding mission be sent to Sialola to ascertain the facts. Botha immediately offered his government's full support

Above
**President Kenneth Kaunda
of Zambia**

Opposite Above & Centre
**The Cape Town Highlanders
— first Citizen Force
regiment to be mobilised for
service in Operation
Savannah — pulls out of
Cape Town station on
January 5 of 1976 in
traditional fashion, with a
piper playing the regimental
march, "Cock o' the North"**

Left
**Whatever their superiors
might have thought, the
South African soldiers (like
this one at Pereira D'Eca)
were glad to turn their
backs on Angola's depressing
vista of ruined buildings
painted with the
vainglorious slogans of
one or the other of the
warring movements**

Below
**Bag and baggage, their
trailers heaped with such
homely impedimenta as
issue rubber dustbins,
packing-case tables
and "liberated" deck-chairs
— anything to keep the
bounteous mud at a
distance — the South
Africans
began to leapfrog back
towards the border**

Above
**Sean McBride, UN
Commissioner for Namibia**

Above Right
**Although only days
away from withdrawal in
mid-March of 1976, these
South Africans remained
ready to fight in case the
situation worsened
suddenly. Here, in between
rain-showers, an infantry
company goes through the
time-honoured daily ritual
of rifle inspection**

and co-operation. The offer was not taken up, however, and the Security Council (with the United States abstaining) settled for condemning South Africa for its "armed attack"; to date the Sialola incident has never been impartially investigated.

The Sialola incident was just another symptom of the distinct deterioration in South Africa's once reasonably close relations with Zambia, its former ally of Operation Savannah days. In the ensuing months there were to be numerous cases of cross-border fire and other incidents as the Zambians threw their support behind Plan.

Caprivi, once the focus of action on the border, had become very quiet now, partly because of intensive SADF patrolling and hearts-and-minds activities, partly because of neglect by Plan since it now had free direct access to Ovamboland and partly because of internal squabbles between Swapo and Canu. The relationship between the two organisations had been bad for some time by now – dating back to when Canu had objected to Swapo deploying its members in Ovamboland instead of Caprivi.

September was a quiet month, with the insurgents maintaining a low profile and avoiding direct contact with the security forces in spite of Swapo claims from Lusaka which insisted that Plan was applying heavy pressure in the operational area. Such incidents as took place were few and low-level, and the most notable event was the search for a South African soldier named Rifleman Eugene de Lange, who disappeared in the operational area when he took a wrong turn while driving an army vehicle to a refugee camp and ended up in Angola, where he was taken prisoner by MPLA soldiers. A military spokesman claimed the scale was tipping slowly but surely towards the security forces, thanks to the "calm, friendly but stern" attitude towards the local population and the compassion shown to the Angolan refugees, many of whom were related to inhabitants in the area.

October was just as quiet, with the insurgents' activities still hampered by the dry season, and the authorities took advantage of the lull to start constructing what later became known as the "Jati

Strip" or just "the Jati", an area of cleared land 1km wide and 420km long along the "Cutline", or border with Angola.

Fenced off with barbed wire more than two metres high, the Jati was a free-fire zone which was to be constantly patrolled on a shoot-first basis. Progress was swift, with the first 20km of fencing being completed by October 26 (like Ohopoho, Caprivi, Wenela and various other ethnic-sounding place-names, "Jati" only seemed indigenous – in actual fact it was a contraction of the first names of Jannie de Wet, Commissioner-General of the Indigenous Territories, and Timo Bezuidenhout, a senior South African official seconded to the Ovamboland internal government.

The lull continued till December, although the insurgents did not cease their activities in spite of the unfavourable dry conditions and killed two South African soldiers in a contact in late October.

In December, however, activities started picking up. Reliable reports filtered through to Windhoek that four of the "front-line states" – Tanzania, Zambia, Mozambique and Angola - were co-operating in airlifting small arms, munitions and rations to Swapo bases in preparation for a renewed wave of infiltration early in 1977. According to the reports there had been two lifts, both in September of that year, which had brought in 15 tons of cargo on aircraft of the Mozambican state airline Comag, refuelling at Ndola in Zambia under the personal supervision of the Zambian army chief. The reports added that future airlifts had already been organised by Comag.

Plan activities from early December onwards were focused on traditional figures of authority, who tended to be conservative and pro-government. On December 6 two insurgents crossed into Ovamboland from Angola but ran into a government patrol before they could carry out their assigned tasks, one being killed and the other wounded; on the same day, however, another group kidnapped Chief Zacharia Kanim and his daughter from their kraal near the border, while on December 7 Deputy Chief Hausiki Enkaile was murdered by a group of seven or eight insurgents in camouflage uniform,

Page 65

and the son of Chief Willipard Enkale was abducted to Angola.

Some light relief was afforded on December 11 by the aged UN Commissioner for South West Africa, Sean McBride, who told reporters in an interview in Lusaka that South Africa had placed 50 000 men, armed with such "sophisticated" weapons as helicopters, tanks, artillery and hundreds of armoured cars, in jump-off positions in the Caprivi Strip for an impending invasion of Angola which would be justified by claiming that MPLA and Cuban troops had joined hands with Plan insurgents.

McBride added that the Rhodesian government had built three new air bases - one of them in Caprivi - and said this indicated preparations for a prolonged counter-insurgent war.

"We have information that these plans being hatched in Pretoria and Salisbury should mature some time next month," he said. "I am very concerned. The situation is extremely serious. From the middle of January we are entering a new situation which involves the destabilisation of Angola."

It was a patently ludicrous accusation - for one thing, South Africa could not have put such a force in the field without a wholesale and very public mobilisation - and P W Botha pounced on it with glee, challenging McBride to come to Caprivi and point out the alleged Rhodesian airstrip. Wisely, McBride did not take up the challenge.

In late December there were several cases of Plan insurgents taking up position on Angolan soil and then firing at security force patrols moving on the South West African side of the border. Such exchanges usually did no harm to either side, but the possibility of fatalities was always there, and in one incident Corporal Benjamin Johannes Schoeman of Potgietersrus was killed when the insurgents fired on a temporary camp close to the border. In another case, Angolan-based insurgents fired at a SAAF Cessna light aircraft which was inspecting the new border fence.

Military strategists speculated that Plan was trying to tempt the security forces into launching

impromptu hot-pursuit operations, which could then be ambushed and also blown up into international incidents to prove South Africa was bullying Angola. It was a form of harassment which was to be seen again and again in the next 12 months, before it became obvious that as far as the South Africans were concerned the former sanctity of international borders was a dead letter in the border war.

So the year ended, with the border war rumbling on. According to Major-General Wally Black, the SADF's Director-General (Operations), 21 South African troops had been killed in action or had died of wounds in 1976, with another 31 accidental deaths.

Above
Freshly equipped and ready to fight, Citizen Force troops started pouring into Angola from early January of 1976, and for the first time the South African strength level rose above its previous high point of about 3 000

Below
Soldiers of the Chipenda-faction FNLA at Chitado, just north of the border. Unable to return home, they faced an uncertain future — which the South Africans were soon to resolve

The new year started on an ominous note. On January 15 reliable Angolan sources confirmed the reports of arms shipments to Plan in September and added that a large and well-equipped insurgent operational base had been set up at Mulemba, about 350km inside Angola, under the personal supervision of Plan supreme commander Dimo Hamaambo.

Large numbers of insurgents were massing at the base, the sources added; a further shipment of 45 tons of weaponry was expected in the near future, and an unknown number of heavy vehicles which included armoured cars had been seen travelling to Mulemba under Cuban escort early in the new year.

It was an alarming report, but nothing happened immediately; in fact, the whole of January was the quietest period in a long time, even though the rainy season was at its height and conditions for insurgent raids and ambushes were at their best, and the only security force casualty of the month was killed by a landmine explosion rather than in a contact.

Army intelligence officers noted that the insurgents were lying low, concentrating on activation, intimidation, mine-laying and firing across the international border. In one case in mid-February this last tactic caused a minor international incident when Plan insurgents took up station behind an MPLA strongpoint at Santa Clara and fired at the South African observation post at Oshikango on the other side of the wire. The insurgents sprayed bullets so enthusiastically that some of their shots hit the MPLA strongpoints. The MPLA, not unnaturally, assumed that the South Africans had decided to attack them and fired across the border, to which the South Africans replied with mortars and small arms.

Late in February Caprivi saw its first incident since July of 1975 when a Plan group fired on a South African patrol base near the Angolan and Zambian borders of the territory, wounding three soldiers. The attack took place in broad daylight – an unusual timing for which the attackers paid dearly: return fire from the patrol base killed three of them, and a subsequent follow-up as the insurgents retreated towards the Zambian border cost them another nine confirmed dead in two contacts before the group managed to reach the Cutline.

Several mine-laying operations took place in Ovamboland in March. In one case, three insurgents blew themselves up when they accidentally detonated the mine while planting it; it had happened before, and was testimony to the fact that as yet Plan members were not receiving adequate training. No doubt the same lack of expertise was to blame for a lucky escape later in the month when an entire vehicle convoy drove over an anti-tank mine which did not detonate because it had been incorrectly laid.

In most of the incidents the insurgents concerned did not attempt to lose themselves in the local population but moved back into Angolan territory as soon as possible, since at that time the international border still represented something.

Meanwhile the SADF's hearts-and-minds operation was going into full gear: on March 22, 76 selected national servicemen were detached from other duties, given special crash teaching courses and deployed to black schools in the border area.

The extent of the fighting was graphically depicted by a statement in Parliament from P W

Botha on March 31. In the two-year period starting on April 1 of 1975, he said, a total of 231 insurgents had been killed in Ovamboland, Kavango and East Caprivi. Security force operational deaths in the same period totalled 33, and the insurgents had murdered 53 members of the local population.

April saw an upswing in the tempo of the war, perhaps a final effort on Plan's part before the rainy season ended and conditions began to favour the security forces. During the first 20 days of the month there were two cases of the now-familiar exchange of shots across the border, and 20 insurgents were killed in no less than 14 separate incidents, ranging from firefights to ambushes; in virtually each case the surviving insurgents fled over the border into Angola.

The fighting continued into the following month. On May 5 there was a bizarre encounter when insurgents fired on two government soldiers manning an observation post in a tree. The soldiers vacated their post at great speed and called for help; soon a detachment of infantry with armoured cars in support attacked the insurgents, who had received about 30 reinforcements in the meantime. The insurgents fired at the infantry and armoured cars with mortars and machine-guns, then fell back over the border when the follow-up force attacked. No casualties to either side resulted from this brisk encounter.

In addition to the skirmish around the tree OP, the first week of May saw a South African soldier killed by a mine, while a small patrol came across a group of about 20 insurgents and, in accordance with the SADF's doctrine of aggressive action, attacked them and killed two, after which the others withdrew. In another action a South African patrol let three insurgents walk into an ambush and killed two, the third managing to escape on to Angolan soil.

By mid-May a total of eight insurgents had been killed without loss to the security forces. On

Above
With Operation Savannah nothing but a memory, the South Africans came to grips with the new dimension in the border war: a hostile Angola, giving sanctuary and help to the insurgents. To a large extent — although not for much longer — it was still a war in which one waited for something to happen, like this soldier peering into Angola from the observation post on top of "Echo Tower", at the Oshikango border post. Each of the large water towers was given a code letter because they made such handy reference points in the flatness of Ovamboland

Opposite
Another of the water towers used as observation posts; this one in Ondangua, the major air base in northern Ovamboland.

May 25 there was an exchange of shots in Caprivi when a South African border patrol moving along the Cutline in Caprivi was fired on by Zambian soldiers. The patrol returned the fire.

June brought no let-up. South African patrols were fired at from across the border on several occasions, a Plan temporary base was knocked out and three insurgents killed and various firefights took place. Plan members mortared a small security force base from near a Zambian immigration post on the Caprivi border, and were mortared in turn; in two cases the Ovambo home guard clashed with infiltrators, killing and wounding several.

In one case, which South African intelligence officers found rather intriguing, a Plan group tried to ambush a South African supply convoy but withdrew when the soldiers in the convoy counter-attacked. This unusual contact was attributed to a food shortage in Plan's ranks – because they had to move far and fast, insurgents could rarely afford to carry enough food in their packs, particularly the tinned meat whose protein they needed for their sometimes incredible feats of endurance (one insurgent, wounded in a contact, ran through the bush for 25km and finally eluded his pursuers).

This was no idle speculation: the problems of getting enough to eat, particularly meat, were discussed in several letters found on Plan field commanders who had been killed or captured.

Reviewing the situation at the end of the month, SADF planners concluded that in general the insurgents were still avoiding contact with the security forces, concentrating instead on intimidating and activating the local population, apparently in preparation for a forthcoming election. There might also be a link, they thought, with Swapo's

internal problems: numerous members of the organisation, including Andreas Shipanga, who had questioned Nujoma's leadership, were still languishing in Zambian and Tanzanian prisons.

Activity dwindled during July, but a significant incident took place at Cuangar, a once-busy little ghost town situated on the Okavango River and clearly visible from South African border observation posts in Kavango. One day early in July an OP spotted a Russian-built Antonov transport aircraft coming in to land on Cuangar's airfield. The aircraft put down at 12.50pm, unloaded about 30 Angolan soldiers and what looked like items of equipment, then took off again in a westerly direction. At 1.10pm, when it was about 30 metres off the ground, it turned sharply north, emitting clouds of black smoke. Then more black smoke mushroomed out behind it and it crashed about 3km from Cuangar; according to the area commander, Colonel Johan van der Spuy, it looked as if the aircraft had been hit by an RPG-7 anti-vehicle rocket.

Van der Spuy added, with complete truth, that the region across the river had been completely controlled by Unita for some time. The significance of this last remark was not, perhaps, immediately obvious to the South African public; but what it meant was that Jonas Savimbi was back in business, thanks partly to his own perspicacity and the MPLA's difficulties in getting itself sorted out – and partly because he was getting South African help, although this was to remain clandestine for years to come.

On July 30 Major-General Jannie Geldenhuys was appointed General Officer Commanding South West Africa Command. Although Geldenhuys, who was then 42, was not well-known outside the military at that stage, those who had had dealings with him knew it was a good appointment. Geldenhuys was an old South West Africa hand – he had served there from 1970 to 1974 and, as Army Chief of Staff, had been deeply involved in Operation Savannah. In addition he had a knack for diplomacy and was just as at home with political matters as he was with military affairs. It was a good combination for what was fast becoming the most sensitive command appointment in the SADF.

P W Botha's comment on announcing Geldenhuys's appointment was an interesting one, although likely enough its intent did not mean much to people outside the military: it was "in accordance with the policy to build and develop an independent and complete defence force for South West Africa".

Geldenhuys's first important public move came on August 19 – the day the security forces and Ovambo home guard shot and killed their 21st insurgent since the beginning of the month – when he addressed a vexed matter which had plagued the security forces since 1975: allegations of misbehaviour and irregularities in the operational area.

While some of the allegations had obviously been part of the Swapo propaganda campaign, others had not, and it had all become a running sore on the military's flank. Now Geldenhuys announced the establishment of a board of inquiry into all such allegations, inviting aggrieved persons to submit written complaints to SWA Command Headquarters and undertaking to transmit findings of possible criminal acts to the Attorney-General of South West Africa.

That Geldenhuys was not merely trying to pacify public opinion off his own bat became clear a day later when the Chief of the SADF, General Magnus Malan, confirmed his action. The announcements cleared the air to some extent, although the accusations were to continue at intervals to the end of the border war, and lead to various criminal prosecutions.

In the meantime the war continued, although there was a certain lull, so that on September 9 SWA Command announced there had been no security-force casualties for three weeks.

On September 22 representatives of Britain, the US, France, West Germany and Canada (the so-called "Western Five") arrived in Pretoria for further settlement talks amid rumours that the South Africans were to be presented with a plan – said to have been drawn up by the US's President Jimmy Carter and Tanzania's President Julius Nyerere – that required the South African forces to withdraw and be replaced by a Swapo army as a run-up to independence. The rumours added that, needless to say, any such suggestion would be rejected out of hand.

The talks did not get off to a good start. According to senior diplomatic sources the Western representatives proposed a rapid withdrawal of all South African troops except a small token force in order to allay Swapo fears of intimidation in the proposed independence elections. However – and this was what caused such a sharp reaction that the talks came close to collapse – Plan camps on the Angolan side of the border were to be left intact under UN supervision.

The South African reaction was so strong that the talks were postponed till September 23 so that the Western team could explore alternatives. In truth they had little room for manoeuvre, since they knew that Swapo had flatly refused to take part

in independence elections while any SADF troops remained in the territory.

Next morning the talks resumed, but only for two hours, after which an unsmiling Foreign Minister Pik Botha issued a brief statement saying only that there would be further discussions on September 24.

The talks ended on September 26 without agreement having been reached. Neither side was willing to issue any statement about the proceedings, except to say that the Western representatives would report back to their governments.

In spite of fears that Plan would mount a renewed effort in view of the talks, there had been only two minor incidents by the time the talks ended. Immediately afterwards, however, a string of incidents took place. There were three cases of an exchange of fire across the border, and one contact during a follow-up which resulted in three insurgents being killed, two others escaping over the border into Angola.

In early October two South African soldiers died, one in a mine-blast and the other in a fire-fight. Worse was to follow: two patrols met in the bush, and a soldier from one fired in the wrong direction and killed four men from the other.

Barring cross-border shooting, the insurgents were still keeping a low profile at this stage, no doubt waiting for the short rainy season to begin in November. In the meantime they continued to concentrate on activating the local population; intelligence officers began receiving reports that Plan groups were carrying first-aid bags and treating local inhabitants' ailments for them in an effort to persuade them not to attend state and mission hospitals.

The security forces made maximum use of the dry weather to harry the insurgents at every possible turn. As a result the kill-rate for September and early October was 50 percent higher than it had been in the preceding eight months.

Above
A variety of landmine-protected vehicles soon appeared in the operational areas adjoining Angola and Zambia. This version was also used in the Rhodesian War.

Opposite
Zairean troops, part of about 1 000 men sent to fight off an invasion of Shaba (formerly Katanga) province by veterans of the 1960s Katangese Gendarmes, who had been given refuge in Angola. The attack, permitted by the Angolans to express their displeasure at Zaire's support of Unita, was a military disaster for Mobuto and he had to call in Moroccan help to defeat the veterans. The following year the Gendarmes did it again; once more Mobuto's troops cut and ran, and he prevailed only with the help of French paratroopers

a calculated risk, so he called for assistance and then attacked.

The contact soon turned into the nearest thing to a full-scale battle South West Africa had seen since the defeat of the Germans in 1915. Hasty reinforcements, which had been helicoptered in, evened up the numbers and a running fight developed which swayed back and forth across the Cutline, the South Africans drawing fire from three other Plan positions situated in Angola.

The fight carried on into the night, resumed next morning, went on all day and did not end till after a skirmish with the northernmost Plan base, by which time the South Africans had penetrated 21km into Angola. The South Africans withdrew, having destroyed two Plan bases, badly damaged a third and killed a known 61 insurgents for a loss of five dead and one man mortally wounded.

While claims and counter-claims flew about - Swapo spokesman Peter Katjavivi had claimed in London on October 30 that South African losses had been in "double figures" and that the fight had actually taken place at Ondangwa, 55km south of the border, an assertion inhabitants of the large air base there found interesting - South African intelligence analysts were puzzling over why such a large concentration of insurgents had suddenly appeared in one place after a year of avoiding contacts with the security forces where possible.

One explanation was inefficiency on the part of the Plan field commander. On the other hand, on October 28 there had been a contact in which another large insurgent group of between 20 and 30 had walked into a small security force ambush, the result being one insurgent and one South African lieutenant dead and four insurgents wounded. The final conclusion was that it was part of a Swapo attempt to reinforce its image as a presence to be reckoned with in the international negotiations on South West Africa's future.

Katjavivi later also announced that Plan had attacked the large border base of Eenhana in one of the worst battles of the border war, killing and wounding "many" South African soldiers and forcing them to abandon it. The Plan fighters had then destroyed the base, along with "their radio communications system, military installations, vehicles and equipment".

The claim, an obvious attempt at refurbishing Plan's reputation after the October 27-29 battle, contravened the basic ground rule of propaganda, namely that a lie must be convincing and not too easy to refute. Geldenhuys promptly short-circuited it by inviting the Windhoek press to visit Eenhana, which they did; as one journalist later wrote, the only change since a visit he had made to Eenhana two months earlier was that the new chaplain had put up a different signpost to his chapel.

November saw efforts by Plan to revive the virtually moribund Caprivian insurgency, aided and abetted by what appeared to be an increasing paranoia among the Zambians. On November 2 the Zambian army claimed it had shot down a South African Cessna light aircraft near Sesheke. The Chief of the SAAF, Lieutenant-General Bob Rogers, promptly denied the claim and by way of proof produced the Cessna's pilot, Captain Koos Loock, who said he had been travelling at 16 000 feet on a routine flight at least 4km south of the Cutline and had not even known he was being shot at till ground control had told him and ordered him to return to Mpacha airfield.

Later a Plan group inside Caprivi fired mortar-bombs at a security force patrol on the Cutline,

Nevertheless the border war showed no signs of abating. Insurgents often operated in large groups and did not hesitate to fight if contact was made. In certain sectors of the South African public the erroneous conclusion was reached that Plan members always ran if attacked. In fact, this tactic was usually the only one that made sense. A typical contact consisted of a short, fierce fire-fight, after which the insurgent group usually gave way and headed for the Angolan border or dispersed into Ovamboland's endless stretches of bushland; to do otherwise would be to provide a sitting target for the SADF's helicopters and reaction-force units.

On October 25 Major-General Wally Black told a meeting of the Associated Scientific and Technical Societies of South Africa that contacts were running at a rate of about 100 a month; about 300 insurgents were active in Ovamboland at any given time, while 2 000 more were lying up in Angola and about 1 400 in Zambia, near the border with Caprivi. South West Africa, he added, was now in the classic third stage of insurgency, which was characterised by open revolt, internal unrest, terrorism and sabotage.

Black described the border struggle as "the corporal's war", because "the corporal with his section of 10 men makes the contact with the terrorist. He has to make the on-the-spot decisions and take the action."

But two days later, on October 27, the days of the corporal's war seemed to be over. An unusually large group of at least 88 insurgents crossed the Cutline into Ovamboland and after covering about 1km ran into a security force patrol. Although the patrol was vastly outnumbered, its commander decided his only salvation lay in taking

about 8km from the Caprivian capital of Katima Mulilo. The patrol fired back with rifles and mortars and the insurgents moved over into Zambian territory, by which time the patrol had also been fired on by Zambian soldiers.

Then followed a potentially nasty incident in which Zambian soldiers mortared an observation post on the southern bank of the Zambesi River. The South Africans fired back, setting off an hour-long duel during which some Zambian bombs fell on Katima Mulilo. The townspeople took it with relative aplomb: there had been sporadic firings over the river at the town since 1974, and since two similar incidents earlier in 1977 slit-trenches had been dug, houses facing the river sandbagged and an alarm system set up.

How much of this was the result of Zambian co-operation with Swapo and how much simple hubris was difficult to tell. Later Geldenhuys opined that he did not believe the attacks had come about "as a result of direct action involving the Zambian government. Personally, I do not believe these attacks occur on official instructions from the Zambian government".

Casualties on both sides continued to mount as the year wore on. Patrols were fired on from Angolan soil, two soldiers died in a mine-blast and 10 insurgents were killed when a group of between 40 and 50 attacked a patrol with machine-guns and RPG-7s. On November 23 another three insurgents were killed and two wounded in three separate fire-fights.

Analysis of the actions provided unmistakeable evidence that although the insurgents had been unable to expand their activities beyond the operational area immediately south of Angola, their standard of training had improved significantly due to the activities of Cuban instructors. They also seemed to have a larger supply of the latest land-mines and were certainly making greater use of light mortars than before.

On December 2 the protracted international negotiations on South West Africa's future resumed when the Western Security Council's team returned to Pretoria after consultations with Swapo and the governments of Tanzania, Zambia, Angola and Mozambique.

The main issue was still the South African troop presence in South West Africa, and seasoned observers found little hope that anything would be achieved while Swapo continued to insist on a total pre-independence withdrawal of the SADF, since Vorster was unlikely to budge past his last offer, namely to reduce the military presence to 4 000 troops, including a total of 1 500 fighting men, which would be based in two camps under UN control.

The greatest unanswered question was whether the Western team had obtained enough support, particularly from Tanzania and Angola, to persuade Swapo to moderate its demands. The answer to that came in a radio and television broadcast featuring Pik Botha on December 11, by which time two more soldiers had died in action, and it was "no".

South Africa was committed not to withdraw all its troops from the territory, he said. "The size of the force in the territory is always dependent on the nature and size of the threat," he added. "If the threat is great, severe and imminent, you would have more troops. If a procedure can be evolved in terms of which the threat can be diminished, then naturally there will be a decrease in the number of troops. It is as easy as that."

So the year ground to an end. According to Wally Black, speaking on Christmas Eve, security force casualties were down by 10 percent on 1976, but there were still between 250 and 300 insurgents operating inside South West Africa, with another 2 200 in camps in Angola and about 800 in south-western Zambia.

According to official statistics, 88 members of the security forces and 363 insurgents had died between 1966 and the end of 1977: modest numbers, perhaps, by the standards of international warfare, but heavy for the small populations from which they were drawn. But these figures were soon to escalate steeply, especially in the case of the insurgents, because the era of the "external operations" was about to dawn.

Some time in December, Prime Minister Vorster and his defence advisers held a long, very secret meeting at his holiday cottage at Oubos, an East Coast seaside resort. Details of the meeting have never been revealed, but what it amounted to was that Vorster was told that if projections about the likely future course of the insurgency were to be believed it would soon be necessary to take much stronger military and political measures against Swapo.

The insurgency could not be stopped by fighting an essentially defensive war in which the security forces sat in South West Africa and only reacted when insurgents crossed the border. Action must be taken to stop them from crossing the border or even being able to do so. What that implied was pre-emptive attacks on selected Plan concentrations in Angola, employing far larger force levels than had been used since Operation Savannah.

It would appear that Vorster was not wildly enthusiastic about taking the war into Angola. He was not a daring innovator by nature, and he had not forgotten the costs, in terms of wasted effort and world opprobrium, of Operation Savannah. On the other hand, even his enemies conceded that he was not one to shirk a hard decision, and so he approved the principle, although he ruled that all such operations must be approved at the highest political level.

It was a landmark decision, a watershed which would have as great an effect on the border war as the withdrawal from Angola in 1976 which had presented Swapo with its safe border.

Above
Prime Minister John Vorster's holiday home at Oubos, where in December of 1977 he conferred with his military chiefs and took the fateful decision to allow large-scale attacks into Angola to pre-empt insurgent infiltration

Following Page
Ever-lasting vigilance in the midst of heat, dust and boredom: this was what the border war required in 1977, when Plan activities escalated as a result of Angolan help. Here members of one of the countless patrols sent out take no chances as they search one of the thousands of little kraals dotting Ovamboland

1978

No immediate action followed the Oubos decision, but the border insurgency got off to an early start in the new year. On January 2 a security force patrol was fired on by a Plan group, which lost two killed in the ensuing clash. On January 4 an Ovambo was shot dead when he fled from his kraal on the approach of a Plan group.

That same day a South African patrol was attacked by a heavily armed group of insurgents and lost two dead. On January 5 another Ovambo was found dead about 20km from Oshikango; a spent AK-47 rifle cartridge-case lay near him, among spoor showing tread-patterns of the type found on boots issued to Plan.

On January 8 four Ovambos died and six were badly wounded when their vehicle detonated a Plan landmine, and another soldier was killed when his patrol was jumped on the Cutline by a Plan group which then retreated into Angola again. Further clashes took place later in the month.

On February 7, while Western negotiators were meeting in Windhoek to hold talks with the various local political parties, including Swapo's "internal" wing, insurgents assassinated Toivo Shiyagaya, Minister of Health and Welfare in the Ovambo tribal government. On February 10, as the Western diplomats gathered in New York with Pik Botha and Swapo leader Sam Nujoma for what was regarded as "last chance" talks on a negotiated settlement, another Plan group attacked a security force patrol but was beaten off and chased into Angola, where it was cornered and 18 of its members shot dead.

On February 19 a group of Zambian-based insurgents crossed over into Caprivi and killed four South Africans by firing an RPG-7 rocket into their vehicle. In Ovamboland insurgents killed two soldiers in an attack on a military water-point and lost two of their own men in the follow-up operation. On February 21 a Plan group kidnapped a teacher and 119 children from St Mary's Mission, a large Anglican church and mission station situated just south of the Cutline, and marched them into Angola. Three of the children later escaped and reported that they had been taken to a Plan training camp. Just afterwards Plan overran a small temporary base and captured an engineer, Sapper Johan van der Mescht, its first-ever South African prisoner.

The New York talks, not unsurprisingly, proved fruitless. Swapo's demand that Walvis Bay be incorporated into an independent Namibia was turned down flat by the South Africans, and agreement could not be reached on where South Africa's 1 500 fighting troops should be located during the run-up to the proposed pre-independence election. Swapo wanted them stationed at Karasburg, far down in the south, whereas the Western nations (no doubt realising that Pretoria would never agree to this) proposed that they be confined to the operational-area bases of Grootfontein and Oshivelo.

On February 28 Sam Nujoma personally (although possibly unwittingly) torpedoed what hope remained of achieving consensus when he delivered himself of a variety of intemperate remarks in a television interview with Cliff Saunders of the South African Broadcasting Corporation.

Nujoma flatly denied that Swapo was guilty of any atrocities, murders or intimidation. He added that the landmines which had killed so many civilians had actually been laid by the SADF, and that the SADF was in the habit of firing indiscriminately at civilians and then reporting the casualties as Plan members. He promised that when Swapo came to power "the people" would "do away with" a variety of South West Africans in the armed forces and other "traitors", not to mention the "puppets" belonging to the non-Swapo political parties.

Then Saunders asked him if he did not think Swapo would be "left out in the cold" if a non-Swapo government took power on independence. Nujoma's spectacularly tactless reply was: "The question of black majority rule is out. We are not fighting even for majority rule. We are fighting to seize power in Namibia, for the benefit of the Namibian people. We are revolutionaries. We are not counter-revolutionaries."

Embarrassed Swapo spokesmen like publicity secretary Mokganedi Tlhabanello later tried to suggest that Nujoma's remarks had been taken out of context, but observers who saw the relevant portion of the interview - which the SABC triumphantly screened several times - agreed it had obviously not been tampered with, and Nujoma himself made no attempt, then or later, to repudiate his statements.

In spite of the failure in New York the border was very quiet during most of March. Then on March 27 large-scale violence broke out again, heralded by the assassination of Chief Clemens Kapuuo, chief of the Herero tribe, chairman of the multi-racial Democratic Turnhalle Alliance and an inveterate enemy of Swapo. Within days infiltrations shot up almost to the January and February high, so that by April 4 no fewer than 12 insurgents had been killed.

Serious planning had now begun on the first of the external operations approved by Vorster the previous December. Nicknamed "Bruilof" (Wedding), it was scheduled to take place late that same month and envisaged simultaneous attacks by mechanised infantry and paratroopers on six Swapo bases in the vicinity of Chetequera, about 25km inside the Angola border on the Ovamboland front. Bruilof was so far advanced that troops had already been called up when it was abandoned for reasons that remain unclear. Most of the planning, however, was simply expanded into a much more ambitious operation, nicknamed "Reindeer", and scheduled for May 4.

Reindeer envisaged a drop by 257 paratroopers on the former iron-mining town of Cassinga, 250km inside Angola, with simultaneous land attacks on the old Bruilof targets around Chetequera and a straggle of confirmed and suspected Swapo bases some distance to the east of Chetequera.

While the military planners burnt the midnight oil, insurgent activity remained high. On April 21 the Ovambo Minister of Justice, Tara Imbili, had a narrow escape when an insurgent planted a mine on the road leading to his house; fortunately for Imbili the insurgent was none too expert or the mine was defective, and he blew himself up in the process. Next day a group of insurgents hijacked a bus travelling between Oshakati and Ruacana with 73 passengers and drove it over the border into Angola, passengers and all.

International peace talks were still in progress, and on April 25 South Africa formally accepted the Western proposals for a South West African settlement, a list of elaborate arrangements covering everything from a ceasefire and a reduction of SADF troops to the holding of an election and the formation of a constituent assembly. Anti-war elements in the South African press and political world hailed Pretoria's acceptance of the proposals, even though Swapo had not accepted them and the UN General Assembly had just started a 10-day special session which was scheduled to attack South African intransigence and inflexibility over South West Africa, and call for an unconditional withdrawal, on pain of economic sanctions.

In the meantime Major-General Wally Black rattled a few chains with a public warning that the acceptance of the proposals would mean an increase rather than a decrease in violence in the operational area, adding that there had been an upward trend in the pattern of incidents in the past four months.

Events soon proved him right. On April 28 the largest Plan group ever to exfiltrate from Angola – about 100 men – indulged in a fierce fire-fight with a security force patrol which did not result in large casualties (the insurgents lost two before pulling back into Angola) but confirmed information contained in Swapo documents found in a base earlier in the month, that the war was to be intensified.

In the next two days determined efforts were made to assassinate several Ovambo leaders by mining their private homes and even the regional legislative assembly at Ongwediva; then, on May 1, two security-force soldiers died when they detonated anti-personnel mines while their patrol was following up on fire directed at them from across the border. In a separate incident a group of between 12 and 15 insurgents were surprised in a village about 5km from the border, where they were drinking beer. A brief fire-fight took place which left two insurgents dead, the rest retreating over the border.

It is possible that the South Africans might have stayed their hand and cancelled or postponed Reindeer in the interests of keeping the Western nations' settlement alive, but no doubt the on-going campaign by Plan had an effect on their thinking, and a May 3 speech by Nujoma at the UN special session, during which he vowed that Swapo "will persevere and intensify the armed liberation struggle" almost certainly knocked out any chance of this happening.

Reindeer was the first and probably the most important external operation, not only in the sense that a failure might well have caused Vorster to pull in his horns but also because of its long-lasting effects on Plan. In some aspects it was also the most hazardous of them all.

Scheduled for the beginning of May, Reindeer was altogether more ambitious than Bruilof. The Chetequera network remained a target, but was no longer the main objective. Instead, Reindeer was to consist of simultaneous attacks on three widely separated targets.

Target Alpha (or "Moscow", as the insurgents called it) was the former copper-mining town of Cassinga, 250km inside Angola, which military intelligence had identified as Swapo's major forward operational headquarters for southern Angola and a training camp capable of housing up to 1 200 insurgent recruits.

Target Bravo ("Vietnam" to Swapo and the Angolans) was the network of six bases at Chetequera, which among other things contained Swapo's forward headquarters for Western Ovamboland and a major supply depot.

Target Charlie was a series of small bases and suspected bases between 17 and 21km east of Chetequera.

Below
A SAAF gun-camera photograph shows how it looked to the Mirage and Buccaneer pilots who dived through heavy anti-aircraft fire to strafe the town

In the case of Cassinga it was an ambitious operation, considering the South Africans' limited resources and the nature of the target.

In the first place, Cassinga was perilously deep inside Angolan territory when it was considered that the paratroopers would have to be extracted by helicopter (which was why it had been excluded from the Bruilof planning).

Secondly, the town would be no push-over. Swapo spokesmen and sympathisers later denied that Cassinga was an armed installation, describing it as a camp for refugees from "South African repression" with only a 300-man "camp defence unit", but aerial photographs showed the town had an extensive network of deep Russian-style zig-zag trenches, bunkers and various other indications of strong defences meant for a much larger force (mercifully for the South Africans' peace of mind, they did not know that it also deployed some anti-aircraft guns).

Another complicating factor was that a force of tanks and mechanised infantry, manned by Fapla and some Cubans, was stationed at Techamutete, just 16km to the south. Although the force was small - four or five World War II-vintage T-34 tanks and about 24 old BTR-152 armoured personnel carriers - it posed a threat out of all proportion to its size because the paratroopers' strongest firepower would consist of their small 60mm patrol mortars and what RPG-7s they could take with them.

In addition, there was always the possibility of hostile air attack, since MiG-21 fighters had been spotted in Angola as long ago as 1976.

The plan called for a softening-up aerial attack by SAAF fighters and bombers. Transport aircraft would then drop a small force of paratroopers, the assault being led by Colonel Jan Breytenbach, generally regarded as the SADF's most experienced fighting soldier.

The planners proposed to overrun Cassinga by means of a swift, violent assault, if possible capturing the Plan commander, the veteran Dimo Hamaambo. The paratroopers would destroy all munitions, equipment and weapons, bring back trained insurgents for interrogation and confiscate documents and other intelligence material, particularly ones which showed that Swapo was directly linked with the Soviet Union.

The paratroopers were given an extra task of great psychological importance: they were to liberate Sapper Johan van der Mescht, still the

only South African soldier ever to have been captured by Swapo, who was reportedly being held in Cassinga.

Once finished, the attackers would be evacuated by waves of helicopters which had refuelled at a temporary base or "helicopter administrative area" (HAA) which was to be established at first light on D-Day, 22km from Cassinga.

To do all this Breytenbach would have an assault force of just over 250 men, backed up by a 120-man mobile reserve which would be held airborne along the Cutline for the duration of the operation. In terms of both men and weapons the force had been stripped to the bone. Each of the three rifle companies consisted of only two platoons, and the two independent rifle platoons of two instead of three sections apiece. The only support weapons would be four 60mm mortars without baseplates, equally divided between two of the companies, and some captured RPG-7 anti-tank rocket-launchers.

Incredibly, the size of the attack group and its reserve was dictated not by pure military considerations but by the fact that the SAAF did not have enough fixed-wing transports for carrying the paratroopers, or enough helicopters with which to bring them back - thanks to the arms boycott the SAAF possessed so few models of its largest helicopter, the Super Frelon, that most of the paratroopers would have to be retrieved by its smaller Pumas, some of which were distinctly old and short-ranged.

All in all, the margin for error was lethally small and the chances of walking out if the extraction

Above
A paratrooper heads for the ground ... and a disastrous landing, followed by a hard fight

Above Right
A rough dressing covering the wrist wound he sustained while taking personal charge of the attack, Colonel Jan Breytenbach, commander of the assault force, speaks to one of his platoons. Facing him is Brigadier M J du Plessis, who had overall responsibility for the operation

Right
Several insurgents took cover under this Landrover at one stage in the fight. It did not save them from being shot dead

failed were even smaller; more than a decade later, hindsight makes it clear that the Cassinga drop still ranks as the most chancy of all the South African border operations.

But Breytenbach and his paratroopers brimmed over with confidence and a strong case for going ahead was presented by the Chief of the Army, the ascetic yet combative Lieutenant-General Constand Viljoen. An artilleryman turned paratrooper, Viljoen argued that the potential benefits far outweighed the risks, and in the end he had his way.

By comparison, the attacks on Chetequera and Charlie were straightforward, although the former was also a fairly formidable target - the bases were manned by an estimated 900 to 1 000 insurgents, and were known to be heavily defended with deep trenches and bunkers and a variety of support weapons which included 82mm recoilless guns, 82mm mortars, RPG-7 rocket-launchers and 14,5mm anti-aircraft guns.

Chetequera itself was to be attacked by an under-strength mechanised battle group known as "Juliet", manned by national servicemen, most of them unblooded, with a very thin sprinkling of Permanent Force members, commanded by the highly experienced Commandant Frank Bestbier.

While Bestbier was attacking Chetequera, two independent combat teams were to assault the southernmost bases. When the fighting was over he would link up with them for the withdrawal southwards to the border.

Charlie's bases were to be overrun in sequence by five rifle companies of 32 Battalion's expatriate Angolans under Commandant Deon Ferreira, who would be backed by air and artillery support.

After nerve-racking last-minute delays Reindeer was implemented on May 4 - the very day on which the General Assembly was preparing to vote overwhelmingly for a South African withdrawal - with a devastating air attack at 8am which caused such heavy damage and casualties that the base's defensive reactions were temporarily paralysed.

This made up for a disastrously off-target drop (the cause of which remains in dispute to this day) which resulted in many paratroopers having to ford a nearby river before going into action. However, the success of the air attack bought the paratroopers enough time to change the direction of their main attack from west-east to south-north. Just after 2pm they had achieved most of their aims - although the commander, Dimo Hamaambo, had escaped in time to save himself and the

prisoner, Van der Mescht, turned out to have been moved elsewhere - and the helicopter extraction started.

The extraction was bedevilled now by the approach of the Techamutete force, a situation made even more ticklish by the fact that Constand Viljoen had actually flown in to be with the troops at Cassinga and at least stood a chance of being captured.

The Techamutete force was beaten off by SAAF Mirages and Buccaneers and the paratroopers themselves, although two tanks came to within whites-of-the-eyes range of the landing zones. One was knocked out with air-to-ground rockets and the other was neutralised by repeated low-level "buzzing" by a Buccaneer pilot who had run out of ammunition. Eventually the evacuation was completed, and that evening the entire assault force was back at the Eenhana border base with the exception of one soldier who disappeared so totally that no trace of him has ever been found.

The other casualties amounted to three dead and 11 wounded. It was an incredibly light toll, considering the hours of heavy fighting; by the SADF's count at least 1 600 Cassinga inhabitants were killed, most of them uniformed Swapo members, and another 340 wounded, while 16 members of the Techamutete column had been killed and 63 wounded. Materially, too, the attack had cost little. The parachutes and some minor items of equipment had had to be left behind and two Buccaneers had suffered minor damage.

At Chetequera the attack also went off successfully, in spite of a hitch when Battle-Group Juliet's main attack went in slightly askew. This necessitated an unscheduled return sweep through a portion of the base, but eventually Chetequera was completely overrun at a cost of two fatalities and a small number of wounded. The independent combat teams inflicted some damage on the southern bases, and by mid-morning of May 5 the total force was back over the Cutline.

The 32 Battalion force made its first contact of May 6, when it chased some insurgents out of a base at Minquila. By May 8 it had overrun and destroyed a string of other camps - some defended and others evacuated - unfortunately suffering several casualties from its own artillery fire because of a communication problem.

Operation Reindeer had been an unqualified success. Plan had lost a total of about 1 000 members killed and 200 captured, while its infiltration effort had been very seriously interrupted and large

Above
A paratrooper chivvies a bunch of captured insurgents towards the battalion headquarters, a "liberated" Swapo carbine dangling from one hand

Following page
Huge clouds of dust and smoke leap up from Cassinga as 450kg bombs dropped by SAAF Canberras explode all the way down its spine — the north-south road leading to Techamutete

Insets Top Left
Back from the softening-up attack, Mirage pilots discuss their first strafing runs over Cassinga

Bottom Left
The medical team tends to two wounded paratroopers as the first casualties of the fighting start coming in to the temporary battalion headquarters

Bottom Right
Obeying the unwritten rule that South African soldiers bring back their dead unless it is absolutely impossible, paratroopers carry the body of one of their comrades to a waiting helicopter as the evacuation begins

dd 4. Mai 78

amounts of valuable intelligence material had been captured.

Operation Reindeer caused an unprecedented furore, particularly the attack on Cassinga. Swapo immediately charged that almost all those killed had been women and children because it had been a lightly defended refugee camp, not a heavily fortified insurgent training base and forward headquarters, as the South Africans claimed.

The South Africans stuck to their guns, while admitting that some of the dead had been women and children living with the insurgents, and others female Plan members in uniform. They followed this up by releasing Swapo documents they had looted. Five days later Swapo took a party of journalists to Cassinga and showed them two mass graves which they were told contained a total of 582 bodies, many women among them.

More than a decade later Cassinga is still being touted in some circles as an infamous massacre of the innocents. Claims and counter-claims aside, the South Africans' insistence that it was indeed a military target is reinforced by unfakeable aerial photographs showing the extensive fortifications and the resistance offered by the defenders, which was so stiff and protracted that the paratroopers stayed much longer than they had planned and had to leave the garrison still holding part of the town.

Whatever the finer details, there can be no doubt that the attacks on Cassinga and Chetequera had a catastrophic effect on Plan's fighting ability, so much so that according to one expert military analyst, H R Heitman, the organisation suffered a loss of trained and partly trained manpower from which it never fully recovered.

For many months afterwards Plan was forced to retain most of its surviving skilled men as instructors and field inadequately trained recruits, sending them over the border in unwisely large groups so that they could be led by the minimum of experienced fighters. This caused further heavy losses because the large groups were easier to detect, while their members were below standard in combat and anti-tracking skills.

The official statistics for 1978 tell their own story. Apart from the dead of Cassinga, insurgent losses totalled 971 – an average of 80,9 a month. The security forces' total operational death-toll was 44. In the future the ratio differed from time to time, but up to 1988 the annual Plan losses varied from a high of 1 494 to a low of 584, while the figure for the security forces varied from 100 to 30. An insurgency is not won or lost by body-counts, but the figures say that Operation Reindeer inflicted a well-nigh mortal blow on Swapo's military capability.

It also provided the South Africans with much food for thought. The most important lesson was obviously that launching external operations was definitely the way to go. Heavy patrolling and civic action could suppress the insurgency, but by the nature of things the initiative would almost always remain in the hands of the insurgent unless the war was taken to him.

By launching external operations, maximum advantage could be taken of the SADF's strong points: its conventionally trained manpower assets, its heavy weaponry and its control of the air. Swapo would be forced to move its headquarters and jumping-off points inconveniently deep into Angola, and its leadership would live in constant apprehension of a sudden South African onslaught. Combined with normal pacification operations inside

northern SWA/Namibia itself, it would be possible to grind down the Swapo war effort from both ends and lessen the advantage of the safe border.

Whatever its effect on Plan's campaign, Operation Reindeer also put paid to the chances of a South West African settlement, at least for 1978. On May 8 Nujoma and his negotiating team packed up and left the latest round of settlement talks in New York, saying the negotiations would serve no purpose at that stage – although Nujoma did not slam the door entirely and said Swapo still desired a negotiated settlement in South West Africa.

Late in May Andreas Shipanga was finally released and made his appearance in London, claiming that numbers of his fellow-dissidents were still being held. Although unshaken in his convictions about South West Africa's ultimate destiny, his experiences had disillusioned him about the Swapo leadership and the validity of the armed struggle as the sole means of achieving independence, and so he returned to the country soon afterwards to found a political party called the Swapo-Democrats.

In August 1985, by which time he had become one of the most influential politicians in the country and a minister in the internal government, he explained the reasons for his return: "I've no doubt about the bravery of the fighting members of Swapo, the Plan soldiers. They are brave, but they do not have proper political and military leadership. Swapo cannot win the war only by military means. But it is too proud and too afraid to negotiate with anyone else diplomatically and politically. Sam (Nujoma) has said he is not prepared to share power."

Three months later Reindeer's final shot was fired when Plan bombarded Katima Mulilo in Caprivi with mortars and 122mm rockets emplaced on Zambian soil. The SADF, which had got to hear about the intended attack, prepared for retaliatory action and sat down to wait. In the early hours of August 23 something like 30 122mm missiles were fired at Katima Mulilo, and a little later Zambian 82mm mortars fired at both the capital and one of the border bases, Wenela. Only two of the missiles inflicted any damage. One damaged a school in Katima Mulilo's black residential area and another demolished a bungalow in the military base, killing 10 soldiers and wounding another 10.

Above
Commandant Frank Bestbier (right) discusses the coming attack with his second-in-command, while all around him his men are preparing for the push over the border to Chetequera

Above Right
As he heads for Eenhana in one of the helicopters, the smile on this paratrooper's face says it all. He has experienced death and wounds and fear, and at the end of it he is alive and going home

Opposite
A convoy of Ratels crosses an oshona as Battle Group Juliet closes in on Objective Bravo — the base at Chetequera

Above
Troopers prepare their Eland-90 armoured cars for the attack on Chetequera. As always, the tough little vehicles were to play an important role in the attack

Centre
Tired paratroopers begin to mop up as Cassinga smoulders around them

Below
A medical orderly watches over a wounded soldier as he lies next to a Ratel, a drip running fluid into his shock-flabby veins. There were few seriously wounded in the attack

The South Africans fired back and then launched their ground troops. The first small combat team moved out of Mapacha airfield half-an-hour after the end of the bombardment and struck into Zambia, heading for a known Swapo camp 30km north of the Cutline. Another combat team crossed into Zambia just after 7am and ran into the retreating insurgents' rearguard. Within a few hours armed Alouette helicopters and para-troopers also entered Zambia.

The operation went on for several more days and nights, and eventually involved additional ground troops as well as Buccaneer strike fighters and Canberra light bombers, while two more artillery and mortar duels took place between Katima Mulilo and its Zambian opposite number, Sesheke. By the time the ground operations ended on August 27, a total of 16 insurgents had been killed.

In terms of casualties inflicted and damage done the South Africans' retaliation did not do a great deal to avenge the losses they had suffered, the highest in any single action of the border war up to that point. But it accomplished a greater purpose: for practical purposes it quashed the insurgency in Caprivi.

The pacification process was aided by a long-standing difference of opinion between Swapo and the Canu, the main point of dispute being the Caprivians' unwillingness to be deployed in Ovamboland rather than on their home ground. The dispute did not turn into an irreconcilable split till 1981, but it helped to ensure that the "armed struggle" was a dead letter in Caprivi from 1978 onwards. Many disgruntled Canu members took advantage of an amnesty offered by the South West African administration and returned to their homeland, and by the time the war ended in 1988, Caprivi had enjoyed 10 years of peace.

The most important effects of Operation Reindeer and the Katima Mulilo incident came in December of 1978, when further hitches in the settlement talks persuaded Pretoria to hold its own election for a multi-racial constituent assembly in South West Africa. In an attempt to keep people away Plan escalated its activities and Angola massed troops along the border, but South West African voters turned out in such vast numbers that

MASSACRE AT KASSINGA

CLIMAX OF PRETORIA'S ALL-OUT CAMPAIGN AGAINST THE NAMIBIAN RESISTANCE

Special bulletin of the South West Africa People's Organization (SWAPO) of Namibia. June 1978

in Ovamboland extra ballot-boxes had to be rushed to some polling centres.

In the end jubilant South African officials announced a 78 percent poll, with the multi-racial Democratic Turnhalle Alliance of Dirk Mudge taking 41 of the assembly's 50 seats. It was incontestably a free and fair election, conducted under the eyes of a number of Western observers, but the international community did not recognise either the election or the assembly because Swapo had not taken part, an attitude which did absolutely nothing to increase South African flexibility.

Above
A Swapo "special bulletin" put out in June of 1978, claiming the SADF had carried out a "barbaric attack" on a refugee camp which had resulted in the massacre of hundreds of "women, children and old men". According to the pamphlet, Cassinga's only defenders were 300 lightly-armed camp guards, who managed to kill more than 100 paratroopers. On the cover is a picture of a mass grave full of dead civilians

Below
Ten soldiers died when a Plan 122mm rocket demolished this barrack hut at Katima Mulilo during the August bombardment

Right
Troops who took part in
Operation Rekstok stand by
to board the approaching
Puma helicopters which will
take them back to their
border bases

The new year began peacefully, with Plan still maintaining a low profile. During the lull the partly-foundered settlement negotiations were resurrected with such apparent success that early in February Foreign Minister Pik Botha stated in public he did not see why implementation of the independence process could not begin before the end of the month.

But once again the war intervened: on February 13 an estimated 250 insurgents took advantage of a blinding summer rainstorm to attack the Nkongo base, about 15km from the border.

The assault was not pressed home and did not achieve anything much beyond wounding seven of the occupants before the attackers withdrew and got clean away, thanks to the rain, which cut visibility and washed out their tracks. But it was an embarrassing episode, and the South African government immediately fired off a strong note of protest to UN Secretary-general Kurt Waldheim, warning that "the whole delicate edifice of agreement which we built so carefully over the past period is in danger of collapse in the light of Swapo's dastardly attack".

The note went on to ask whether Swapo had accepted the settlement proposals and whether, as scheduled, the United Nations Transitional Agreement Group's troops would arrive by the end of the month and set the independence process in motion.

Waldheim's reply was, to put it bluntly, less than adequate. He failed to give an assurance that the troops would be arriving as scheduled, and according to one report he also opined that any delays were being caused by South Africa, not Swapo.

In addition, Sam Nujoma held talks with UN Special Representative Martti Ahtisaari and then announced that in the event of a settlement Swapo fighters would not be restricted to their bases in order to be monitored, and that South African troop levels would have to be reduced irrespective of whether a visible peace should come about.

Botha reacted by vowing that not a single soldier would be withdrawn unless a visible ceasefire was brought about, adding that a reduction in strength would take place only if Swapo stopped committing acts of violence.

"Swapo will only be allowed into South West Africa if they return unarmed to participate peacefully in elections," he said. "They will only return through previously stated points. Intimidation by Swapo, in any form whatsoever, will not be tolerated for one moment."

Plan responded with a rash of attacks on Ovambo civilians in the next fortnight, and on February 26 another attack on a security force base, this time the one at Elundu, from which 32 Battalion had carried out its sweep north of the border during Operation Reindeer.

1979

A party of Rekstok raiders load some of the equipment at the Obembo base on to a helicopter. Although Rekstok and a simultaneous operation into Zambia, Operation Saffraan, were largely fruitless, they helped to prevent a quick recovery by Plan, which was still reeling from the damage suffered in Operation Reindeer

Above
**UN Secretary-General
Dr Kurt Waldheim**

Below
**South African ambassador
to the UN Riaan Eksteen**

It was not an action of great moment – the insurgents opened up on the base at long range for about 15 minutes and then decamped, having caused no damage because all the projectiles missed the target. However, it achieved large newspaper headlines, which was the object of the exercise, and this was followed up by a Swapo statement issued in London and quoted by the Angolan news agency Angop which claimed that in the past three months Plan had killed more than 300 South African soldiers, destroyed two military bases, shot down two reconnaissance aircraft, knocked out 40 military vehicles and captured large quantities of arms and ammunition.

This rather naive attempt at disinformation was soon overtaken by harder news. In addition to stepping up its patrolling activities, the SADF launched two modest simultaneous six-day external operations on March 7, nicknamed "Rekstok" and "Saffraan". Operating from Ovamboland, the Rekstok forces swept through a series of known and suspected Swapo bases at Mongua, Oncocua, Henhombe, Heque and elsewhere, while Saffraan jumped off from Caprivi and did the same in south-western Zambia. Neither achieved much material success, although several large and hastily vacated Plan bases were destroyed and forthcoming insurgent infiltrations were badly disrupted.

Rekstok and Saffraan were followed by aerial attacks on targets inside Angola. The targets and the results of the raid or raids have remained unidentified to this day, and the whole episode might well have remained a secret except that one Canberra light bomber was damaged – apparently by ground fire – and crashed, killing its crew. The Angolans promptly claimed they had shot down six SAAF aircraft, during repeated bombing raids between March 6 and March 15 in which 132 tons of bombs had been dropped, killing 12 people and wounding 30. An SADF spokesman riposted with the remark that the Angolan statement contained "certain delectable untruths".

Plan continued to avoid contact with the security forces and concentrate on attacking civilians. By May 11 the year's death-toll stood at 61 civilians, mostly blacks but also a handful of whites who had been murdered in a short-lived Plan foray into the Tsumeb-Otavi area, south of the operational area, 11 soldiers, five Ovambo home guards and one policeman. The SADF responded by increasing its counter-insurgency activities and providing certain tribal chiefs and other civilians with bodyguards and special constables for round-the-clock protection.

As a result Plan attacks on civilians began to slow down by mid-year, but the insurgents switched their attention back to harder targets, among other things hitting at Ruacana's hydro-electric works with rockets and mortar-bombs fired from Angola. It was a brief attack which ended after the Ruacana protective element fired back.

Plan's activities around this time tended to disguise the fact that it was still suffering from the after-effects of Operation Reindeer, not to mention such actions as Rekstok and Saffraan and an increasingly sophisticated counter-insurgency force. Between April and the beginning of July it had lost at least 55 dead and most contacts were initiated by the security force.

Interrogation of prisoners and reports from SADF intelligence sources in the operational area and Angola painted a gloomy picture of low morale, repeated public executions of would-be deserters and increased abductions (there were to be more

than 450 by year's end) to make up for a dearth of volunteers. Thanks to the interruption of supply lines by Unita activities there was such a lack of food in some base camps that there had actually been cases of insurgents dying of hunger; many insurgents infiltrating into Ovamboland were interested less in fighting the security forces than foraging for food or even stealing it from their fellow Ovambos.

Small wonder, then, that on September 11 General Geldenhuys – never one for making over-optimistic statements – told reporters that he believed the tide had turned in South West Africa, although, he added, a long struggle still lay ahead.

On September 11 Angola's President Agostinho Neto visited Moscow and died there, allegedly under somewhat mysterious circumstances. It was an unexpectedly abrupt end for a man who had survived not only Operation Savannah but at least two attempted coups which were said to have been sparked by his preference for appointing light-skinned mulattos like himself to senior military positions (years later, in 1984, South Africans serving on the Joint Military Commission noticed that very few Angolan senior officers were blacks).

In mid-September there was another brief and fruitless bombardment of Nkongo with mortars and small arms which did not disguise the fact that 13 insurgents had been shot dead within the space of a week – two of them at the hands of Ovambo home guards following yet another bungled attempt to assassinate the homeland's Minister of Justice, Tara Imbili. By September 26 another 38 insurgents had died, bringing the total of known deaths to almost 350 since the beginning of April; according to the SADF this was partly because Ovamboland inhabitants were passing on more information on Plan movements than ever before.

On October 1 the settlement talks went into yet another round when South Africa's UN ambassador Riaan Eksteen was handed a revised independence plan drawn up by the Western nations, together with a suggestion that "proximity talks" be held as soon as possible. Among other things the new plan envisaged South Africa being allowed to retain five bases within a 50km-wide demilitarised zone along the border for the first three months of the independence process. South African troops would be confined to these bases for 12 weeks and then withdrawn altogether; Swapo would be totally excluded from them. The Untag force would patrol the DMZ to ensure that all the provisions were being complied with.

The plan was greeted with less than total joy by the participants in the border war. Swapo stated it would not react till the text had been formally presented to it; African sources openly expressed the belief that South Africa would insist on its original demand for control to be exerted over Swapo, and that in any case the South Africans would not react till they had some idea of the likely outcome of the Zimbabwe-Rhodesian negotiations which were then taking place in London.

While the politicians pondered and prevaricated, Plan losses in South West Africa continued to rise. By October 18, according to Geldenhuys, Plan had suffered almost 500 confirmed dead since the beginning of May. On October 31 he expanded on his earlier statements. Since May, he said, the security forces had killed or rendered "inactive" about 2 000 members of Plan's fighting strength. This represented between 12 and 15 percent of its total trained or partly trained men, 6 000 to

8 000 of whom were stationed in Angola and 1 000 to 2 000 in Zambia.

Numbers of Plan deserters were now living in South West Africa again and others had surrendered to the host countries in which they were based, he added, and it seemed that still others wanted to lay down their arms as well, since tribespeople had reported that insurgents calling at their kraals had told them how weary they were of the armed struggle.

Geldenhuys quoted reports that group leaders sometimes had to use physical violence to maintain discipline, and explained that one reason why insurgents were operating in larger groups was that it enabled leaders to keep a wary eye on potential deserters.

At the time there was much speculation at Geldenhuys's use of the phrase "rendered inactive". As he later explained in a newspaper interview, he meant insurgents who had been "permanently or temporarily put out of action", including deserters and wounded.

Geldenhuys has also long believed that Plan fatalities through the years have been far greater than could be confirmed by actual body-count or other reliable evidence, the reason being that the insurgents had never had adequate medical facilities to treat wounded. As a result, according to circumstantial evidence, great numbers died from comparatively minor wounds or ailments which were neglected either because the circumstances did not allow immediate treatment or because no treatment was available.

Swapo's permanent UN representative, Theo-Ben Gurirab, promptly discounted the figure of 2 000 given by Geldenhuys as "day-dreaming" and added: "He is busy with wishful thinking. If he wants to live in the world of Alice in Wonderland, let him do so." Swapo was in South West Africa to stay, he added, and was busy restructuring its armed forces to intensify the armed struggle.

The intensification did not eventuate, however, and by November 30 a total of 147 insurgents had been killed for a loss of three security-force members. The biggest single "kill" occurred late in the month when a security-force element clashed with a Plan group in Ovamboland, killed seven, then followed the survivors into Angola and hit several bases, killing another 68.

On December 5 the South African government formally accepted the concept of a demilitarised zone, subject to six conditions; meanwhile, the killing on the border went on. By the end of December, 25 insurgents had died for a loss of four security-force soldiers. Of this number, 21 were lost during a three-day follow-up action which started after a patrol had surprised the Plan group as it was crossing into South West Africa. For Plan it was a disastrous end to a generally disastrous year in which strenuous efforts had achieved little except a high death-toll of 915 known dead for a loss of 50 security-force members.

On the other hand, it had been a rough year all round. According to figures released later by Geldenhuys, the number of incidents had gone up from just under 500 in 1978 to more than 900 in 1979, and there had been more than 300 contacts, almost double the 1978 figure. In addition to the abduction of more than 450 people, 55 local inhabitants had died in landmine explosions and 102 had been murdered, among them 18 tribal headmen and six whites. More than 50 cases of sabotage had taken place, mostly of telephone and power lines or water pipelines.

Food supplied for humanitarian purposes by various sympathetic Western countries like Denmark and organisations like UNICEF did not necessarily end up feeding refugees but often went straight to the insurgents

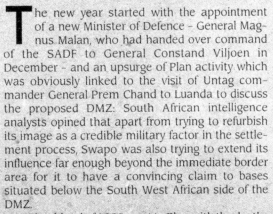

1980

The new year started with the appointment of a new Minister of Defence - General Magnus Malan, who had handed over command of the SADF to General Constand Viljoen in December - and an upsurge of Plan activity which was obviously linked to the visit of Untag commander General Prem Chand to Luanda to discuss the proposed DMZ: South African intelligence analysts opined that apart from trying to refurbish its image as a credible military factor in the settlement process, Swapo was also trying to extend its influence far enough beyond the immediate border area for it to have a convincing claim to bases situated below the South West African side of the DMZ.

First blood of 1980 went to Plan with the deaths of two security-force soldiers in a contact on January 20. Less than a fortnight later six soldiers and 19 insurgents died in a contact and its resultant follow-up. More contacts followed thick and fast, so that by February 15 a total of 77 Plan members had been killed since the beginning of the month, as well as several more security-force soldiers.

Operation Sceptic: Having run a gauntlet of anti-aircraft fire from a Plan 14,5mm gun hidden in a thicket nearby, a Puma helicopter takes off with the casualties. The smoke from the knocked-out Ratel can be seen at left

Inset
A more seriously wounded soldier is carried to the helicopter. At the time it was thought he would die, but within months he had recovered

That same month a Plan group ventured far south of the operational area, penetrated the Tsumeb-Grootfontein-Otavi triangle and killed two white civilians. The security forces got on their trail and by February 22 had killed 19 of the raiders for a loss of one white soldier and a Bushman tracker. The chase continued, and at the end of the first week in March the group headed back to Ovamboland, having killed another soldier and suffered a further 11 deaths (three at the hands of the local population, two of them being shot dead by the 15-year-old daughter of one of their victims).

The scale of the fighting then diminished, but not by much. In the next two weeks another 13 insurgents were shot dead, while one infantryman was killed in action and three army engineers died in a mine explosion, bringing total security-force deaths for the past six weeks to 22, 14 of them in February - the heaviest in a long time.

In the meantime Dr Jonas Savimbi was making his voice heard in the settlement talks. On March 6 - as UN officials and South African government representatives were holding constitutional talks in Windhoek - he delivered a letter to P W Botha in Cape Town, demanding to be included in the DMZ talks because he and not Luanda controlled the Angolan shallow area in which the no-go area was supposed to be established. He added that he would not tolerate a new intervention of foreign forces after having been engaged in a struggle against first the Portuguese and then the Russians and Cubans.

If the UN forces tried to interfere with the people of southern Angola without Unita's authority, he warned, he would take such steps as were deemed necessary.

Since Savimbi was indisputably in control of the proposed DMZ area, this was a matter of extreme embarrassment to the MPLA, and when the press quizzed Foreign Minister Pik Botha about Savimbi's demand he would say only that he did not wish to comment on the letter at that stage. According to political observers, however, the South African leaders were not too upset by Savimbi's protest; although extremely unwilling to be branded as wreckers, they were none too happy about proceeding with the DMZ concept because Robert Mugabe's overwhelming victory in the Zimbabwe-Rhodesian election had aroused so much ire among their supporters that the prospects for settlement had suffered.

In April the intensity of the South West African fighting slowed down but did not stop, and 21 insurgents and one security-force member had died by the end of the month.

On May 1 P W Botha came out in public support of immediate home rule for South West Africa, even though the territory was not yet independent. Speaking in the 1980 defence debate in Parliament, he said that his government was willing to hand over many territorial administrative functions, including control over local members of the security force (although the significance of this last did not become apparent till August).

This did not rule out an internationally acceptable independence, he hastened to add, pointing out that Western countries did not accept the view that Swapo was the sole voice of the South West African people and expressing the hope that the insurgents would seek a joint solution together with the leaders of the territory's democratic parties.

"A political solution for South West Africa is absolutely essential," he added. "It is not South Africa that is causing delay in finding a political solution."

The formation of the home-rule government was, in fact, already cut and dried, and on May 14 Dirk Mudge, whose Democratic Turnhalle Alliance held the vast majority of seats after the election of December 1978, announced that in future South West Africa would be governed by a "Council of Ministers" to which Pretoria would increasingly transfer its powers (the Council of Ministers was inaugurated on July 1, along with a separate South West African civil service). Mudge was at pains, however, to emphasise that the new dispensation would not be "a disguised form of independence", as the council would still fall under the jurisdiction of Pretoria's Administrator-General.

While all this was happening on the political front there was a dramatic upsurge of action in the border war. By mid-May 26 insurgents had been killed in two separate operations, and a few days later four soldiers of 41 Battalion, a multi-racial unit entirely recruited from South West Africans. Then five security-force soldiers and 81 insurgents died in the bloodiest single incident since August of 1978: a patrol of unknown size had walked into a huge Plan ambush and lost the five dead in the initial exchange of fire. The patrol then counter-attacked, at the same time calling for reinforcements. In the ensuing shootout the 81 insurgents were killed and large amounts of weapons,

ammunition and equipment were captured.

The contact brought the total deaths for the year to 30 security-force members and 324 insurgents (as well as at least 40 civilians), but the fighting was not over yet. The air base at Ondangwa came under a brief stand-off mortar bombardment which, however, inflicted only minor damage, and in the last week of May, 15 insurgents were killed in various contacts.

The bloodletting continued into the next month. On June 5 a soldier was killed and on June 7 another two. On June 9 a fourth soldier died, as well as five insurgents.

But now the border war was temporarily overshadowed by another development: Operation Sceptic, the largest mechanised-infantry assault carried out by South African forces since World War II, the first phase of which had already been launched on May 25.

A far more ambitious venture than any of the previous external operations, Sceptic was aimed at taking out Plan's command-and-control centre for the entire operational area, which was located at Chifufua (nicknamed "Smokeshell"), about 180km due north of the Cutline but about 260km by road. Commanded by Plan's Dimo Hamaambo, Smokeshell consisted of 13 sub-bases spread over 45 square kilometres, so well-camouflaged and dug in that the only way of destroying it was by an extensive ground attack.

The plan was that three battle-groups would cross the border under the control of a temporary tactical headquarters set up by Brigadier Rudolph Badenhorst, OC Sector 10, at Eenhana base.

On May 25 a force consisting of 54 Battalion, plus two companies of 32 Battalion and one parachute company, all under Commandant Anton van Graan, crossed the border and secured the area up to Mulemba, about 90km north of the Cutline, where it established a helicopter administrative area. Around June 1 three mechanised-infantry forces – Battle-Group 10 under Commandant Chris Serfontein, Battle-Group 61 under Commandant J M Dippenaar and Battle-Group 53 under Commandant Jorrie Jordaan occupied themselves with training and mock area operations at various locations far removed from the scene of action.

On the afternoon of June 9 the three battle-groups converged on Eenhana. Having refuelled, they crossed the Cutline at last light and headed

Right
Eyes staring with shock, a wounded infantryman whose Ratel has just been knocked out by a battery of Plan guns is hurried to a waiting helicopter by two of his mates

Opposite Top — Bottom
Commandant J M Dippenaar (in beret, right rear) holds a last-minute order group in the bush, part of the way to Smokeshell. At this stage the attack was running late, thanks mainly to very bad terrain on the approach route

A Plan insurgent who survived the fighting sits bound on a Ratel, waiting to be taken back across the border and into captivity

A high-level observer — the Chief of the Army, Lieutenant-General Constand Viljoen — talks to some of the troopies. Spruce and steel-calm as always, there is nothing about him to indicate that a little earlier the Ratel in which he had been riding had detonated two linked mines, blowing him clear out of his hatch

In accordance with standing orders, the burnt-out Ratel is taken back so that it cannot be used for propaganda purposes. It was so badly damaged that the tiffies had to cut the hull from the suspension, then load both on to a supply lorry

for Chifufua at top speed. Leaving Jordaan behind to carry out area operations in the Chitumba area due east of Mulemba, Serfontein and Dippenaar travelled almost non-stop through the bitter night cold and hit Smokeshell around 2.30pm on June 10, just after a softening-up artillery and aerial bombardment. Incredibly, the attack took the defenders by surprise, but the shock was diminished by the sheer size of the objective and what ensued was the most bitter infantry action of the border war at this stage.

Sceptic was to have ended on June 16. Instead, thanks to additional intelligence garnered on the spot, it turned into a much wider operation against bases to the west of Smokeshell and was not completed till June 30.

Although marred by some organisational hitches, there was no doubting the fact that Sceptic had been an overall success. Plan operations had been seriously disrupted, huge amounts of food, equipment and weapons had been captured or destroyed, much valuable intelligence had been gathered and a total of 360 insurgents were known to have died. In addition the South Africans had acquired valuable semi-conventional battlefield experience.

At the same time it had cost them 17 dead, the largest death-toll in one operation so far, and it had given some unsettling indications of things to come: for the first time, during the extended post-Smokeshell phase, the SADF had come up against semi-mechanised Plan elements, and during the withdrawal an Angolan column attacked one of the battle-groups instead of staying out of what amounted to a domestic squabble.

This last was a worrying phenomenon. SADF policy was to avoid contact with the Angolans except if Plan insurgents were inextricably mingled with elements of Fapla, but in the future it was obviously not going to be so easy to apply, and this proved to be the case.

On June 23, while Sceptic was still in progress, the settlement talks got under way again after a fashion, with Pik Botha offering to reduce operational bases from 40 to "20 selected locations" in the proposed DMZ on certain conditions which included the disarming of all insurgents seven days after the holding of a free and fair pre-independence election; an undertaking from Swapo that it would abandon its claim to bases inside South West Africa, as distinct from bases in Angola; and an undertaking by Waldheim himself not to give effect to the General Assembly resolution which had proclaimed Swapo as the only authentic representative of the South West African people.

Waldheim accepted the offer, noting that the frontline states and Swapo regarded the 20 bases as unnecessary but had agreed to the provision "in the interests of obtaining a settlement". Angola and Zambia had undertaken to ensure that Swapo would accept the outcome of the election, and if South Africa agreed to the DMZ the UN would not insist on Swapo internal bases after a ceasefire. Waldheim also pledged that in spite of the 1976 resolution "the principle of impartiality has been and will be consistently followed".

The South West African internal parties reacted to Waldheim's letter with caution or pleasure, according to their various persuasions, while DTA leader Dirk Mudge would say nothing till his party's executive council had studied it. Some observers commented that nothing had really changed, because if the reply was stripped of its fine words it went no further than Resolution 435.

Above
The mechanised infantry goes into action. In war films an attack looks spectacular. In real life its portrait is painted in shades of khaki and pale dust and black oily smoke ... and you might never see the man who kills you

Below
Near the half-way mark to the objective, the 20km-long column halts briefly to sort out its kinks

Less than a fortnight later Waldheim seemingly backed up their view by mounting a strong attack on South Africa for launching Operation Sceptic. Pik Botha responded coolly that while he was "surprised" by the Secretary-General's remarks, "Dr Waldheim's attack on South Africa is nothing new. He does it regularly when he visits Africa, to, among other things, hide the incapability of the United Nations to do something positive about the development of Africa".

In the meantime the effects of Sceptic were clearly to be seen in counter-insurgency operations on the border. Not only had Plan operations been temporarily beheaded, but many insurgents who had escaped or had been in the field when the attack took place found themselves without communications or food at a time when southern Angola was already going hungry because of a drought.

Sixty-five insurgents were killed in Ovamboland during July. Security forces reported many of them appeared to be wandering aimlessly, sometimes singly, sometimes in twos and threes, their main object not fighting but finding food. One group

was surprised in the act of slaughtering a purloined goat and another was found hiding in a kraal.

On July 30, with the furore raised by Sceptic scarcely settled, South African troops headed back into Angola for another pre-emptive strike, Operation Klipkop. Klipkop was a tiny affair compared to Sceptic, aimed at wiping out a Plan logistical and transit base at the little town of Chitado, 5km from the border and 35km east of Ruacana; no doubt the desire to discourage further mortar attacks on the hydro-electric scheme (there had been another one a few days earlier) was a secondary object.

Soon after first light on July 30 an 80-man force was dropped by helicopter a short distance from Chitado. Then, waiting only for SAAF aircraft to drop 20 000 leaflets explaining that Angolans were not in danger unless they fired on South Africans, the raiders went in, supported by armed Alouette helicopters. After a brisk but brief fight in which 27 defenders were killed (which were Swapo and which MPLA was impossible to tell, since all were wearing the same uniform), the raiders captured and destroyed the base.

Ever mindful of the publicity angle, the SADF then flew a party of journalists in, gave them a battlefield briefing and flew them out again. Then the attackers withdrew, blowing up the MPLA headquarters and barracks.

Two days later, on August 1, the South West Africa Territory Force was officially founded. It was a modest organisation, comprising a few local infantry battalions and some headquarters and support elements, but in just eight years it was to grow to such a size that border service became the exception rather than the rule for fighting troops of the South African Defence Force.

In Ovamboland the insurgents were still suffering from Operation Sceptic's disruption. As in July, many of them wandered about aimlessly

in twos or threes, intent on finding food rather than fighting and often fleeing without firing a shot; one group was so dispirited that a security-force patrol sneaked up on them and caught them as they lay listlessly in ambush. The security forces kept up the pressure, hunting them down whenever possible and often with the help of information given by the inhabitants.

In the first two weeks of August 73 insurgents were killed without loss. Then the guerrillas began to recover. On August 16 a security force element lost four men in a shootout with 70 insurgents, 29 of whom were killed. On August 20 another soldier was killed, and two more on August 26.

September, however, proved a bad month for the insurgents. On September 15 one soldier was killed in action, but the security forces, acting on information from local inhabitants, pounced on an unprecedentedly large 150-man group led by a seasoned Plan field commander called Kelola. After four days 81 of the group were dead, including Kelola himself. Kelola's mission was the subject of much speculation at SWATF Headquarters, where General Geldenhuys was busy handing over to his successor, Major-General Charles Lloyd, so that he could take over as Chief of the Army.

In the end it was agreed that Kelola had probably been tasked to carry out some headline-grabbing missions aimed at restoring Swapo's tarnished military image. Military observers noted that Kelola's infiltration had come just before Swapo leaders were to attend an international conference in Paris. Had he been waiting for the right moment to strike so that Nujoma could announce a military success at the conference?

Many smaller contacts took place as well, and by the end of the month 170 insurgents had died. The intensity of September carried over into October. On October 14 security forces killed two insurgents comparatively far south at Kamanjab;

a few days later they discovered that Plan had sent another small unit into the Otavi-Grootfontein-Tsumeb triangle and launched a week-long hunt that resulted in the deaths of eight insurgents. Around October 20 a small pre-emptive raid on a Swapo base inside Angola left 22 insurgents and MPLA soldiers dead. In the next 10 days 38 insurgents were killed in several small actions. In all, 130 had lost their lives since the beginning of the month, bringing the year's toll, including losses suffered in the external operations, to over 1 300.

The fighting slowed down in November, but in late December several Swapo bases inside Angola were raided. At first no public revelation was made, but then the raids were announced by Swapo's secretary of administration, Moses Garoeb, who claimed they had been repulsed with severe losses for the security forces.

General Lloyd rejected Garoeb's claim in a radio broadcast on December 31, confirming raids had taken place in the past few days but denying the security forces had suffered losses. There was no way in which the security forces could hide their casualties, he said.

Lloyd went on to say that the security forces had taken the initiative and were acting "aggressively" against Swapo; they knew where the insurgent bases were located in Angola and attacked them at will. He had information, he added, that there was a large dissident element in Swapo ranks and expected significant increase in the number of insurgents seeking amnesty in the coming year.

So ended December, with a series of bangs rather than a whimper. It had been a year of grievous casualties for both sides. The security forces had lost 100 men, their highest-ever fatality figure, then or later; the insurgents had lost 1 447, a staggering number that was to be surpassed only once in the next eight years.

Above
The Plan gunner who knocked out the Ratel lies dead at his 14,5mm gun, his clothes blown off him by the impact of the high-explosive 20mm shells fired at him by another Ratel almost immediately afterwards. The Plan gunners served their guns to the death. By the time this photograph was taken the South Africans had removed the gun's barrel

1981

The war did not take long to resume after the New Year. A fortnight into January, as South Africans, Swapo and members of the internal parties were attending a spectacularly unsuccessful meeting in Geneva (which degenerated into a shouting-match over the UN's alleged pro-Swapo bias), the security forces and the insurgents clashed again. Soon afterwards the South Africans announced that two soldiers and 35 insurgents had died in a two-day follow-up operation in "the northern operational area". This year the phrase meant more than just Ovamboland: for the first time since 1966 Plan was trying to activate Kavango. The effort was not to prove immediately fruitful, but Kavango was to stay a Swapo target – and a security-force headache - for the next three years.

On January 18 the Angolan news agency Angop claimed that seven days earlier the South African Air Force had carried out reconnaissance flights over Angolan soil, after which a motorised-infantry company had crossed the border near Chiede. The following day army units backed by six Puma helicopters and a squadron of Mirages had attacked Angolan troops near Cuamato. Fierce fighting was still taking place, Angop said, and both sides had suffered dead and wounded. A South African spokesman responded by referring inquiries to its earlier announcement.

The greatest sensation that month, however, was not the border war itself but sensational claims made in the British press by one Trevor Edwards, a British national and former Rhodesian soldier who had spent eight months serving in the shadowy 32 Battalion and now went public with horrific claims of atrocities he and his men had allegedly committed on the Angolan population while engaged in external actions - there was always a 32 Battalion element operating in Angola from its base at Buffalo, near Rundu, he claimed.

Edwards's allegations in the press were followed on January 29 by his appearance on a British television programme, in the course of which he repeated his earlier allegations. These were categorically denied by the SADF on February 7, although by this time the issue had been largely overshadowed by yet another sensation, a South African special-forces raid on the African National Congress in Maputo, capital of Mozambique, on January 30.

A different perspective on the border war appeared in print on February 17, when Nicholas Ashford, a correspondent for The Times newspaper in London, ended a border tour laid on by the SADF for correspondents with a feature in which he said he had come back with two clear impressions, firstly that the South Africans believed they had Swapo on the run, and secondly that they were opposed to the establishment of a demilitarised zone along the border because they calculated they were winning the war.

Ashford said that the SADF's "civic action" programmes had achieved some success in Kavango and Caprivi, but had been an almost total failure in Ovamboland. However, the South Africans seemed confident enough of the outcome, and their camps were larger than ever and had an air of permanence about them.

Confident the South Africans might have been, but the border war was far from over. A total of 77 insurgents died in February, and March saw a dramatic upsurge in the fighting. By mid-month 58 insurgents had been killed; 43 of them in 13 incidents which all took place during one sanguinary weekend. In one contact a Plan group ambushed a police counter-insurgency patrol near Ondangwa but failed to inflict any casualties, whereupon the policemen proceeded to fight their way out, killing five of the ambushers in the process. Later that same day a police patrol encountered another Plan group only 8km from the scene of the earlier incident and killed 16 in a furious fire-fight.

The latest losses brought Plan fatalities to 283 since January 1, but more clashes were to follow. Soon after mid-month - not long after Swapo warned from London that there was an unprecedented military build-up in South West Africa and the SADF tartly replied that "history has proved that we do not need massive troop concentrations to wipe out terrorists, wherever they might be" - SAAF aircraft ventured deep into Angola to attack the large Swapo administrative and transit camp at Lubango, the former Sa Da Bandeira. Timed to hit the camp during the lunch-break, the attack came as such a surprise that the aircraft encountered almost no defensive fire and returned safely to their base.

Meanwhile in the operational area the security forces killed another 35 insurgents in 20 skirmishes during the week ending on March 19. In the same period at least 10 civilians died - two murdered by the insurgents, one killed in the cross-fire during a contact and seven blown up by a land-mine - while various insurgent groups damaged a water pipeline east of Ruacana and a low-water bridge near Omaumba, and blew up six telephone poles west of Ombalantu.

Another lull then followed, but in mid-April six civilians and 13 insurgents were killed in just two days. Of the insurgents, 10 died in minor skirmishes, but the other three were members of a group about 30 strong which had crossed the southern border of the operational area and penetrated the so-called "Mangetti Block", a white farming area. The foray was not notably successful: two insurgents were killed by the security forces before they reached the Mangetti Block and the third on a farm near Tsumeb; after this the group split up and took refuge in the nearby mountains.

Opposite
Operation Protea: Ratels cross the bridge at Xangongo, while one of the former occupants lies dead nearby — whether he is Swapo or Fapla is difficult to tell, since they serve side by side, often in the same uniforms. To the Ratel gunners it was enough that he was there, and belonged to the other side; there is no time or inclination for splitting hairs when you are being shot at. And so he lies dead while the Ratels rumble on

Below
Operation Protea: Before or after an action, what a soldier likes to do is sleep, either to restore his squandered energy or to try and store it up for the bad times ahead. These soldiers and their bedding are still clean, but it will not be so for much longer. Warfare is a dirty business in more than one sense of the word

This brought the year's death-toll to a confirmed 365 insurgents killed and at least 60 civilians; the overall count since the war had begun, according to SADF Chief Magnus Malan, now amounted to about 3 600 insurgents and 128 security force members (Malan added that 38 percent of the soldiers deployed on the border were now South West Africans, an indication of the rapidly growing size of the SWA Territory Force).

Further contacts - and deaths - continued to be reported: in late May, for example, a landmine explosion killed three soldiers. Thanks to a local famine in southern Angola the operational area was crawling with insurgents - three times as many as usual, so that security force patrols were facing an average of between 500 and 600 at any one time instead of the more usual 150 to 200.

The military's reaction was to intensify patrolling in the operational area and follow up as aggressively as possible, even if this involved violating the border. A better flow of intelligence from the local population and increasingly refined tactics all helped to push up Plan losses: in the first week of July, the bloodiest of the entire year, security forces killed 93 insurgents in seven days. Nineteen more had died by July 11, when the SWATF's Lloyd reported announced that the security forces had forged a "buffer zone" by carrying out a series of raids east of Oshikango featuring specialist airborne troops.

"We are not allowing Swapo the opportunity to establish bases within striking distance of South West Africa," Lloyd declared.

The killing carried on. By July 24 another 43 insurgents had died, bringing the month's total to 178. By late August the monthly insurgent toll was an unprecedented 225. Then on August 24 there was a massive escalation on both sides as the SADF mounted its largest external operation to date: Operation Protea.

Protea had several aims, all deriving from the threatening situation developing in and near the operational area. Firstly it was aimed at knocking out the Plan headquarters at Xangongo, the former Vila Rocades, and Ongiva, the former Pereira d'Eca. Secondly it was intended to destroy the enormous quantities of heavy weapons and conventional-warfare equipment the Angolans had been assembling at Ongiva, a stone's throw from the border. The Angolan armed forces were becoming increas-

ingly sophisticated, and in addition to having the use of copious supplies of ground-warfare armaments they and the Cubans were constructing a comprehensive network of radar and anti-aircraft rocket installations in the south which boded ill for the SAAF with its jealously hoarded inventory of virtually irreplaceable combat aircraft.

The run-up to Protea had actually started some time before August 24, with a series of foot-mobile operations east of Ongiva, which played havoc with the Plan infra-structure. One of these, Operation Carnation, was still in progress when Protea itself was launched.

Operation Protea's opening move consisted of a force of SAAF fighter-bombers which screamed over the border at low-level on August 23 and seriously damaged the Angolan air-defence radar installations at Cahama, 130km inside Angola and north-west of Ongiva. Then a mechanised force crossed the Cunene River near Ruacana and travelled up the river. At Humbe, directly across the river from Xangongo, it dug in to prevent any force advancing south-eastwards down the main highway towards, or any Plan elements from escaping northwards from Xangongo.

In the meantime another mechanised force crossed the border north of Ondangwa and arrived at Xangongo on August 24 after an all-night advance. Having detached elements to block a Fapla force at near-by Peu Peu and clean up satellite Plan camps in the vicinity of Xangongo, the main body assaulted and defeated a combined Plan-Fapla force dug in on Xangongo's southern outskirts, the Peu Peu element meanwhile warding off an attempted Fapla break-through.

With Xangongo subdued and being mopped up, the South African force then headed towards Ongiva. It broke up an attempted holding action by Fapla artillery and mechanised forces at Mongua and on August 26 fell on Ongiva, which it took after a two-day battle against a strong Plan/Fapla force consisting of infantry, tanks and artillery. Strong semi-permanent garrisons were left at Xangongo and Protea, and by September 1 the raiders were over the border again with about 2 000 tons of looted ammunition, anti-aircraft guns, vehicles ranging from lorries and recovery tractors to scout cars and tanks, and many other items.

The South Africans rode out the ensuing international political storm, knowing what a

Above
South African generals tended to risk their necks in the bush war by going right up to the "sharp end". Here the new Chief of the Army, General Jannie Geldenhuys, changes his socks during a halt while travelling with soldiers engaged in Operation Daisy

Right
Operation Protea: Dismembered by a direct hit, its menace dissolved into scrap iron, an old Soviet-built 14,5mm twin-barrelled anti-aircraft gun — not very effective against fast aircraft any more, but deadly when firing armour-piercing shells at light armoured vehicles — sprawls on the back of a burning lorry at Ongiva

staggering blow they had dealt the insurgents and their allies. For the loss of 10 security-force soldiers they had killed more than 1 000 Plan and Fapla members, including several very senior insurgent officers and Russian attached personnel, seriously disrupted the insurgent command and supply structures and captured vast quantities of top-secret material.

Most of all, the garrisons left behind at Xangongo and Ongiva – whose very existence was to be strongly denied in the months to come – would ensure that the shallow area stayed firmly in the hands of the South Africans and their Unita allies, who by now were active almost everywhere in the south and east.

For Fapla Protea had meant a humiliating defeat on its home ground, the loss of many soldiers and large quantities of weapons and equipment and a blow to its efficiency in prosecuting the burgeoning war against Jonas Savimbi. Most of all, the Angolans had been told in no uncertain terms that if they actively supported the South West African insurgency it would cost them dear.

On the other hand, Protea was also the first time that the South Africans had found themselves facing substantial Angolan interference in their anti-Swapo operations. The good old days when Fapla tended to stand aside in such confrontations was clearly a thing of the past, and future external operations would have to be larger and more heavily armed and equipped than in the past.

The valuable intelligence picked up during Operation Protea was largely responsible for a second 1981 external, Operation Daisy, which started on November 1 when a mechanised force crossed the border, set up a tactical headquarters at Ionde, 120km inside Angola, and then proceeded further north to attack a Plan headquarters and a base area at Bambi and Cheraquera respectively.

After a softening-up strike by SAAF aircraft the ground troops captured both objectives, killing about 70 insurgents for a loss of three and destroying large amounts of food, equipment and munitions. They then mopped up and swept the surrounding area before pulling out on November 20.

Daisy was not a headline-making operation and did not yield spectacular results like Protea, but it undoubtedly achieved the planners' aim. It

had served to further disrupt the Swapo operational and logistical machine, and as the deepest external raid since Operation Savannah it had driven home the message that there was no absolutely safe refuge for Plan anywhere in southern Angola.

It had also brought home a fairly unpleasant message to the South Africans. Although the Angolans had not become involved on the ground this time, their MiG-21s put in several appearances and one of them, apparently flown by a Cuban, was shot down by a SAAF Mirage which was carrying out a combat air patrol. This occurrence was celebrated by SAAF pilots because it was the first fighter South Africans had downed in aerial combat since the Korean War, but gave their superiors further food for thought, since it provided additional evidence of the Luanda forces' increasing reluctance to simply stand by when their territorial integrity was violated; it was evident that the old-style external operation, in which air superiority was more or less taken for granted, was fast becoming a thing of the past.

The effects of the loss of trained manpower and operational planning caused by Daisy was being seen now in the operational area. A series of relentless follow-up operations, starting while Daisy was still in progress, resulted in the deaths of 114 insurgents in the middle fortnight of November; security forces reported that the Plan members were suffering from low morale, weak discipline and lack of food. All the same, the security situation in Ovamboland was such that the area did not take part in the November 11-13 elections in which most of the other ethnic groups elected their regional authorities (except the Basters, who had recently held just such a poll, and the Bushmen, who had decided that they did not want an ethnic authority).

The year ended with a total death-toll of well over 2 500 insurgents – a confirmed 1 479, excluding the two external operations, with an estimated 200 to 300 killed in aerial attacks on Cahama and Xangongo during Protea. Total security-force losses were 56 killed, a considerable drop on 1980, but civilians had suffered heavily. According to official statistics 92 were murdered by the insurgents and 62 others died in landmine explosions, while 91 were either abducted to Angola or left voluntarily to join Plan.

Above
Operation Protea: A Fapla T-34 tank burns after being knocked out during the attack on Xangongo. At this stage the Angolans were using their tanks in a mainly static role as direct-fire artillery support instead of unleashing them as mobile destroyers

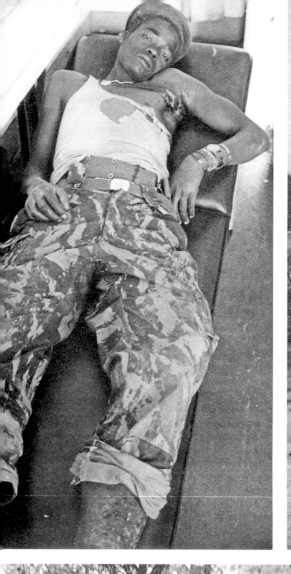

1982

January of 1982 - the year South West Africa's progress towards independence was recognised by a change in its official name to "South West Africa/Namibia" - saw the security forces suffer a series of multiple losses for little gain. In the first week a helicopter was shot down during a follow-up, killing the three-man crew (one of whom was the only son of the Chief of the SAAF, Lieutenant-General Denis Earp). A few days later two Natal national servicemen were killed in action. A fortnight later two more national servicemen were killed in a landmine explosion.

The following day three more soldiers were killed by a landmine, two of them twin brothers the SADF had foolishly allowed to serve together. Within days another two soldiers were killed in action.

February was relatively quiet from a military point of view, but renewed accusations of security forces brutality were made by the Rev Peter Storey, president of the South African Council of Churches, who claimed the army and police were responsible for 90 percent of the atrocities committed in Ovamboland. Later in the month opposition politician Hans Rohr of the Namibia Christian Democrat Party claimed that the security forces had been guilty of harassing and intimidating local inhabitants of Kavango, where Swapo was engaged in an activation campaign.

Both these verbal attacks were rejected by the SADF, but a fortnight after Rohr's complaints Magnus Malan announced that he had set up a board of inquiry into specific complaints raised by Rohr.

In the meantime both the shooting and the propaganda war were hotting up again. In the first week of March Plan attacks on the kraals of two senior Ovambo headmen were beaten off by special constables and a soldier was killed in action, while Swapo's Luanda office claimed that Plan had destroyed a military base at Okahe, killing and wounding more than 100 soldiers, and also wiped out a 28-man mounted infantry patrol and three accompanying helicopters - both of which items of news intrigued the security forces, since no helicopters or "mounties" had been lost for some time and no military base existed at Okahe.

The first external operation of the year came in mid-March. Operation Super, as it was retrospectively named, happened almost by accident when a small raid suddenly escalated into an action of considerable size.

Super resulted from Swapo's decision to open up a new infiltration route, running from southwestern Angola into the desolate and almost uninhabited Kaokoland area, then swinging eastwards into Ovamboland, the idea being to provide a new corridor into the main operational area and at the same time over-extend the thinly spread security forces.

South African intelligence got to hear about this new development and identified a transit camp which had been set up in the Marienfluss area just north of the border; in due course a few Puma and Alouette III helicopters and 45 men of 32 Battalion were sent to take it out. The foot-soldiers were dropped off by the Pumas and proceeded to capture the camp in an action extending over eight hours, with the Alouettes providing close support. A total of 201 insurgents were killed for a loss of three soldiers, and the new infiltration route was effectively closed down.

April saw one of Swapo's rare essays at escalating its activities from the intimidation-and-activation stage to true guerrilla action. Nine heavily

armed groups of Plan's special "Volcano" unit - composed of picked men trained in Eastern Europe - slipped out of Kaokoland, Ovamboland and Kavango and headed southwards on either side of the Etosha Pan to attack the mainly white Tsumeb farming area. Speedy action by the security forces stopped both of the western groups and two of the eastern groups well before their target, and another two eastern groups were wiped out when they reached the Mangetti Block, north of the farming area.

The other three groups got through, however, and set off on a six-week rampage in which they ambushed their pursuers, mined roads, killed civilians and committed various acts of sabotage. It took about two months of unremitting effort before the raid ended with 76 of the insurgents dead and the rest dispersed. By that time 10 soldiers and policemen had died, as well as seven civilians.

From one viewpoint it was an exercise in cynicism by the Plan leadership, since the raiders had been sent on a virtual suicide mission because they were operating far from any sanctuary and could not possibly have made a significant difference to the war. From another viewpoint the raid was a great propaganda success, enhancing Plan's battered image and causing such consternation that Magnus Malan had to run the gamut of hostile questions in Parliament. It was not repeated, however, and eventually its impact was obscured by other events.

While all this was happening Plan remained active in Ovamboland and Kavango, and in the latter area accounted for two security-force members a fortnight into May - one of them a national serviceman who was killed when the school at which he had been teaching was subjected to a storm of mortar and small-arms fire.

The SADF's riposte was to launch a long series of small pre-emptive and follow-up operations into the shallow area north of the border. By May 20, 512 insurgents had died since January 1 and a Russian helicopter had been destroyed on the ground by SAAF fighters. In the course of these raids the SAAF suffered a serious loss when one of its most experienced ground-attack pilots, Major Eugene Kotze, was lost on a mission.

In this period, too, the military set up a special liaison committee into security-force misconduct following fresh allegations by Roman Catholic churchmen of widespread atrocities. Announcing the inquiry, spokesman Commandant As Kleynhans said the number of complaints had decreased considerably as a result of measures taken by the SADF and SWATF, but added: "There are still atrocities ... we simply cannot screen every soldier who comes to Ovamboland. But we're getting to the bottom of it, and any soldier caught by the Defence Force faces severe punishment." Every soldier, he said, now had to sign a special card stating that he would respect members of the local population and would never resort to physical violence against them.

A little later the board of inquiry into misconduct set up in March announced that it had investigated 40 allegations, of which some had been disproved, others "settled locally to the satisfaction of all concerned" and still others referred to the police. Various persons would be prosecuted, one had already appeared in court and action was to be taken against certain members of the security forces whose supervision had been unsatisfactory. In addition, the board would reopen so that subsequent complaints could be investigated.

Above
The Rev Peter Storey

Opposite
Top Left
Wounded and captured at Xangongo, an enemy soldier awaits medical treatment at a forward hospital. The Fapla uniform means nothing. If he speaks Portuguese, he is probably an Angolan. If he speaks Afrikaans, he is probably a SWA/Namibian. Even that rule of thumb is not enough in a border area where a wire fence divides people of the same tribe

Top Right
While its crew members block their ears against its horrendous noise, a 5,5-inch medium gun fires a 140mm shell at Ongiva, its barrel recoiling and the "spades" on the ends of its trails kicking up dust as they dig into the ground

Below
Reflecting, perhaps, on what might have been, a crew-member of a Ratel-90 tank destroyer drags on his cigarette soon after the vehicle detonated a mine while careering through a Plan base near Xangongo. At this stage of the war, Ratel-90s were still something of a semi-secret weapon

Above
A tired Captain Jan
Hougaard of 32 Battalion,
commander of the ground
forces during Operation
Super, checks over the
weapons and ammunition
captured. In the background
is Major-General Charles
Lloyd, General Officer
Commanding SWA
Territory Force

Just over a week later a hastily-convened separate board of inquiry into allegations that SWATF soldiers had beaten up members of a church congregation issued an interim report that one man had already been court-martialled and several others were likely to face the same ordeal. General Lloyd said he condemned such misconduct in the strongest terms and gave his assurance that such occurrences would be stamped out.

Soon afterwards a complaints office was opened in Windhoek for the specific purpose of receiving complaints about misconduct towards civilians, and in the years to come a considerable number of soldiers and policemen were to be tried and convicted for acts ranging from rape and robbery to murder and assault.

By mid-year the death-toll stood at 594 insurgents and 47 members of the security forces, while eight civilians had died in cross-fire, 79 had been murdered by Plan and 63 had been abducted into Angola as part of Swapo's intimidation campaign. In spite of this dismal evidence that the war was still raging, however, yet another attempt at settlement was on the cards, as Pik Botha revealed on June 17 at a press conference at Oshivelo while on a routine visit to the operational area.

South Africa was willing to accept the first two phases of the Western nations' plan, he said, but added that the withdrawal of the Cuban troops from Angola was the most important part of the settlement – "the Cubans must withdraw and the South African troops would gradually be reduced".

On July 21 the negotiators duly met in New York. The talks began on a rather ominous note because South Africa immediately handed a letter to UN Secretary-General Javier Perez de Cuellar accusing the Angolan government of colluding in Swapo plans to escalate its "armed activities in the region". The letter asked Perez de Cuellar to intercede with Swapo; if the insurgents ignored him and went ahead with their activities, it warned, the South African forces would retaliate.

This sparked immediate fears that the South Africans were about to launch a new external operation, but it did not torpedo the talks. The Angolans stood firm on the point that the Cubans would not withdraw till SWA had become independent and all the South Africans had gone. The record of proceedings was never published, but according to reliable sources the South Africans agreed to a compromise plan which stipulated that after the ceasefire went into effect the Cubans would stay north of the 14th parallel – about 240km from the border – and Plan would be confined to bases no closer than 350km inside Angola.

On July 29 Pik Botha surfaced in Windhoek with the message that the target date for a cease-fire in SWA/Namibia was August 15, barely a fortnight away. Some issues still had to be resolved, he added, and as time passed it would be decided if August 15 was a reasonable date.

At the UN headquarters in New York, meanwhile, it was reported by some officials that South Africa no longer demanded a total Cuban pull-out as a pre-condition to its own withdrawal, but Swapo's permanent representative there, Theo-Ben Gurirab, was less than enthusiastic about the settlement talks. He rejected a recent Botha claim that Sam Nujoma had eliminated all his internal opponents as "unfounded" and "a characteristic smoke-screen to create the pretext for another mass invasion of Angola".

Gurirab added: "I don't think (an August 15 ceasefire) is possible. It is certainly not true that all parties have agreed." It would be at least another month before the Security Council would give the UN operation the go-ahead, "and there will be no going to the Security Council till we have settled all the outstanding issues".

Gurirab's pessimism was well-founded. By early August it was clear that the chances of an early settlement were fading. None of the parties concerned would say why, but newspapers quoted a senior UN source as saying that the South Africans had imposed a new settlement pre-condition which Swapo was unlikely to meet. One reason why the 1978 talks had broken down, the source recalled, was because South Africa had insisted that the UN monitor Swapo's bases in Angola and Zambia. The front-line states had finally prevailed on Swapo to accept this; now the South Africans had demanded that in addition the insurgents must be disarmed while in their external bases.

Apart from this issue, however, there was no agreement as yet on the core issue of the Cuban withdrawal timetable, and by now it was obvious that the August 15 ceasefire date could not be adhered to. Instead, various participants began talking of September 15 as possible ceasefire date.

At this stage (August 10) Defence Headquarters revealed that it had been engaged in a drawn-out external strike into Angola which it called Operation Mebos. A very clandestine affair involving a small but potent heli-borne force of paratroopers and members of one of the SADF's reconnaissance regiments, it is possible that Mebos would not have been made public except that its "own" casualty rate was so unexpectedly high that a full explanation was obviously required.

Mebos had actually started at the beginning of July when South African intelligence sources had discovered that Plan and the Angolans were hatching plans to retake Xangongo and Ongiva. The South Africans established that Plan's new central headquarters for the eastern operational area was located at the villages of Evale and Ionde and hit both locations on July 16, only to find that they had been vacated.

It was soon discovered that the headquarters was now established in the vicinity of Mupa, further north. On July 22 the Mupa headquarters was attacked, resulting in the death of 18 insurgents and the discovery of documents outlining plans to assassinate prominent SWA/Namibian politicians and build up in-country arms caches.

The core of the headquarters had escaped, however, and been re-established even further northwards. Another attack found this camp, too, deserted, but on August 2 the South Africans struck pay-dirt when they located a base near Cassinga which was occupied by a Plan battalion. Soon afterwards they hit this base and killed 106 insurgents, losing 15 men when a Puma was hit by ground fire and crashed while ferrying in a full load of paratroopers at low level.

The surviving insurgents disengaged during the night and retreated northwards. The South Africans followed up; next day - by which time they were something like 200km inside Angola - they finally came on the elusive headquarters and wiped it out in a brisk fire-fight which cost the lives of 118 insurgents.

Although several senior Plan commanders escaped with their lives in the final attack, Mebos was accounted a success because it completely disrupted Plan's command-and-control machinery in the eastern region for a considerable period. By the time it was finally called off it had resulted in the deaths of about 345 insurgents and the capture and destruction or evacuation of valuable intelligence material and a large quantity of stores and munitions, including 1 000 landmines. But the price had been heavy: 29 "own forces" dead, more than had been suffered in any of the larger external operations like Protea and Smokeshell.

Mebos did not do the settlement negotiations any good. On August 13, as the operation was winding down, a Swapo statement issued in London claimed Plan insurgents had shot down two helicopters, damaged seven others and killed 30 soldiers (which Defence Headquarters described as "a figment of Swapo's already overworked imagination"), and added that the New York settlement talks were a "diplomatic charade, orchestrated by the Western five (nations) to mislead world public opinion that progress is being made towards a peaceful solution of the conflict".

The front-line states were still persevering with settlement plans of their own, however, and on August 16 a well-connected political correspondent, Hennie Serfontein, published an intriguing report from New York in various South African newspapers.

The front-line states, he said, recognising that a Cuban withdrawal was even more important to the Americans than the South Africans, had come up with a plan which allowed such a withdrawal on condition it was not linked with a SWA/Namibian settlement. In return the United States would recognise the Angolan government and supply it with aid; South Africa would pledge to stop attacking Angola and supporting Unita; and the US would undertake to hold South Africa to its promise.

Serfontein quoted "UN and black sources" as saying they were optimistic that "it is now only a matter of phraseology and detail and not substance", and that if South Africa did not accept this deal it would be proof that Pretoria was not interested in settling.

As laid out by Serfontein, however, the front-line states' compromise had a fatal flaw: it did not address the cause of the South African operations beyond the border, namely Luanda's willingness to allow Swapo to use its soil as a jumping-off place for infiltration into SWA/Namibia. The external operations were never more than extensions of the counter-insurgency campaign, and Angola could have stopped them at any stage simply by forbidding Swapo to operate southwards.

The September 15 ceasefire date was never really a viable proposition; in the opinion of at least one observer, none of the parties to the settlement were hurting enough to make the final and inevitably painful compromises necessary for a genuine and lasting peace.

And so the war went on. The South Africans sat tight in Xangongo and Ongiva; the Angolans continued to expand their network of radar installations and SA-3 and SA-6 high-altitude anti-aircraft rockets; and on the border contacts continued, with 20 insurgents being killed in a joint land-air pursuit 10km south of the border around August 20, and another 17 on the Ovamboland-Kaokoland border a few days later, after having been patiently tracked for over 100km.

The ceasefire receded even further on August 30, when Angolan Foreign Minister Paulo Jorge flatly rejected linkage between the Cuban and South African withdrawals. The Americans, on the other hand - as President Ronald Reagan made plain in a letter to the front-line states which was written about this time, still regarded the continuing presence of the Cubans as the main obstacle to a settlement.

So September 15 came and went with the various participants in the negotiations still locked into their respective positions.

A few days later the echo of an almost-forgotten war was heard in Caprivi when five Plan soldiers presented themselves at Katima Mulilo and asked for amnesty, claiming that Swapo discriminated against non-Ovambos. According to a military spokesman 16 others had given themselves up earlier in the month, also complaining of racial discrimination; since the amnesty had been declared in 1980, he said, 155 people had come

back. Of these at least 115 had been trained insurgents, all Caprivians except for two Kavangos, one Herero and one Ovambo.

A Swapo UN representative subsequently described as "blatant lies" all allegations of ethnic discrimination by Swapo, including claims by returned female insurgents that their babies had been taken away to be raised for Swapo, although he conceded that Swapo children had to receive education.

Angola had been making such wild claims about South African military concentrations and activities in its southland - including continual reconnaissance flights by jet fighters, air attacks, artillery bombardments, 5 500 troops massed north of the border and another 30 000 poised in the operational area - that it came as quite a surprise when a SAAF Mirage shot down a MiG-21 early in October.

According to the SAAF two Mirages were jumped by four MiGs while escorting a reconnaissance aircraft which had been photographing missile launching sites, Swapo concentrations and logistical installations. A dog-fight ensued in which one of the MiGs was shot down, at which the others broke away. The Angolans promptly issued a counter-claim which said that its aircraft had chased away three South African machines after a brief encounter in which one of the MiGs had been damaged. An SADF spokesman equally speedily issued a counter-counter-claim accusing the Angolans of "a pathetic attempt to disguise their loss".

Magnus Malan, when questioned by a reporter, made no effort to hide the continuous South African violations of Angolan airspace. The reconnaissance flights over southern Angola, he said, were "quite normal - if they violate our borders we must do something about it. If they don't stop, we must do something about it".

On December 8 the drawn-out settlement talks resumed with an historic encounter: the first-ever talks at ministerial level between South Africa and Angola. At Sal international airport on one of the Cape Verde Islands - a routine stop-over for South Africa, Angola and Cuba alike - a delegation led by Foreign Minister Pik Botha held detailed discussions with an Angolan group under Luanda's Minister of the Interior, Lieutenant-Colonel Alexandre Rodrigues.

The negotiators came away tight-lipped, with Pretoria spokesmen willing only to confirm that a meeting had taken place and a stony silence emanating from Luanda, but it appears that the hostile border situation between Angola and SWA/Namibia was discussed, as well as the implementation of Resolution 435, although the contentious issue of Angola's Cuban presence was not touched on.

The meeting ended with an agreement that there would be another round of talks in the near future, and arrangements were made for senior officials of both countries to maintain contact. The delegations then jetted home, the Angolans taking with them the South African positions, to which they would respond at the next meeting.

No immediate follow-up meeting took place, however, possibly because a few days later South Africa was embroiled in a new international outcry when one of its special-forces groups raided 12 houses in Maseru, capital of Lesotho, in an attempt to forestall a threatened African National Congress bombing campaign on "soft" targets such as supermarkets during the festive season. The raiders killed 30 people later described by General Constand Viljoen as ANC terrorists - a claim hotly disputed by the next-of-kin of some of the dead - while five women and two children died in the crossfire (UN Secretary-General Perez de Cuellar later put the total figure at 42, 19 of them registered refugees).

The raid occasioned an immediate General Assembly debate which inevitably spilled over on to the subject of other South African transgressions. The UN Council for Namibia tabled a new set of resolutions which deplored the West's "collaboration" with Pretoria and condemned South Africa and the United States for trying to link the settlement to a withdrawal of Cuban troops from Angola, and delegate after delegate attacked the US for insisting on a Cuban pull-out.

By the third day of debate the Western contact group had had enough. Speaking on its behalf, the French ambassador to the UN, Luc de la Barre de Nanteuil, accused the Council for Namibia of failing both to recognise the gravity of the SWA/Namibian question and to seize the opportunity to arrange a peaceful settlement.

The five Western nations still believed, De Nanteuil emphasised, that a settlement could be achieved through negotiation, but he was careful to side-step the contentious American-South African demand for what was now being called "linkage". At the same time the Western nations made their attitude about the Maseru raid quite clear by joining in a unanimous Security Council vote against South Africa's "premeditated aggressive act".

The year ended in yet another public wrangle, albeit of far lesser intensity, resulting from remarks by the acting SWATF commander, Brigadier Willie Meyer, at a press conference in Windhoek on December 29.

Noting that a total of 1 286 insurgents had died during the year, as well as 77 security-force members and at least 139 civilians, he said that Plan's military activities had decreased markedly during 1982. In 1981 there had been 1 059 incidents but only 787 in 1982, and Swapo now had only 6 000 men in Angola, compared to up to 8 000 in 1980. Swapo's spokesman in Western Europe, Peter Manning, promptly rejected Meyer's statements, claiming the majority of those killed had been "Angolan civilians murdered by the South African military forces", although he did not offer any confirmatory evidence.

Below
Sacks of maize-meal — part of the supplies found in the Plan camp after the Marienfluss battle during Operation Super. Most of it was destined for caches in the main operational area

1983

In the first week of January six Citizen Force soldiers were killed and two others mortally wounded when their vehicle detonated a land-mine in the Kaokoland sector, which had been quiet ever since Operation Super. Helped by heavy rains which hampered the automatic follow-up opera-tion, the perpetrators got clean away to Angola.

In the same period SWATF soldiers uncovered a large cache in Ovamboland containing six crates of Russian and British anti-tank mines and various anti-personnel mines of Warsaw Pact origin; and in Kavango Plan was commencing an even more intensive activation campaign than the previous year.

Immediately afterwards, on January 10, Dirk Mudge of the Democratic Turnhalle Alliance tendered his resignation as chairman of the Council of Ministers after the Administrator-General, Dr Willie van Niekerk, had rejected a Legislative Assembly bill on public holidays. The other ministers resigned en bloc soon afterwards, and within a few days the assembly was dissolved and direct rule by Van Niekerk reinstated.

Late in January rumours of an impending ceasefire and a continuation of the December 8 talks on the Cape Verde Islands began to circulate in both Europe and South Africa.

In Lisbon a Portuguese news agency reported that the two countries had already agreed to a temporary ceasefire and the establishment of a buffer zone in southern Angola.

This was followed by claims from Western and African diplomats in Lisbon that at the December 8 talks South Africa had proposed that Angola's Cuban and other foreign troops be withdrawn to the 14th parallel, about 150km north of the border, and that a temporary ceasefire come into effect on February 1. Angola, on the other hand, had suggested the creation of a 50km-wide demili-tarised zone on either side of the border.

Pretoria and Luanda were very close to reaching basic agreement on a DMZ, the diplomats said, but warned that many obstacles still stood in the way of a firm agreement. In the meantime both sides were still trying to gain the military ad-vantage on the ground in order to improve their negotiating positions.

In Cape Town Pik Botha was almost equally sanguine in a briefing to political journalists. Agreement on a withdrawal of Cuban troops – estimated at 30 000 by South Africa at this stage, although Western sources suggested the figure was about 18 000 – would be enough to overcome obstacles to a peace settlement in SWA/Namibia, he said, and while "we still have to talk on other outstanding matters ... I do not see anything which could not be speedily resolved".

Pressed on the question of a Cuban withdrawal, he opined that it was up to the US to secure agree-ment on this. When a journalist pointed out that Angola had indicated it would refuse to discuss the subject, Botha replied that he had not raised the matter in the December 8 talks.

So far Luanda had not made any public reference to the December 8 talks, but on January 28 the silence was broken when Franca van Dunem, Angola's ambassador to France, was quoted by the Angop news agency as formally denying that his country had reached any agreement with South Africa on the subjects discussed – primarily SWA/Namibian independence and the situation in southern Angola – although he added that the contacts had been "promising and encouraging". He did not elaborate on this last remark.

Speculation continued to grow in the next few weeks, however. On February 18 it was reported from Washington that South Africa's ambassador in the US, Dr Brand Fourie, was on the point of leaving the American capital in the next few days for further negotiations with the Angolans.

The reports came amid increasing rumours of a de facto border ceasefire (stoutly denied by SWATF) and a report in the Washington Post news-paper that the conclusion of a disengagement agreement was imminent. As it transpired, a cease-fire or disengagement was nowhere in the offing, but February 24 had been designated as the start of a second round of talks which would centre on Angola's response to the South African proposals.

In the meantime Swapo had launched its most serious assault on SWA/Namibia for some years. Since May of 1982 East German, Russian and Cuban instructors had been training Volcano members for a special mission, turning them into the toughest and most resourceful fighters Plan had ever had. Sometime in late January Swapo had begun moving the men down to southern Angola, something like 1 700 of them - virtually the entire strength of the special unit. There they were formed into 14 com-panies of between 40 and 50 men each and given final preparation.

From February 13 all but one company were launched over the border to infiltrate into Kaoko-land, Ovamboland and Kavango to engage the attention of the security forces there while the remaining group slipped further southwards to hit the white farmers in the Kamanjab-Outjo-Tsumeb-Otjiwarongo area.

SWATF reacted on February 15 by mounting Operation Phoenix, an internal counter-action, and within days the fighting began in various widely-spread locations. By February 22, on the eve of the second round of Cape Verde talks, a total of two security-force members and 129 insurgents - 109 of them positively identified as Volcano members - had died in a week of intermittent fighting, but it was obvious that the Plan incursion was far from over. Questions had been asked in Parliament about how an estimated 200 men could penetrate so deep into SWA/Namibia when the SADF was supposed to be in complete control, and Windhoek was awash with rumours that up to 2 000 insurgents were running wild south of the border.

Not surprisingly, the Plan incursion exercised a baleful effect on the talks when they began on Sal Island on the evening of February 23. Although the Angolan delegation was again led by the Minister of the Interior, Alexandre Rodriques, the South African group consisted entirely of officials and military officers, which was interpreted by observers as a sure signal of Pretoria's anger at the latest fighting.

The level of South African representation did not go unnoticed, and according to rumours Cape Verde's Prime Minister at first declined to host the negotiations because of the imbalance. However, real and imagined difficulties were sufficiently overcome to allow the talks to start, although Rodriques absented himself in protest at South Africa's calculated snub in not sending someone of equal rank.

The meeting lasted exactly two hours and 20 minutes, after which the two delegations packed up and flew home. By Rodrigues's account in a subsequent interview the Angolans opened by protesting against the down-grading of the South African delegation. The cessation of hostilities between the two countries and the implementation

Top
**Dr Willie van Niekerk,
SWA/Namibian
Administrator-General**

Above
**Dr Brand Fourie, Secretary
for Foreign Affairs**

of Resolution 435 were then discussed, but the negotiations produced no positive results because they did not flow logically from the December 8 talks and therefore it had not been possible to discuss South Africa's response to counter-proposals the Angolans had made to the original positions put forward by Pretoria.

Thus the second round of Cape Verde talks ended without having achieved anything. The only bright point was that both sides had agreed to meet again in the near future; Rodriques said that Angola "had not turned its back on the talks" and was willing to resume negotiations at any time.

The situation in SWA/Namibia continued to worsen, so that by February 28 the southernmost Volcano group was within 50km of the Mangetti Block, with security-force elements close on their heels, while their colleagues were busy elsewhere in the operational area.

By March 3 the overall death-toll since mid-February had risen to 155 insurgents; 25 black civilians had been shot dead by the intruders or killed in mine-blasts, another 10 had been seriously wounded and 45 children as well as two or three teachers had been abducted to Angola. In the next 24 hours another 17 insurgents were killed in the Tsandi area of Ovamboland and in western Kavango.

Within the next day or two between 20 and 30 Volcano fighters crossed into the white farming areas, having evaded their pursuers, and one group shot dead two soldiers who were guarding an isolated homestead near the Etosha game reserve. The same day another soldier was killed in action elsewhere in the operational area, bringing the security forces' dead to 12 since the incursion started and the insurgents' fatalities to 187.

In the next six days another 15 insurgents were killed, and in the following week 24 more, for a loss of a further three security-force members. Follow-ups claimed two more insurgents in the Kamanjab area, south of Etosha.

On March 27 Swapo issued a statement from Lusaka saying that its forces had killed 28 South African soldiers since the beginning of the month. The figure was vastly inflated, but the reality was bad enough: 17 soldiers and policemen dead for a loss of 227 insurgents, and on March 25 the security forces' toll rose to 18 when a policeman was killed in a contact.

By this stage the daring Volcano penetration southwards had more or less run out of steam; on April 10 SWATF announced that four insurgents killed in western Ovamboland were thought to have been among those involved in the farm attack earlier in the month (this was later confirmed). In the end the southern raid had been a failure: only 12 men of the company had managed to reach their objective, and all had died, then or in later follow-up operations.

On April 15 Operation Phoenix was wound down. It had been a sanguinary episode, almost unparalleled in the war. In exactly two months of fighting 309 insurgents and 27 security-force members had died, while by SWATF reckoning the insurgents had killed 33 civilians and carried another 161 off to Angola.

This long and bloody raid was to be the apogee of Swapo's efforts to extend the war southwards from Ovamboland. Volcano did not launch another foray of significant size in the years to follow, and in fact was so little heard of after that time that in November of 1986 the then General Officer Commanding SWATF, Major-General Georg Mei-

ring, gave it as his opinion that the unit had been disbanded altogether (although a Swapo spokesman immediately retorted from Luanda that "that is just the speculation of the Boers").

Plan remained active in various parts of the operational area. One of its mines killed nine Ovambo civilians when their lorry detonated it south of Ruacana, while several of its members who were engaged in the energetic effort to activate Kavango captured seven unarmed local security-force recruits and bayoneted them to death, the story of their gruesome end being brought back by one of the group who had been wounded but had managed to escape.

But the main attack had been smashed, and for several months the border was to be relatively quiet, although Plan activity remained comparatively high in parts of Kavango. In fact, the February-April incursion is seen by most South African military observers as the final turning-point in Plan's "armed struggle". Swapo's military operations had peaked in 1980 and then steadily declined to an all-time low point in the second half of 1982 after the first Volcano stab at the white south. The February 1983 incursion had revitalised it, but only for a time, and after that Plan's military effort went into a decline which was protracted but irreversible.

The war continued in other ways, however. In mid-April civil claims involving a sum of no less than R420 000 were instituted against the government by 22 Kavango and Ovambo civilians who said they had been assaulted by soldiers and policemen in November of 1982, and this was followed by a call on the government from the Synod of Bishops of the Church of the Province of South Africa for an immediate withdrawal of all SADF troops from SWA/Namibia and the urgent implementation of Resolution 435.

The bishops said members of the synod who had visited the operational area had been "appalled beyond words at the destructive effect of violence on people, communities, property and land, as well as upon those who perpetrated it". They said most of the important contributions made by churches to SWA/Namibia in the fields of education, medicine and community development had been halted by the enforced closure of schools and hospitals, the destruction of buildings and the harassment of clergy, Christian workers and the local population.

On April 26, at a conference on SWA/Namibia which was being held in Paris, Algerian UN ambassador Mohamed Sahnoun (who was also head of the UN Special Committee Against Apartheid) accused South Africa of mounting a commando raid into Angola which had caused damage of R46 million to Luanda's oil refinery and had come within an ace of destroying it completely, except that one of the raiders had been blown up while planting a bomb.

True or false? Even now it is difficult to say. The South African government's response was a blanket refutation, and Sahnoun did not say when the raid had taken place or produce any evidence to back up his claim. Some observers speculated at the time that Angola was up to its old strategem of blaming a Unita attack on the South Africans to avoid giving the insurgents any sort of recognition; but the matter was never taken any further by any of the interested parties.

On May 4 Prime Minister P W Botha reacted to the Anglican bishops' call for an immediate withdrawal from SWA/Namibia in an open letter containing a blunt rejection. He reiterated his consistent stand that the South African forces were in SWA/ Namibia "at the request of the territory's elected leaders", and added:

"On February 25 and 26 last year I put the direct question to all the political parties taking a constitutional approach in SWA/Namibia: 'Do you want South Africa to withdraw from South West Africa, militarily or otherwise?' None of the delegations answered yes or conditionally yes."

He had also posed the same question to the SWA/Namibian Council of Churches, which had replied that it was not a matter for the church but for the politicians, he said.

"The answer to your call for withdrawal of all military presence in SWA/Namibia at this stage is therefore very clear. As far as South Africa is concerned, it is an unequivocal no."

Botha noted that the government would be "equally pleased" if, by letting the territory achieve independence, it could withdraw the vast sums it currently made available.

This included R70 million annually for the railway service and R60 million South Africa had provided for drought relief in 1982; since 1973 the government had provided SWA/Namibia with loans and direct contributions totalling more than R2 000 million.

"Will the international community take over this burden?" Botha asked. "I doubt it very much."

On July 20 Namibia Christian Democratic Party leader Hans Rohr had made fresh allegations of security-force misbehaviour in Kavango, and to the military's deep embarrassment a respected middle-of-the-road journalist, Bill Hulme, was robbed of some beers at a roadblock in Eastern Caprivi.

A few days later Nujoma claimed in Lusaka that 100 000 South African troops were massed in SWA/Namibia and recruiting blacks in "a desperate attempt to repulse freedom fighters" and vowing to "intensify the armed struggle until the borders of freedom are on the origins of the Orange River". It was a blatant untruth, considering the known force levels of the SADF, and a military spokesman scornfully replied: "He obviously does not care about the desperate plight of his terrorist bands, and his assessment of the situation in South West Africa is also a vivid example of the unreal world he lives in."

Not much came of Nujoma's vow to intensify the struggle, although on August 1 a South African soldier was killed in a landmine explosion in the operational area, and later in the month two others were to die in Kavango. But events on the border were soon to be overshadowed by what was happening in Angola.

On August 12 Luanda's news agency, Angop, claimed that eight SAAF aircraft, four Canberra light bombers and four Impala ground-strike fighters, had repeatedly bombed and destroyed the small but important rail and communications centre of Cangamba about 500km from the border in south-eastern Angola. Angop added that South African "tactical groups" had moved into the Moxico, Cuando-Cubango and Cunene provinces in the past four days. A South African military spokesman promptly replied that the SADF did not wish to comment on "such blatant propaganda".

But something was obviously brewing in southern Angola. Just before mid-month the Angolans claimed their garrison at Cangamba had beaten off a full-scale Unita attack but warned that the South Africans were rushing to the rebels' aid. Unita rejected the Angolan claims and stated it had captured the town after an 11-day siege, as part of a new offensive that had left it in control of large areas in the south and east of the country. The offensive would continue, Unita spokesmen said, while renewing its offer of talks with MPLA.

In Pretoria, the SADF's Constand Viljoen pooh-poohed the Angolans' claims that the SAAF had bombed Cangamba, although he conceded that South Africa had been forced to undertake reconnaissance flights over Luanda's territory "because the Angolan regime allows and actively supports Swapo aggression from their territory ... I can mention that these towns fall completely out of the action range of an Impala with a weapons load". The Angolans spurned this explanation by pointing out that Canberras and Impalas could refuel at Rundu in Kavango.

The Angolans persisted in their accusations. On August 16 it was claimed in an Angop broadcast that the South African and SWA/Namibian troops still in Ongiva and Xangongo had been reinforced by 10 000 more, and that there had been an incursion by "regular forces" in the region of Mavinga, halfway between Rundu and Cangamba. The South Africans vehemently denied the allegations, no doubt acutely aware that UN Secretary-General Perez de Cuellar was considering a quick visit to Pretoria, SWA/Namibia and possibly Angola on a fact-finding tour aimed at speeding up the independence process.

The Angolan accusations continued. On August 17 they said their forces had evacuated Cangamba; it had been hit by devastating South African fire-bomb raids and then attacked by helicopter-borne South African "regular forces", "mercenaries" and Unita insurgents. On August 18 Angop radio broadcasts monitored said the situation was "deteriorating" as the 10 000 South African regulars and mercenaries advanced northwards. The SADF intended tightening its stranglehold on the southern regions, it added, while advancing inland.

Newspaper correspondents based in Lisbon, where all of these claims were released, consulted diplomatic sources and reported that most of the Cubans in Cangamba had helicoptered to safety before the town fell, although not before 120 of Castro's legionaries had been killed, according to Unita.

Did South Africa help Unita in the capture of Cangomba? At the time most South Africans believed the answer was "yes", mainly because the years of clandestine operations, the bland denials which were followed in so many cases by startling revelations, had robbed official announcements of a great deal of credibility. On the other hand, Savimbi's biographer, Fred Bridgland, says he believes – though his conviction is "far from absolute" – that Unita's version of the battle is nearer the truth.

The Unita version is that after six months of starving out the 3 000 defenders, Savimbi started the battle on August 3 by shelling the town with some of the Russian-made 76mm artillery pieces he had captured from the Angolans three years earlier. Then he sent in three "brigades" (reinforced battalions by South African standards) of semi-conventional troops and a large number of irregulars and commandos. The infantry spent eight days breaching the complex of defensive minefields and trenches around the town, losing many men to the mines, the garrison's fire and strafing from MiG-21 fighters and Mi-8 armed helicopters operating from Luena against which the rebels had little effective protection at that stage of the war.

By August 11 they had breached the defences in so many places that more than 100 surviving Cubans, led by their commanding officer, were lifted out by helicopters. The rebels finally took Cangamba on August 14, having killed 829 Angolans and Cubans and captured 328 for a loss of 63 killed and about 200 wounded; a few days earlier they had also beaten off an attempt by two Angolan battalions to capture a nearby centre called Tempue, inflicting a loss of 72 troops.

Bridgland says he tends to believe Savimbi's version because at all stages the Angolans reacted to Unita accounts of the battle, whereas "if there had been a heavy South African involvement the MPLA would surely have alerted world opinion much earlier in the fighting, for it could have been sure of obtaining general condemnation of South African military actions so far inside Angola. And of the 1 100 enemy the MPLA claimed to have killed, it said all of them were Unita guerrillas: not one was a South African".

At the time some European observers believed Unita's capture of Cangamba had been a turning-point in Savimbi's eight-year war against Luanda. This is probably not quite correct, although it is true that the fall of Cangamba had cleared away a dangerous threat and made it easier for Savimbi to extend his semi-conventional operations northwards to Luena and the Benguela railway.

However, it would be accurate to say that the Cangamba victory made it plain to the world at large that Unita was no longer merely a regional menace but was spreading its activities over areas far beyond its stronghold in the remote south-eastern Cuando-Cubango province, which, up to the time of writing, the Angolans were never to recapture.

According to various reliable sources Unita now actually controlled about 25 percent of Angola's land area, mainly in the south and east, and operated on a more or less continuous basis in another 50 percent of the huge country. Even the Angolans accepted this, and in fact had admitted for the first time that very month that Savimbi's forces were operating in the central province of Bie, only 300km from Lobito, and were actually straddling the Benguela line.

Unita had gone a long way since it had consisted of a few hundred ill-armed guerrillas of 1975. It was now said to be a force of about 35 000 trained and partly trained fighting men, and was receiving so much help from African and non-African states like Zaire and Zambia that it was no longer as dependent on Pretoria's support as it had been in former years.

It had become a power in the land. It had a "liberated zone" in the south-east, which was not only good for its prestige but also gave it a firm base of operations. It controlled the strategic Cazombo Salient, a square block of territory jutting eastwards into Zambia, and the rest of Angola's 1 000km border with President Kaunda's country. It had cut off road access to the diamond mines in the north-east, and had so completely encircled the important railway town of Luena that the Cuban/Angolan garrison there was being supplied by air. Several of Savimbi's "regular" (semi-conventional) battalions were pushing north-east and north-west of Huambo.

What all this meant was that Savimbi was an even more valuable ally for South Africa than ever. While he was in place Swapo would never be able to mount a full-blooded incursion into Kavango or eastern Ovamboland; in addition, he posed such

a severe threat to Luanda that more than 80 percent of Plan's trained fighting strength was permanently in Angolan service, some on rear-areas security duties and the rest deployed along the north-western rim of the liberated zone. This was why South Africa was willing to endure almost any condemnation in the years ahead to render assistance in both cash and kind to the charismatic man from Cuando-Cubango province.

The Unita victory at Cangamba was to have a negative effect as well, from the South African-Unita point of view. Alarmed by the increased vulnerability of their client, the Soviet Union sent at least 10 ships, loaded with everything from T-62 battle tanks to helicopters and high-altitude anti-aircraft missiles. Cuba sent 5 000 extra troops, bringing its commitment to an estimated 25 000-plus.

Perez de Cuellar's lightning visit to South Africa and SWA/Namibia finally took place late in the month. He touched at Pretoria, spent two days in SWA/Namibia and on August 26 arrived in Luanda, where President Dos Santos personally welcomed him and lost no time in presenting new conditions for withdrawing the Cubans which, observers believed, spelt out a more amenable attitude: the unconditional and immediate withdrawal of all South African troops in southern Angola; the rapid implementation of Resolution 435; the ending of all South African "aggression" against Angola; and the suppression of South African support for Unita.

Dos Santos and his visitor then drove to the presidential palace to meet with Sam Nujoma, where the Secretary-General was later reported by Angop to have told a welcoming throng that he had come to speak to the Swapo leader "as the representative of the people of Namibia" – a remark which did nothing to allay South African suspicions about UN bias towards the insurgents.

In the meantime the Kavango insurgency was dying down, at least for the moment; in mid-September two groups of about 50 insurgents each who had crossed over from Angola earlier in the month retraced their steps over the border, and a SWATF spokesman claimed: "Everything is under control," although security-force sources warned that the groups had probably cached weapons and munitions in preparation for the coming rainy season – an accurate prediction, as it turned out, for 1984 was to see such heavy Plan concentration on Kavango that (as one officer reported two years later) "at one stage we thought we'd lost the war."

On September 29 the internal effort towards settlement assumed a new shape when virtually all the political parties in the territory – the outstanding exception being Swapo's "internal" wing – announced that they intended to form a conference which would endeavour to find non-violent ways of leading SWA/Namibia to independence.

The border war remained at a low ebb for the next two months: public attention in October was gripped not by news of fighting but by church moves against the war and a BBC documentary film making strong claims of further security-force atrocities.

On October 23 the Cape Town diocesan synod of the Church of the Province voted 140 to 130 in favour of a motion calling for the withdrawal of all its chaplains serving with the SADF in SWA/Namibia. Speakers in favour of the motion said Anglican chaplains with the SADF were perceived as being part and parcel of the armed forces' "illegal" presence in the area; one speaker said that

Opposite
A captured Russian light gun taken during the early stages of Operation Askari, is hooked on to a Ratel so that it can be towed back to SWA/Namibia to join South Africa's large inventory of weapons and munitions brought back as booty from earlier operations

chaplains should minister to all, but only in ways consistent with the Gospel. "Jesus went to Hades," he added, "but He didn't go in the Devil's pay or in the Devil's uniform."

After hot debate the motion was amended to call for a "more acceptable" method than the present system of ministering to its members who were serving in the armed forces on both sides of the conflict.

The film - clandestinely shot by a BBC crew posing as tourists and led by producer Geoffrey Seed, who had earlier made a similar documentary about Russia - made specific claims that the security forces had inflicted a variety of tortures on civilians.

The BBC men were arrested and deported, but by that stage they had obtained the film they needed and it was later screened in Britain; when Geoffrey Seed was asked at a special press preview why the film had not dealt with alleged Swapo atrocities, he replied that his aim had been to show how the South Africans were administering the territory, and most of the filming had been done in the south, away from the operational area.

On October 27 SWATF spokesmen fired off a counter-blast at allegations made earlier by Terry Waite, the Archbishop of Canterbury's special adviser on foreign affairs, which applied just as strongly to the BBC film.

The spokesmen noted that "the security forces are continually being accused of atrocities. Swapo's atrocities, on the other hand, are not given the same prominence and an incorrect picture of the situation is presented". The accusations against the security forces were usually vague and "based on hearsay evidence and normally appear in the media as part of a propaganda campaign before, if at all, being reported as a formal complaint to the security forces".

The spokesmen then handed out a list of reported Swapo atrocities committed between 1979 and September of 1983, as well as the names of security-force members who had been tried and convicted of such offences against the local population. According to the list, 303 civilians had been killed and 513 wounded by landmines since 1979, 366 had been murdered and 1 341 had been abducted and taken to Angola.

The debate about Cuban "linkage" with the implementation of Resolution 435 in SWA/Namibia continued into the following month. On November 13 - the day after SWA/Namibia's new "Multi-Party Conference" held its first session in Windhoek - leaders of the six front-line states met in Lusaka and condemned both the US and South Africa for insisting on linkage. Next day Britain's Foreign Secretary, Sir Geoffrey Howe (no doubt with an eye to the Commonwealth heads of state conference in London towards the end of the month) called for change in South Africa and asked both South Africa and Swapo to respect the sanctity of international borders.

Swapo should understand that attacks would merely "strengthen (South African) intransigence", he said, while by destabilising its neighbours South Africa "risks precipitating the situation they fear most: making the Russians and their surrogates a more powerful factor in the equation".

Howe's speech did not have any effect on either of the combatants. Less than 10 days later 11 Ovambo civilians died in one of the worst incidents of its kind in the border war when their vehicle detonated two mines the insurgents had planted in a dirt road.

By now the South Africans' efficient intelligence-gathering system was picking up strong indications that Plan intended to launch a far heavier infiltration than usual as soon as the long rainy season started in January. The South Africans sent out small deep-penetration scouting teams and stepped up SAAF reconnaissance flights - one of which nearly came to grief when an Impala II returned from a mission in the Cahama area with the unexploded warhead of an SA-9 missile protruding from its tail.

The SAAF responded by attacking various Angolan air-defence installations, and in one case a small task force of artillery with a protective and covering element proceeded up the road from Xangongo till it was close up to Cahama to shell other missile anti-aircraft sites. It was the forerunner to a new external raid, Operation Askari.

Askari was born in peculiar circumstances. In November Russian diplomats in Washington or at the United Nations - the venue remains unclear to this day - approached one of their South African equivalents and handed him a message for transmission to his government.

The contents of the message were straight and to the point: South Africa's continued occupation of Angolan soil and support for Unita was unacceptable to Moscow. The Americans would not achieve a Cuban withdrawal as a prerequisite for SWA/Namibian independence under any circumstances, since the "Chester Crocker cycle" had now ended, and it would be in South Africa's interest to acknowledge this reality. The USSR was tied to Angola by an agreement of friendship and co-operation, and would give Luanda all the support it needed to protect its sovereignty and territorial integrity.

The message should not be regarded as a threat, the Russian said in conclusion. It was meant to make South Africa aware of the "logical and reasonable consequences" of its actions, and to ensure that Pretoria came to the "right conclusions".

The South African replied that his government would find it difficult to see anything other than a threat in the Soviet message; "if this is the case, the South African government will see the message in an extremely negative light, and South Africa will not allow itself to be intimidated by threats."

So Askari went ahead, but in spite of the South Africans' brave words the Russian warning hung over it like a cloud from beginning to end.

The operation itself began in the first week of December, with additional ground reconnaissance designed to obtain more information which could be used to develop a proper intelligence picture so that operational planning could take place. As the intelligence picture began to take shape the operation escalated. One by one the South Africans sent in four battle-groups, each comprising about 500 mechanised infantrymen, and several smaller motorised-infantry groupings, the idea being that the latter would sweep the area closer to the border while the mechanised forces would hit specific "hard" targets.

The South Africans' planning was crystallised by news that seven companies of insurgents, numbering a total of between 800 and 1 000 men, had been transported to Jamba, north of Cassinga, and were scheduled to move southwards. Operation Askari moved into high gear. Primarily it was aimed at disrupting or destroying Plan's logistic and command infra-structure by attacking a number of bases and headquarters both on the ground and from the air. Insurgent elements and arms caches which had been prepared for the forthcoming incursion were to be located and destroyed, but the raiders were strictly enjoined to make all possible efforts to isolate Plan groups from Angolan and Cuban troops before attacking them.

By this time the Angolans were well aware of the increased South African activity. On December 16 Angop claimed SAAF reconnaissance flights had increased and said that four days earlier one of four South African "columns" had moved to Mulondo in Huila province and fired on Fapla forces there; the South African activity, the agency claimed, was aimed at reducing pressure on Unita. The SADF blandly denied everything.

The Angop claims came just after South Africa's ambassador to the UN, Kurt von Schirnding, delivered a letter to the Secretary-General which contained a surprise offer drawn up in Rome a few days earlier by Chester Crocker and Pik Botha: South Africa would be willing to disengage all its troops from Angola by January 31 of 1984, "on the understanding that this gesture would be reciprocated by the Angolan government, which would assure that its own forces, Swapo and the Cubans would not exploit the resulting situation, in particular with regard to actions which might threaten the security of the inhabitants of SWA/Namibia". The proposed action would remain open for 30 days, the letter added, but could be extended on condition that non-interference provisions were adhered to.

For a number of solid reasons the offer was a sincere one rather than an essay at stone-walling. Powerful and increasing international pressure was being exerted on South Africa to remove her semi-permanent presence from Angola, and on the part of Crocker it was an attempt to seize what he saw as the last chance of achieving a peaceful resolution of the Angolan civil war, the departure of the Cubans and independence for SWA/Namibia before President Ronald Reagan's term of office ended (as it transpired, he was re-elected).

Sincere or not, it was rejected out of hand by Angola within five days. It certainly had no effect on the fighting, and the South Africans' instructions to separate Plan elements from host-country troops proved hard to apply because the Fapla forces in the vicinity showed themselves to be less inclined than ever before to allow the South Africans free rein in hunting Plan.

Near the town of Caiundo a Fapla force ambushed a SWATF reconnaissance element, killing five soldiers, capturing one (he was exchanged for a number of Angolan prisoners late in 1984) and laying hands on a Unimog lorry and various small arms and equipment. The Angolans triumphantly announced this action, and it was reluctantly confirmed by SWATF spokesmen. The Fapla garrison at Mulondo clashed with the South Africans when it came to the rescue of Plan troops the latter were attacking; the Fapla force at Cahama sent a detachment southwards to cover the withdrawal of about 200 insurgents whose camp south of the town came under attack.

By this time Angop was issuing a stream of accusations. South African jets were attacking targets up to 300km inside the country, it claimed on December 20, and some aircraft had bombed Caiundo for eight hours, killing dozens of civilians and destroying schools and a hospital; on December 22, just after the UN Security Council had demanded the immediate withdrawal of the troops Pretoria had in Angola, it broadcast government claims that for days the South Africans had been bombarding towns and villages in the south, and that some of the raiders' armoured vehicles had been knocked out in continued fighting.

In Pretoria, however, SADF spokesmen stuck to their earlier position that the only military presence in southern Angola consisted of troops engaged in hot-pursuit operations against Plan insurgents, who would be sought out and destroyed "wherever they are", even though it was patently obvious by now that a large-scale external raid was in progress.

The Angolans' claims became wilder as time passed, till Deputy Foreign Minister Venancio de Moura was claiming that the South Africans had penetrated more than 200km from the border and occupied Cassinga, had deployed three motorised brigades and kept 100 aircraft in the air at all times. One genuine attack the Angolans did not mention, probably because it was too embarrassing, took place on December 29 when four Mirages hit Lubango, not only to stress its vulnerability but also to create uncertainty about whether it might be attacked by ground forces as well.

On December 26 the US State Department called on both sides to "exercise restraint", a spokesman saying that the South African offer to disengage by January 31 was likely to provide "a useful basis for exploring practical ways to implement a ceasefire, which should be the first step towards a broader settlement". Continued fighting, he warned, might jeopardise the chances of the offer being accepted.

The warning did not have any effect. The South Africans were now fully engaged not with the Plan fighters, most of whom had retreated well to the north, but with increasingly aggressive Cuban/Fapla forces, and a major confrontation was looming.

On January 3 one of the mechanised battle-groups was engaged in attacking an important Plan tactical headquarters and logistics base about 5km north-east of the town of Cuvelai when it was set upon by 11 Fapla Brigade, reinforced by two Cuban battalions; to their horror the South African troops found themselves facing T-54/55 battle tanks, used in their proper mobile role instead of as static artillery as had been the case in Operation Protea.

A short but ferocious battle followed, which ended with the South Africans capturing Cuvelai after knocking out 11 tanks and killing a confirmed 324 members of Plan and the Angolan/Cuban attackers for a loss of seven of their own men.

Veterans of the battle later spoke feelingly about the appalling conditions of rain and mud in which they fought, and the difficulties of breaching the well-laid-out defensive system of 16 separate minefields, all covered by artillery firing air-burst shells, which made it extremely difficult for the South Africans to debus from their Ratel infantry fighting vehicles. In fact, the largest single South African loss occurred when a T-54 knocked out a Ratel which had bogged down in a minefield, killing five of the occupants.

However, the battle was the turning-point of the incursion; the Angolan/Cuban/Plan resistance collapsed, and the South Africans were able to spend the next few days scouring the area, seizing great quantities of weapons, equipment and munitions, and destroying what they could not take back with them.

They were still mopping up when, on January 5, Swapo's Nujoma sent a letter to Perez de Cuellar in the middle of a Security Council debate on the incursion, asking him to arrange direct ceasefire negotiations between the insurgents and the South Africans as soon as possible, "in order to contribute meaningfully to an early ceasefire agreement". This rather surprising approach was obviously at the behest of the Angolans, whose President Dos Santos had earlier informed the Secretary-General that Angola was willing to test the previous month's South African offer of a 30-day truce from January 31, but that this would require Swapo's consent as well.

The offer did not do much to appease the UN General Assembly, which passed a resolution calling for punitive sanctions against South Africa. In the Security Council the resolution was firmly vetoed by the United States, with Britain and France objecting to some of the more extravagant wording used, but on January 6 the council made its general feeling known when it strongly condemned South Africa for the incursion and demanded that Pretoria's forces leave Angola instantly.

This was more or less a case of shutting the stable-door after the horse had escaped, for the South Africans had completed their mopping up and demolition and began to withdraw on January 7. It was a slow business. Routes had to be swept for mines, while the fiercest rains in living memory had turned roads into a quagmire and placid streams into foaming torrents over which bridges had to be built.

On January 9 Nujoma apparently reversed himself, when he sent a message to an anti-apartheid function of the Greater London Council denouncing the South Africans' trial ceasefire offer as "hypocrisy" and insisted that Pretoria would have to be forced to allow SWA/Namibia to become independent. No Plan members had been killed or wounded in the fighting, he insisted, brushing aside documentary and other evidence produced by the South Africans; all the attacks had been directed at "Angolan military, civilian and economic targets".

No doubt he was playing to the gallery, because on the following day Swapo did another about-face and repeated its January 5 call for direct ceasefire talks with the South Africans. The statement said it hoped the South Africans would not turn any direct talks into "a public relations charade" like the Geneva meeting in January of 1981.

Swapo made it clear, however, that its participation in face-to-face talks was contingent on the ceasefire being the first step in implementation of Resolution 435. Since the South Africans had made it equally clear that they would refuse to proceed with implementation unless the Cubans withdrew from Angola, the offer was dead before it got off the ground; on January 11 Pik Botha blasted the insurgents for trying to make "cheap propaganda points" in their "provocative" response to South African efforts to find a peaceful solution in SWA/Namibia.

The organisation responded with a vow that it would intensify the "liberation struggle" if South Africa was not prepared to start talking to it about a ceasefire. On January 12 Swapo spokesman Peter Manning called on the international community to take note of South Africa's "blunt and arrogant refusal" to proceed with implementation of Resolution 435.

On January 15 the last of the raiding force rolled over the border into SWA/Namibia, and the South Africans could reflect on the lessons learnt. Askari had borne considerable fruit. A total of 25 light and heavy tanks had been knocked out, Plan operations had been badly disrupted and the South Africans had proved that even when outnumbered they could defeat a conventional force on the battlefield by dint of better tactics and battle-handling.

On the other hand, the fighting around Cuvelai had been a very sobering experience for the South Africans. They had not encountered a mobile tank

Above
A Puma helicopter of the South African JMC component screams over the dense bush of southern Angola, flying just above tree-top height in order to evade missiles, on its way to investigate a violation of the agreement by Plan insurgents

Opposite
A platoon of 32 Battalion troops outside the Mupa mission church when they escorted Colonel Dippenaar to a goodwill meeting with the local inhabitants. Afterwards the "buffalo soldiers" handed out ration-pack sweets to the children

Left
An Angolan map enlargement of the positions around Cuvelai, captured from Fapla's 11 Brigade by the South Africans in the climactic battle on January 5 of 1984 which signalled the effective end of Operation Askari. It was later annotated by the SADF and put on public display. The elaborately lettered title was probably done to pass the time

Above

**Citizens of Ongiva
had worked up a good
relationship with the SADF
and SWATF during the long
post-Protea occupation, and
when they heard that the
South Africans were
withdrawing as part of the
peace-making after
Operation Askari, they held a
protest meeting at which
they demanded to be
allowed to go along. But
they had to stay behind**

force on the battlefield before, and were intensely conscious of the fact that only poor handling by the other side had kept their casualties down to a comparatively low figure (21 for the entire operation).

In addition, it was the first time that the Angolans/Cubans had reacted so aggressively - General Constand Viljoen spoke no less than the truth when he said the fierceness of the attack had "surprised" the South Africans. It was obvious that the days of relatively easy external operations was over. From now on the South Africans could expect both ground and air attacks if they ventured north of the line. Then, too, it was the first time that Russians had taken an active part in the fighting (among the hundreds of documents the South Africans brought back was an operations order prepared for an Angolan field commander by one of his advisers, written in Russian and then translated into Portuguese).

And, of course, there had been that ominous Russian warning in November of 1983; not to mention the threat of punitive sanctions, which had contributed to an early end to the operation.

All this time the insurgency remained at a low ebb, its command-and-control system still trying to cope with the massive shock administered by Operation Askari. Insurgents in the field wandered around leaderless and others filtered in over the border to escape from the havoc in southern Angola. On January 17 it was reported in Windhoek that three insurgents had been shot dead near Nkuren-kuru in Kavango, while security forces were on the trail of five others who had crossed the line after Askari, passed through Kavango and were now near Tsinsabis, 70km north of Tsumeb; within a week four of them had died in action.

The South African offer of a 30-day ceasefire ran into further trouble on January 18, when Angola set a list of conditions which had to be met before any halt to the shooting war. The major stumbling-block, as had previously been the case, was the question of a withdrawal of the Cuban troops, now estimated to number 30 000. The original South African proposal had not contained a reference to the Cubans, but the latest Angolan pre-conditions included a requirement that Pretoria agree to implement Resolution 435 "without considerations foreign to the resolution". What this meant in plain

language was that South Africa was required to drop its demand that a Cuban withdrawal was a prerequisite for settlement.

Next day Pik Botha responded by saying that the original offer to stop external operations was aimed at defusing the situation and was purposely not linked to a Cuban withdrawal.

"It is therefore a reasonable test to see if the Angolan government is genuinely interested in peace," he said. "But the Angolan government does not want to be tested because (it) now demands that South Africa back down from its standpoint that the Cubans must be withdrawn before a settlement be implemented."

Angola knew, Botha said, that his government could not back down from this standpoint because a "free and reasonable" election could not take place in SWA/Namibia if South Africa was required to reduce its troop strength to 1 500 while 30 000 or more Cubans were stationed north of the border.

While all this public fencing was going on, however, South Africa was already involved in further behind-the-scenes peace talks. Senior Foreign Affairs official Dave Steward had just visited the Cape Verde Islands for further talks with government officials there, and on January 24 the United States Deputy Assistant Secretary of State for African Affairs, Frank Wisner, arrived in Lisbon from the same destination.

Wisner himself made no statement on his arrival and the US embassy would say only that he had had discussions with a ministerial-level Angolan delegation. According to Portuguese and Cape Verdian sources Wisner had discussed the SWA/Namibian deadlock with Angolan and South African officials, but a US State Department spokesman said Pretoria's representatives had not taken part in the talks - apparently the truth, since Steward had returned to Pretoria by January 19.

This did not prevent the release on January 25 of an angry Angolan note to the Security Council, claiming that South Africa still had eight battalions in Angola which were occupying the towns of Otchinjau, Xangongo, Quiteve, Ongiva and Mupa. Another battalion, the note said, was lying east of Caiundo, and the SAAF had flown 17 air reconnaissance missions over Angolan territory between January 15 and January 17. An SADF spokesman retorted that the Angolans seemed still to be referring to the now-defunct Operation Askari, all the forces of which had returned to their bases by January 15 - neatly side-stepping the fact that South Africa's semi-permanent presence dating from Operation Protea in 1981 was still in place.

On January 26 Angola's President Dos Santos lifted the veil of secrecy slightly when he disclosed in Lisbon that his government had begun to negotiate with the US, adding that he would back direct talks between South Africa and Swapo.

By this time the peripatetic Chester Crocker and his team were in South Africa, conferring deep into the night with Pik Botha and senior Foreign Affairs officials at the historic Fleur du Cap wine estate near Stellenbosch. Crocker conveyed Luanda's message to Botha and also raised the subject of new tripartite talks between the US, South Africa and Angola.

That same day promising noises emanated from Swapo's headquarters in Lusaka, when a two-day meeting of the political bureau of the organisation's governing central committee ended with publication of a statement noticeably devoid of the usual anti-South African rhetoric. Swapo "once more reiterates its readiness to talk to South

Africa as the other party in the armed conflict in Namibia", the statement said, and went on to ask the international community to pressure South Africa to implement Resolution 435, although still "firmly" rejecting linkage of the Cubans and the settlement process.

This was followed on January 29, the day Chester Crocker flew into Lusaka to visit President Kaunda, by another Swapo statement quoting Nujoma to the effect that the organisation would accept a ceasefire if Pretoria would agree to a face-to-face discussion on implementation of Resolution 435.

Just two days later, however, it appeared Swapo had reversed its viewpoint again. Speaking in Tanzania, Nujoma was quoted by the state-controlled radio service as bluntly rejecting the ceasefire offer as "a diplomatic ploy intended to hoodwink the people of Namibia"; in London, a Swapo spokesman said the ceasefire was a matter for negotiation between South Africa and Angola and, unlike one instituted in terms of Resolution 435, would not be under UN supervision. He added that Swapo was sceptical about whether South Africa would withdraw its remaining forces from southern Angola and said Pretoria had not indicated whether the ceasefire would extend to SWA/Namibia as well.

The Swapo positional switch anticipated an announcement in Parliament by Prime Minister P W Botha, speaking during the traditional no-confidence debate, that "on the basis of assurances" received from the US during the Fleur du Cap talks "I wish to confirm the Republic of South Africa's decision to begin disengaging its forces in Angola with effect from today". The success of the withdrawal operation and the chances of implementing a possible ceasefire, he added, now depended on all the parties concerned.

At a press conference later in the day he declined to elaborate on the nature of the US assurances he had mentioned in Parliament, but said that the government now expected Swapo not to take advantage of the military situation by such strategems as bringing in new forces, crossing the border and continuing attacks inside SWA/Namibia.

Asked about Nujoma's categorical January 30 rejection from Tanzania, he said he had not seen the statement but expressed uncertainty that it had been made by Nujoma – an uncharacteristically cautious reply which, some observers felt, could be seen as an indication that Nujoma had given either the Angolans or the US an undertaking to honour the terms of the ceasefire (although a Swapo spokesman would later deny that there had been any direct contact between Crocker and Nujoma on the matter).

Whether this was so or not, there can be little doubt that Botha's statement of intent was a sincere one. The plain fact of the matter was that South Africa's semi-permanent presence in southern Angola, while it had served its purpose remarkably well, had turned into an intolerable political burden that was poisoning the country's relations with the rest of the world, not to mention the fact that SWA/Namibia was turning into a financial albatross (later Botha was to state that in total South Africa's involvement north of the Orange had cost it well over R1 000 million in just two years).

Swapo gave no immediate indication of how it intended to react to the ceasefire offer, although informed sources said that within a few days the organisation would "react positively", but would make its offer conditional on direct talks with South Africa about implementation of Resolution 435.

What actually happened, however, was that large numbers of insurgents began infiltrating into SWA/Namibia in the wake of the withdrawing South Africans. P W Botha's response was to halt the withdrawal, while at the same time (on February 6) proposing immediate tripartite military discussions to establish a proper framework for a South African disengagement. Angola and the US agreed to this, and Botha ordered that the withdrawal continue, with all troops to be out by February 15 except about 300 men who were tasked to monitor Swapo movements.

Preparations were already under way by February 8, when Pik Botha told foreign correspondents in Cape Town that a de facto ceasefire was "in practice at this moment" in southern Angola. There was "a very promising climate" for an extended halt to the border war, he added, and "steps are being taken by the South African government and, I believe, the Angolan government, to put into effect a ceasefire for 30 days and, I hope, beyond".

The same day Nujoma told reporters in Rome that his organisation "will observe the so-called 30-day disengagement of forces, provided that after 30 days there will be talks between Swapo and South Africa to sign a ceasefire". He added that Swapo was suspicious about South Africa's motives in unilaterally starting to disengage, but would respect the pull-out nevertheless.

Although no-one but a few top-level officials realised it, the entire conflict was about to enter into a unique phase of its long and bloody course.

On February 13 high-level parties of South Africans, Angolans and Americans jetted into Lusaka for two days of intensive talks at the city's Mulungushi conference centre, which had been placed at their disposal by President Kaunda. The talks culminated with the drawing up of a document known as the "Mulungushi Minute", a one-page list of nine points, quoted below verbatim:

1. Both sides agreed that a Joint South African/Angolan Commission will be constituted as soon as possible to monitor the disengagement.
2. The first meeting of the Commission will occur in Lusaka on February 16, 1984.
3. The Commission, with a parity of forces from both sides, will be located at Ongiva, a mutually agreeable location within the area in question.
4. The Commission will be empowered to travel in the area in question as necessary at the behest of either or both of the parties.
5. The purpose of the Commission will be to monitor the disengagement process and to detect, investigate and report on any alleged violations.
6. On the day on which both sides agree that the Commission is in operation on site, a 30-day period will commence which will conclude with the final withdrawal of all South African forces from the area in question, aside from those attached to the Commission and its joint monitoring teams.
7. Both sides believe that a symbolic American observer presence in the activities of the Commission would be useful.
8. The Angolan side reiterated its firm commitment to restrain Swapo as the process proceeds, including no Swapo or Cuban presence in the recovered territory.
9. Both sides agreed that the disengagement process, including the successful operation of the

Above
Freshly arrived on the scene of the violation, the South African component chairman, Colonel J M Dippenaar, debriefs a very dirty captain of 32 Battalion, co-commander of a joint patrol which ambushed and shot up a Plan logistics group which had been ferrying supplies southwards in spite of the ban on insurgent movement in the Area in Question. Like all white members of 32 Battalion, he is "blacked up" while in the field

Joint Commission, would be an important step in establishing conditions leading to the peaceful resolution of the problems of the region, including the question of the implementation of UNSC Resolution 435.

On February 16 there was another meeting at Lusaka, this time involving Colonel J M Dippenaar of Smokeshell fame and three other middle-level SADF officers, who were to constitute the South African component of the Joint Monitoring Commission.

After long hours of negotiation between the South African, Angolan and United States delegations the meeting ended with agreement on a 17-point disengagement plan based on the Mulungushi Minute.

In summary the agreement provided for the following:

● The "Area in Question" (the area to be monitored) would be bounded in the south by the SWA/Namibian border and in the north by an imaginary west-to-east line running from Marienfluss near the Cunene River mouth to Iona, Mulondo, a point 10km north of Cassinga, the Cubango River and then southwards along the river to the SWA/Namibian border. No South African troops would be permitted north of the JMC Headquarters (this imaginary east-west boundary later became known as the "monitoring line") except those involved in the monitoring operation.

● The JMC headquarters would be established at Cuvelai, where it would stay for a week, while joint monitoring teams composed of equal numbers of South African and Angolan soldiers swept the area down to Mupa to ensure that it was clear of both Swapo and SADF/SWATF forces. The JMC HQ would then move down to Mupa and, at one-week intervals, to Evale, Ongiva and finally the border post of Oshikango, the joint monitoring teams carrying out a Cuvelai-style sweep at each stage.

● As the JMC moved southwards, Fapla elements would move in and occupy each "swept" area.

● The first meeting of the JMC would take place at Cuvelai on February 25. At this meeting senior officers would plan the joint lifting of minefields between Cuvelai and Techamutete to the north of it, and the commission would decide when its joint monitoring forces were capable of effectively performing their functions, at which time the 30-day clock would be started.

● Prior to February 25 Angola and South Africa would communicate by way of a same-day facility set up for this purpose by the US, whose observers would not be on the spot but would be located in Windhoek.

● The question of Calueque, which had been left to the JMC to handle, would be dealt with when the northern border of the Area in Question reached it. Till then the South Africans would continue to be responsible for the protection and maintenance of the pumping station.

Then followed days of intensive staff work by Dippenaar's group and equally frenetic activity by the other people involved in the disengagement, which after several days of namelessness was christened "Operation Flamingo" (this was later changed to "Operation Sclera"). In the meantime a South African force was working its way up to Cuvelai to set up the JMC camp; on February 24 – the same day the Multi-Party Conference in faraway Windhoek published its "Declaration of Basic Principles" and announced that MPC leaders would be going abroad for talks with other African leaders – all preparations were complete and on February 25 the first JMC meeting was held at the new headquarters.

By this stage, however, although no-one realised it at the time, the disengagement was already showing the flaws that were to destroy it. Principal among these was the fact that, thanks to the on-going war with Jonas Savimbi's Unita, the Angolans could not afford to go through with a process which would lead to the establishment of a non-Swapo government in Windhoek.

After nearly nine years the civil war had reached such proportions that to stay in power the MPLA needed not just the Cubans but Swapo as well. In addition, the Angolans regarded a Swapo-ruled SWA/Namibia as strategically essential because it would guard their southern flank while they dealt with Unita, which was still receiving help from South Africa. As a result their enthusiasm for making the JMC work did not burn very brightly – although the Angolan officers on the ground worked hard at first – and at no stage amounted to anything more than the bare minimum required of them, and sometimes not even that.

The consequence was that Plan movement southwards through the Area in Question and into SWA/Namibia never ceased and in fact intensified, in spite of repeated Angolan promises to crack down on the insurgents. The insurgents continued to flow over the border, not only into Ovamboland but into Kavango; in Lusaka and elsewhere Nujoma still professed support for the disengagement process while at the same time denying any of his men were operating from Angola because they were all in SWA/Namibia already. This was to be Swapo's consistent attitude, even when indisputable evidence to the contrary was found.

The South Africans reacted by mounting one anti-Swapo sweep after another, both in the operational area and in the tract between the border and the imaginary "monitoring line". The insurgents

Below
Lieutenant Fred Turner of 32 Battalion (second from right, in cap) his face still blackened with camouflage cream and his wounded left leg roughly bandaged, undergoes an informal debriefing at Cuvelai immediately after being evacuated following a Plan mortar attack on his joint monitoring patrol in the first days of the JMC operation. Turner's return co-incided with a visit by SADF chief Jannie Geldenhuys (in background, third from left). Colonel Buks Koen of the South African JMC component (far right) looks on

suffered particularly heavily in Kavango, and it is a fact that Swapo lost interest in Kavango from this time on, so that the territory was never reactivated to any large extent.

The statistics tell of the intensity of the struggle. In the first days of March, while the JMC operation was still in the process of coming on stream, Ondangwa air base was mortared but not damaged. On May 2 SWATF Headquarters reported 23 insurgents had been killed in two days and 200 new arrivals in Ovamboland had split up into smaller groups which were difficult to pursue because of the heavy rains. In the next few days hundreds more insurgents crossed the border southwards. By March 5 the number of incidents had risen from 21 in December to 34 in January and 58 in February – 44 of the latter being recorded after February 14. Among other things two border posts had been subjected to mortar and RPG-7 fire, eight telephone-poles had been blown down, the home of an official had been damaged by mortar fire at Opuwo in Kaokoland and numerous insurgents had been shot dead.

On March 7 a defiant Nujoma warned from his headquarters that Swapo would intensify its struggle against the "occupation forces" in SWA/Namibia in spite of the Lusaka agreement, and angrily dismissed charges that the movement was hindering disengagement: "Freedom fighters are not operating in Angola, they are operating inside Namibia. As long as an inch of Namibian territory is occupied by South Africa, Swapo's resistance against such occupation will continue."

The same day a spokesman for the South West Africa Police announced that Plan had opened a new front near the Botswana border, over which 14 insurgents had infiltrated (it was a short-lived incursion, however: three insurgents died in separate contacts and nine others vanished, apparently back to Botswana).

In Kaokoland two soldiers and a civilian were wounded when their vehicle detonated a landmine north of Opuwo; a few days later police shot dead two insurgents at Omitara Dam, only 130km north-east of Windhoek, and insurgents hit the Oshikuku security-force base in Ovamboland with a long-range mortar bombardment which, however, missed the military camp and wounded two civilians in a nearby kraal.

Widespread security arrangements were now being made, with heavily manned roadblocks springing up and constant small-scale clashes taking place. During three days in mid-May an army staff-sergeant and 33 insurgents died in action in various skirmishes.

On March 20, in a telephone interview with the South African Press Association in Windhoek, Nujoma appealed to the South African government for urgent talks with Swapo to bring about "a climate of peace"; given the heightened tempo of the war, it was hardly surprising that Pretoria did not even bother to respond.

By March 18 Angola's Dos Santos had muddied the water even further by arriving in Havana on a surprise visit which ended with a joint statement by himself and Fidel Castro which expressed admiration and solidarity with "the heroic struggle being waged by the peoples of Namibia and South Africa under the direction of their sole representatives, Swapo and the African National Congress".

On March 20, Pik Botha – having got hold of the statement's full text – angrily asked how the Angolans could co-operate in a joint force which had already engaged Swapo insurgents in southern

Angola, and at the same time support Swapo. Did it indicate, he asked, "a call for the end to the activities of the Joint Monitoring Commission by the Luanda regime?"

The Angolans responded confidentially by giving their assurance of continued support for the Lusaka Agreement; according to reliable sources they also told the South Africans that the whole affair had been wrongly handled by the Cubans. The emphasis of communique was to have been on the fact that both governments had agreed to a phased withdrawal of Cubans, subject to certain conditions; the meeting had been far from cordial and in fact Dos Santos had been treated brusquely and even with a certain degree of impoliteness; and the Cubans had assured them that the communique would not be made public, then broke their word almost immediately.

It was a strange episode; were the Cubans, acting on behalf of the Russians, trying to drive a wedge between Angola and South Africa? No immediate answers could be found, and the incident took its place in the growing body of discord within the JMC operation.

The Plan movement inside and outside Angola continued. On March 19 a joint patrol clashed with a Swapo group in the Area in Question, and on March 26 a SWATF spokesman announced that 17 insurgents had been killed in skirmishes during the past week, while a civilian had been killed when a lorry hit a mine in western Kavango. In the next 10 days another nine insurgents were killed, bringing the total since mid-February to 135; security-force patrols reported that generally speaking the Plan fighters were maintaining a low profile and avoiding contact.

All this activity badly disrupted the withdrawal timetable, which should have brought the JMC Headquarters to Ongiva – its last stop before the border post at Oshikango – within a month of commencement. Instead it was not till May 3 that the components arrived there. By this time the

Above
Lieutenant-General Jannie Geldenhuys greets Major Carlos Xavier, head of the Angolan component of the JMC, on arrival at the JMC headquarters at Cuvelai during one of his flying problem-solving visits in the early stages of the disengagement. Between them is Major-General Georg Meiring, GOC SWA Territory Force. In the background at right, wearing a peaked cap, is Lieutenant-General Denis Earp, Chief of the SAAF. At right, wearing glasses, is Colonel J M Dippenaar, chairman of the South African component. The white band on Xavier's arm is the JMC armband which was worn by both components

Above
Operation Sclera participants were issued with white or red armbands and could buy cravats and T-shirts, all emblazoned with the JMC's clasped-hands logo

Previous Page
Heavily laden 32 Battalion troops emplane to be flown to the starting-point of their joint patrol in the first few weeks of the JMC operation. On the helicopter's door is the JMC recognition sign: a large cross made of "Dayglo" orange adhesive tape

Insets Left to Right
**Fapla troops and 32 Battalion soldiers pass one another on the road to Mupa.
Colonel J M Dippenaar addresses Angolans in the large church at Mupa prior to returning a statuette of Christ looted by a South African serviceman during Operation Askari and subsequently intercepted. His speech finished, a South African and an Angolan soldier unveil the returned statuette. At a meeting outside later Dippenaar and Fapla officers explained the JMC operation to the local population.
A discussion at the scene of the first Swapo violation. From left are a South African interpreter, Commandant W J le Crerar of the South African JMC component, Captain Gouveia da Costa of the Angolan component and a South African soldier**

goodwill had started to evaporate, as was noted at the first joint meeting at the new location next day, when Angolan Deputy Foreign Minister Venancio de Moura, who had flown in to attend it, made such an intemperate attack on South Africa that his component's resident diplomat later apologised to Dippenaar.

An ambitious but fruitless essay at bridge-building took place between May 10 and May 13, when the Multi-Party Conference joined representatives of Swapo and South Africa at a peace conference at Lusaka which was chaired jointly by President Kaunda and the Administrator-General of SWA/Namibia, Dr Willie van Niekerk. Three days of talking about the territory's future ended without agreement, and the various parties jetted home.

On May 18 Herman Toivo ja Toivo, speaking at a press conference in London, laid the blame for the conference's failure squarely on the South African delegation, accusing it of going to Lusaka "with the objective of trying to sidestep the United Nations plan for achieving Namibia's independence as contained in Resolution 435". The reasoning behind this statement was curious, however, considering that, by his own admission, Swapo had adopted a position on the linkage of Cuban troop withdrawal with implementation which it knew in advance the South Africans would not even consider: "The meeting broke up without a final declaration," he said, "because the South African delegation was not prepared to agree to a text which called for an early implementation of that resolution and which rejected the so-called 'linkage' issue."

Toivo admitted that the JMC operation was causing "difficulties" for the insurgents. However, he added, there was no question of abandoning the armed struggle, although "we are ready to talk" if the South African government was sincere about a ceasefire and the implementation of Resolution 435. But he made it clear that talks could take place only on Swapo's terms: there was no point in reconvening the Lusaka talks after the May 10-13 failure unless Pretoria was prepared to forget about linkage and commit itself to Resolution 435.

On May 21 - while an MPC delegation which had arrived in Washington prepared for talks with Crocker and his superior, Secretary of State for Foreign Affairs George Shultz, followed by a visit to Perez de Cuellar in New York - Pik Botha struck an optimistic note by saying that the South African withdrawal had reached an advanced stage and could be completed within days rather than weeks. Speaking at Lusaka after a three-hour meeting with Angola on the possibility of setting up a joint permanent commission to carry on the JMC's work after it had been dissolved, he admitted that the participants had encountered a number of problems, but added that these were not insurmountable and the peace commission meetings would continue.

Botha could not have been as optimistic as his words indicated. The JMC operation was in grave difficulty by this time and the Angolans had proved distinctly lukewarm towards the idea of a joint permanent commission, claiming it would not work unless the insurgents were involved in the peace process and an early start was made towards implementing Resolution 435.

The truth of the matter was that for practical purposes the move to Ongiva marked the end of serious co-operation as laid down in the Lusaka Agreement; the JMC was to remain bogged down there for the next 10 months, hampered by Angolan prevarication and with relationships at both

governmental and operational level deteriorating by the day. The Angolans provided minimum co-operation in patrolling and scouting the AIQ, Plan violations increased dramatically and the South Africans began picking up hard evidence that Fapla elements were actively aiding the insurgents - only to find that their protests fell on deaf ears.

Angola made no secret of its new hard-line attitude. On June 22, just after Swapo had flatly rejected an invitation to take part in the MPC's deliberations, Luanda's Foreign Minister, Paulo Jorge, told reporters in Stockholm that South Africa was continually inventing excuses to slow down its withdrawal, adding: "Personally, I believe they are delaying because they do not know what to do next, because they realise that the next step must be negotiations with Swapo."

Jorge flatly denied that the Lusaka Agreement had placed any obligations on Angola, and said it had not changed Swapo's position in the country in any way - "ask Swapo if we have ever hindered them from doing anything in Angola".

The South Africans, now seriously concerned that the Lusaka Agreement itself was about to fall apart, called yet another ministerial meeting in the Zambian capital on July 2. This time some progress was made - or seemed to be made; by now the South Africans understood only too well that Angolan undertakings were usually built on sand. The leader of the Angolan delegation, Lieutenant-Colonel Alexandre Rodrigues, accepted in principle the concepts of a JPC and a treaty governing the operation of Calueque after withdrawal, but qualified his acceptance with the routine rider that Angola was having difficulty in controlling Swapo because the organisation was not involved in the peace process.

The upshot of this meeting was an eyeball-to-eyeball encounter between Sam Nujoma and the Administrator-General of SWA/Namibia, Dr Willie van Niekerk, on the Cape Verde Islands on July 24. Van Niekerk laid down two pre-conditions: firstly, that without a firm commitment on a Cuban withdrawal there could be no suggestion of talks on the implementation of Resolution 435; and secondly, that the two delegations could discuss the statements they would convey to the UN Secretary-General and Swapo's peaceful participation in the internal democratic political process in SWA/Namibia.

Nujoma responded by saying he had not been informed of the pre-conditions and that Swapo would end hostilities only if both delegations agreed to send messages to the Secretary-General asking for immediate implementation of Resolution 435. Van Niekerk could not agree to this, however, and the meeting ended after only two hours. Several days later a Swapo spokesman in Luanda blamed the failure of the talks on Van Niekerk, saying: "The truth is that it was South Africa and not Swapo who turned down the offer of a ceasefire and cessation of hostilities contained in a Swapo proposal."

South Africa responded by drawing up new ceasefire proposals, to which Swapo promptly replied by rejecting any suggestions which fell outside the UN settlement plan.

The proposals for a JPC and a Ruacana-Calueque treaty both fell flat as well, thanks to postponements and prevarication by the Angolans, who could not be brought around to making any concrete undertaking. In the meantime the situation on the ground was worsening. On August 3 SWATF Headquarters announced that 322 insurgents had now been killed in action since mid-February, among them six senior field commanders, while another two, Ben Nikanor and Joseph Manegange, had surrendered.

By now, too, the Angolan JMC component was making continual claims of impossibly large numbers of SAAF overflights (although there had been none since August 12), and a meeting between Pik Botha and Rodrigues at Lusaka on August 17, to follow through on the issues raised at the previous talks, achieved nothing worthwhile, partly because Rodrigues was interested only in the alleged SAAF overflight violations.

Meanwhile at the JMC the Angolans continued to report more and more mythical violations of their airspace by the SAAF. At times the number of alleged aerial violations reached ridiculous size – it was claimed, for example, that there had been no fewer than 83 during August 17 to 18.

The atmosphere improved somewhat after a high-level JMC meeting on September 2 which was attended by Geldenhuys and an unexpectedly conciliatory Lieutenant Ngongo Monteiro, his opposite number, and the conference ended with both parties agreeing that there should be another get-together similar to the original one at Mulungushi, at which the creation of a JPC could be discussed. In concrete terms, however, this meeting achieved as little as its predecessors, although for a while the Angolan JMC component became more helpful.

Angolan demands for South Africa to move faster now dwindled, and in Pretoria the military planners concluded that this was because the situation might suit the Angolans very well: it had allowed them to re-occupy the south, it gave them the pretext for keeping their Cuban garrison in place and it was a good guarantee against fresh external operations, so that they could devote their attention and resources to dealing with Unita.

The situation did not help the South Africans much, on the other hand. The counter-insurgency campaign carried on at full tilt - by September 11, 86 insurgents had been killed in just six weeks, a total of 411 since February 16 and 471 since January.

On the political front, meanwhile, the United States and other Western nations were pushing hard for a settlement, but an October 4 address to the UN General Assembly by Cuba's Foreign Minister, Isidoro Malmierca Peoli, did little to bring any clarity to the situation. Peoli declared that the "strict application" of Resolution 435, which included the withdrawal of South African troops, "will make the withdrawal of Cuban troops from Angola possible … In their attempts to delay, boycott and impede the independence of Namibia, the imperialists and their ally, the racist Pretoria regime, recur (sic) to lies, diversionism, coercion, pressure and blackmail. Whom do they expect to deceive?"

Dos Santos told a different story in an interview in the Washington Post of October 14 (granted, it was speculated, in an effort to counter a successful Unita public relations effort in the US). He was committed to sending Cuban forces home in parallel phases with a South African withdrawal from SWA/Namibia, he said; although he then made the mandatory accusation that South Africa was to blame for the stalled disengagement, he went on to add that Angola was "prepared to live in an atmosphere of tolerance" with Pretoria after SWA/Namibia became independent, and would regard apartheid as an internal matter.

Dos Santos offered amnesty to Unita members, but made it clear that Savimbi and other high officials faced certain death if they returned to Luanda. Unita's roving Foreign Minister, Jeremias Chitunda, replied from Washington with a defiant prediction (which proved to be unfounded) that the rebels were poised "to fight in the streets of Luanda" within three months, claiming that arms caches had been established and that Unita fighters had been infiltrated into the capital and its environs for a final push.

The US was now pushing even harder for a SWA/Namibian settlement. In mid-October Crocker's assistant Frank Wisner flew to Luanda for talks which, as a State Department spokesman guardedly announced, "concern the conditions under which a Cuban troop withdrawal could take place". No more was said on the subject till October 22, when the State Department announced that Wisner had returned with a concrete Angolan offer on Cuban withdrawal which "we are reviewing … in expectation of further talks in the near future"; according to informed sources Dos Santos had told Wisner he was prepared to offer a "commitment" on a Cuban withdrawal schedule which would co-incide with South Africa's departure from SWA/Namibia.

The background to these talks has never been officially revealed, but a fortnight later one of South Africa's most respected political observers, London-based Anthony Delius, threw some light on what had gone on in Luanda. After drawing on his many overseas contacts, Delius came to the conclusion that the JMC's "slow-motion exercise" had been "far too much for the Angolan nerves and economy", especially when one of the central figures in the Angolan government was the hard-lining Paulo Jorge, a veteran of the Agostinho Neto days, who was "regularly rumoured to be particularly determined not to be talked into doing any sort of a deal over the Cubans …"

The trouble with the JMC operation, Delius opined, was that "neither (the Angolans nor the South Africans) could trust the other side to play fair … Both Mr Wisner and Dr Crocker could never

Above
A typical meeting of the Joint Monitoring Commission. At far right is Colonel Dippenaar, leader of the South African component; next to him is Major Xavier. Although relations were cordial during the first three months, they began to deteriorate sharply after the JMC headquarters arrived at Ongiva in May

Above
A soldier of 32 Battalion hands out sweets culled from ration-packs to Angolan children outside the church at Mupa. Apprehensive at first in the presence of "Os Terrivis" (the Terrible Ones), the youngsters soon overcame their reticence and dug into the first gob-stoppers they had seen in many a day

assure themselves that President Dos Santos had explained the rules exactly to Mr Paulo Jorge, or had even dared to do so ...

"President Dos Santos has frequently been said to be on the verge of accepting a deal which would involve a swop - South African soldiers leave SWA/ Namibia in return for Cuban troops leaving for Cuba ... (in October) President Dos Santos appeared to have made a desperate new bid, a last-minute move ...

"When Mr Wisner went across to Luanda to find out what was bothering President Dos Santos, he discovered that Angola's foreign-affairs people were continually having holes talked in their heads by nervous advisers. Besides, all this international dilly-dallying was wrecking whatever finances Angola had for patching up the territory".

Neither the Angolans nor the South Africans were ready for a meeting of minds, he said. The South Africans felt they needed more time to win hearts and minds, while the Angolans felt they would rather make final arrangements about borders and SWA/Namibian independence "more directly with the Americans. Besides, the Angolans were fairly sure they would be able to get more money from the Americans in special aid than they would from the South Africans. The Reagan dollar, they heard, was better to have than failing gold. Added to which, the presence of Unita in Angola meant far more to South African security than it did to America's.

"Nevertheless Mr Wisner, after a great deal of intense argument, was able to go back to Washington with a reasonably fair assurance that he had the word of the parties concerned that the Cubans and the South Africans might be expected to go home, however cautiously.

"As a sign of Luanda's good word, Mr Jorge was pushed out of control of the movement of Cubans and the South Africans agreed to continue their departure if there was a joint effort to keep Swapo out till Namibia was prepared to receive them.

"So the position rests, while the Americans decide what degree of urgency to give it for the next four years".

Wisner was still in Luanda when, on October 17, the SWATF's Meiring announced that Plan's

commander in Kavango, one Akushinda, had been captured on October 12 and his six-man headquarters group "eliminated". Akushinda's capture elated the South Africans. He was an old hand at insurgent warfare and for nearly two years he had slipped through their fingers again and again. Now he was behind bars and the headquarters from which he had orchestrated all of Plan's activities in Kavango was permanently out of action. By this stage 520 Plan guerrillas had died since January, 55 of them in Kavango, and according to Meiring there were now "at worst, not more than 51" insurgents operating in the homeland, who were suffering from low morale and being hampered by the locals' co-operation with the security forces. By October 31 another six of the 51 had been killed as well, along with 11 insurgents in other parts of the operational area.

On October 31 and November 1 Crocker and Van Niekerk met on the Cape Verde Islands for another round of talks on Cuban withdrawal and SWA/Namibian independence. On the table were the latest Angolan proposals, envisaging a phased pull-out which would see the departure of 20 000 Cubans over three years, while another 10 000 remained behind in northern Angola, the withdrawal to start when implementation of Resolution 435 commenced and South African troop strength in SWA/Namibia had been reduced to 1 500 men. All Unita bases inside SWA/Namibia (locations unspecified) were also to be dismantled and Pretoria was to "commit itself from the very start to cease all support to Unita".

The South Africans, on the other hand, proposed that the Cuban troops should be reduced to 12 000 six weeks after implementation of Resolution 435 began, then to 8 000 three weeks later, with all of them out after 12 weeks. The Cubans were not to be replaced by any surrogate force, Angola was to provide detailed lists of all Cubans and communist-bloc advisers stationed in Angola, the number of advisers was to be kept at 1978 levels and a joint peace-keeping commission was to be established to supervise and verify the withdrawal. No reference was made to the Angolan demand that all ties with Unita must be severed.

The two countries' positions were still poles apart, although this was not general knowledge because it had been agreed that the details of both sides' proposals would be kept secret. However, November 12 saw Pik Botha making another prediction that South African troops could be out of Angola "within days", speaking this time at Munich after a meeting in Frankfurt with his West German counterpart, Hans-Dietrich Genscher.

"Unless there are large-scale Swapo incursions in the Ongiva region, disengagement could be completed even within days of the JMC meeting on November 15," he said, although he admitted that he could see "difficult negotiations" ahead on the question of a Cuban troop withdrawal. Nevertheless, the MPLA's agreement in principle to a withdrawal was "a very important step forward", and Pretoria was still finalising its detailed response to the Angolan proposals.

Botha admitted that there was a widening gulf between his government and the MPC, whose leaders had totally rejected Resolution 435 and were insisting on a conference similar to the one at Lancaster House at which the Zimbabwean constitution had been hammered out. However, he added, while South Africa continued to be guided by the wishes of the SWA/Namibians, it could not allow its interests to be endangered - a clear

indication that Pretoria remained committed to Resolution 435.

Asked whether South Africa would be willing to mediate between Unita and the MPLA, Botha responded that Pretoria did not want to become involved in Angola's civil war, "but if we are asked to mediate between Unita and the MPLA we would render what assistance we could", which neatly sidestepped the indisputable fact that South Africa was still aiding Unita.

But this latest plan, too, was destined to go nowhere. Later in November highly-placed government officials in Havana were telling reporters that Fidel Castro was ready to sign a four-party agreement on a Cuban withdrawal from Angola, but comments published in Granma, the Cuban Communist Party newspaper, made it plain that the new plan would be nowhere near the South Africans' minimum requirements.

On November 19 high-level South African and Angolan delegations arrived at Ongiva for the first JMC meeting in several months. No statement was issued after the meeting. The contents of the Cape Verde Islands proposals were still secret at this stage, but not for much longer: on November 25 the Angolans unilaterally took a full-page advertisement in the London Times newspaper in which they published the text of a letter Dos Santos had sent to UN Secretary-General Perez de Cuellar, which contained their proposals and the South Africans' in precise detail.

The letter contained a remark which was all the more telling for being perfectly true: some Cuban troops would have to remain behind even after SWA/Namibian independence, Dos Santos said, because "Angola cannot make concessions which amount to suicide for its national integrity and socio-political development".

The comment finally disposed of the hoary myth, sedulously promoted since 1975, that the Cubans were in Angola to defend it against the depredations of the racist South Africans. It also explained why the Cubans and their ally, Paulo Jorge, had made such efforts to prevent the vacillating Dos Santos from giving in to South African and American demands for a total withdrawal. If the entire garrison was withdrawn and the MPLA government collapsed, it would be an unendurable blow to Fidel Castro, who had spent at least 1 000 of his men's lives in Angola and was also still smarting from the humiliating way in which the Americans had closed down his Grenada operation in 1983.

The Angolans' decision to go public was a clear breach of the undertaking they had given at the Cape Verde talks, and Pik Botha gave them a public tongue-lashing, saying their action had placed a question-mark over their ability to negotiate seriously.

There the matter rested for the moment, although behind-the-scenes diplomatic activity continued.

So ended 1984, with 39 security-force members and 584 insurgents dead, including the losses incurred during Operation Askari. In addition 196 civilians had died as a result of Plan activities, while 265 had been wounded and 103 abducted. It was a sad toll for a year which was supposed to have brought SWA/Namibia nearer to peace.

Above
The JMC as it looked in the early days of warm co-operation — a group photograph outside the tent in which the daily conferences took place. At centre in front are the two chairmen, Dippenaar and Xavier. The flags are carefully arranged so that the Angolan one is to the north of the camp and the South African one to the south

1985

While the JMC stagnated quietly at Ongiva in January, the security forces inside SWA/Namibia braced themselves for a new incursion to start as soon as the wet season began in earnest. They knew that the Plan field commanders, having been driven out of the shallow area by the constant sweeps, had set themselves up at Cuvelai in the theoretically Swapo-free Area in Question, and captured insurgents had revealed that infiltrators were receiving refresher training there in preparation for the arrival of the rains. In addition, reports were coming in that the insurgents were moving into a new area south of Cuvelai.

Late in January the annual SADF/SWATF military exercises took place in Ovamboland and inevitably sparked rumours that a new incursion was imminent. SWATF spokesman Colonel As Kleynhans denied the rumours, pointing out that the main exercise, nicknamed Vuiswys, was not linked to an incursion because it was to practise conventional rather than counter-insurgency skills. A smaller exercise near Ruacana by 61 Mechanised Battalion, however, was based on a strike into Angola. Would there be such a strike? Well, Kleynhans replied, in spite of Operation Sclera "we are still at war with Swapo ... We are expecting an infiltration to take place and it is not excluded that we might decide to go for Swapo headquarters again. However, there's no decision at the moment".

In fact there was little chance of a South African incursion. The SADF and SWATF were still at liberty to operate between the border and the imaginary east-west "monitoring line" which now ran through Ongiva, and there were heavy political implications involved in any venture further northwards; among other things it would instantly kill the ailing disengagement process, which the South Africans still hoped to revitalise.

The insurgents suffered from no such inhibitions, at least in spirit. Almost immediately after Kleynhans made his comments, Swapo's information secretary in London, Hidipo Hamutenya, contradicted him by saying in a BBC radio interview that insurgents had been crossing into SWA/Namibia since before the rains had started in order to build up strengths on the ground and intensify the sabotage campaign.

This was in response to South Africa's refusal to make any concessions to facilitate a political settlement, and also to consolidate Plan strength in the operational area, Hamutenya added; Swapo respected Angola's disengagement agreement, but the pact related only to parts of southern Angola previously occupied by South African troops and did not extend to other areas.

There was no immediate flare-up in the border fighting, but the verbal war resumed in early February, with Dos Santos alleging that Unita was an "integral part" of the SADF and that South Africa was involved in "a vast destabilization plan which has as its main objective the overthrow of the Angolan government". This was immediately denied by Pik Botha, who described Unita as "an Angolan nationalist movement" and charged that there could be no doubt that Angola was actively supporting the violent overthrow of the South African government.

"It plays host to several thousand members of the African National Congress and has put at their disposal several camps which are used for the training of anti-South African terrorists," he said. "It has given indispensable support to Swapo in its terrorist attacks against South West Africa/Namibia."

The Lusaka Agreement had not led to the total disengagement of South African forces, he said, because the Angolan government had been unwilling or unable to comply with one of its central provisions - that Swapo elements should not be allowed into the area vacated by South African forces.

In spite of all this thunder and lightning, however, the disengagement process had not disintegrated, and talks between Botha and Crocker in Pretoria on February 9 and 10 ended with the American boosting expectations by telling reporters: "We hope the agreement on disengagement will soon be totally complete." What the US wanted, Crocker added, was to see all foreign troops, especially Cubans, withdrawn from Southern Africa. Botha would say no more than that the Cuban withdrawal had been a key issue. No doubt his reticence resulted partly from disappointment at the results of the talks. Pretoria was willing to synchronise a Cuban withdrawal with implementation of Resolution 435, but the Angolans were insisting on retaining a substantial 15 000 in Luanda and northwards for another three years after the withdrawal of the main body.

On February 11 the two men continued their talks in Cape Town - but this time they were joined by Jonas Savimbi. At the conclusion of the talks none of the three was willing to make any significant statement, but observers interpreted Savimbi's presence as a sign that the Americans would not abandon him in the event of a South African withdrawal.

At this time the security forces were engaged in some of the fiercest fighting of the war as large numbers of insurgents continued to cross the border, aided by sporadic but heavy rainfall. By mid-February small groups totalling more than 700 insurgents were said to be active in the operational area, many of them members of Plan's "Typhoon" deep-penetration unit. Most of the action was in central Ovamboland; activity in Kavango remained low-key, thanks to the previous year's counter-insurgency campaign, and in Kaokoland consisted mainly of some mine-laying - although this caused the highest security-force loss for some time, five soldiers dying when their vehicle was blown up. By February 15 a total of 130 insurgents had died for a loss of seven, the largest Plan death-toll for the first seven weeks of any year since the war had begun.

The feebleness of the JMC's monitoring operation was revealed four days later by one Josephus Nikodemus Kalenga, a Typhoon section-commander who had been wounded and captured in SWA/Namibia and was allowed to be interviewed by the press.

Kalenga said he was actually a youth organiser, but because of Plan's manpower shortage he had been drafted into operational tasks and appointed to lead a special-unit group into SWA/Namibia to recruit in central Ovamboland and commit acts of sabotage. Plan knew about the Lusaka Agreement, he said, and had been told to keep away from Fapla positions in the Area in Question. They had done so, and in moving southwards through the Area in Question had not once encountered any joint monitoring patrols. They duly crossed the border, but on the second day in SWA/Namibia they had been attacked by the security forces and all but he had been killed.

Over the border the Angolan civil war was also at a high pitch, if Unita statements were to be believed. On February 26 a spokesman claimed that the rebels had overrun the Fapla garrison at Mandimba in the extreme north-eastern Zaire province, killing 46 troops and seizing "much war material". A spokesman also claimed that in the preceding 11 days Unita forces had shot down two transport aircraft and killed 316 government soldiers, including 31 Cubans. In addition, the insurgents had destroyed a military train en route to the central provincial capital of Malanje and captured "great quantities" of war material and equipment it had been transporting to Fapla's Cuban-supported 81 Brigade there. Malanje had been attacked the same day in a separate operation, the spokesman said, adding that in the past four months Unita saboteurs had carried out a series of attacks on Luanda itself. None of these statements could be independently confirmed, but there was no doubt that heavy fighting was in progress, and diplomats in Lisbon – a traditional source of information about Angola – said it appeared Savimbi was trying some sort of envelopment of the capital.

The border war continued to escalate. On March 5 the SWA/Namibian police commissioner, Lieutenant-General A J C Gouws, announced that with effect from March 11 a security area 1 000km long and about 130km deep would be proclaimed in Kaokoland, Ovamboland and Kavango, and another about 450km long in East Caprivi. Permits would be needed to enter these areas, he said. The new measures did not have an immediate effect, and it came as no surprise when, on March 16, a government spokesman told reporters that South African and SWATF troops would stay up to 40km inside Angola because the Luanda regime had not succeeded in "disciplining" Swapo members as it had undertaken to do at the Lusaka talks.

Chester Crocker, meanwhile, had initiated yet another round of talks on SWA/Namibian independence. On March 19 – the day SWATF announced that 19 insurgents had been killed in the past fortnight, bringing the year's total to 207 – he met an Angolan delegation on the Cape Verde Islands and then arranged to visit Cape Town to lay a set of compromise proposals before Pik Botha.

No details of the proposals were known, but according to diplomatic sources the US had dropped its demand for a total Cuban withdrawal and was now prepared for an arrangement in terms of which 10 000 troops would leave immediately and the rest would be gradually reduced. Observers agreed that the Angolans would not be amenable to Pretoria's raising the ante, particularly in view of the on-going Unita activity, and that at the same time it would not be easy to convince the South Africans that the plan had any merits.

On March 25 a delegation of the Multi-Party Conference met P W Botha in Cape Town to submit proposals for the establishment of a "transitional government" to take over the reins of government from the Administrator-General and rule the territory till an independence settlement had been arrived at. Reliable sources said that the government would consist of a national assembly, a council of ministers and a constitutional council, formed from members of the MPC; if Botha accepted the proposals the MPC intended to form a government within six weeks. Botha duly took receipt of the proposals and promised to deliver an answer within one month.

Angered and dismayed by this turn of events, the contact group of five Western nations began girding their loins to object strenuously. No doubt the MPC's proposals had a malign effect on the

following day's talks with Chester Crocker, which ended without fanfare and obviously without success (one informed source later claimed that P W Botha had been so displeased that he had given Crocker a "dressing down").

The JMC was now on its last legs, having become almost totally irrelevant. By April 13, when 142 violations of the Lusaka Agreement had been recorded since moving to Ongiva, with the SADF and SWATF found responsible for only four, the South African government decided to pull out, and the decision was announced at the April 15 JMC meeting. On April 17 the South Africans left, with the exception of 60 men who remained at Calueque pending the sorting out of that long-standing problem before the commission was formally wound down on May 16.

The South African component marched over the border at Oshikango in good style, a band playing and flags flying, but all the pageantry could not disguise the fact that the South Africans had got the worst of the deal that had been hammered out with such high expectations at Lusaka little more than a year earlier.

At a brief press conference Constand Viljoen put the best face on the withdrawal, saying it was a "sign of hope" and an opportunity for both South Africa and Angola to learn from their mistakes of the past nine years and ensure they were not repeated.

He admitted, however, that "by giving up a military area we do have to give up a certain amount of military advantage", adding that he "sincerely hoped" that no further external operations would be necessary, but if the Angolans allowed Swapo to use the shallow area as a springboard for infiltration again, the SADF would always be ready (as he put it) to defend the people of SWA/Namibia. Observers interpreted this – correctly, as events were to prove – that the South Africans were expecting Plan activity to increase and would not hesitate to mount fresh external operations if it suited their purpose.

On April 18 P W Botha announced in Parliament that he had accepted the MPC's proposals. The government was still trying to achieve an internationally recognised settlement, he said, and was not trying to delay or jeopardise the implementation of Resolution 435. By transferring some official functions back to the territory, the people there would be able to govern themselves till agreement on a Cuban withdrawal from Angola made it possible for implementation to take place.

Botha said the transitional government would be able to promulgate a bill of rights, and establish a constitutional court and constitutional council. It would also be able to negotiate with all parties, including Swapo, about independence for SWA/Namibia. So as not to hamper the international settlement plan, he said, the South African government would retain all powers invested in it, including defence and foreign affairs, and all laws passed by the new legislature would have to be signed by the Administrator-General.

The Western Five nations all expressed concern about the development, pointing out that any unilateral move to set up an interim internal government would have no validity, and any constitution but one drawn up in terms of Resolution 435 "would be without effect".

All things considered, Botha's announcement did not create as much of an uproar as some political observers had expected; a spokesman for the major partner in the group, the United States,

said that an interim government would not affect the UN effort to gain independence for SWA/Namibia, noted that South Africa had pledged to co-operate with the UN initiative and added: "We expect South Africa to keep its word".

In Windhoek the leaders of two major MPC groupings, Dirk Mudge of the Democratic Turnhalle Alliance and Moses Katjiuongwa of the mainly Herero South West African National Union, said the plan was not a violation of Resolution 435 and added that the conference would persist with its efforts to reach an understanding with the international community.

In the meantime, however, "we cannot wait forever. Nobody can expect us to sit back and see our own situation deteriorate in our country just because there are political parties such as Swapo who claim to be the sole and authentic representatives".

To no one's surprise, Swapo gave the idea of a transitional government a frosty reception, describing it as a South African attempt to "impose" a "pseudo-independence" on the territory.

Just 12 days after the withdrawal at Oshikango, the Angolan propaganda campaign restarted. "Regular South African army units" were still stationed 12km inside Angola, the Angop agency said in a radio broadcast, while large contingents of "anti-guerrilla fighters", "cavalry" and police were in position along the border; all this was causing "great tension" in Cunene province and "made imminent the threat of renewed aggression or invasions".

Angop then deflated its own indignation by making it clear that the "units" still inside Angola consisted of the 60 soldiers stationed at Calueque and those at Ruacana, which was on SWA/Namibian soil, and by quoting Lieutenant-Colonel Sabiano Siquiero of the Angolan JMC component as saying that there had been no incidents involving the South Africans and that their withdrawal was to be discussed at top level within the next few days.

General Constand Viljoen correctly described this shabby little essay at disinformation as "absolute nonsense", pointing out that South Africa had fulfilled its part of the agreement "to the letter"

and that final arrangements following the Oshikango withdrawal were continuing smoothly, with daily meetings between the commanders of the South African presence in SWA/Namibia and the Angolan border troops taking place at Santa Clara, the Angolan section of Oshikango.

The JMC itself lingered on for another month; the Angolans proved unreceptive to a South African suggestion that a permanent joint peace committee be established, and on May 16 the commission was disbanded.

And so it was back to Square 1. In the final analysis the only ones who had benefited by Operation Sclera had been the Angolans, since they had been able to reoccupy large areas of their southland from which they had effectively been barred by South African and Unita operations. The South Africans had killed large numbers of insurgents - 629 since the beginning of 1984, for a loss of 37 men - but were nowhere near bringing an end to the fighting, although the end of the rainy season had brought a measure of relief.

Swapo was very much intact, too, although the cumulative effect of several years of losses had seriously reduced its manpower and the response to recruiting drives among the Ovambos had been so poor that it had taken to abducting older school pupils again - the worst occurrence being on May 12, when insurgents abducted about 80 students aged between 15 and 20 from the Ongha secondary school in the Okwanyama tribal area about 30km north of Oshakati, and took them at gun-point into Angola. Sixteen of the victims managed to escape en route, but the kidnappers got clean away with the rest because security forces which were following up were under orders not to cross the border.

As the JMC finally became a footnote to SWA/Namibian history, the top-secret withdrawal plan Chester Crocker had laid before the South African government late in March became the subject of a strong protest in the US Senate, with Senator Steven Symms denouncing it and saying that it "could well have been devised in Moscow or Havana".

According to Symms, the plan - which was apparently leaked to him by Unita's chief foreign envoy, Jeremias Chitunda - called for Luanda to repatriate 12 000 Cubans over eight months while South Africa reduced its military presence in SWA/Namibia to 1 500 men and pledged to uphold Angola's territorial integrity by cutting off support to Unita and refraining from hot-pursuit operations after fleeing insurgents; after 12 months Angola would be allowed to retain 15 000 Cubans for an "indefinite" period as long as they were not used in an offensive manner.

The US State Department refused to be drawn. A spokesman would only confirm that "compromise proposals" had been placed before both sides, adding that the figures Symms had quoted were "inaccurate" and "that's all we're going to say". The South African Department of Foreign Affairs was even less forthcoming: a spokesman said that it refused to comment because the whole matter was still under discussion by the US, South Africa and Angola. Next day, however, Howard Phillips, who was leading a group of conservative American business men on a tour of South Africa at the time, denounced the plan as delineated by Symms and said that when he had discussed the matter with Deputy Foreign Minister Louis Nel on May 17 "Nel was outraged that Crocker would retreat from his commitments ... to the government of South Africa". Nel could not be reached for comment.

Also on May 18, Angola's Dos Santos was quoted by Angop as saying that some South African troops were still in Angola in spite of the Republic's much-vaunted withdrawal at Oshikango, and that Pretoria had left bands of Unita rebels behind in areas which it had vacated and was supplying them with arms and transport. A Department of Foreign Affairs spokesman refused to comment on the allegations about Unita, but confirmed that 60 South Africans were still at Calueque, adding that they were there at the request of the Angolan government and serving alongside Fapla troops.

The exchange was a typical example of the public and private relationship between the Angolan and South African governments. In private the Angolans were relatively accommodating; in public they played the theme of "racist aggression" to the hilt, not hesitating to make wild and usually unsubstantiated accusations about South African intentions and actions when it suited their political purposes.

They never tired, for example, of accusing South Africans of launching attacks - even palpably unlikely ones - when the allegations helped them to disguise the fact that the war with Unita had now spread far afield from Savimbi's original "liberated zone" in the Cuando-Cubango province.

In early May the rebels claimed to have shot down an Mi-24 helicopter gunship, killed 29 Fapla soldiers in an attack on a military post in Cuanza-Sul province, wiped out a supply column on the road between Huambo and Luanda and ambushed another convoy in Cuanza-Norte province, killing 31 soldiers and destroying nine lorries. Later in the month they claimed to have shot down another Mi-24 and killed 161 government soldiers in a series of co-ordinated attacks carried out in seven different provinces. The fact that these claims could not be confirmed from other sources could not hide the fact that the war was much more widespread than the Luanda government was prepared to admit.

On the other hand, there was no gainsaying the fact that the South Africans had not broken their ties with Unita and were unlikely to do so while the Angolans allowed Plan to use their territory as a springboard for attacks into SWA/Namibia; Pretoria was painfully aware that if Savimbi went under it would mean that the infiltration rate would go up by several hundred percent because all the Swapo troops serving permanently with the Angolan forces would be available for incursions over the border. This ancient Angolan thorn in the peacemakers' flesh stung as sharply as ever, no matter how desperately they tried to ignore the pain.

Strangely enough, at this time the Luanda government was not dismayed by the spreading civil war but actually more confident about its fighting ability than ever before, according to one well-qualified military observer - Dr David Albright, professor of national security affairs at the United States Air Force Air War College, who arrived in Cape Town after a month's African visit.

According to Albright it appeared that the Angolans "have become convinced that they really have the capability for handling Unita, even if the Cubans are gone. They seem to believe they have made progress in training their own forces - that in the final crunch they can handle Savimbi".

Asked if it was not true that Fapla had been unable to eliminate Unita because of low battle-worthiness and bad logistics, combined with the fact that most Angolan soldiers were trained for a conventional defensive role rather than a mobile aggressive one, he replied: "This is a different reality they perceive that has produced the kind of confidence that is necessary. I don't know if they understand (that one cannot wage a defensive war)." This lack of comprehension he put down to bad advice from the Russians, who knew a great deal about fomenting insurgencies but not much about fighting them.

He suspected, he said, that the Angolans' attitude was "very Soviet-orientated, very conventional, with a large logistic tail", and "if it's not very well-organised the tail falls apart ...

"The truth is that the Soviets have had very little experience in this kind of warfare. Part of the Angolan confidence in this respect probably reflects part of the myopia of the Soviets. The Soviets have apparently been telling the Angolans that they are doing better, and the Angolans are believing this".

On the other hand, Albright added, Savimbi was also becoming increasingly self-confident, and "the fundamental question is this: can either participant be persuaded that they are winning without being tested on the battlefield? We are dealing here with perceptions which are clearly at odds, and frankly I don't see a way of altering (their) perspectives".

It was an eerily percipient comment which was to be answered within a few months at the Lomba River in the south-east.

One incident the Angolans did not make up, however, and which was to be a cause celebre for months to come, was revealed on May 22, just six days after the JMC had been wound up, when Luanda claimed to have killed two heavily armed South African "commandos" and captured another in the Cabinda enclave as they were about to sabotage a refinery in the Malongo oil complex.

The SADF promptly denied that it was involved in any operation in Cabinda. Faced with this blunt disavowal and aware of the mendacity of the Angolans' propaganda, South African newspaper commentators speculated about the possible identity of the raiders. Among the theories offered were that they were South Africans seconded to Unita or its feeble Cabindan ally, Flec (Front for the Liberation of the Cabinda Enclave); and that they were former refugees who had served with the SADF before becoming insurgents.

On May 23, however, Constand Viljoen called a press conference and admitted that the SADF had "small groups" of soldiers deployed in northern Angola, although he would not confirm Luanda's casualty figures. The soldiers were tasked with gathering information about "hostile elements which threaten the safety of South West Africa and South Africa", such as Swapo, the ANC and "Russian surrogate forces". He added: "At the moment there is concern because contact with such a small element has been broken. This element was gathering information about ANC bases, Swapo bases, as well as Cuban involvement with them in the area south and north of Luanda."

There was an instantaneous and powerful reaction from virtually every quarter, both inside South Africa and out. The US State Department deplored the incident and demanded a "full explanation", and other governments followed suit, while the SADF sorrowfully watched its painfully acquired credibility seep away. The Cape Times newspaper of Cape Town spoke for many people when it published an angry editorial saying: "Who will now ever again accept the word of the South African Defence Force? Or, indeed, of the Department of Foreign Affairs or the South African government itself? What is left of the diplomacy of Nkomati and the Lusaka Agreement? Are the Departments of Defence and Foreign Affairs at cross-purposes?

"…What does the Minister of Defence, General Malan, have to say in the matter? Why does he remain silent and leave it to General Viljoen to do the talking?

"As things stand, General Malan owes South Africa, Angola and the world an explanation. Meanwhile, the disinvestment lobby is rejoicing at this unexpected bonanza while Dr Crocker and the advocates of "constructive engagement" are left mortified. If he cannot give a satisfactory explanation, the Minister of Defence should resign."

The Angolans played their propaganda coup to the hilt. They screened film showing the two dead men and the prisoner, and all three were soon identified. The wounded survivor was Captain Wynand du Toit and the dead were Sergeant Louis van Breda and Corporal Rowland Liebenberg.

On May 24 Pik Botha told newsmen in Cape Town that the South African government was eager to discuss the Cabinda incident with the Angolan government and arrange for the return of Du Toit and the bodies of his comrades. Botha also released the text of a long self-exculpatory message Pretoria had sent to the Angolan government. In it he reminded the Angolans that they had ignored repeated requests from Pretoria to desist from training and aiding ANC insurgents; "disconcerting evidence" was available to show that Angola was allowing both movements to use its soil as a training

Below
A haggard, wounded Captain Wynand du Toit in a Luanda hospital soon after being captured in Cabinda

area and launching-pad.

"It is an established principle of international law that a state may not permit or encourage on its territory activities for the purpose of carrying out acts of violence in the territory of another state," the message read. "It is equally well-established that a state has the right to take appropriate steps to protect its own security forces and territorial integrity against such acts.

"That is why the South African government ... has no alternative but to take whatever action it deems appropriate for the protection of the people of South Africa from such acts of violence."

Viljoen issued another statement in which he denied that Du Toit and his group had been trying to blow up oil installations or had been carrying sabotage weapons, in spite of the Angolans' insistence that the men had been armed with silenced firearms, incendiary bombs and 16 "contact mines", although it was not clear whether the last referred to pressure mines (devices set off by pressure) or adhesive ('limpet') mines.

The Angolans immediately rejected Pretoria's overtures, disclosed further details of the abortive raid and announced their intention of laying a complaint with the UN Security Council. On May 28 they paraded a haggard Du Toit at a press conference, where he read out a halting but detailed description of how he and his group had been on the way to blow up a key oil depot in order to cause a "considerable economic setback to the Angolan government" when they were discovered and attacked. He added: "We were not looking for ANC or Swapo, we were attacking Gulf Oil." Du Toit also made the damaging admission that he had been carrying Unita propaganda leaflets which were to have been left at the scene because "our attack was to have been claimed by Unita". South African psychologists examined the film and concluded that Du Toit had been brainwashed to some extent, but this did little to soften the embarrassment. The South Africans had been caught with their hands well and truly in the cookie jar.

Department of Information and Propaganda director Paulino Joao told the assembled journalists that if the attack had succeeded "we would have lost 30 million dollars" worth of crude oil, 200 million dollars in equipment and another 250 million dollars in lost production during reconstruction ... This action was undertaken to destroy Malongo and to cripple the Angolan government".

Joao's statement was no exaggeration. Cabinda was so important to Angola that it could be described as Luanda's Achilles heel. With the Benguela railway unable to perform its most lucrative function - transporting copper ore from Zaire and Zambia - and the north-eastern diamond mines unable to work at full capacity because of Unita activity, the oil pumped out by Gulf Oil and other American companies was responsible for about 90 percent of Angola's foreign-exchange earnings and enabled it to pay for the 30 000-odd Cuban troops who kept it in power. That made it a prime economic target, and in the eyes of the world the circumstantial evidence was strong enough to condemn the South Africans; and so in the next few weeks the South African government was subjected to a sustained attack of abuse such as it had not had to endure for a long time.

By coincidence the annual defence debate took place just after the Cabinda incident. In his opening speech in the House of Assembly Magnus Malan denied accusations that South Africa was engaged in destabilisation or had violated the Lusaka Agreement, and dismissed as being "out of touch with reality" any claims that the incident had created a credibility problem for the SADF. The Cabinda incident, he contended, had not involved destabilisation of Angola or interference in Angola's affairs because the target had been not the state of Angola but the ANC and Swapo.

This did not appease the Leader of the Opposition, Dr Frederik van Zyl Slabbert, who accused Malan of that most heinous of crimes, telling "obvious lies" to Parliament. During Operation Savannah, he recalled, Parliament and the rest of the country had been the "victims of systematic deception" because John Vorster and the Cabinet "simply deliberately did not tell the truth to Parliament ... And now the government quite blatantly admits that we were correct then, and if necessary they would lie to us again and do the same thing all over".

One of Slabbert's co-members of the Progressive Federal Party, Graham McIntosh, went even further and accused Malan of exporting "sabotage, destabilisation, covert operations and insurgency" which "has been covered up for most South Africans by lies, denials, black propaganda, disinformation and the cynical use of the Defence and Internal Security Acts". Malan, he said, was "the Gaddafi of Southern Africa", a remark he later withdrew, along with various others, after being reprimanded by Slabbert.

Criticism from overseas was equally ferocious. The prestigious Washington Post said the raid could have been timed to damage an Angolan mission to the United States which had arrived to seek capital with which to expand the Cabinda oil installations (the loan was granted, mainly as a result of lobbying by the American companies involved there). In Havana, Fidel Castro came out on May 29 with a pugnacious speech in which he vowed that his soldiers would stay in Angola till SWA/Namibian independence was assured, and that if necessary he would send extra contingents.

The Angolans informed Pretoria that as a result of the raid they were breaking off all negotiations with South Africa; Pik Botha hit back by saying that it was "revealing to note that the Luanda government has not denied that it is providing facilities to the ANC and Swapo, and that it is assisting them in their planning of acts of violence against the peoples of South Africa and SWA/Namibia", hinting that the government might start moving towards an internal settlement on its own initiative if the United States was agreeable.

Unita, meanwhile, issued a statement denying that a South African unit had been responsible for the raid, since "only the ingenuous could believe the South African government would in any way attack the interests of the United States, wherever they may be". At the same time it did not directly claim responsibility for the raid. In view of the overwhelming evidence to the contrary, this denial was not accorded any respect.

The Unita denial was obviously the result of top-secret talks Pik Botha held with Savimbi in the first days of June, but which would not be revealed for another three weeks. The talks centred on the implications of the Cabinda incident; Savimbi assured Botha that he would be willing to hold talks with Luanda in a bid for national reconciliation, and that he would not attempt to attack the Gulf Oil installations if the company management was willing to sit down and talk with him.

On June 3 the South African government was compelled to give its assurance to the US ambassador in South Africa, Herman Nickel, that the country would not be a party to any attacks on American installations or personnel anywhere in the world, but also took the opportunity to add that the Angolans were using the Cabinda incident as a pretext for breaking off negotiations on the main obstacle to implementation of Resolution 435 – the withdrawal of Cuban troops. He also warned that although the 60 South Africans who had been stationed at Calueque had now been withdrawn, after an undertaking by the Angolans to provide the necessary security, "South African forces would have no alternative but to take appropriate action" if a 1978 situation recurred and Swapo bases were established in the shallow area north of the border.

The assurance did not mollify the Americans. On June 4 Frank Wisner said he was prepared to take note of South Africa's assurances that US property would not be attacked, that Pretoria remained committed to Resolution 435 and that the Calueque detachment had been withdrawn "but we are not out of the woods. The issue remains very active and of great concern to the United States government. We are continuing our discussions on an urgent basis with the South African government". The US still had doubts about parts of the South African explanation of the raid, he added, and confirmed that one of them concerned the reports that the South Africans had been carrying explosives when they were supposed to have been on an intelligence-gathering mission.

On June 6 the Angolan ambassador to the United Nations, Elisio de Figueiredo, added fuel to the flames by claiming there were still South African troops north of the border "in spite of the pathetic lies of Mr Botha". It was "difficult to specify figures", he added, "but we know and we have proof of the continuing presence of certain South African forces within the Angolan territory". But De Figueiredo did not produce such proof, and his statement elicited no more than the standard condemnatory phrases.

On June 13, however, an Angola Defence Ministry statement broadcast by Angop accused South Africa of 22 airspace violations and said it had massed 20 000 men and 90-odd aircraft along the border, adding that "previous experience has shown that an increase in activity by the South African Air Force and Army at the start of the dry season is a sign that a new invasion of our territory is being prepared". The following day Angola called for an urgent Security Council meeting to discuss the alleged threat; in his letter to the council De Figueiredo claimed that a threat to international peace and security existed because of "the continuous acts of aggression and violence perpetuated (sic) by the racist armed forces of South Africa, resulting in the violation of the territorial integrity and national sovereignty" of Angola.

At the same time the US displayed its distinct displeasure by having its UN ambassador, Jose Sorzano, describe the situation as "very serious" in the Security Council and urge that "we speak together with one voice" in rejecting the forth-coming transitional government as a body with "no conceivable purpose".

He added that "no one can be permitted to take power into their own hands, or to proclaim themselves the leaders of the Namibian people or the government of Namibia", although (as the cynics in South Africa observed) this was more or less what the General Assembly had done by declaring Swapo to be the only legitimate voice of the SWA/ Namibian people, without making any effort to seek reliable evidence about the popular will.

Sorzano struck a comparatively conciliatory note, however, by maintaining that a Cuban withdrawal from Angola was a practical possibility through continuing negotiations, and adding: "Even in the wake of the events of the past few days, it is our view that the door remains open to a settlement." While deploring South African violations of Angolan territory and complaining that the achievements (unspecified) of the Lusaka Agreement had been marred by the Cabinda incident, the US was "heartened by South African withdrawal from Calueque, and the reports that co-operation between South African and Angolan forces continued along the border."

But the deterioration in South African-American relations had not been arrested. On June 17 – just two days after P W Botha formally installed the "Government of National Unity" in Windhoek – a US Embassy spokesman in Pretoria announced that ambassador Herman Nickel had been recalled, and spoke rather unguardedly about the South African attack on the Malongo depot. Pik Botha immediately counter-attacked with a statement in which he took great exception to these remarks, saying he had "personally conveyed the facts" to Nickel, and that when invited to produce proof that an attack instead of reconnaissance had been intended, Nickel "relied on statements made by Captain Wynand du Toit ... I pointed out that it was obvious that Captain Du Toit was either drugged or forced under duress to make that statement, or both".

On June 20 the US State Department leaked a story to the press that its detailed investigation of the Cabinda incident "casts doubt on all the assurances South Africa has given". For one thing, one source said, Pretoria's version was full of "glaring geographical and mileage errors" because "Malongo just wasn't on any logical route between where they say they landed and what they say they were looking for". A week later the State Department announced that Herman Nickel's return to South Africa would be postponed a while longer to see whether Pretoria's actions – not just the Cabinda raid but another on the Botswana capital of Gaborone in search of ANC operatives – were "simply an aberration or something long-term".

To the South African public it was becoming increasingly clear that the elaborate JMC operation had accomplished nothing, and this was confirmed on June 30 when Major-General Georg Meiring announced in Windhoek that a two-day external raid nicknamed "Operation Boswilger" had just ended.

Boswilger – a follow-up operation which had escalated as it went on, rather than an elaborately planned incursion like some of its predecessors – was set in motion when insurgents operating from bases in the shallow area detonated an explosive charge which damaged a bridge between Epali and Ondangwa, sabotaged 20 telephone poles, un-leashed a brief stand-off mortar bombardment on the Eenhana base and detonated a bomb at the Ongwediva Teachers' Training College.

On June 29 the follow-up began, with SWATF reaction teams setting off on the insurgents' trail in mine-protected vehicles, their orders being (as the OC Sector 10, Brigadier Joep Joubert, said later) to follow the spoor "even if this meant crossing the border. In other words, the order was for the execution of a hot-pursuit operation".

The teams rolled over the border at 9am, killed nine insurgents in the initial contact and then followed the others up to 40km inside Angola, systematically wiping out their bases. On the first day 43 insurgents were killed in 23 different contacts, and on the second day 14 died in 13 contacts. The force then withdrew, having lost one man and captured large supplies of weapons and ammunition. The South Africans had taken care to warn the Angolans that they were coming, and on the one occasion when the two forces had come face to face, Joubert said later, they "parted on friendly enough terms".

Obviously mindful of international sensitivity about actions against Angola following the Cabinda incident, Pik Botha wasted no time in claiming that the raid was in accordance with the letter and spirit of the Lusaka Agreement, since "the government (of Angola) undertook to see that Swapo would not continue to carry out its campaign of terror against South West Africa from Angolan territory". In addition, he added, the operation was in accordance with accepted principles of international law because its aim had been "to protect the people of South West Africa against aggression which is being planned and executed from outside South West Africa".

On July 3 Joubert made South Africa's attitude clear by warning that more operations like Boswilger would take place if Swapo activities continued inside SWA/Namibia. The "unseasonal upsurge" in Plan activity, he said, was due to the cessation of security-force activities after the withdrawal from Angola; since the JMC had been dissolved there had been 82 abductions, 29 murders, 37 landmine explosions, 41 acts of sabotage, 21 attacks and 10 ambushes, with a total civilian death-toll of 34.

Boswilger brought Plan losses for the year to 375 and knocked out an estimated 18 percent of the insurgent cadres in the shallow area, but according to military intelligence an estimated 150 to 250 insurgents remained active – a large number by the standards of the low-intensity border war.

None of these were operating in Kavango, however, where June had seen the end of what had remained of the Plan campaign that had been crippled by the capture of Akushinda in October of 1984. To make sure it did not recur, the security forces were set to implementing two custom-designed projects, Operation Opeet, an intensive patrol programme later described by the OC Sector 20 (Kavango), Colonel Deon Ferreira, as "the most successful border-control operation we've ever had", and Operation Concert, aimed at the restoration of sound civilian administration.

The Angolan civil war across the border was raging as well, to judge by unconfirmed reports from both Angola and Unita. On July 9 Fapla had killed 2 486 Unita soldiers in the first half of the year and given amnesty to 111 more, according to Angop, which added that more than 1 000 weapons and 180 000 rounds of ammunition had been confiscated, and more than 40 tons of arms, equipment and explosives parachuted to Unita from SAAF aircraft had been seized at Malanje. Angop added that South Africans were still occupying part of Angolan territory (although it did not specify where) and had concentrated 20 000 troops with 80 to 90 aircraft along the border, ready for an "invasion … at any moment". There had also been 71 known violations of Angolan airspace by SAAF aircraft (an SADF spokesman noted merely that "this is the same propaganda already distributed on June 12 … and is aimed at obtaining international reaction").

Unita, on the other hand, claimed to have killed 15 Fapla troops and five Cubans in raids in three provinces between June 27 and July 4 and shot down a MiG-21 near Luena. In the next fortnight or so it claimed to have killed 91 Fapla and five Cubans in nine days of fighting in six provinces for a loss of seven killed and 11 wounded, and then 112 Fapla and 10 Cubans between July 18 and 25, capturing large quantities of arms, for a loss of 11 killed, 27 wounded and three missing.

In mid-July the Angolans' war effort received a blow when the Reagan government repealed the "Clark Amendment" of Operation Savannah days, the result being that for the first time in nine years the Americans could openly provide Unita with military aid. Needless to say the repeal so deeply angered the Angolans that they broke contact with the US, but its usefulness as a means of coercing Luanda into addressing once more the issue of withdrawing Angola's 30 000-odd Cubans could not be denied and was subsequently proved valid.

The MPLA had more pressing matters to occupy its attention. For some time it had been setting the stage for an attempt at annihilating Unita. Earlier in the year its East German-trained internal security service had launched a campaign to infiltrate Unita, kill or capture its agents and activate the local population against the rebels. Now Luanda was assembling all its available assets for what it had nicknamed "Operation Congress II", the largest offensive it had ever mounted against Unita. Led and advised by Russians and Cubans, it was a force of impressive size by Southern African standards: thousands of men - including a large number of Swapo's semi-conventional troops and ANC members who happened to be training in Angola - backed by tanks, artillery and late-model Soviet aircraft. The intention was to place Unita's lightly armed forces under maximum strain by advancing simultaneously on the Cazombo Salient in the east and Mavinga in the south-east, thus forcing Savimbi to fight on two fronts with no hope of reinforcing his presence on either. It would appear that the Angolans hoped to have taken one or both of their objectives by September 3, when a conference of non-aligned nations was scheduled to start in Luanda.

At the end of July Congress II began to roll, and soon the combatants were involved in running fights of various degrees of intensity. Fighting on their home ground, the Unita forces visited much death and destruction on their slow-moving opponents, but the Fapla columns proved unstoppable, and by early September they were uncomfortably near the outer defensive lines of both Cazombo town and Mavinga.

In SWA/Namibia Brigadier Joubert's "unprecedented upsurge" continued. In August there were 20 mine incidents – an activity previously unknown at this time of the year - and sabotage cases had increased by 100 percent since the beginning of the year. In addition, military intelligence began picking up evidence that Swapo planned to launch a major infiltration as far as Tsumeb and Windhoek when the short rainy season started in November.

Years of attrition and poor recruiting had cut Swapo's available trained manpower from about 16 000 in 1977 to about 8 500, of whom only a fraction were available for deployment in SWA/Namibia, but the insurgent high command had addressed this deficiency by taking the unusual step of withdrawing several hundred men from its Eighth Battalion - one of the "conventional" battalions which was permanently deployed in support of Fapla along the rim of Savimbi-held territory - for retraining in insurgency-style bushcraft. The plan

was to concentrate the new men in the Evale-Anhanca-Dova area, give them several weeks of motivational and operational instruction, and then launch them over the border as soon as the rains began.

The South Africans did not take immediate action. Then on September 14 they captured two insurgents from Plan's "Charlie Detachment" and tracked their 30 or so comrades till the spoor disappeared into Angola. Joubert then obtained permission to launch a pre-emptive operation, which was nicknamed "Egret", and on September 15 just under 500 men of 101 (Ovambo) Battalion's vehicle-mounted "Romeo Mikes" (reaction-force teams) crossed into Angola.

Egret was South Africa's first deliberate incursion into Angola since Operation Askari, and the raiders operated under strict constraints. They were instructed to avoid contact with Fapla, refrain from operating further north than 120km from the border and stay at least 5km from any population centre which had a military presence (there was one accidental encounter when a Romeo Mike team burst out of the bush and found itself within pistol-shot of a Fapla-held village; negotiations took place in an amicable spirit and the team vanished into the bush again, its commander heaving a sigh of relief).

For several days the highly mobile teams combed the almost trackless bush of the Evale-Anhanca-Dova area, relying on their expert trackers and on information freely supplied by the local inhabitants. SAAF aircraft flew a number of reconnaissance flights and carried out at least one ground attack, in the vicinity of Nehone. The Romeo Mikes killed 15 insurgents in nine separate contacts, captured another 103 (including 49 in civilian clothes), turned up several large arms caches and scattered the prospective infiltrators, hundreds of whom hastily headed northwards on foot, on bicycles and in vehicles to escape what might well have been a large South African operation. Fortunately for the fleeing Eighth Battalion men, who proved to be totally ignorant of standard bush-warfare techniques like anti-tracking tactics, the attackers lacked both the manpower and the freedom of action to follow through.

As was to be expected, Egret set off a renewed international uproar composed of equal parts of indignation, cynicism and confusion – the last coming about when Angola's ever-agile propagandists seized on this heaven-sent opportunity to accuse South Africa of sending in troops and combat aircraft to help Unita to fight off its Fapla attackers in the Mavinga-Jamba area. This was patently untrue, at least as far as the Romeo Mikes were concerned, since the Fapla-Unita fighting was taking place hundreds of kilometres to the east, but the Angolan claims and South Africa's diminished credibility after the Cabinda incident served to muddy the waters so thoroughly that Egret and the Mavinga-Jamba fighting became inextricably connected.

The United States deplored the incursion, saying that "no previous facts were brought to our attention (by the South Africans) that would warrant such an action"; France condemned the attack as being "in disdain of international rights"; the Portuguese expressed "deep concern"; and the British conveyed their displeasure through diplomatic channels. Swapo spokesmen in London declined to comment on the raid "because it does not involve Swapo". Considering the indisputable evidence found, this was an outright lie.

Above
Operation Egret:
With the strong possibilities that insurgents are lurking near by, this 101 Battalion soldier throws the traditional courtesies overboard and enters a kraal by pulling loose a stake in the rear part of the stockade

Below
Operation Egret:
Huddled in front of the radio set in the forward compartment of the command Casspir, a team commander issues orders to elements of his small, highly mobile force

The uproar obscured the fact that Savimbi was in serious trouble, with heavy pressure being exerted on him on both the Mavinga and Cazombo fronts. On September 18, as the Romeo Mike teams roamed around the Dova-Evale-Anhanca area, he had to make a painful choice and decided to abandon the Cazombo front in order to concentrate his assets on preserving Mavinga.

In the final analysis there was no real choice. Mavinga was the key to Savimbi's success and, indeed, to his continued existence. If the Angolans took it they would control the all-weather runway that was Savimbi's door to the outside world, and would also have acquired a handy staging-post for the attack on his headquarters 270km away at Jamba. Till this time Jamba had always been virtually immune from attack because of the threat of aerial retaliation from the Mapacha air base in Caprivi, but for the increasingly confident Angolans, backed now by the extensive air defences they had been steadily building in the south, the SAAF threat was not as frightening as it had been. It was clear that they would head for Jamba if Mavinga fell, and the rains were still at least a month away. Morale was still high among Savimbi's men, but he and his officers knew that Mavinga – and thus Jamba – were under such serious threat that they were ready to move their headquarters to an alternative location deeper in the bush.

The quantity and quality of aid he was receiving from South Africa remained a burning but unanswered question. Angola continued to accuse Pretoria of sending combat aircraft and troops to Unita's aid, to which Magnus Malan would say only that Pretoria was providing "material, humanitarian and moral" aid to the rebels. Savimbi admitted that South African as well as French and International Red Cross doctors were treating his wounded, but strenuously denied that South African troops were fighting alongside his forces and actually offered to take journalists to see for themselves (confirmation of a circumstantial kind is that the only known South African fatality in the fighting was a medical orderly, Lance-Corporal Hans Fidler). Weeks later he was quoted by London Times correspondent Michael Hornsby as telling of Unita "having been given more arms by Pretoria (in September) than in the previous 10 years". At no stage, then or later, would Savimbi admit that his troops had enjoyed SAAF combat support, but it is known that during September the South African high command authorised limited air strikes at Fapla concentrations and sent Savimbi a small artillery force.

Vague though it was, Malan's statement on aiding Savimbi was a milestone of sorts, since it was the first time the South African government had openly admitted that it had continued to support Unita after Operation Savannah, but his amplifying remarks were more important than that long-delayed admission. South Africa would lend such aid "when necessary and in our security interests", he said, and was prepared to cease doing so "on condition that all foreign forces are withdrawn from Angola". Malan's statement made it clear that Pretoria's belief in the value of Savimbi had not changed, and that it was regarded as essential for Unita to stay in place till the short rainy season started in November and forced the heavily motorised Angolans with their notoriously feeble logistic back-up system to abandon the offensive.

By September 22 Operation Egret was over and the Romeo Mikes were back at base. In spite of the furore the operation had caused, the South Africans were satisfied with the results. They had thoroughly disrupted the intended rainy-season infiltration and had captured a rich harvest of documents; one letter, taken from the pouch of a dead intelligence officer, provided much food for thought because it confirmed that Plan morale was low at ground level.

Simultaneous internal action taken by the police while Egret was in progress resulted in the arrest of five agents and the confiscation of grenades, assault rifles, mines and 384kg of explosives – 124kg of it in Katatura township, where most of Windhoek's blacks lived.

Unita suffered further reverses as the month drew to a close. By the last week in September

Left
**Operation Egret:
A young Swapo officer
grimaces in agony after
a rifle-shot broke his leg
while he was running
across open ground**

the rebels had been driven out of the Cazombo Salient and the southern Fapla column was menacing Mavinga. The ground troops had already crossed the Lomba River, a little over 30km to the north, while MiG-21 and MiG-23 aircraft from the air bases at Menongue and Lubango regularly bombed the increasingly battered little town's vitally important runway on which SAAF transports carrying supplies landed every night after hedge-hopping across the border to keep below the Angolan radar coverage.

Then the tide turned. The Fapla force crossed the Lomba River and was within 32km of Mavinga when it was stopped in its tracks by a combination of Unita ground troops, South African artillery fire and SAAF bombing and strafing attacks. After some brisk fighting by the Unita ground troops, the Angolans began to withdraw to avoid being trapped by the fast-approaching short rainy season. Savimbi – and the South Africans – had achieved a few months' breathing-space, but the Unita leader did not rest on his laurels. His men stayed active, not only in the south but also in other areas further afield, where he had taken the opportunity of stepping up the insurgency's tempo while resident Fapla troops were away serving in Congress II.

Unita continued to claim that large numbers of Russians were stiffening the Angolan troops, and on September 28 one of its Lisbon spokesmen warned that if Moscow's military involvement did not cease "we would not be surprised if South Africa, determined to protect its interests in the region, decided to make war on Angola to force the Soviets out. There is a clear danger of the conflict escalating to unprecedented levels because of the massive Soviet involvement in Angola". This was not quite true, since Soviet personnel continued to be specialists rather than fighting troops, but what worried Unita was that the Angolans had not yet quite given up on Congress II and were engaged in rebuilding its forces for a resumption of the operation in mid-December.

The Angolans apparently concurred with Savimbi's view that a South African intervention

was not to be dismissed. Spokesmen said that Luanda feared a major South African attack, noting repeated references by Pretoria to the "Soviet threat" and pointing out that "they have used this pretext before for major incursions. We seem to be seeing a renewed build-up of pressure by Pretoria". In the meantime, the spokesmen added, the South Africans were flying repeated ground-attack sorties against the Fapla troops, had shot down six helicopters during the attack on Mavinga and had infantry serving with Unita. To all these accusations the SADF replied only by referring to Malan's earlier statement about providing Unita with "humanitarian, material and moral" support.

Meanwhile, the Angolans' deepest suspicions had been aroused by a visit to the State Department on September 26 by two high-ranking South African foreign-affairs officials, former UN ambassador Dave Steward and Les Manley, both veterans of the diplomatic wars. A State Department official refused to discuss the visit, but the Angolans believed the South Africans were there to persuade the Americans to back Unita, and they were right. The Clark Amendment had been repealed, but the Americans were still in two minds as to the form of help they should give, and Steward's task was to prod them into action.

By now the vigorous Unita public relations and lobbying campaign in the US had found many influential supporters, among them various anti-communist and right-wing parliamentarians whose suspicions had been aroused by the enormous shipments of Russian weapons and munitions to Fapla since 1982, and it was reliably reported that both the Department of Defence and the Central Intelligence Agency were urging the US government to resume military aid to the rebels. On the other hand, aid for Savimbi was equally strongly opposed by an unlikely amalgam of left-wingers, liberals and oil executives whose companies enjoyed a lucrative and contented relationship with the Angolan government – in fact, the US had R1 350 million invested in Angola and was Luanda's biggest trading partner.

On September 27 in Windhoek, meanwhile, the National Assembly unanimously passed a bill empowering it to establish a constitutional council.

On October 2 the Angolans' suspicions about Steward's and Manley's visit were confirmed when parliamentarians Claude Pepper of the Democratic Party and Jack Kemp of the Republicans, introduced a bill in the House of Representatives which would provide Unita with the equivalent of R35 million for humanitarian aid, and news leaked out that the National Security Council was engaged in reviewing the policy banning military aid to Savimbi.

The following day an unrepentant South Africa was given its second Security Council drubbing in a fortnight. Ambassador Kurt von Schirnding warned that a major Russian-led offensive was advancing on its territory and that "Swapo is sending major units southward as part of the Soviet-directed offensive" in Angola, then unexpectedly tabled a draft resolution calling for the withdrawal, "forthwith and unconditionally", of all foreign forces from Angola and requesting states to refrain from interfering in Angola's domestic affairs "so that self-determination can at last be achieved". The resolution achieved nothing: British delegate Sir John Thompson mocked it by saying: "We agree … What business, then, do the South African forces have in Angola, fighting the legitimate government?" Thompson did not expand on his definition of legitimacy, which was just as well,

seeing that the MPLA had elected itself by force of arms.

Von Schirnding also called for a resumption of talks between Pretoria and Luanda, describing them as "more urgent than ever"; South Africa's call for a total withdrawal of foreign troops from Angola, he said, was a "sincere and serious" attempt to work towards peace. It was a waste of breath. On October 8, after yards of further rhetoric, the Security Council unanimously called on South Africa to get out of Angola and stay out, and recommended (with one abstention, that of the US) that Luanda be helped to strengthen its defences against Pretoria's "escalating aggression". The South Africans were also told to pay the Angolans "full and adequate compensation", which Pretoria ignored as it had ignored similar demands made in the past.

The extent of the Lomba River victory was underlined less than 24 hours later, when the Security Council decided to send three senior diplomats and a support staff of 12 to south-eastern Angola to "evaluate the damage resulting from the invasion by South African forces" before and during the battle at Mavinga: an embarrassed Perez de Cuellar was forced to ask Von Schirnding if South Africa could co-operate in guaranteeing the party's safety. While his staffers grinned openly, Von Schirnding courteously tendered his regrets that he was unable to do so, and said the Secretary-General would have to discuss the matter with Unita, which was in control of the area.

Since this alternative was out of the question, Perez de Cuellar had no option but to entrust his representatives to the protection of Fapla. As a result the mission was a total failure. The team duly visited Cazombo and assessed the damage there, but the nearest they could get to Mavinga was the Menongue military base, where they "heard statements and saw human and material damage", as they put it to him later, before returning to New York.

All this time Savimbi's US representatives continued with their public relations efforts. The MPLA struck back by hiring a PR firm as glossy as Savimbi's, which laid on a goodwill tour led by the chief executive of Sonangol, the Angolan state-owned oil company, and then took the extraordinary step of scheduling a rock concert in Luanda for December 14 and persuading such musicians as Bruce Springsteen, Stevie Wonder and Miles Davis to perform in it.

On November 4 Unita announced in Lisbon that it had killed "at least" 93 government soldiers and one Cuban during the past two weeks in attacks and ambushes which included an attack on a diamond mine. While the figures could not be confirmed, the report indicated that the insurgency was reviving in the north-east, even though the Cazombo Salient was still in government hands.

On November 13 a small group of Plan insurgents carried out a brief stand-off bombardment of the Ruacana scheme. An immediate security-force reaction resulted in six of the group being shot dead and one captured, while another decamped with a follow-up force hot on his heels. He was shot dead on November 14, the day UN ambassador Von Schirnding found himself back in the dock before the Security Council, which was sitting to hear argument in favour of comprehensive sanctions against South Africa to dislodge it from SWA/Namibia.

Von Schirnding sprang a surprise on the council by stating that the South African govern-

Above
A captured insurgent, his eyes covered with a makeshift blindfold fashioned out of a wound dressing, is brought in to the team headquarters to be picked up by a helicopter and taken back for interrogation

Below
The team commander stands astride the wounded man after saving his life by running to him, forcing the over-excited soldiers to stop shooting at him. The medical orderly (left) assesses the wound before applying a pressure bandage and splinting the insurgent's broken leg

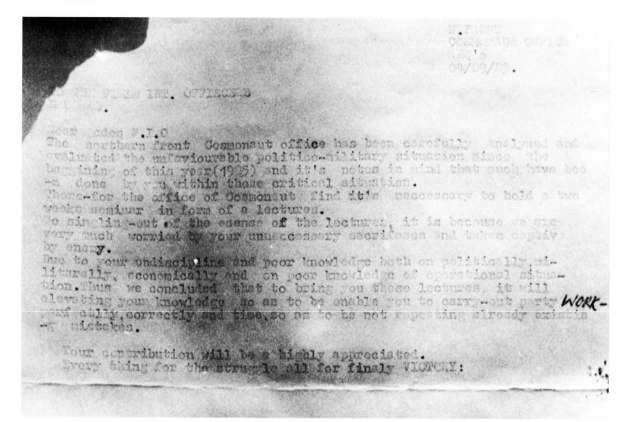

ment had formally opted for an electoral system of proportional representation instead of Whitehall-style constituencies represented by single members, thereby facilitating the movement towards independence, although he said the government was acting at the request of the territory's transitional government, which the UN did not recognise. While some African diplomats reportedly regarded Von Schirnding's announcement as a hopeful sign, it did absolutely nothing to take the steam out of various council members' demands for sanctions.

Late in the month the American government finally opted for direct military aid to Savimbi. While briefing newspaper editors and columnists on another matter, President Ronald Reagan said his government felt that covert aid for Savimbi "would have much more chance of success right now" than any of the humanitarian-aid bills presently pending in the US Congress – a mystifying statement except to those who understood American political practice, and knew that covert aid needed only to be approved by the intelligence committees of the House of Representatives and the US Senate, whereas an overt aid package would have to be put to a full vote of both houses.

Reagan's disinclination to put the issue to a full vote was vindicated when his announcement was greeted with opposition from an assortment of anti-Savimbi enthusiasts, ranging from 101 parliamentarians to lobbyists, business men and political activists. A White House spokesman back-pedalled by saying that Reagan had not yet made "final decisions" on the matter, but to many observers it was a foregone conclusion that the president would follow the wishes of his basically conservative anti-communist constituency.

Strangely enough, this did not prevent another round of peace talks between the US and Angola taking place – the first since the repeal of the Clark Amendment in July. On November 26 Chester Crocker arrived in Lusaka for a two-day meeting with Interior Minister Alexandre Rodrigues. The talks ran their full course, after which Crocker said guardedly that "from the standpoint of the US

Government we had a useful discussion", adding that Washington wanted to "re-energise" the relationship which had broken down after the Clark Amendment's repeal. Rodrigues was somewhat freer in his comments, describing the talks as "very useful" and saying that there would be a follow-up meeting in Luanda within a few weeks.

As Crocker headed for home, the UN mission which had failed so completely to reach Mavinga in October finally issued a report which placed the material damage done by South African forces in the recent fighting at 36 million dollars. In Cazombo, the report said, the mission had been told of extensive South African supply airlifts and the attachment of South African specialists to Unita units; during the Unita withdrawal "largely deliberate and systematic" damage was done, assessed at 604 000 dollars. Because the mission had not been able to visit Mavinga, it had had to rely on accounts of how the Fapla advance had been stopped by Unita and South African troops and SAAF air strikes. The total cost amounted to 36,7 million dollars, and the "real cost (was) substantially higher". It was an interesting document but totally irrelevant, since the South Africans simply ignored it.

The extent of Angola's financial problem was revealed on December 3, when Dos Santos told a party congress that because of the threat from South Africa and Unita, more than one-third of Angola's budget would be spent on defence in coming years. According to informed sources the increase was not due simply to the war, however, but also to a miscalculation by the Angolan government, which had not taken into account the steady drop in the world price of oil – the mainstay of the national economy – which declined from 25 US dollars a barrel in 1975 till it bottomed out at less than 10 dollars in 1986. The sources said that because of the projected shortfall the Angolan government was being forced to raid some of its cherished educational and social-welfare budgets to obtain the means with which to prosecute the war, which still took top priority.

In fact, as Dos Santos addressed the congress Luanda was already preparing to launch another offensive against Unita as soon as the short rainy season ended. It was an unusual time for a Fapla attack, but it was obviously aimed at disrupting insurgent activity once the long rainy season began in late January. Long convoys began heading towards Menongue and Cuito Cuanavale, and as many as 15 flights of aircraft a day were ferrying arms and equipment to the base from Luanda and Lobito.

On December 8 Unita's Lisbon spokesman, Alcides Sakala, broke the news of the build-up and claimed his organisation had already killed 28 Cubans and shot down two helicopters in an attack on a resupply convoy of 230 lorries headed for Cuito Cuanavale. On December 9 Sakala reported Unita had shot down a MiG-23 and an Mi-8 helicopter in separate actions, adding that the rains were creating a mud problem and "it is not known at this stage if they are going to utilise tanks, the soil is getting soggy". On the same day another Unita spokesman claimed there had been "saturation bombing" of rebel territory and that 3 500 Fapla troops, aided by a 1 500-man Cuban regiment, had begun moving south from Cuito Cuanavale. It was moving slowly, however, and there had not been any battles yet, he added.

Some observers suggested at the time that Unita was stressing a Cuban and Soviet build-up in an attempt to pressure the "doves" in Washington who had persuaded the Reagan administration to hold off temporarily on providing covert military support for Unita, and the events of the next few days indicated that there was some truth in this belief, although there is no doubt that a continuation of Congress II was in motion.

On December 9 the usually well-informed Washington Post quoted official sources as saying that the US government had "tentatively" decided to give Unita about 30 million dollars (about R65 million) as the first instalment of a covert aid programme, but added that the payment had been delayed till at least January because the State Department hoped to use the threat of support to Unita to pressure the Angolan government into negotiating on the withdrawal of its Cuban troops; the decision had been taken informally at an inter-agency meeting in mid-November at which Secretary of State George Shultz had been able to fend off CIA and Department of Defence pressure for an immediate commencement of aid.

Two days later the US Senate voted 58 to 39 against a Republican-sponsored attempt to attach a 125 million-dollar overt-aid amendment to a huge omnibus spending bill totalling near 1 250 billion dollars, on the grounds that it was not germane, although the senators in favour of the amendment argued that the funds were desperately needed to help the rebels to defend themselves against a major Russian-backed offensive. The Senate vote was interpreted as a sign that the US Congress would not approve overt aid for Unita before the end of the year – although, thanks to the peculiarities of the American parliamentary system, Reagan could provide "covert" aid by the simple expedient of obtaining the support of the congressional intelligence committees, and according to congressional officials it was likely that a firmer government decision would be taken after Crocker's scheduled meeting with Rodrigues in Luanda later in the month.

Around this time the Fapla force about which Unita spokesmen had screamed so loudly finally ran into the rebels. A two-day fight ensued which cost 127 Fapla and 12 Cuban soldiers were killed, and for practical purposes this ended the advance.

Till December 20 nothing more was heard of either the Angolan fighting or the SWA/Namibian peace negotiations. Then, as Crocker and Rodrigues met in Luanda and agreed in principle that the Cuban troops would leave Angola after 10 years of support for the Luanda government, informed sources in Pretoria said that a small contingent of South Africans had penetrated deep into Angola. The SADF declined to comment, but additional information was that the raiding party had travelled all the way to Cuvelai, where it had killed at least six insurgents and captured extensive munitions and supplies which included Libyan and, for the first time, Kenyan uniforms. The news then achieved quasi-official status when the South African Broadcasting Corporation confirmed that the incursion was still in progress.

The raid had nothing to do with the now-abandoned offensive against Unita, but, as with Operation Egret, was immediately connected to it. The Angolans were not about to let such a good opportunity go by, and two days later issued a statement saying that four South African battalions, backed by tanks and aircraft, had moved into Angola between December 15 and 17 "under the false pretext of an alleged pursuit of Swapo fighters". They had now been reinforced by a fifth battalion, while two motorised-infantry brigades were waiting near the border, "ready to launch a new large-scale aggressive action", and SAAF aircraft had been making frequent flights deep into Angolan territory in south-east Moxico and Cuando-Cubango provinces, where Unita was resisting the government offensive.

SADF spokesmen declined once again to comment on these allegations, but a Swapo spokesman in Luanda was less inhibited. "No Swapo guerrillas were killed in these last few days," he insisted. "South Africa always finds an excuse to invade Angola. In the areas where the South African troops are reported to be now, we have only refugees."

There was some truth in the Angolan allegations about troop movements, although not as regards their tasking or areas of activity. Security-force elements had crossed the border to sweep the shallow area, and more troops had been deployed in parts of Eastern Caprivi after military intelligence had reported that Swapo had decided to reopen a front there.

In the meantime, the US State Department's resistance to immediate aid for Unita was beginning to crumble under a combined assault by a coalition of "hawks" which included the armed forces, the CIA, the National Security Council and various conservative parliamentarians.

The State Department's view was that aid to Savimbi, widely regarded as a South African surrogate, could ruin the US's role as a mediator and torpedo the negotiations on a Cuban withdrawal and thus the entire SWA/Namibian independence process. The pro-Unita lobby dismissed these arguments with increasing success, so much so that according to government sources it was possible the first sums of money would be flowing to Unita through CIA channels by February unless Crocker produced an 11th-hour solution. The Washington Post claimed the initial sums might be between R21m and R40m, while congressional sources added the aid might include anti-tank missiles and Red-Eye and Stinger anti-aircraft missiles.

Within SWA/Namibia the security forces were meanwhile preparing for Plan's traditional rainy-season offensive, following intelligence reports that supply convoys were moving south from Swapo bases in central Angola to cadres lying up in the shallow area, accompanied by political commissars tasked to brief the insurgents before they exfiltrated.

Cautious optimism prevailed about the size of the infiltration, however. Plan activity over the past 12 months had been the lowest in three or four years; the security forces had initiated almost all contacts and, although there had been no major operations, had killed more insurgents (590) than during the equivalent period in 1984 – but 56 civilians had died in landmine and other incidents and 179 had been abducted.

The simple fact was that Plan's trained manpower reservoir, which had always been comparatively small, was beginning to run dry as a result of losses in external operations, the steady attrition inside SWA/Namibia and its heavy commitments in Fapla's war against Unita. It was part of a downward curve, and at SWATF Head-quarters General Meiring confidently predicted that Plan was likely to continue following "the path of least resistance" by concentrating on sabotage attacks, which had the lowest risk factor of any insurgent activity.

Scenting success, the South Africans kept up the pressure. On December 26 SADF sources leaked the news that the Cuvelai raiding party was still in Angola, and that so far it had killed 15 insurgents in eight contacts, destroyed seven caches of arms and knocked out a temporary base. The sources added that the sweep in the shallow area was still in progress and that the insurgents had withdrawn from Caprivi, although they were expected to try again by another route.

On December 30, as Angola sombrely cele-brated its 10th year of MPLA rule, Savimbi had the last word for 1985. In an article published in the Political Review, magazine of the Heritage Foun-dation, he predicted that 1986 might be a watershed year in the Angolan war, and that the expected American decision on whether or not to aid Unita could be the determining factor on whether the entire region fell under Soviet domination.

"Not Unita alone, but all of central and southern Africa, awaits the decision by the United States," he said. "With your military and political support, other nations will follow your lead and give us aid … Hesitation, and the refusal to aid Unita in its fight, against the Cubans and Soviets, will be taken as a signal by all the countries in the region that the United States has abandoned them to the Soviets as the West abandoned Czechoslovakia and Eastern Europe to Hitler in 1938 … Zambia, Namibia and Botswana … will be forced to make their political accommodations with the Soviets just as most of eastern Europe fell under Nazi political domination without a shot being fired."

Savimbi made no bones about the fact that he received help from South Africa, adding: "But it is hypocritical of the Soviets to claim that this means we somehow endorse the Pretoria govern-ment. Nor did my acceptance of Chinese military training and aid – when no other nation would help me – make me a Maoist in economics or politics."

Savimbi's analogy between the Angolan situation and pre-World War II Nazi expansionism was finely calculated to stir up as many guilt feelings among the Americans as possible, for he was playing for high stakes. Before the US Congress were two bills asking that Unita be given 27 million dollars in military aid and the same amount in humanitarian help, and the Reagan government was still trying to make up its mind about covert support.

The year began with the South African government still wading through a fog of complaints about its actions against its immediate neighbours, ranging from claims that Pretoria was enforcing strict border control on Lesotho (which was true) to accusations that it had killed nine people in a raid on the Lesotho capital, Maseru, on December 20 (which it strenuously denied and which was probably not true).

Pretoria in turn warned Botswana not to harbour African National Congress insurgents. President Quett Masire promptly denied doing so, then called in various friendly ambassadors to tell them it was feared that the South Africans would soon raid Botswana again. In short order this led to a British call for restraint and a warning by the Commonwealth that any such attack would undermine its current efforts to make an end to apartheid, seeing that it was about to send a seven-member "Eminent Persons Group" to visit the Republic shortly.

In between, almost unnoticed, the border war claimed its first victims during the first days of the new year, when the security forces shot dead four insurgents during a follow-up into Angola which had been launched after a Plan group had killed an Ovambo civilian near Nkongo and wounded another.

On January 9 the yearly war of words began with a Fapla spokesman claiming that a South African force of unspecified size had penetrated 150km into Angola's Cunene province and kidnapped two militiamen near Mupa, adding that SAAF aircraft had been making frequent flights over the southern provinces in the past few days. The SADF refused to comment in any way. This was followed by claims from Dos Santos that three battalions of "regular" troops, backed by armoured vehicles and air support, were operating in the southern Cunene province.

Amid this furore Chester Crocker flew into Luanda on January 9 for a follow-up meeting on his visit in December. His reception was slightly frosty, because news had leaked out that Savimbi was soon to arrive in Washington: according to Angop Dos Santos welcomed Crocker but asked if Savimbi's trip to the US would amount to "a declaration of war" by Washington. Crocker replied that he had come to Luanda for negotiations to "end a sad time for the peoples of Angola and Namibia". According to Angolan officials Dos Santos was considerably more blunt about the issue when the talks began, flatly informing Crocker that Luanda would view as an unfriendly act any resumption of US aid to Unita.

When Crocker had finished in Luanda he flew on to South Africa for talks with government leaders, businessmen and academics. He was still there when, on January 12, Angop claimed that South Africa had formed mixed battalions of its own troops and Unita members and deployed them in Angola, where they had already killed six Fapla soldiers and wounded 47 in an ambush of a military column between Menongue and Cuito Cuanavale. The SADF refused to comment.

There was a grain of truth in this allegation, it would appear from facts which began emerging in 1989. After finally turning back the last-gasp Fapla advance in December, Savimbi had wasted no time in pumping men and material into the Cazombo Salient, where the Angolans had not been able to leave anything but a thinly-spread presence. According to reliable sources it appears SAAF transports were used to ferry the rebels from Mavinga to airstrips north and south-east of Mavinga, and possibly also in lifting supplies and equipment to another airstrip at Lumbala, the former Gago Coutinho, close to the border with Zaire. Savimbi also intensified the insurgency in central Angola and elsewhere.

In Windhoek, meanwhile, security-force analysts were investigating unconfirmed reports that between 48 and 300 Plan insurgents had assembled along Botswana's border with SWA/Namibia. Police mounted what were described as "precautionary" patrols along the Botswana border, with the army standing by in case it was needed because south of the designated operational area it could only act in aid of the civil power.

Announcing this possible new development, General Meiring expressed surprise that Plan had not yet launched an infiltration attempt into the Tsumeb-Grootfontein-Otavi triangle. However, he said, there were indications that the insurgents in Angola had not abandoned their preparations for a seasonal strike southwards.

For the next few days, public attention was taken up by the overthrow of Lesotho dictator Chief Leabua Jonathan and his replacement by a military regime friendly to South Africa, followed by the jailing of a Koevoet sergeant for committing two murders, and a South African national serviceman for raping an Ovambo woman.

At the end of January, Savimbi arrived in Washington with a 17-person entourage and was received, to Luanda's chagrin, like a head of state. He was met by Reagan, visited the Pentagon and given lavish TV prime-time coverage. He left on February 6 with (according to reliable sources) a firm commitment of support from the US government and an assurance that he would soon be receiving supplies of weapons such as the Stinger, which was considered to be possibly the most advanced manpack anti-aircraft missile in the world. To avert a parliamentary backlash that might lead to the atmosphere in which the Clark Amendment had been passed 10 years earlier, Reagan ordered his senior officials who most ardently opposed sending weapons to Unita, Chester Crocker and George Shultz, to appear before congressional committees and support the government's intentions. This so enraged Luanda that Dos Santos broke off all contact with Crocker for more than a year.

While Crocker and Shultz reluctantly fought the Reagan government's battles in the panelled committee-rooms of Washington, the wars on both sides of the border continued. North of the border, as Fred Bridgland says, "clashes between the MPLA and Unita were now occurring at some place or other in Angola on a daily basis, unseen and little regarded by the world's press".

Little regarded they might have been, but Savimbi's widespread depredations were giving the MPLA acute pain. During February and March the rebels captured at least three towns and harried the Fapla presence in the central provinces of Cuanza Norte, Uige, Huila and Lunda provinces; his operations with Flec in Cabinda caused so much trouble that in late February the Fapla high command moved an extra 2 000 hard-to-spare troops to the enclave.

Many of the attacks were on foreigners helping to keep Angola's rickety economy going. Unita claimed to have killed Cuban soldiers and Bulgarian and Romanian contract-workers, and on March 1 overran the main MPLA diamond-mining town of Andrada, 1 000km north of Jamba, in a two-hour battle. Nearly 200 foreign mineworkers were captured, ranging from Filipinos and Portuguese to Britons and West Germans. They were marched for 15 days into Zaire's Shaba province and left at a remote Methodist mission, from where they were taken home by the International Red Cross. The Unita soldiers carried off diamonds worth more than R12 million, large quantities of food and weapons and 1 000 head of cattle belonging to the government. It was a vicious blow to the Angolan economy: production of diamonds - its largest source of foreign revenue after oil - had been dropping since 1984 because of Unita activities, and this latest raid resulted in a zero production figure for January-March of 1986.

Luanda fought back by boosting Operation Iron Fist, which was beginning to make some headway, and laying great stress on its amnesty offers. In addition it was busy planning an even larger anti-Unita offensive than Operation Congress II.

In SWA/Namibia the long-awaited seasonal infiltration from Angola had got under way in the first half of February. The first kills were reported 13 days into the month, when 37 insurgents died in a single contact in eastern Ovamboland; another six were killed next day. By now the long-awaited infiltration was in full swing and deaths began to mount. On February 23 four people were wounded when some security-force members went on a Sunday excursion with their families and detonated a landmine; that same weekend 15 insurgents were killed, bringing the toll to 116 for the year.

February 19 saw the Angolans publicly admit for the first time that they were in desperate economic straits, thanks to the war and the still-falling oil price. On that date Dos Santos announced that because of the price deterioration he was cutting the 1986 budget, which would mean shelving at least one-third of the country's planned development projects, cancelling or renegotiating contracts with foreign firms and cutting air travel overseas - a luxury beyond the reach of the average Angolan but still indulged in by the MPLA elite. Further budget cuts, he warned, were in prospect if the price of oil continued to drop.

On March 2 Angop renewed its complaints. In recent weeks, it said, South African soldiers and aircraft had violated Angolan territory in a "provocative and destabilising" way; units of the South African and Unita forces were active near Oncocua, Mucope and Caiundo in southern Cunene province and were also operating near Cuito Cuanavale. The SADF refused to comment, but at least one incursion certainly took place north of eastern Ovamboland, and although no figures were given, a SWATF officer later said in an unguarded moment that the Plan local presence had been "badly mauled".

On March 4 P W Botha, while addressing a joint sitting of the three houses of Parliament, suggested that Resolution 435 be implemented from August 1, "provided a firm and satisfactory agreement can be reached before that date on the withdrawal of Cubans". The people of SWA/ Namibia had "waited long enough" for independence, he said; the last remaining obstacle in the way of a settlement was the "continuing threat" posed to SWA/Namibia and the southern African region by the Cubans.

Speaking at a press conference later, Pik Botha said the head of state had proposed a specific date "in order to make it possible for Luanda to come forward with more concrete proposals ... (his) statement is equivalent to an invitation to Luanda to get down to it - we want them to get around a conference table". The government was "ready to attend a conference tomorrow" at which Swapo, the Multi-Party Conference, Angola and Unita were represented, he said. Swapo's reaction to this offer was not enthusiastic. The joint secretary for foreign affairs, Niko Bessenger, commented that the statement had not brought the independence process "one bit closer" to implementation of 435, and added: "There is no room for optimism in this speech at all."

UN Secretary-General Perez de Cuellar, however, welcomed the offer as "an important development" - but neatly evaded the core issue and thereby completely vitiated the initiative by criticising as "extraneous" Pretoria's continued insistence on a Cuban withdrawal because, as one of his spokesmen said, "the Secretary-General has repeatedly emphasised that the question of Namibia should be regarded as a primary issue in its own right". Angola reacted by saying that the Cuban presence "is a question only concerning the Angolan and Cuban authorities, and cannot be used as a condition for granting freedom to Namibia". In Luanda, Swapo spokesman Sackey Namutongo said the proposal "has nothing new for us. It's just the same language of linkage".

Chester Crocker nevertheless seized on the offer without delay. He wasted no time in setting up a meeting in Geneva with his Soviet counterpart to tackle the primary issue of the Cuban presence, and sent his deputy Frank Wisner on a series of visits which started in Lisbon and then took him to Southern Africa.

No solution manifested itself, however, and by April it was back to business as usual in the border war. On April 7 an Angolan Defence Ministry communique quoted by Angop claimed its air force had shot down a SAAF C-130 which was dropping supplies to Unita, and damaged another one. The communique gave no further details, however, and an SADF spokesman reacted by saying: "We deny (this claim) categorically ... I don't know what they shot down, but it wasn't one of ours." A week later, however, Angop quoted the Angolan armed forces chief of staff, Colonel Antonio dos Santos Franca, as saying that it had happened while the SAAF aircraft had been shielding behind civilian airliners and using international air routes while dropping supplies to Unita (an inquiry by the International Air Transport Association subsequently proved that the Angolans had actually shot down one of their own civilian C-130s).

The Angolans' preparations for the new push against Unita were now taking shape under the direction of a Russian general named Konstantin Shagnovitch, an Afghanistan veteran who had arrived in December of 1985 to assume supreme command of all the Angolan forces and their allies.

Enormous amounts of late-model Russian weaponry and equipment streamed to Luena and Cuito Cuanavale; according to Bridgland the Russians dug so deeply into their inventories that "Moscow even committed planes that were part of its strategic assets for any major conflict in Europe". With them came nearly 1 000 Russians to occupy training and command posts, not to mention about 2 000 East Germans who whipped Fapla's intelligence and communication services into shape. About 20 000 Fapla soldiers, 7 000 Swapo fighters and 900 ANC members were concentrated at the two centres - a massive force by the standards of both the border and Angolan civil wars - and Dos Santos visited Moscow to ask for a stronger Russian commitment to the offensive as well as more high-altitude anti-aircraft missiles (the latter duly arrived in mid-June).

Savimbi's reaction was to step up a guerrilla campaign aimed at disrupting Fapla's lines of communication and tie down its troops in both the south and in the north (he had managed to recruit and activate large numbers of former FNLA members who had been left leaderless and aimless by Holden Roberto's flight from Angola in 1975). He also visited Cape Town early in May and successfully sought P W Botha's promise that the South Africans would continue to support him and that they would not withdraw from SWA/Namibia till the Cubans had left.

While all this was going on, Sam Nujoma claimed in Harare on April 7 that "renegade" elements of the old Rhodesian army had been drafted into the SADF and were responsible for killing civilians in SWA/Namibia. In addition, he claimed, South Africa was forcibly recruiting blacks into the "repressive" SWATF and had "Namibianised the war because white soldiers are afraid to face the Swapo freedom fighters. They are now using blacks as cannon fodder in their puppet army". A military spokesman said Nujoma's "meaningless rhetoric" was "no more than another poor attempt to boost flagging morale … it is suggested that he substantiate his claims before making ludicrous public statements".

The accusations were "ironic", he added, when it was considered that between January 1979 and March 1986 Plan had murdered 430 civilians, killed another 359 by means of landmine explosions and abducted at least 1 629 women and children.

The insurgency continued. On April 7 two SWATF members and 23 insurgents were killed in a skirmish in the operational area. Another 19 insurgents died in the next three weeks, including three of a group which fired furiously but inaccurately with RPG-7 anti-tank rockets, mortars and small arms at a village near Oshikuku, only to be fought off by the village home guard unit and then pursued by a follow-up force. It brought the year's total insurgent losses to 283.

This was to be the pattern of the border war for the next few months: a myriad small, often fiercely fought actions that caused a never-ending dribble of casualties. But the border fighting was once again overshadowed by events in Angola and further afield.

On May 19 simultaneous SADF special-forces raids against ANC targets in Botswana, Zimbabwe and Zambia caused a huge uproar which summarily torpedoed the Eminent Persons Group's visit to South Africa.

On May 26 the Angolan Defence Ministry made detailed claims of South African incursions. Between May 1 and May 22 South African forces of varying strength had been detected in the environs of Chiede, Nehone, Nehone, Namacunde, Buabua, Evale, Virei, Donguena and Nainane-Calueque. On May 6 six Pumas flew over Chicupa region and fired on Fapla troops with machine-guns, on May 10 a 67-vehicle column crossed the border and reached Buabua, 75km from Ongiva and on May 13 troops supported by two helicopters had occupied Iona. Angop did not give details about these alleged forces' activities except in one instance, where it claimed that a South African group using armoured vehicles and heavy artillery had killed 53 Fapla and wounded five in an attack 35km south-west of Xangongo while the latter were engaged in anti-Unita operations on May 22.

Just one day later, on May 27, Shagnovitch's "big push" started. It has since been revealed that during the planning there arose serious differences between the Angolans, who wanted to seize the centre and north of the country before tackling the south-west, and the Russians and Cubans, who believed that an attack in the south-east would damage Unita's ability to mount its own offensives in other parts of Angola and force it to call in some of the troops with which it was fighting there; most of all, a successful conclusion would obliterate what Savimbi called "Free Angola".

The Russian/Cuban position carried the day. From Luena two large armoured columns set out, one heading westwards to Savimbi's birthplace of Munhango in central Angola and the other proceeding due south towards the town of Lumbala, formerly known as Gago Coutinho. The third left Cuito Cuanavale and made for Mavinga. Slowly but inexorably they ground towards their targets, while swarms of small Unita groups plagued their supply-lines, their striking power vastly enhanced by the Stinger and anti-tank missiles which had started arriving at Mavinga from Zaire around April.

On June 5 Angop went public with an incident which even now remains shrouded in mystery - officially, anyway. Before dawn the previous day, it said, one of the South African Navy's fast strike craft had slipped into the harbour of Namibe and fired a volley of missiles at an oil depot, destroying two storage tanks and damaging another. At the same time it deployed frogmen who mined three freighters tied up in the harbour, sinking one and heavily damaging the other two (the Soviet Union later identified the sunken ship as the dry-cargo vessel Havana, which had been carrying 6 000 tons of food, and the other two as the Russian freighters Kapitan Visblokov and Kapitan Chirkov). The attacking ship and its saboteurs then got clean away, the Angolans said.

An SADF spokesman said he had no comment to make over the spate of recent allegations, saying that it was "easy to blame everything that happened in the southern hemisphere on South Africa", but that it should be realised that there was "a civil war in Angola and anything is possible". To South African and other observers, however, the action had all the earmarks of a special-forces raid.

The SADF has never admitted to attacking Namibe, but intelligence officers in Pretoria later told correspondent Anthony Robinson of the Financial Times that the story was true and that the attack had been mounted to disrupt MPLA arms supplies to Cuito Cuanavale; indirect evidence indicates that the underwater saboteurs were members of the SADF's amphibious-warfare unit.

On June 8 the Soviet government said by way of a statement issued by the Tass news agency that it "most categorically condemns the actions of the Republic of South Africa in attacking Namibe", and added that "actions of this kind cannot be left unpunished. Responsibility for this is also shared by those who patronise the Republic of South Africa, above all the United States". The statement did not give any hint as to what actions were contemplated, and none took place; and the Namibe raid succeeded in seriously affecting the activities of the Cuito Cuanavale-Mavinga column because the rebels carried out one raid after another on the road from Menongue, severely disrupting the column's supply-lines.

On the same day Angola claimed that South Africa now had seven battalions stationed on its soil and lodged what it described as an "urgent appeal" with the UN to take appropriate action. True or false? Outside of those involved, no one knew, and observers had learnt not to take Angolan accusations or South African denials at face value.

Meanwhile the Fapla advance continued, albeit very slowly. In the first week of June the Luena-Munhango column had captured the important Unita-held town of Cangombe, about 60km away, the Luena-Lumbala column was labouring southwards and the Cuito-Cuanavale column was making heavy weather of the advance to Mavinga, thanks to very heavy Unita attacks on its lines of communication and also the transfer of three of its brigades to the far north, where Savimbi's insurgency had gone into high gear.

The next few weeks brought tidings of further intermittent blood-letting north and south of the border. By the first week in July SWA/Namibian security forces claimed to have killed 408 insurgents since the beginning of the year; by late July the Fapla offensive had bogged down, defeated once again by heavy resistance and the Angolans' old weakness, their inability to supply the large "conventional" forces they put in the field. According to Bridgland the column from Cuito Cuanavale had advanced no more than 15km by this stage, the Lumbala column was beleaguered in Lucusse, 80km south of Luena, and the Munhango column had made little progress since capturing Cangombe. Savimbi was confident that the Angolans had been turned back once more, and seemingly the Angolan rank and file thought so too: according to at least one source, the generally anti-South African Guardian newspaper, streams of deserters and draft-dodgers were flowing into Zaire and Zambia.

Angola continued to beat the anti-South African drum. On July 29 Dos Santos, who was addressing an Organisation for African Unity summit meeting at Addis Ababa, claimed that South Africa was preparing to carry out an external operation at any time and had massed 20 000 troops in northern SWA/Namibia, along with 120 tanks, 350 heavy artillery pieces, 800 armoured cars, 60 ground-to-air missile systems, 90 military aircraft and 50 combat and transport helicopters. In addition, he said, five South African battalions stationed along the border were carrying out regular attacks on army installations and economic targets (although there was none of either within several hundred kilometres of the border), and SAAF aircraft were dropping arms to Unita.

Dos Santos also attacked the US for backing Unita, saying that Reagan was retaliating against Angola for supporting black nationalist movements in South Africa and SWA/Namibia; the alliance between the US and "the apartheid regime" constituted a significant shift in US policy in the region.

An SADF spokesman replied curtly that Dos Santos's statements were "typical of the kind of rhetoric (at) this kind of gathering", which was probably the most accurate way of putting it, since Dos Santos's figures were wildly inflated (for example, the SADF had no tanks deployed in the border area and its total inventory of artillery pieces, including its ancient 25-pounders of World War II vintage, was about half the figure mentioned by the Angolan president).

What Dos Santos did not say was that exploratory peace talks had started in London between the MPLA Foreign Minister, Alfonso van Dunem, and Savimbi's third-in-command, Tito Chingungi. It was an historic encounter in more ways than one. The MPLA and Unita had maintained low-level contacts for years, but this was the first time that they had got together on a high-level basis. According to Bridgland "the purge of hardliners from the MPLA at the December 1985 congress had put pragmatism in the ascendancy in Luanda. But it was clear that no formula could be devised to enable Cuban and Soviet personnel to withdraw, without loss of face, before the dry-season warfare gained full momentum and ran its course ahead of the arrival of the rains in October". Thus ended what might have been the most significant meeting in the history of the Angolan civil war.

It is likely that Dos Santos's wild claims at Addis Ababa were meant to build up an alibi in case Cuito Cuanavale was attacked by Unita. This duly happened, but not till the August 1 target date set by P W Botha had gone by without a suitable reaction from the MPLA. In a statement to the press that day, Pik Botha blamed Angola for failing to respond with concrete proposals for a "realistic timetable", adding:

"The South African government again appeals to the Luanda regime to come forward with proposals for a realistic programme of withdrawal … it is unacceptable that the political future of SWA/Namibia should be determined through violence by an organization which intends to impose its will on the territory, backed by some 40 000 Cuban troops stationed across the border in Angola. It should be clear that the people cannot wait indefinitely for a breakthrough regarding withdrawal.

"Should it eventually become evident, after all avenues have been thoroughly explored, that there is no realistic prospect of attaining these goals, all parties most directly affected will have to reconsider how internationally acceptable independence may best be achieved in the light of prevailing circumstances."

On August 9 and 10 the expected assault on Cuito Cuanavale took place. It was carried out by about 4 000 Unita troops, with some South African assistance. Exactly what that assistance consisted of is still an official secret, but from scraps of information that have leaked out, it would appear that the South Africans' support consisted mainly of artillery bombardments and ground attacks by fighter aircraft. Some infantry - probably drawn from 32 Battalion - were also involved, but it is thought that their role was mainly to carry out "area operations" in order to secure the guns and supply routes.

Details of the attack were never released. A Unita communique released on August 11 said only that its forces had attacked Cuito Cuanavale after 24 hours of bombing by MiGs, "all piloted by Cuban crews", at the end of which the base's radar installations had been destroyed, along with all the anti-aircraft guns, most of the artillery and stocks of bombs and other munitions. It was clear that Savimbi's forces had not actually captured the base, and observers at the time noted that it appeared as if all or most of the damage had been done by the long-distance South African shelling - a close replay of what was to happen a year later - and that the Unita troops had either concentrated on chasing the outlying Fapla elements into the base perimeter or had carried out an assault and been repulsed. What was not announced was that the bridge over the Cuito River, just east of the base, had also been attacked by a party of mysterious raiders (whose identity remains shrouded in mystery to this day) and so severely damaged that it was incapable of carrying any vehicular traffic.

True to form, the Angolans blamed the entire attack on the South Africans, claiming it had been carried out by 32 Battalion, which had attacked twice and been thrown back on both occasions. In successive statements Luanda claimed that three (this later became four) South African battalions had been involved, and that 40 of the attackers had been killed and four captured, while two Fapla troops and 23 civilians had been killed by the shelling. Four days later Angop quoted the Angolan Defence Ministry as saying that the siege was still in progress and that 95 "invading South African troops" had been killed so far. No further mention of the four alleged prisoners of war was made, and Luanda did not respond to a Unita challenge to produce them.

The SADF's only comment was that the Angolans had had to resort "to unadulterated propaganda to convince the world that all is well", because according to its analysis there was a massive build-up of Fapla, Cuban and Soviet forces and "sophisticated hardware" for "what appears to be a last-ditch attempt to unseat Unita in southern Angola".

The Americans accepted the Luanda version of the attack, and a State Department spokesman said reports of the attack appeared to be quite true. He added: "We do not condone any South African raid into Angola, nor can we accept the justification for such action on the basis of South Africa's illegal occupation of Namibia." Britain and West Germany were more cautious and said only that they were awaiting independent confirmation.

It did not really matter. The attack had achieved its purpose by neutralising Cuito Cuanavale. Shagnovitch could not very well take on Unita on its home ground without the use of Cuito Cuanavale's air support, especially with the rainy season drawing near, so he began pulling back to regroup at Lucusse, Munhango and Menongue, deploying fighters and gunship helicopters at the last base to provide air cover in case of any Unita counteroffensives. Although there were subsequent reports that Shagnovitch appeared to be massing his troops for another essay eastwards, the Fapla offensive did not resume, and once again Savimbi - and the South Africans - had bought some breathing-space.

All this time the border war continued on both the fighting and propaganda fronts. On August 12 SWATF announced that a South African soldier and three civilians had been killed in stand-off bombardments on Oshakati and Ruacana (in the case of Oshakati, six B-10 shells and three 82mm mortar-bombs were fired at the base but hit the black residential section instead; a follow-up operation resulted in the deaths of four of the insurgents involved). Three weeks later Swapo spokesman Johnny ya Otto was quoted by Angop as saying that in the first six months of the year Plan had killed nearly 600 South African troops and shot down four transport aircraft and five helicopters. The SADF described this ludicrous claim as a "blatant distortion of reality".

The SADF retort was, in fact, no more than the truth. The war had been going badly for the insurgents, particularly in Kavango - so much so that by September 12 the OC Sector 20, Colonel Deon Ferreira, felt confident enough to say that Kavango was free of Plan activity. Operations Opeet and Concert had succeeded so well, he said, that "we've broken the terrorists' ideological backbone to a large extent ... they're back in the organisational

phase; we have won the shooting war". The figures quoted by the SWATF supported his optimism.

At that stage the active insurgent presence in the entire operational area was estimated at a mere 70 effectives, and comments by the GOC SWATF, Major-General Georg Meiring, during an interview with this writer that same month, provide a good indication of how the military were thinking:

In this long war there are two statements which were accepted in the past but which we have proved to be false.

Firstly, that time is always on the side of the terrorists. Wrong. We have been fighting for 20 years, and they are deteriorating.

Secondly, that you can't win a counterinsurgency war. You can. They are losing here and at the same time we are winning, which are two different things.

The terrorist can't win because each terrorist is a political commissar (but) his fighting ability is not too high. Yet you must have a reasonably fighting capacity ... After 20 years you'd expect that any decently motivated people would have achieved something ... 1979-1980 was the high point (for Swapo). In the first seven months of this year there were one-third less incidents than last year. Most of the local population deaths have been due to hard intimidation and mine deaths, and only two percent to five percent in crossfire.

By this morning 526 (insurgents) had died ... The reason why they are not so successful, we think, is due to the number of arms caches found in South West Africa and Angola before and after the turn of the year - 58 were found internally and 90 externally. The landmine war is also being won - 609 were lifted in 1986. In the past we were lifting one for every three detonated. Now it is three or four for every one that went off.

But the main reasons why we think we are winning are the following:

In 1983, 64 percent of the population (in the operational area) came forward to give us information about Swapo activities. In 1984 the figure was 317 percent. In 1986 it was almost 600 percent. This tells me the population is doing its bit. The more they do, the safer it is for them, and we are really in the process of winning hearts and minds, and Swapo doesn't have the influence it thinks it has.

There are two aspects to this.

Firstly, when we allocated strengths (for SWATF) last year, we decided to add 205 men to 101 Battalion, and over 3 000 Ovambos reported for attestation.

Secondly, the terrorists can't be in (the operational area) for more than six days before the information reaches the security forces, and this is in the heart of Central Ovamboland: the relationship between the military and the Ovambos is very good ... as a fighting force Swapo has nothing. The only thing keeping them (alive) is the hostile element north of the border.

In this whole process we have to do with politics - international politics, internal politics and so on. I think that (as regards) internal politics we are making progress as well. There is no real animosity - far less, I think, than in any place in South Africa. The reason, I think, is that people have started to conduct their affairs in an atmosphere without intimidation. We are only involved to the extent that intimidation is kept very low.

In South Africa people expect quick results. But imagine trying to form a government which incorporates the Conservative Party and the South African Communist Party.

(The transitional government) are providing good government on the ground, and good government is the essence of winning hearts and minds and the counter-revolution ... Remember that each (party) has a great love for South West Africa. They might differ, but when it goes about South West Africa they usually talk with one another.

When will it end? We must put all our efforts into the last stretch, so that the vehicle won't run down the dune again. Everything Swapo stood for has been achieved without its contribution. Apartheid is gone, the country is on the way to independence and so on. But the fact is that if Swapo lays down its arms it can take part in the political process.

At this stage the annual infiltration-time was approaching as the short rainy season commenced. On November 7 Angop claimed that South African troops had pushed 150km into Angola but had then been "forced to retreat" to near the SWA/Namibian border "after the intervention of the Angolan army". No casualty figures were given, and it is not known whether any such incursion ever took place. If it did, it obviously had no connection with a small pre-emptive raid announced by SWATF on November 14, when it said two security-force soldiers and 39 insurgents had been killed during an attack carried out on a Plan training camp two days earlier, acting on information obtained about preparations for the expected infiltration. There had been no contact with Fapla during the operation.

The latest deaths brought the year's insurgent death-toll to 606, the figure being announced just before correspondent James MacManus wrote in an in-depth article published in Britain's Sunday Telegraph newspaper that although the operational area appeared to be ideal country for Plan to operate in, "it is the South African army and local security forces that are winning the war with a successful counter-insurgency operation along the border".

The South Africans were distinctly confident about their chances at this stage, although an estimated 1 100 insurgents were believed to be moving southwards, aiming at infiltrating by way of the traditional routes through Kaokoland, central Ovamboland and Kavango. By November 25, when the insurgent death-toll for 1986 had risen to 614, Meiring stated in an interview in Windhoek that no Plan members were operating in either Kavango or Kaokoland, and that there were only "an estimated 35 terrorists" in Ovamboland.

A Swapo spokesman in Luanda replied that Plan intended to step up its bombing campaign in major centres like Windhoek, Swakopmund, Tsumeb and Walvis Bay because "we intend to take the war to new areas, to targets in the cities. We will make the price of their occupation of our country a high one". Security-force planners found the statement a revealing one because it indicated that the remorseless pressure of the past few years had forced Plan to adopt new tactics: planting a bomb is low-cost in terms of effort, risk and logistics, and is almost guaranteed good publicity - particularly when the dead are foreigners, like a United States military attache who died in an explosion at an Oshakati garage in 1985.

Earlier in November Dos Santos ceremonially buried the doomed-from-birth Alvor Agreement which had enabled his party to seize power in 1975. Savimbi had been campaigning with varying degrees of success in Western Europe, calling on various nations to force the MPLA into implementing the 1975 elections, and this helped (according to Fred Bridgland) to "provoke Eduardo dos Santos into a hardline response". Speaking at a rally marking the 11th anniversary of the independence, Dos Santos declared: "Recently references have been made to the so-called Alvor Agreement. All Angolans know that this document lost its validity long ago. It has become obsolete and should lie in our museum ... Everybody knows that there is no true liberation struggle in the world that does not have the direct or indirect support of the USSR or Cuba."

A decade earlier Dos Santos's contemptuous dismissal of the Alvor Agreement might have raised an international outcry. Now, in late 1986, it caused barely a ripple. The MPLA had achieved legitimacy simply by being able to hang on to power for 11 years, and the rights or wrongs of the matter were of interest to no one, including those who were calling so fervently for a "fair and free" UN-sponsored election next door in SWA/Namibia.

Except Savimbi, who was prosecuting his lone war against Luanda as vigorously as ever. His forces saw action in many parts of the country as he set about reconquering central Angola and also expanding to the north to take advantage of the support he had garnered there.

The year ended with 645 insurgents dead for a loss of 33 security-force soldiers and 116 civilians. According to SWATF spokesmen, Plan was on the run and the progression of the war had been reversed, so that the insurgents were back to where they had been five or 10 years earlier.

But if the quality of insurgent activity had degraded, Plan itself was far from giving up the struggle, as the new year was to prove. And some of the heaviest fighting the South Africans had seen since World War II still lay ahead - not in SWA/Namibia, but once again in Angola.

On January 7 of 1987, in one of his last public statements before handing over the post of GOC SWATF to Major-General Willie Meyer, General Meiring noted that about 60 Fapla soldiers had died in clashes with the South African and SWA/Namibian forces during 1986, and warned that it would be only a matter of time before Fapla would feel sufficiently confident to take on South African forces, most probably in aerial combat.

Meiring was to be proved absolutely correct, but it was to be more than half a year before his prediction came to pass; in the meantime the border war restarted as the rainy season arrived. On January 8 three South Africans and eight insurgents died in a follow-up operation in the operational area. Then a pre-emptive attack into the Angolan shallow area left another 56 insurgents and six SWATF soldiers dead in four days of fighting.

As this bout of fighting ended news came that a 700g time-bomb had exploded at a petrol station at Gobabis, about 200km east of Windhoek, killing a man and causing damage estimated at R45 000. Another bomb was discovered nearby and defused. Police said they believed that the man who had died in the blast had planted both, then blown himself up by accident while arming the second one. There were some fears that this was the start of the bombing campaign Swapo had threatened in

late 1986, but it did not eventuate. Small-scale clashes in the operational area continued, however, and by January 22 100 insurgents had been killed since the beginning of the year.

On January 25 the Angolans claimed that South African troops had attacked their forces on January 12 and January 19, although they did not give any details as to location or losses, and said the South Africans were massing troops inside Cunene province for "a major armed aggression". An SADF dismissed the accusation as being "similar to claims made by Angola recently", but to some observers, who knew that the SADF and SWATF were engaged in continual pre-emptive sweeps in the shallow area, it was obvious that sooner or later security-force and Fapla elements were bound to run into one another, considering how closely Plan was integrated into the Angolan forces.

In fact the first such clash had already taken place, although the Angolans apparently did not know about it when they issued their statement. On January 24 a SWATF element tracked a group of insurgents back to a base they were sharing with Fapla in the vicinity of Mongua, about 75km north of the border. The Fapla garrison opened fire on the SWATF group, which promptly called in reinforcements and attacked. By the time the fighting ended 72 insurgents and two SWATF

Below
As his forces brace themselves for the coming Lomba River offensive, Jonas Savimbi briefs the international press on the situation at his headquarters at Jamba

soldiers had died, as well as some Fapla members. Asked later how many Angolans had been killed, SWATF spokesmen would not go further than coyly saying "a number", but Windhoek sources said the figure was 40.

The killing continued into February. By mid-February another 63 insurgents and two SWATF members had died in clashes inside the operational area. In the next week another 19 insurgents and two SWATF soldiers were killed, and another 18 insurgents and two SWATF members in the week after. By February 26 the insurgent death-toll for the year stood at a high 272.

In the meantime Savimbi had been busy. His expansion northwards in the first two months of 1987 took on such dimensions that his lines of aerial communication with Mavinga became uncomfortably long, so much so that the Americans began to prepare the long-existing air base at Kamina in southern Zaire as a supply-base to Unita; there was a rash of newspaper reports that Savimbi was planning to move his main headquarters from Jamba to an unspecified location further north, near the Zairean border, or at least establish an alternative headquarters there.

Some observers took this to mean that Savimbi was contemplating cutting himself loose from South Africa, at once his military saviour and his political albatross, but it did not happen, for two very good reasons. In the first place, "Free Angola" was still very vulnerable to a threat from the Menongue-Cuito Cuanavale direction. Secondly, the loss of his "liberated zone" would be a devastating psychological blow to his cause and his troops' morale; and thirdly, Savimbi realised very well that whereas the Americans might supply him with Stingers, only the South Africans were willing to lend him the on-the-ground fighting assets like artillerymen, pilots and infantry he would need in the event of another Fapla offensive. The wisdom of this realisation was to be amply proved before very long.

Savimbi went further. In February, by arrangement with President Denis Sassou-Neguesso of Congo-Brazzaville, several hundred members of Flec arrived in the south-east to be trained as insurgents and cycled back to Cabinda (which in due course resulted in a noticeable increase in the insurgency level in the enclave).

By now General Shagnovitch and the Cubans and Angolans were preparing for the next "push" against Unita. Fresh supplies of weapons and equipment were flowing into Angola on a daily basis: tanks, guns, armoured fighting vehicles, radars, fighters and fighter-bombers, helicopter gunships, air-defence rockets - some of the items so modern that Western evaluation experts had never laid hands on them. The Soviet Union was like a martial cornucopia, showering Angola with a king's ransom in military hardware (according to various observers the equivalent of about R2 billion worth between mid-1986 and mid-1987, most of it in the latter period).

From Luanda and the other arrival points the new weaponry was fed down to the combat zones in two streams. Most of it was despatched to Shagnovitch's forward base at Menongue, from where it was sent on the base at Cuito Cuanavale, the jumping-off point for the advance on Mavinga. The rest went to the eastern regional headquarters at Luena, where the town of Lucusse was being developed as a forward base. Troops were beginning to concentrate at Cuito Cuanavale and Lucusse as well, pulled in from as far afield as Cabinda, even when they were actively engaged in counter-insurgency operations.

Neither Savimbi nor the South Africans had any doubt that Shagnovitch was preparing for another offensive, one that would be vastly larger than its predecessors, and that this time he meant to win at almost any cost. It was an expression of Luanda's desperation. Angolan prestige had been badly dented by the ignominious failures of 1985 and 1986; the economy was still deteriorating almost daily and popular discontent was growing; the MPLA's Russian and Cuban sponsors were growing restive at its lack of success; and the longer Savimbi remained at large, the bolder and more painful his activities became. If Mavinga could be taken, Fapla could sit out the rainy season there and attack Jamba as soon as the 1987 wet weather was over, and if partial or total control over the Benguela line could be obtained Angola would be able to use it not only for earning foreign revenue but also for facilitating the resupply of troops.

Savimbi reacted, as he had done in previous years, by starting a campaign of continual harassment of Fapla lines of communications and staging areas, and also by launching offensives elsewhere in the country to hamper Fapla time-tables for concentrating troops. Many of these operations were small, but others were much larger, to judge by the reported casualties: another diamond mine was raided in the north-east, and a few daring, if not really damaging, sabotage attacks were carried out in industrial areas on the outskirts of Luanda.

While Savimbi and Shagnovitch prepared for their confrontation, the South Africans' war continued on several fronts. In March, 71 insurgents were killed in the operational area for a loss of four security-force members, and another seven in the first week of April, along with two SWATF soldiers, while Plan landmines killed five civilians and wounded another three. On April 9 Pretoria became involved in another squabble with Botswana when a minibus filled with explosives blew up in a residential area of Gaborone, near the head-quarters of the Botswana Defence Force, killing three Batswana and destroying two houses (Botswana President Quett Masire subsequently claimed it had been detonated by the South African Police to destroy the evidence of an abortive undercover operation; the Department of Foreign Affairs replied that the minibus had been used to ferry arms and munitions to and from Botswana for the African National Congress).

On April 21 the South African government publicly warned Zambia for the second time to restrain an ANC force which, it said, was about to infiltrate into the Republic. The Zambians spurned the warning with the comment that Pretoria was looking for a scapegoat for the difficulties it was facing in the forthcoming May general election, in which the government was facing strong opposition from the white far right. In Zimbabwe and Mozambique, both of which had received similar warnings earlier in the month, the authorities were preparing for what they believed were imminent South African pre-emptive raids.

Fighting along the border continued. By April 23 a total of 446 insurgents had been killed since January 1, along with two more civilians, and 12 pupils had been abducted from a school and taken to Angola. Just five days later Pretoria set off an almighty international row when it sent in a special-forces group to raid ANC houses in the Zambian town of Livingstone, killing four people whom the Lusaka authorities identified as Zambian citizens. The uproar had barely subsided when the Mozam-bicans announced on May 29 that SADF "com-mandos" had shot up two ANC-occupied houses and two private residences in Maputo, killing two Mozambican citizens; three of the raiders had been captured, the state news agency, AIM, reported.

The South Africans flatly denied responsibility, then and later, with Pik Botha stating that the incident had resulted from a factional struggle within the ANC. Since the South Africans had never previously hesitated to admit their involvement in similar incidents, and the Mozambicans failed to produce either the alleged captured raiders or any confirmatory evidence, then or later, observers tended to agree with Botha.

International opinion was not so easily pacified, however, and amid the international uproar little attention was attracted by an announcement on June 8 by General Willie Meyer, that a security-force element had followed a Plan group to a Fapla base at Anhanca, attacked after being fired on and killed all 20 insurgents as well as various Angolans without any "own" losses. Neither did a routine

Angop claim that SAAF aircraft had bombed Ongiva and army units backed by helicopters and armoured cars were preparing for a major assault.

In the next few weeks more such claims flowed from Luanda as the Angolans began setting the stage for their new offensive, knowing full well that when it started Savimbi was sure to call on Pretoria for help, and that Pretoria was sure to provide it. On July 8 Angop claimed that throughout June Fapla had been subjected to attacks by more than 6 000 non-existent South African troops, armed not only with the obligatory aircraft, tanks and artillery but also with unspecified "banned chemical weapons" and napalm, adding that the intruders had been chased back to SWA/Namibia after suffering "incalculable" (but unquantified) casualties.

An SADF spokesman replied that "it is ... common knowledge that it is the Russians and their surrogates who resort to chemical weapons when hard-pressed", adding that the claims were an "obvious attempt to minimise (Unita successes) by blaming South Africa". In fact, although this was not made public at the time, the South Africans had picked up incontrovertible evidence that the Angolans had been using some type of chemical weapons against Unita, and this had been confirmed by civilian doctors who had examined some of the rebel wounded.

For the SADF it was a deeply worrying development, because while it had anti-CW equipment, this was not very practical to wear in the Angolan and SWA/Namibian theatres, partic-ularly in summer, when soldiers could not fight effectively in the ferocious heat and humidity unless they stripped down to the bare minimum of clothing and equipment. Nevertheless, soldiers undergoing refresher training at the Army Battle School were instructed in anti-CW techniques, no doubt with the twin purposes of boosting morale and making sure the news leaked out to the Angolans that the SADF was aware of what was going on and would retaliate in kind if necessary.

In the first fortnight of July four security-force soldiers and two insurgents were killed in action, and some minor sabotage took place in Ovambo-land; but the border war was about to be eclipsed by happenings in Angola.

On July 1 General Magnus Malan had warned that now that the dry season had arrived in Angola it was "almost time for another Soviet-planned and supported offensive executed by its Cuban mer-cenaries". It was a statement of fact. Shagnovitch was waiting for the ground to dry out enough for his heavily motorised and mechanised forces to operate at their best; while he waited, the sinews of his campaign continued to roll in.

Washington Post correspondent William Claiborne had a rare opportunity to see the build-up in progress when he obtained permission to visit southern Angola early in the month. "During one four-hour period at Lubango's airport," he reported, "a constant stream of Soviet Aeroflot transport planes landed and their cargoes, including air-to-air missiles, were quickly unloaded by Cuban and Angolan troops ... The scene at Luanda's airport was similar, with long lines of Aeroflot transports waiting on the taxi-way for their turn to take off at intervals of only a few minutes." The London Times graphically reported that "air resupply of such towns as Cuito Cuanavale and Menongue provides the most striking reminder of Afghanistan, with Soviet-built Antonov transport planes spiralling down onto airstrips from great heights, spewing flares in an attempt to mislead the American anti-

Opposite
Unita soldiers clamber over the remains of a MiG-21 shot down by a Stinger air-defence missile during the Lomba River fighting. The MiGs were very wary of the highly effective Stingers

aircraft missiles which have recently proved so effective in Unita hands".

It was quite obvious that the Angolans intended to launch another simultaneous attack from Cuito Cuanavale and Lucusse, and some time in July the South Africans activated Operation Modular on the instructions of the Chief of the SADF, General Jannie Geldenhuys. At that stage it was a modest affair. The SADF would assist Unita in developing an anti-tank plan in the south, and if necessary the SAAF would be called in. As these things will, Modular was to escalate a good deal before it ended, although the entire South African presence never amounted to more than about 2 000 men at its peak.

In mid-July Chester Crocker flew to Luanda for another round of peace talks. Three weeks earlier Soviet Foreign Minister Eduard Shevardnadze had warned him that the meeting would fail, but to his pleasure it took place in what he later described as "a business-like atmosphere. That is to say, the two delegations did not throw water-pitchers at each other, or ash-trays, or something".

He returned with raised hopes that the Angolans were moving towards a peaceful rather than a violent resolution of their war situation. Subsequent remarks he made about this meeting tend to indicate that he believed the substantial group of "doves" within the MPLA high command would be able to exercise a dominating influence - possibly resulting from the confusing array of personal and ideological factions, and the fact that the Angolans denied up to the end that an offensive was impending. If so, it was a wrong assumption. The Angolans were set on a military solution to the Unita problem; within a week of the meeting Shagnovitch was ready, and sent his forces rolling out of Cuito Cuanavale and other bases.

It was a bitter disappointment for Crocker. On July 22, speaking from Washington in a three-way press conference linked to Lisbon and London, he said with undisguised anger that hopes of a breakthrough in Angola and SWA/Namibia had been brutally dashed.

"All the advance indications that we had received (at the mid-July meeting), that they were now ready to do serious business, proved to be hollow and proved to be false. Therefore we have nothing from the Angolan side which provides a basis for our going to the South African leadership in an effort to move rapidly and energetically towards a compromise. Those are the cold, hard facts ... There may also be a sense that the Angolan leadership is still not united about which way it wants to move - under very heavy external pressure.

"We have no doubt, for example, that the Cubans do not want to see their expeditionary force asked to leave. In fact they have tried to link the Cuban presence in Southern Africa not only to Namibia and so forth, but to the ending of apartheid in South Africa, which sounds to us like an open-ended hunting licence for the indefinite future for Fidel Castro ...

"(The talks) raised the most basic questions about the independence and the African character of that government."

On July 27 and 28 a sizeable clash by border-war standards took place in the shallow area, when a SWATF follow-up force chasing about 120 insurgents drove into a combined Plan-Fapla ambush. The SWA/Namibians attacked and the ambushers withdrew. The SWATF force set off in pursuit, caught up with their opponents and defeated them in a bloody encounter which, a spokes-man in Windhoek said later, cost the lives of 190 insurgents and Angolans with no losses to the security forces except one officer slightly wounded and several vehicles damaged.

Sam Nujoma immediately responded to this announcement with a statement from Addis Ababa in which he said that no insurgents had been killed in the battle, only civilians. The Swapo London office followed this up by saying the SWATF communique was "an utter fabrication ... there are no Swapo forces in any Fapla base in Angola ... On the contrary, we know that the South African racist troops have been engaged in fierce battles with the Angolan forces in recent days in the area of Ongiva, and that the South Africans have suffered serious casualties".

By early August, five of Shagnovitch's brigades were advancing from the Lucusse area towards Cangamba and Lumbala, supported by ground-attack aircraft based in Lucusse and Luena; three more brigades were stationed in the Munhango area and Shagnovitch's main force, consisting of 16, 21, 47 and 59 Brigades, was on the way to Tumpo, east of Cuito Cuanavale, where another brigade, numbered 25, was already lying up.

Shagnovitch's intentions, as later reconstructed by the South Africans, were to have the Lucusse brigades capture Cangamba and Lumbala in a simultaneous assault, then swing westwards to hinder Unita's ready access to the Benguela line and establish a good jumping-off place from which to attack the insurgents' base areas during the 1988 phase, in the process tying down as many of the rebel forces as possible. The three Munhango brigades, although under-strength and probably not part of Shagnovitch's assault forces, would be handily placed to hinder Unita from using the central Angolan no-man's-land and could later serve as a base from which to block it off. Meanwhile Shagnovitch's southern force would steamroller eastwards from Cuito Cuanavale and capture Mavinga with a two-pronged attack across the Lomba River.

It was a daunting scenario that made a defeat for Savimbi only too easy to visualise. By now a number of experienced South African officers who were familiar with the terrain had been attached to the Unita forces to analyse the enemy's approach routes and work out ways of dealing with Shagnovitch's very heavy armoured element. In spite of contemporary newspaper reports, no South Africans were attached to the force tasked with fighting off the Lucusse brigades except two medical orderlies, although contingency plans were prepared to send liaison teams there if Unita requested them.

In the event the Lucusse brigades presented no problem. They advanced a certain distance and were then brought to a halt by fierce resistance from mobile, heavily armed Unita elements operating in front of them, on their flanks and behind them. After taking considerable losses they withdrew to Lucusse again, having failed to capture either Cangamba or Lumbala.

The southern advance was another story. The Cuito Cuanavale brigades arrived at Tumpo, and on August 14 headed for the battle area: 16 and 21 Brigades advanced eastwards, the intention being that at a given point they would swing directly southwards and advance on Mavinga, while 47 and 59 Brigades moved south and south-eastwards and then headed eastwards towards Mavinga.

The brigades advanced very slowly - about 4km a day - thanks to heavy bush and thick sand, the ever-present danger of Unita ambushes or lightning South African mechanised attacks and a determination not to stray outside their air-defence umbrella in case of SAAF strikes. The brigades were also suffering from supply problems because of Unita raids on their lines of communication and a mysterious sabotage raid (blamed on the South Africans, probably correctly) early in September which damaged the vital bridge over the Cuito River to such an extent that supplies had to be helicoptered from one bank to the other.

It was soon clear that Savimbi would need more than advice, and the SADF launched "Operation Modular". At first this consisted of no more than attaching one battery of 127mm multiple rocket-launchers and another of 120mm mortars, each protected by an infantry company, to the forward elements of the Unita forces. The two batteries caused considerable damage to the advancing Angolans, but they did not have the firepower to stop the advance, and 47 Brigade was now moving along the southern bank of the Lomba River with the intention of covering the impending crossing by 59 and 21 Brigades.

It was obvious that something more potent was needed if the Fapla advance was to be stopped, so a small mechanised-infantry force - a detachment from 101 Battalion, a mechanised-infantry and armoured car group drawn from 61 Mechanised Battalion, a G-5 battery, a 127mm MRL battery and a 120mm mortar battery - was deployed south of the Lomba. The Lomba was not much of an obstacle in itself, being a fairly small river which was, moreover, fairly dry because the rains had not yet started; but both its banks were bounded by 2km-wide dry and very soft oshonas, or flood-plains, and this feature was to work in the defenders' favour because it drastically slowed down Fapla movement.

On September 10 two battalions of 21 Brigade and five T-55 tanks struggled across with the help of a bridge-laying lorry, only to be set upon by the South African force and Unita. In the ensuing battle one battalion was practically wiped out and the other badly cut up, while three of the tanks were destroyed by fire from missiles and "Ratel-90s" (anti-tank Ratels armed with 90mm guns). The other two tanks then retreated to the north bank, accompanied by the surviving Fapla infantry, hotly pursued by the erstwhile defenders. Some more fighting followed in which further damage was done to the Angolan forces, although without loss to the Unita or South African troops, who then pulled back over the river.

While all this was happening, weeks of high-powered negotiations brought the release of Wynand du Toit, more than two years after his capture in Cabinda, when he was exchanged in Maputo for 133 Angolan soldiers and two foreign nationals charged with terrorism. It was an odd interlude, considering that at the time South Africans and Angolans were squaring up to one another near the Lomba River.

Just three days later, on September 13, the shooting war resumed. At this stage 21 Brigade was still licking its wounds, but two battalions of 59 Brigade waded through the river, a small detachment of T-55 tanks crossing by means of a bridge-laying lorry. The Fapla force was attacked by the two 101 Battalion companies and a horde of Unita, and heavy fighting took place, ending with three of the tanks knocked out and the Fapla infantry fleeing northward over open terrain, which cost them further casualties. About 300 Fapla soldiers and three South Africans died in this encounter, while a Ratel was knocked out by a shot from a tank.

On September 16 the South Africans attacked part of 47 Brigade, including the headquarters, while it was lying up in an old Unita logistics base. After two days of very heavy fighting the Angolans broke away, managing (to the South Africans' disgust) to save the headquarters, but leaving behind 382 dead and six tanks destroyed, for a toll of six South Africans and about 40 Unita troops.

The brigade now changed its plans and began moving northwards in order to put the Lomba between itself and the South Africans before joining hands with 59 Brigade. It was still engaged in this manoeuvre on October 3 when, while moving across open terrain, it was jumped by a mobile force consisting of the 61 Mechanised Battalion element and some artillery. Although it had no tanks the mobile force went immediately into the attack and chopped up the Fapla formation, killing about 250 men. For practical purposes 47 Brigade now ceased to exist; abandoning their weapons and equipment - including 18 tanks, five armoured cars, three 23mm twin-barrelled anti-aircraft guns and SA-8 and SA-9 high-altitude missiles - the survivors fled over the Lomba under cover of night and were absorbed into 59 Brigade on the northern bank, but next day the Unita forces swarmed across the river and expelled the Angolans from their positions.

The October 3 battle was the turning-point of the offensive. The Angolan advance had lost all its momentum beyond any hope of recovery, and all the brigades began a long but generally orderly withdrawal - no easy task under the circumstances - which eventually took them back almost to where they had started. The South Africans, in turn, were pulled back over the Lomba on October 7, since their immediate task had been completed.

But the fighting was far from over. Two brigades, 16 and 21, were now deployed at the source of the Chambinga River and 59 Brigade and a tactical group were based between the Vimpulo and Mianei rivers. Although all had been damaged to some extent, they were still coherent forces, and the immediate priority was still to prevent their regrouping for another thrust against Mavinga. It was decided, therefore, that the entire Angolan presence must be expelled from the territory east of the Cuito River.

Reinforcements were despatched from SWA/Namibia: a detachment of 4 South African Infantry, some 127mm MRLs, a squadron of the first South African tanks ever to be deployed in Angola - the redoubtable "Olifant", a completely updated Centurion - and a troop of G-6 self-propelled guns, virtual toolroom models, since the huge vehicles were not yet in production (one of them, suitably tarted up, formed part of the South African exhibition at the FIDA 88 arms show in Chile in March of 1988).

While waiting for them to arrive, the South Africans used their artillery and aircraft to pin down the Angolans. In the next few weeks thousands of 155mm shells forced the brigades to lie low, sadly battered the Chambinga River bridge that Fapla relied on for resupply and (from October 9, when the guns got within range) pounded the Cuito Cuanavale base into uselessness and forced the Angolans/Cubans to switch their flying operations to Menongue.

The neutralising of Cuito Cuanavale's air capability was a serious blow. Unlike the South Africans, the Marxists kept their combat aircraft

under stringent ground control, and because this had now to be exercised from distant Menongue the SADF/SWATF elements benefited. In addition, the fuel-gulping Angolan/Cuban fighters now had a much shorter holding time over the battle areas. Thanks partly to these factors, the Cuban/Angolan pilots inflicted minimal damage on the South Africans in the months to come (one G-5, one logistics lorry and one water-bowser hit, and no personnel losses), although they flew more than 1000 sorties over the South Africans.

If Cuito Cuanavale had still been functional there is no doubt the South Africans would have suffered more, since their anti-aircraft capability consisted of little more than some manually operated 20mm guns, a few modern but not-very-mobile 35mm guns and a number of captured SA-7 missiles which frequently malfunctioned through sheer old age.

Almost two years later, the South Africans' intentions as regards Cuito Cuanavale is still a matter for hot debate. According to the Angolan/Cuban propaganda machine the South Africans and Unita assaulted it several times between September of 1987 and March of 1988, but were bloodily repulsed each time; as a result the base has acquired, at least in certain circles, a certain heroic aura of victory which was polished to the greatest possible lustre, even to the extent of issuing hastily minted special campaign medals to the defenders while the shelling was still in progress.

In this effort to snatch a media victory out of what was essentially a military defeat (since Cuito Cuanavale was rendered useless) the Angolans were aided by the silence of the South Africans, who adhered grimly to their policy of saying as little as possible. It was a policy which had been applied at intervals since Operation Savannah and which had evoked widespread criticism, some of it justified. In the past Pretoria's main reasons for doing so centred on the need for security and also on the fact that its forces were often involved in clandestine or semi-clandestine operations. In this case there were additional reasons, which were not apparent till late in 1988 and make interesting reading because they indicate that the official silence was inspired by more than just a wish to prevent the SADF's mainly supportive activities from creating the wrong impression.

This came out when Jannie Geldenhuys, while addressing defence correspondents at Oshakati, mused: "Facts and propaganda (about the Lomba River fighting) are now so intermingled that sometimes you don't know which is which. From the other side propaganda is made from time to time about South Africa being driven out of Angola. Many people believed this because we didn't inform the media properly. We didn't tell as much as we would have liked to, but there were inhibiting factors, such as the fact that it was Unita's war, and in this case we couldn't claim Unita's successes – and the fact is that Unita played a very important role.

"If we had trumpeted about Cuban weaknesses, we would have placed them in the situation where they would have had to regain their prestige. There is also the fact that Russia is a great power and one should not try to humiliate a great power. Perhaps we forget the impact of the fact that wars are no longer declared. A war which is not declared also has a more inhibiting factor as regards the flow of news. There is also the fact that information released while fighting is in progress can help the enemy considerably.

"As a result we couldn't give the press what we wanted (and) it came about that the other side exploited this."

Propaganda aside, however, the Cuito Cuanavale controversy is not as simple as it seems. There remains a substantial doubt as to whether the South Africans and Unita wanted to capture the base. The SADF has maintained consistently that (in the words of one spokesman) "it was at no time feasible or desirable to physically occupy Cuito Cuanavale … (the object was) to render it useless to Fapla".

Jannie Geldenhuys himself has always denied that the South Africans had any such object in mind. On October 10 of 1988 he told defence correspondents at Oshakati: "I want to stress that it was never our aim to capture Cuito Cuanavale. You have it from the horse's mouth. I not only did not order (the South African forces) to attack Cuito Cuanavale but said that we must not attack it unless it fell into our lap, for the following reasons.

"Firstly, we didn't really have well-balanced forces – we had concentrated on equipment in order to make up for the lacks of certain equipment in the Unita forces. But as you know, when you capture an objective you must hold it … There was no point in capturing Cuito Cuanavale if we couldn't hold it (and) it would have been difficult to hold; it is not an area which lends itself to good defence … (Secondly) we placed a very high premium on human life, and that's why, if we could have taken it without fighting for it, we would have taken it, but not by fighting for it if that meant sacrificing life."

At another stage in the briefing Geldenhuys remarked that "tactically it would have been totally unsound to fight across Cuito Cuanavale in the face of a strong enemy. We would have taken another route if Cuito Cuanavale had been the objective."

Discussing the same subject at another briefing in late January of 1989, he said: "A big thing has been made (of the fact) that we were defeated there. I laid down the mission myself and I never said it was an objective. In fact, I made the point that we would not fight for Cuito Cuanavale unless it fell into our lap, for the simple reason that we were on the wrong side of the obstacle (presumably he meant the Cuito River). You need to have your head read if you fight for an objective on the wrong side of an obstacle. We have never intended to stay in Angola (and) Unita would not have been able to hold Cuito Cuanavale by itself in the face of a counter-attack. So there was absolutely no point in going for it, and we didn't."

At this remove one might well make two comments. Firstly, the South Africans did not need to capture Cuito Cuanavale, since their artillery enabled them to neutralise it (to such good effect, let it be added, that eventually the Marxist headquarters was evacuated from the base and relocated elsewhere). Secondly, the South Africans, as far as is known, suffered no losses in the vicinity, whereas one would expect at least a few casualties in any attack on a position as heavily defended as was Cuito Cuanavale.

All this time the South African government was denying its forces had anything to do with the Angolan fighting, no matter how obvious it was that the SADF and SWATF were heavily involved. Its reasons might have seemed sound enough, but there had been too many false denials over the years and obviously it could not divulge the reason for its silence, so that the South African public (and the world at large) did not believe it; and when, on November 2, Defence Headquarters announced that 11 SADF and SWATF soldiers had been killed fighting Plan two days earlier, it was immediately and widely assumed that they had been casualties of the Angolan fighting.

In fact the SADF was telling the truth. The soldiers had been killed - most of them in a single mortar-bomb explosion - when SWATF headquarters had despatched a force to take out a Plan base in the shallow area across the border from central Ovamboland. The operation succeeded and more than 150 insurgents were killed, and it came as such a surprise that it was some days before the news reached the Swapo high command (which then dismissed the whole affair with the statement that "in truth, nothing like this has happened".

The incident came on the eve of the heaviest fighting Operation Modular was to see. On November 9 the SADF/SWATF/Unita force, now a brigade strong, assailed 16 Brigade between the Chambinga and Hube rivers, and on November 11 an element also wiped out the Fapla tactical group between the Vimpulo and Mianei rivers; 59 Brigade was then hastily withdrawn to new positions on the other side of Cuito Cuanavale. In seven days of fighting in thick bush the allied force killed a known 525 men, knocked out 33 tanks - one of them reportedly at a range of just 10 metres - and captured large amounts of weapons, vehicles and equipment for a loss of 16 South Africans.

No further large-scale action was seen - although the artillery continued to pound Cuito Cuanavale and SAAF fighters still raided Fapla convoys setting out from Menongue - and on December 5 Operation Modular officially ended, with General Geldenhuys announcing that the South African and SWATF troops would begin to withdraw, now that they had completed their tasks. Geldenhuys stressed that it was a tactical disengagement, taking place under operational circumstances. This meant that the forces concerned had constantly to be mindful of the conflict which was still in progress, and which could even mean their taking offensive action en passant. This was exactly what happened, and in the months to come the South Africans were frequently accused of going back on their word.

By now, however, the strategic situation had worsened rather than improved. The October defeats had impelled the Marxists to fly in more troops from Cuba. Elements of the Cubans' 50 Division had been arriving since November, and Fapla reinforcements were continuing to flow into the Cuito Cuanavale area, accompanied by T-62 tanks. From the South Africans' point of view, the only consolation was that the new concentrations provided better targets for the G-5 guns, which did much execution, and the fact that the fresh Cuban troops were being concentrated in the south-west, far from the battle areas, in spite of loud boasts from their superiors in Luanda that they had been ordered to drive the South Africans out of Angola.

Nevertheless, the situation caused grave disquiet in Pretoria. It was obvious that a new offensive against Unita might be launched at any time, since the end-of-year rains had been extremely patchy, and in the slightly longer term the new Cubans also posed a distinct threat to SWA/Namibia, since the lightly-armed SWATF battalions would not be able to withstand a "conventional" thrust southwards. Fidel Castro was the joker in the Angolan pack. The self-proclaimed "liberator" of the Third World and a man to whom machismo was as essential as oxygen, he was capable of anything, while the Angolans were

desperate men who would clutch at any straw. In the absence of any intervention from their Russian paymasters, there was no telling what they might not do.

It was decided that Unita, helped by the South Africans, would pre-empt any offensive action by means of a new operation, nicknamed "Hooper" and aimed at clearing all Fapla troops out of the area between the Cuatir II and Chambinga rivers. If this could be done it would not only prevent the resumption of the offensive but would also drastically reduce the size of the Fapla fighting elements, making it easier for Unita to hold the area east of Cuito Cuanavale.

Hooper did not start immediately, because the South African national servicemen were scheduled to finish on December 15 and their replacements had to be worked up to the required level. Meanwhile the G-5s and G-6s continued to hammer various Fapla targets. Supply convoys to Cuito Cuanavale were shelled, the base itself was prevented from operating and repair crews were driven away from the damaged Cuito River bridge (it was later destroyed altogether in an aerial attack using a new SAAF "smart bomb" whose existence was not to be disclosed for nearly a year).

In the meantime Savimbi took advantage of the Fapla defeats to reactivate central Angola. He secured the route to the Benguela railway again, and near the end of December a 900-man Unita force deploying four captured T-55 tanks recaptured Munhango in a 90-minute fight in which 28 Fapla soldiers died and an Mi-24 gunship was shot down. At this stage the rest of the garrison fled. On December 30 a heavily guarded and strategically important bridge over the Cuanza River was attacked and seriously damaged, although who the attackers were has never been revealed (Angola took a week to announce the bridge's "partial destruction" by "South African commandos, using frogmen", while Unita claimed its forces had "totally destroyed" the bridge after a week of intense fighting).

It had been a bloody year for all concerned. Seventy-two South Africans and SWA/Namibian servicemen had died north and south of the border, and 747 insurgents, while one SWA/Namibian soldier had been captured by Fapla in the shallow area. Unita's losses had been heavy, probably several thousand, but it had scored several victories. For the Angolans 1987 had been 12 months of unmitigated disaster. They had lost more than 3 000 men and a vast amount of equipment, weaponry and munitions. Worse than that, they had been forced to retreat in the south and had lost most of their earlier gains in the central part of the country. In provinces far removed from the battlefront the insurgency had flared up again as the local Unita contingents took advantage of the reduced Fapla presence. The national economy, seriously ailing before the fighting started, was now staggering.

Luanda's hawks, some South African observers predicted, had taken such a bloody nose that they had lost their influence. The Lomba River offensive had been their last throw.

But Unita and the SADF knew better, and were preparing for yet another outburst of fighting which was not long in coming.

While the SAAF, the G-5s and G-6s continued to pound the enemy, the South Africans and Unita rounded off their preparations and then proceeded to bide their time, waiting for the right weather conditions: experienced rainy-season fighters by now, what they wanted was bad weather, with low cloud cover and as much rain as possible to thwart the Angolan/Cuban aircraft.

On January 13 conditions were right for their task, the expulsion of 21 Brigade from its fortified positions along the Cuatir II. Aware, no doubt, of the Angolan soldiers' well-known disinclination to fight at night, the South African/Unita force went in around dusk, making the first contact at 6pm. Two hours of fighting followed, after which the Angolans broke and fled, leaving behind about 250 dead and numbers of artillery pieces, tanks, multiple rocket-launchers and supply vehicles. Unita casualties are not known, but the South Africans suffered no losses of men, vehicles or equipment. The Unita troops then proceeded to mop up and settle in.

The Angolans did not react immediately. On January 14 Defence Minister Pedro Maria Tonha was quoted by Angop as saying that the South Africans had shelled Fapla positions 15 times since January 5, while SAAF aircraft had bombed a populated area near Cuito Cuanavale and a military supply column. The South Africans' aim, Tonha added, was to capture Cuito Cuanavale and then extend their activities further to the north.

Then on January 15, around the same time as Pretoria announced that SAAF aircraft had launched a "successful" strike at an unnamed Swapo base in Angola, the Angolan defence ministry made its first reference to the clash. Six thousand South African troops, it said, backed by aircraft, tanks and artillery, had attacked government forces just east of Cuito Cuanavale in a "major battle" aimed at seizing Cuito Cuanavale in order to "ease the infiltration" of Unita into the central highlands and block the rebuilding of the Benguela railway. The ministry did not provide further details or mention the outcome of the battle.

A Unita spokesman in Lisbon was more specific, although his statement, like the proverbial curate's egg, was good only in parts: without any South African aid his organisation had "destroyed the (the) celebrated 21st Brigade" in an eight-hour battle and "completely encircled" Cuito Cuanavale. The truth of the matter lay somewhere in between: the fact that the South Africans suffered no losses whatever would indicate that they were (as Pretoria claimed) acting in support of Unita.

The retreating remnant of 21 Brigade was not pursued, and eventually reached the Fapla logistics base at Tumpo, near Cuito Cuanavale. There, while the other Fapla elements east of the Cuito River absorbed reinforcements and frantically strengthened their positions in anticipation of another South African/Unita offensive, 21 Brigade was reinforced, regrouped and re-equipped.

While this was happening the Angolan propaganda machine ground out claims and allegations that ranged from exaggerated to completely spurious. On January 21 the Luanda correspondent of AIM claimed that Cuban pilots had clashed directly with the SAAF for the first time when they bombed South African military positions as part of a last-ditch effort to prevent Cuito Cuanavale from falling (which an SADF spokesman dismissed as "not a new claim"). On January 22 Angop claimed Fapla had halted the advance of 6000 South African

troops which had been engaged in besieging Cuito Cuanavale, and had shot down about 40 SAAF aircraft which had been providing support, while Tonha made a separate claim that full-scale aerial battles were raging around Cuito Cuanavale and Munhango and added that Pretoria was massing more troops along the border in order "to launch even greater aggression against Angola".

On January 24 Angolan spokesman Major Mario Placido reported that Cuito Cuanavale had been heavily shelled in the course of a concentrated South African attack. This claim has long puzzled military analysts, because none has ever been able to find any evidence, official or unofficial, that the South Africans had any hand in such an attack, if, in fact, one took place at all. The situation is further confused by the fact that on January 25 Unita claimed that the base had been abandoned. Possibly the result of bad intelligence, since the Unita troops were encamped between 7km and 12km east of Cuito Cuanavale, this was totally incorrect and the Angolans quite rightly denied the claim (although they admitted that heavy fighting was taking place around Munhango).

Shortly afterwards 21 Brigade burst out of Tumpo, overcame fierce resistance offered by Unita and reoccupied the positions from which it had been driven less than a fortnight earlier. It did not attempt to capitalise on this victory, though, which meant that much of the possible tactical effect was lost. Strangely enough, the Angolans did not make much propaganda capital out of what was undoubtedly a stunning upset for the allies: Major Placido's version was that Fapla troops, covered by Cuban pilots, had driven "South African" forces back to a position 30km from the base and were strengthening their defences to hold it "at all costs".

Cuito Cuanavale's anti-aircraft defences were very good, he added, and the SAAF had not yet dared to launch any attacks on it - a neat evasion of the fact that air attacks were not necessary, since the base was being pounded non-stop by the G-5s. At one stage it was reported that up to 200 shells were falling on it every day, and the shelling made life there so unbearable that a few days later the garrison commander pulled out and re-established his headquarters at Nancova, about 25km to the north, leaving Cuito Cuanavale manned by an assortment of hardened veterans and almost untrained "youth pioneers" in their mid-teens, all of them growing increasingly hungry because of the paucity of convoys from Menongue.

Nevertheless Placido's statement, like so many others, fell on receptive ears in the absence of statements from the South Africans, who were still maintaining a tomb-like silence in their efforts to avoid stealing Savimbi's thunder. By now their discretion was beginning to backfire, with opposition parties' questions growing more and more direct. On January 27 Progressive Federal Party leader Colin Eglin demanded more facts, saying that South Africans were "concerned and adult enough" to know what was going on. His call was echoed by the Conservative party's defence spokesman, Koos van der Merwe, who said that the tax-paying public was entitled to know what was going on in Angola, because "in general the public should be informed so that they can judge the government's actions".

In the meantime Chester Crocker had managed to restart his limping peace initiative and had organised a two-day meeting in Luanda for January 28 and 29. The talks got off to a good start when Dos Santos made conciliatory noises just before the

Opposite
A group of Unita and South African soldiers cross the Lomba River, just before the wholesale Angolan and Cuban withdrawal towards the protection of Cuito Cuanavale

American's arrival on January 27. He was ready to negotiate on SWA/Namibian independence, he told newsmen in Luanda, and had already presented what he described as "constructive proposals". He did not say who he had presented the proposals to, but it was obvious that the main recipient would be Crocker, and according to observers there were indications that the Cubans – who, at Angola's express request, were to be present for the first time – were willing to entertain the thought of a phased withdrawal of their troops, now said to be 40 000 strong.

Although nothing concrete was achieved at the meeting, Crocker left Luanda on January 31 heartened by the promise of further talks. According to the Portuguese news agency Lusa the participants had decided to break off in order to "analyse new elements brought up in the talks in preparation for future negotiations". The next day, State Department spokesman Charles Redman said from Washington that Cuban and Angolan officials had affirmed for the first time that they accepted a plan to withdraw all Cuban troops from Angola. The next step, he went on, would be for the Angolans "to come forward with specific ways to close the gap on a Cuban troop withdrawal schedule".

US Secretary of State George Shultz expressed his pleasure at the outcome of the talks – it was, he told the House of Representatives Foreign Affairs Committee, "an important development that holds the promise of a settlement in the region", adding that he hoped Angola would now put forward "concrete and realistic schedules" to be passed on to Pretoria.

Pik Botha was less enthusiastic. Speaking at a press conference immediately after Shultz's remarks, he said that South Africa would not be interested in a token withdrawal which merely rearranged the forces in the area while effectively putting a Swapo government in Windhoek and destroying Unita. Angolan and Cuban acceptance of a withdrawal linked to SWA/Namibian independ-

ence was "nothing new", he said. The most important element of the acceptance had been Angola's admission that there were 40 000 Cubans in the country, and he could see nothing positive or constructive in the announcement unless it was accompanied by the "crucial factor" of a timetable.

The "crucial factor" was not forthcoming, no doubt because from Luanda's viewpoint, and especially that of the hawks in Dos Santos's cabinet, no such withdrawal could even be contemplated while Unita had taken the initiative in the southeast (21 Brigade's victory notwithstanding) and was exercising military and administrative control over an estimated 35 percent of the country. Instead, Angola's ambassador in the United Kingdom, Elisio de Figueiredo, said in a BBC interview on February 3 that there had been no change in Angola's position about Cuban troops – the Cubans would leave only after South Africa had stopped supporting Unita and had withdrawn from Angola, and Resolution 435 had been implemented.

In Cuba, meanwhile, the strictly controlled news media made no mention of Angola's acceptance of a linked withdrawal, possibly because of the population's increasing war-weariness (as one Havana journalist told a Western correspondent: "Most Cubans won't say it aloud, but they don't understand why kids should go to a remote African country to get killed.").

The chemical-weapons row between South Africa and Angola had surfaced again by this time. Late in January the South Africans had announced that they were sending a military medical team to investigate persistent civilian reports that Fapla was using poison gas against Unita; on February 3 the Angolans formally denied doing so and accused South Africa of waging a disinformation campaign, and on February 8 went further, with Luanda's ambassador in France, Luis de Almeida, alleging that the SADF had employed toxic gas against Fapla troops after failing to capture Cuito Cuanavale and calling on the international com-

Above
A T-55 tank captured from 21 (Fapla) Brigade during the Battle of Tumpo 1 in January of 1988. Attached to its bows is a mineplough

munity to condemn what he described as the "new racist South African crime".

An SADF spokesman replied that it was to be expected that Angola would make such an accusation, "especially after the SADF has already confirmed that a South African team of medical experts has been invited by Unita to investigate Angola's use of this kind of substance." The South Africans have consistently denied using any chemical weapons against either Fapla or Swapo, be it poison gas or napalm.

There were now strong rumours doing the rounds in London and elsewhere that Angolan peace talks would take place "within a few months", possibly in Portugal, after publication of reports that Soviet leader Mikhail Gorbachev was believed to have grown tired of pumping huge quantities of military aid into Angola, and was pressuring the Angolans while the US was leaning on South Africa and Savimbi.

No obvious signs of such pressure were to be seen on either side, however; on February 11 Pik Botha, while briefing newspaper correspondents on the Cuban withdrawal issue, openly scoffed at the Angolans' attitude. South Africa would welcome progress by Crocker on breaking the deadlock, but proposals put forward so far by Dos Santos were "nothing but a rearrangement of the war theatre ... a man like President Dos Santos would be the least inclined to let go the only force that keeps him in power ... The SA government will not accept any plan which does not ensure that there is genuine withdrawal, with systems to monitor that withdrawal. We're just a bit tired of these deceitful little games, and we trust our American friends will also become tired of them."

Botha noted that he did not believe that the White House had the support of the US Congress on "important foreign policy ventures" like South Africa, and "that makes it risky for my government, or any government, to rely on agreements with the US. This truth is filtering through to quite a large number of countries."

Angola was scarcely less discouraging. Three days later, on February 14, Luanda's Foreign Minister, Afonso van Dunem, said bluntly that the presentation of a withdrawal calendar depended "above all" on the US, South Africa and "other countries" ceasing to support Unita.

On February 15 Dos Santos told journalists during a visit to the island nation of Principe and Sao Tome that South Africa had increased its forces in southern Angola to more than 6 000 men in the past three days, and that its actions were intended to deflect attention from Pretoria's apartheid policies. Dos Santos obviously did not realise that renewed large-scale fighting had broken out on the Cuito Cuanavale front.

The South Africans had been waiting for the right weather again; it arrived on February 14, and around 2pm that day Commandant Mike Muller took 61 Mechanised Battalion into an attack on 59 Brigade, which was lying up at Tumpo, about 20km east of Cuito Cuanavale (to diminish the chances of aerial intervention even more, 32 Battalion had been ordered to attack Menongue at the same time). Hours of fighting ended with 59 Brigade breaking off contact, but only in order to regroup and counter-attack.

The counter-attack failed, however, and 59 Brigade pulled back, having lost about 230 killed and a large amount of weaponry and equipment ranging from tanks and armoured personnel-carriers to anti-aircraft guns, multiple rocket-

launchers and a high-altitude guided missile system. The South Africans lost four men killed, all occupants of one of five Ratel infantry fighting vehicles hit by direct fire during the Fapla counter-attack (two Olifants were also damaged, presumably in the original attack, but were repaired and returned to action before the fighting ended).

At the same time Unita attacked 21 Brigade and drove it out of its positions again, although without inflicting serious damage.

The two brigades retreated some distance and then dug in about 8km east of Cuito Cuanavale, where they stayed while the war of words hotted up once more as the Angolans made wilder and wilder accusations in order to cover up the fact that their offensive had been a total and embarrassingly public failure.

Jannie Geldenhuys announced the SADF deaths, saying that South African forces in the area had been fighting "a guard action on the flank" in response to a Fapla counter-attack, and adding that Unita had made "significant advances" at the weekend. Angop reacted by saying that South Africa had launched a new attack against Fapla positions east of Cuito Cuanavale (which was partly correct, because the agency carefully omitted to make any mention of Unita's action against 21 Brigade), and then went on to say that SADF troop strengths in the Cuando-Cubango province now stood at 7 000 (which was totally wrong). On February 19 Dos Santos put out a statement that in the past 45 days South Africa had lost 140 men, six fighters, 47 tanks and "various armoured cars". An SADF spokesman described his figures as "ludicrous", because "it is common knowledge that the Defence Force announces its operational losses after the next of kin have been informed". This was no less than the truth, and the SADF's figures were never challenged, then or later.

A further humiliation was visited on the Angolans that same day. A bomb had gone off in the First National Bank's Oshakati branch at a time when it was crowded with civilians, most of them black. Twenty people were killed outright and many others were wounded, six critically. One of the latter, ironically, was the daughter of the pro-Swapo Lutheran Bishop of Ovamboland, Cleophas Dumeni. The South Africans immediately stated that the bomb had been planted by Swapo; more to the point, SAAF fighters carried out their first strike at Lubango – southern Angola's largest Fapla and Swapo headquarters – and inflicted severe damage on two targets, Swapo's most important training military institution, the Tobias Hanyeko Training Centre, and an insurgent holding camp about 10km from the city.

Officially the SADF's attitude was that the attack had been simply another part of its war against Swapo; unofficially it was made clear to observers that the raid was aimed partly at expressing anger over the Oshakati blast and partly to show the Angolans that their much-vaunted air defences were anything but invulnerable (just two days later, though, a SAAF Mirage was brought down by gunfire while attacking an Angolan/Cuban position somewhere in the south-east, killing the pilot, Major Edward Every).

Four days later a Swapo spokesman in Luanda denied that any of its installations had been damaged or any of his personnel killed in the attack, claimed the Oshakati bomb had been planted by "South African agents" and then made the grotesque accusation that the Oshakati bank manager and his deputy had left the room a few

Above
Major Dick Every

minutes before the bomb went off, leaving "many black people ... deliberately locked up in the bank (to be) cold-bloodedly killed and maimed in the blast." An FNB spokesman dismissed this allegation as "outrageous", pointing out that the manager, his deputy and the manager's wife had all been wounded in the explosion.

In Angola, meanwhile, there was a lull of sorts. Cuito Cuanavale was garrisoned by a hitherto uncommitted formation, 13 Brigade, and defended on its southern flank by another, 8 Brigade, while 21, 25 and 59 Brigades were dug in on the eastern bank of the Cuito River, the damaged bridge having been made useable although not repaired. The South African G-5s sporadically shelled all these targets, and especially Cuito Cuanavale, to make sure the airstrip remained unserviceable. On February 20 Geldenhuys reiterated that a tactical disengagement was in progress, but warned once again that it did not mean a sudden rush south-wards to the border. Care had to be taken to ensure the safety of the soldiers concerned, and also to make certain that Unita was in a position to keep the objectives the South Africans had helped it to acquire.

To the latter end another battle was fought, this time on February 25, just a day after Dos Santos had told the Angolan parliament that the country would not allow South Africa to force it into accepting a peace settlement with Unita. The Fapla commander had withdrawn 21, 25 and 59 Brigades from the east bank of the Cuito and sent them back to the Tumpo logistics base east of Cuito Cuanavale; that night a combined South African/Unita force under Commandant Mike Muller of 61 Mechanised Battalion assaulted Tumpo, while a Unita force simultaneously launched an attack on another Fapla element positioned at nearby Dala.

This second battle at Tumpo is not as well-known as some of the earlier clashes, possibly because Unita took the entire credit, but it consisted of two days of hard fighting in which the attackers were subjected to heavy and accurate fire from an estimated 58 artillery pieces the Angolans had emplaced on the west bank of the Tumpo River, a constant air threat (59 MiG overflights), thick bush and numerous minefields.

As a result the attack failed in its primary purpose and Tumpo remained in Angolan/Cuban hands. On the other hand, the brigades had been forced to pull back into their main perimeters, so that they were now crammed into a small area, providing a good artillery target if this became necessary, and giving Unita a free hand in the east and south. The Fapla element at Dala, too, had been compelled to abandon its outlying positions.

Unita losses in the Tumpo and Dala fighting are not known and neither are the Fapla casualties, although the SADF later described the latter as "obviously substantial" and a spokesman for Savimbi put the figure at 172 Angolans and 10 Cubans; the South Africans lost three dead, while four tanks were temporarily immobilised and two Ratels were damaged by indirect artillery fire.

This was the last major fighting in which the South Africans took part. Operation Hooper was wound down and replaced by Operation Packer, in terms of which the remaining SADF and SWATF presence - soon reduced by the ongoing disengagement to less than 1 500 men, including both "teeth" and "tail" - remained deployed east of Cuito Cuanavale to ensure that Fapla did not attempt to break out of the Tumpo area or launch another offensive.

Some exchanges of shots were still taking place - on February 28 two South African soldiers were killed by "indirect fire" - but it was doubtful whether, in fact, Fapla was capable of anything but very limited action at this stage, since it had taken a fearful mauling in the fighting of the past six months.

A total of 4 768 of its officers and men were known to have been killed, including a disproportionate number of what armies call "leader group", the precious sprinkling of trained and experienced operational commanders who make the difference between an organised force and a rabble.

It had lost weapons and equipment worth billions, some destroyed and other items captured: 94 tanks, eight MiG-23s, four MiG-21s, helicopters, armoured reconnaissance and troop-carrying vehicles, multiple rocket-launchers, mortars, almost 400 logistics vehicles, SA-8 and SA-9 high-altitude missile systems, artillery, radar systems, anti-aircraft guns and many other items, most of it brand new and some so advanced that Western powers came hat in hand to the South Africans to ask if they might examine it. In Pretoria, jubilant South African analysts calculated that when hidden costs such as running expenses and the training and deployment of new troops was counted in, the entire Angolan military budget for 1988/89 would be absorbed.

In terms of ground lost and opportunities thrown away the picture was even worse. The Fapla brigades were actually at a greater disadvantage than before the offensive, crammed into the Cuito Cuanavale area and kept there by Unita activities and the threat of another South African operation. Cuito Cuanavale remained unuseable, its radars smashed and its runways a shooting gallery for the G-5s; all resupply was by way of frequently-ambushed convoys from Menongue.

No fewer than 12 Fapla brigades were tied down between Menongue and the west bank of the Cuito River because Luanda could not take the chance of Cuito Cuanavale being cut off and either starved out or captured by direct assault. As a result, Savimbi was free to raise the banner of rebellion almost where he pleased, from the Cunene province in the far south to the remote enclave of Cabinda, and he took full advantage of the opportunity, particularly along the Benguela line.

Operations Modular and Hooper cost the SADF and SWATF 31 killed (out of 43 for Angola and the operational area combined) and 90 wounded, with two Mirages and a Bosbok light aircraft shot down, three Olifant tanks destroyed or damaged and captured, four Ratel infantry fighting vehicles destroyed and various other vehicles damaged. Naturally these figures do not give the hidden costs. The execrable operating conditions wreaked much damage on hundreds of logistics vehicles and operating costs had run into many millions, not to mention the expenditure of vast quantities of expensive 155mm artillery rounds (months later Magnus Malan stated in Parliament that the cost of ammunition used in "actual combat", as distinct from that expended in training, had increased from R72,5 million in 1985/86 to R136,8 million in 1986/87 to R328,7 million in 1987/88).

Nevertheless, in terms of objectives achieved there can be no doubt that the South Africans had scored a victory. In addition, the Olifant had proved as sturdy and capable of absorbing punishment as its Centurion ancestor, and infinitely better as regards range and firepower ('in tank against tank fighting we didn't lose one', a senior SADF officer reflected later), and the virtually unique G-6 had not only proved it was viable but could now be thoroughly "debugged" from practical battle experience.

All this time the border war continued - at least in words. On March 6 Swapo alleged from Luanda that its forces had killed 11 South African soldiers, five in a contact near Ohopoho in Kaokoland and six in a landmine explosion, and mortared the base at Okalongo, inflicting heavy losses (unspecified) in men and material. The claim was completely overshadowed, however, by a surprise move from Magnus Malan.

Up to this time the Americans had handled all Angolan peace negotiations. Now Malan made a direct public approach to the Soviet Union which amounted to an offer that if the Russians agreed to install a free, neutral and genuinely non-aligned government in Angola, Pretoria would not insist that it be pro-South African.

The offer from Malan - of all the cabinet ministers, the one who customarily warned the loudest and longest about the dangers of Soviet expansionism - took all the observers, expert or otherwise, totally by surprise. Obviously he had not made the offer off his own bat. That indicated a radical shift in policy. Why?

Various theories were offered. It was pointed out that the South Africans' close relationship with the US was under great strain because Congress had voted in favour of trade sanctions aimed to fight apartheid (although none of the parliamentarians who had sponsored such legislation had explained how the destruction of the South African economy would benefit anyone in the country). One newspaper quoted "government sources" as saying that the offer was intended to emphasise South Africa's status as a regional power and also to send the US a signal that Pretoria was sceptical about the Americans' claims that they were making progress on persuading the Angolans to join with Unita in a government of national unity.

John Barrett of the South African Institute of International Affairs asked pointedly: "The question is, are they trying to put a finger in America's eye, or are they really serious?" Barrett then answered his own question and said that there was evidence Pretoria meant what it said. Russian-affairs expert Philip Nel went further and opined that direct South African-Russian talks on Angola were now a possibility, although he warned that it might be a long time before they actually took place.

No doubt Barrett and Nel understood perfectly well - even if most other observers did not, or did not want to - that Malan's offer was completely in line with South African government policy. The South Africans' support for Savimbi had never been based on simplistic kill-the-commies ideological grounds. They were interested in Angola only in the context of the border war. What it boiled down to was that they did not really care who ruled Angola, as long as the government concerned did not interfere in the border war by aiding and abetting the Swapo insurgents, just as they did not really care who finally ended up in power in Windhoek as long as a future Namibia did not become a thorn in their political flesh.

This being so, a Pretoria offer that would lead to the installation of a neutral government in Luanda, like the one the Soviets were proposing for Afghanistan, made perfect sense. It is certain that the South Africans believed, with some justification, that an immediate government of national unity for Angola was little more than a pipe-dream, considering the vast ideological differences between the MPLA and Unita and the bitter 13-year-old civil war in which neither side would concede either victory or defeat.

Malan's offer got nowhere - for the time being, anyway. Three days later the Soviets turned him down flat. The Angolan and Afghan situations were "completely different", spokesman Gennady Gerasimov said. "We believe that the most important subject on which the South African government does not speak is apartheid," he told journalists in Moscow, "interference in the affairs of their neighbour states, Angola, for example, and Namibia. This is the crux of the matter."

Yet the ice had been broken, and various high-ranking diplomats privately expressed the opinion that the Russians, Angolans and Cubans had become convinced that the key to ending the conflict lay in direct negotiations with South Africa. This was confirmed the same day by a claim from the editor of a confidential Portuguese newsletter covering Angola that President Dos Santos had sent President P W Botha a message by way of Lisbon-based intermediaries, expressing willingness to meet for face-to-face discussions.

Two days later there was partial official confirmation when the Angolan Minister of Industry, Pedro van Dunem, said his government had received indications that the South Africans were considering opening direct negotiations with Luanda, and added that "the time has come to hold direct talks with Pretoria. The US has lost its credibility as a mediator between us and South Africa". Unita was backed by South Africa, which was also engaged in a massive military assault on targets in southern Angola, Van Dunem pointed out, and therefore a peace deal needed to be worked out directly with Pretoria.

This last was no more than a face-saver - the South Africans were sitting tight east of the Cuito River while Unita conducted its wide-spread insurgency - but it proved that the Angolans were serious.

Just how serious can be judged from a report a few days later from a Lisbon-domiciled South African correspondent, Ken Pottinger, who quoted a "well-informed military source" as saying: "The Faplas have taken such a beating in recent months that moderates in Luanda are convinced that only direct talks with Pretoria can prevent further bloodshed." There is another theory, put about by usually well-informed sources but never officially confirmed - that the Angolans decided to make a move because they had got wind of a South African-American-Unita plan to exert pressure on the MPLA to negotiate by having Savimbi unilaterally declare southern Angola independent.

Be that as it may, there seems to be no doubt about the urgency of the Angolan approach. Some months after the event one of South Africa's most senior officials told the writer of this book that the first Angolan approach to Pretoria had been so urgent and pleading in tone that initially the South Africans had been inclined to ignore it as the work of an overwrought or rebellious Angolan official who was acting on his own initiative. Then another approach was made, and the South Africans were astonished to discover that the first one had been completely authentic. The Angolans wanted to talk, and soon.

On March 14 Foreign Minister Pik Botha announced in Geneva, following long discussions with Chester Crocker, that the Angolans had accepted in principle that a Cuban withdrawal

should be linked with implementation of the peace process in SWA/Namibia. He made it clear that he was dissatisfied by the lack of details in the proposals - "numbers, timetables and dates are what I understand by details (and) that is the issue that will have to be taken up now". But, he said, "they apparently acknowledge in principle that there is a linkage between the Cuban withdrawal and the implementation of Resolution 435".

Botha emphasised that South Africa would stand by Savimbi, but it could not prescribe that Unita should be given a role in the government of Angola. That issue was secondary to the Cuban withdrawal, although "the fact is that they enjoy majority support from the people of Angola".

Addressing reporters at Jamba the same day, Savimbi made it clear that he had a very precise idea of what his role should be. He had discussed a joint strategy for negotiations at a secret meeting with PW Botha in Cape Town, he said, and Pretoria was keeping him fully briefed on developments. Talks could soon end the war, he added, noting that the Cubans and Angolans had agreed to a withdrawal and "the Russians now seem to be saying that they would prefer a negotiated settlement to continuing war". There was no question of South Africa leaving him personally out of the forthcoming talks: "I will be there … when you are talking about Unita, you are talking about Savimbi".

No immediate public action followed all these harbingers of peace, except that on March 15 Soviet and Unita officials held very secret talks in Lisbon and Angola returned the bodies of Rowland Liebenberg and Pieter van Breda, the raiders killed in Cabinda in 1985, in exchange for 12 Angolan soldiers captured during the Lomba River fighting. Pik Botha returned from Geneva on March 16 to warn that no "substantial" progress had been made on a regional peace settlement yet, although there were "signals" of direct Luanda-Pretoria talks and the Americans and Russians "could also have important talks in the immediate future" on this subject. At the same time "we are still exchanging ideas on a time-schedule for the withdrawing of Cuban troops and the numbers of Cubans to be withdrawn. No agreement has been reached."

Rumours now began to circulate of a forthcoming peace meeting between Angola and South Africa which would involve Russian, American, Cuban and Unita negotiators as well. Two days later, on March 23, Luanda representative Lopo di Nascimento confirmed that work was proceeding on the text of a peace agreement. Speaking in Harare, Di Nascimento said that "finally we are seeing light at the end of the tunnel and we hope that South Africa does not, at the last minute, once again hide the light we are glimpsing, as it did with Resolution 435". The agreement would be internationally guaranteed by the United Nations, the UN Security Council or the major world powers.

The third battle at Tumpo took place on the same day, March 23, apparently with the aim of clearing the entire east bank of the Cuito. By this time Tumpo was very heavily defended indeed, and the attack was aborted after three Olifants had been disabled in the minefields (to the South Africans' mortification they were salvaged by the Angolans before they could be destroyed). About 13 Unita troops were killed but no SADF personnel, and the South Africans, understandably, made no great fuss about it. The Angolans did not react immediately, possibly because of communications difficulties.

In diplomatic terms Di Nascimento's leaking of news about the four-way negotiations could be only one thing, an attempt to exert pressure on South Africa, and a disgruntled Pik Botha promptly poured cold water on it by noting that it was an example of raising expectations before progress had been made on the most important element, a schedule for a Cuban withdrawal; by this he did not mean that an agreement was impossible, but "we are still very far" from that point.

The following day, March 25, Savimbi startled all the participants - including Pretoria - with an announcement that he had formed a rebel government comprising a prime minister and 16 full and deputy ministers. Angolan and Swapo spokesmen wasted no time in denouncing the formation of the "government" as a cheap propaganda stunt, while Pik Botha would say only that the South African government knew nothing about the matter and he had no comment to make "at this stage". Various Western diplomats saw Savimbi's announcement as an indication that South Africa was indulging in a pressure-play of its own.

None of these manoeuvrings prevented the Angolans from disguising their deteriorating security situation - among other things Unita was in effective control of the Cazombo Salient again, with Fapla holding only a few of the larger towns - by issuing periodical accusations of South African attacks against their forces. One such, however, issued on March 27, contained a grain of truth because it obviously referred to the fighting at Tumpo. Angop's version of the battle was that the SADF had assaulted Cuito Cuanavale between March 18 and 23, but Fapla elements had beaten them off, killing 18 soldiers, destroying four tanks and capturing artillery shells and various documents. None of the documents was made public, however, and since no deaths were announced by the SADF, no great notice was taken of the claim.

Next day Egypt's Minister of State for Foreign Affairs, Boutros Ghali, told reporters in Lusaka that Dos Santos and Savimbi had both indicated to him that they were ready for a face-to-face meeting, with the former setting only one condition - that neither the US nor South Africa be present. Ghali did not say when or where he had obtained this startling commitment, although it was known that Egypt had been trying to mediate between the opponents for some time; in the event, nothing more was heard about any such encounter.

Early in April the US began to exert pressure by spreading the word around Washington that it planned to virtually triple military aid to Unita in an attempt to wean Savimbi away from South Africa and increase pressure on Luanda for internal reconciliation - although observers noted that this was little more than a ploy, since it was unlikely that the intelligence committees controlling "covert" aid would approve any such measure.

On April 17 Angolan Foreign Minister Afonso van Dunem claimed more than 6 000 South African soldiers were preparing for yet another assault on Cuito Cuanavale. Speaking at a diplomatic dinner in Luanda, he said the force was part of a larger South African presence in Angola comprising 9 000 soldiers, 600 artillery pieces and 500 tanks and armoured cars, and reiterated that Luanda refused to participate in any form of negotiations with Unita.

By pure coincidence General Jannie Geldenhuys spoke at a briefing for military correspondents the following day at which he said that the SADF's tactical disengagement from Angola was continuing, although not as fast as had been hoped. The troop level was now considerably less than its high-water mark of 3 000 at the height of the fighting, and "we have also scaled down our equipment. We feel we have safeguarded our interest in south-eastern Angola". At the end of 1987, he said, Swapo had had an estimated 8 700 men, but only a small number was now in the area concerned.

On May 3 the first of what was to be a protracted round of Angolan summit talks opened in London, the main participants being the South Africans under Geldenhuys and Director-General for Foreign Affairs Neil van Heerden, and the Angolans and Cubans, led by Foreign Minister Afonso van Dunem and Cuba's top Africa expert, Jorge Risquet, with an American delegation under Chester Crocker present in a "facilitating" role. Noticeably absent were Unita and Swapo, both of which issued frosty statements about the meeting. Unita's Lisbon spokesman said that "we are going to let the negotiations evolve ... but for there to be peace in Angola, Unita must be part of the negotiating process". A Swapo spokesman in London commented: "If the talks are about Namibia, then the talks should have Swapo around the table."

The talks went well, and the delegations parted after having agreed to meet again in the near future at an unnamed African capital. A joint post-conference statement said only that the meeting had taken place in a "constructive atmosphere" and that progress had been made; London sources said that at the next meeting the Angolans would table specific proposals for the withdrawal of Cuban troops from Angola, and South Africa would contribute proposals for withdrawing its troops across the border and implementing independence in SWA/Namibia.

As the delegations returned to their capitals the SADF announced that Lance-Corporal Hendrik Jacobus Venter had been killed in action in a skirmish against insurgents, while one of his comrades, Private Johan Papenfus, was missing. Some days were to pass before it became known that Papenfus had been wounded and captured, then flown to Cuba for medical treatment.

The London honeymoon did not last for long. Almost as soon as he was back in Havana, Jorge Risquet told a news conference that the Cuban troop presence in Angola had been reinforced. "There were 20 000 Cuban troops in the south and 15 000 in the north," he said. "As there was an increase, now there are more". Just how many more he would not say, but according to Western analysts the figure was now about 40 000. His government's view of the talks, Risquet said, was that they went about securing independence for SWA/Namibia and ensuring that Angola's security was guaranteed. This would require such measures as a withdrawal of South African troops to within the borders of the Republic itself, and an end to US and South African aid to Unita, and "if these conditions are met, the Cuban military contingent will have finished its internationalist mission and will return home".

The Cuban reinforcements came near to provoking open warfare on the border and indefinitely delaying the peace process. During May alone, at the very time that the peace talks were taking place in London and later at Brazzaville, large numbers of Cuban fighting soldiers and considerable amounts of conventional-warfare equipment poured ashore at Namibe, while other contingents were shipped down overland from their posts in the north.

By the end of May about 11 000 infantry had been deployed in southern Angola, as well as 105 T-55 and T-64 battle tanks, an anti-aircraft regiment equipped with guns and high-altitude missiles, an array of advanced radar systems and an artillery regiment with field-guns and multiple rocket-launchers; in addition the old airstrip at Xangongo had been upgraded and extended by 542 metres, obviously to allow its use by high-technology aircraft, while three battalions named "Zebra", "Tiger" and "Lion" – each consisting of about 200 Cubans and 250 Plan insurgents, supported by tank and artillery elements – had been stationed in the shallow area, one only about 60km from the border.

Angolan and Cuban MiG-21s and MiG-23s had also taken to violating SWA/Namibian airspace, usually briefly and at high altitude, so that they were impossible to intercept and could not be shot down because the SADF had no high-altitude missiles (there was one exception, when a MiG-21 flew over Ruacana at low level, frightening the wits out of a pilot who had been stooging around in a light aircraft).

To the South Africans – down to less than 1 000 troops in Angola at this stage – it was a worrying situation. Angolan propaganda to the contrary, the South Africans had virtually no conventional-warfare troops in SWA/Namibia, and the lightly-armed SWATF units could not hope to ward off a sudden Cuban thrust southwards. Likewise, the prospects of external follow-ups against fleeing insurgents were now very slim, because of the backing enjoyed by the Swapo/Cuban battalions. In a sense the South Africans' long-standing practice of undertaking large tasks with forces which were technically far too small was now boomeranging on them.

On the other hand, while feeling rather vulnerable, they were hardly panicky. The Cuban/Angolan ground forces had proved to be no great shakes so far, and neither had their pilots; the South Africans lacked suitable anti-aircraft guns and

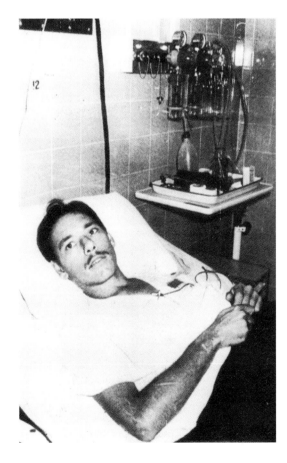

Left
Johan Papenfus in hospital in Havana while undergoing treatment for serious wounds to his left leg

missiles, while years of arms boycotts had left them with obsolescent jet fighters, but the other side had not managed to gain air superiority or inflict much damage during the Lomba River fighting in spite of having top-of-the-line equipment and flying thousands of sorties (one South African unit once racked up a daily total of 59 attacks).

The matter of air superiority was the subject of much public debate in South Africa in the aftermath of the Angolan fighting. Some of the views aired were thoughtful and valid; many of them were grounded in ignorance or malice, or both. Various SAAF spokesmen, including the Chief of the SAAF-designate, Major-General Jan van Loggerenberg, denied and explained, but to little avail.

In October of 1988 Brigadier Jan Steyn, then SAAF Chief of Staff Operations, spoke with unprecedented frankness about the 1987/1988 air war in Angola while briefing a number of defence correspondents.

"The Air Force has the freedom of the air for its own purposes," he said. "There are two very important factors involved: space and time. It is simply not practical to dominate all the airspace all the time. We set limits for ourselves, that is, we avoided direct contact with Fapa (the Angolan air force) as far as possible - one reason being their air-defence network - which raised the risks. At first their aircraft came from Cuito Cuanavale and Menongue, and later from Lubango. From Menongue it took 11 minutes to get (to the fighting zone), and three minutes from Cuito Cuanavale. For us, it was 18 minutes from Ondangwa. So it was difficult to dominate all the airspace."

Steyn went on to reveal other conclusions the SAAF had reached, based on actual observation, debriefings, radio intercepts and other means of intelligence.

The Cubans had played a dominating role in the Angolan fighting. Towards the end, for example, they had taken over operation of up to 90 percent of Fapla's extensive air-defence systems. Joint aircraft formations were almost invariably led by Cubans, who carried out all tasks such as intercepts, while the Angolan pilots "did the donkey work".

Angola had "one of the worst air forces in Africa", but the Cubans, too, had displayed serious weaknesses. In the period under review they had lost aircraft worth 235 million US dollars as a result of bad management, Steyn said. "One year ago the Cubans brought out 10 Sukhoi-22 (fighter-bombers). In eight months they lost seven of them in flying accidents."

Russian doctrine had been stringently applied, with pilots tightly controlled from the ground. As a result, he said, "they stayed high and their target acquisition was bad. They made heavy use of radar; they almost never went outside their own radar coverage, and thus the pilots had very little opportunity for initiative - they made use of their operational doctrine instead."

The SAAF philosophy differed, he said.

"We were flexible. We conducted strikes far beyond our radar coverage and often below it, (and) we had excellent target acquisition. We used a low attack profile, tossing bombs seven to 10 kilometres, with an accuracy of about 200 metres ... Between Cuito Cuanavale and Menongue, 8 (Fapla) Brigade transported a large amount of supplies to Fapla, and the SAAF interdicted it; we lost a Mirage there ... We utilised the air to our advantage, at comparatively low cost ... (but) equipment and lives were very important to us. We were prepared to take operational risks, but not foolish risks".

SAAF losses, he said, had been one Mirage F-1AZ and one Bosbok shot down, while two other F-1s, an AZ and a CZ, had been damaged. The Cubans and Angolans had lost nine MiG-23s, three MiG-21s and three SU-22s, with a total replacement cost of 408 million US dollars. They had launched a confirmed 111 surface-to-air missiles and achieved a success-rate of only 4,5 percent; the total damage of their ground attacks had amounted to hits on one bomber, one G-5, one Samil lorry and one water-bowser.

Asked about the future, Steyn replied: "Remember, that depends on strategy - whether it's offensive or defensive; it's senseless to use your weak points against the enemy ... The technological lag is there, but we're working on it. So although Fapla and the Cubans had better equipment and defences, the results do not show it. One can't make any other conclusion but that the Air Force's strategy worked."

The massive Cuban march to the south, meanwhile, was a mystifying business to insiders and outsiders alike. Had the decision to flex all that Cuban muscle been taken in Havana or Luanda? Most of the newcomers were reportedly from the all-regular 50 Division, said to be the best in the Cuban army and which had been described as Fidel Castro's personal division, and Castro was said to have personally ordered that the offensive take place. Since Cuba was hopelessly in Moscow's debt, what role were the Russians playing?

A fortnight later the knowledgeable Jannie Geldenhuys, addressing defence correspondents in Pretoria, cast the clearest light on the subject when he pointed out that in the past the Angolans and Cubans had "often" taken military decisions independently of one another. The southward influx appeared to be a "purely Cuban move", although "it is also possible that the Angolan government knew about it but did not approve" (Geldenhuys might simply have been exercising tact; one reliable source who was present at the Brazzaville talks later told this writer that the Angolan diplomats present had reacted with distinct signs of surprise when the Cuban delegation had announced the southward move).

As to the motive, Geldenhuys said, he could find "no other explanation" than that the Cubans were trying to obtain the best pre-negotiations position with a view to the implementation of Resolution 435. A secondary consideration could be a "show of force on the part of the Cubans to provide a stronger platform for the (Angolan) and Cuban delegation" in the on-going peace talks.

He agreed that the move might also be a form of psychological warfare because "it is not the type of force for which one can see a military purpose in Cunene province, so it would seem there are other aims such as intimidation", and conceded that the advance might be a "taunting manoeuvre", but added that when such an action was taken "the possibility always exists that you can succeed, and then you have a war - and this is not the time to start a war".

The United Nations, so quick to condemn South African incursions into Angola, was of little help. On May 27 Secretary-General Perez de Cuellar, while attending an OAU meeting in Addis Ababa, expressed his great concern about the South Africans' operations in Angola (even though these had been wound down to a large extent months earlier) and gave it as his opinion that the sole obstacle to SWA/Namibian independence was South Africa's insistence on making the implementation of Resolution 435 conditional on "resolving a wholly extraneous matter", the presence of Cuban troops in Angola.

Further pressure was exerted on both sides when a summit meeting between Ronald Reagan and Mikhail Gorbachev opened in Moscow on May 30. At first the Soviet government sent some confusing signals about the situation. The Soviet Union, said Deputy Foreign Minister Vladimir Petrovsky, wanted to "unblock the Angolan situation", while lower-ranking officials suggested to reporters covering the talks that the immense Soviet military investment in Angola had been "useless expenditure" and the Russians would be able to organise a peace treaty between the Angolans and Unita provided the US could depose Savimbi as rebel leader.

The summit ended with both countries agreeing that a concrete peace plan must be evolved by September 29, the 10th anniversary of Resolution 435 - and, not coincidentally, just before the US presidential elections. It was no secret that the US government would like nothing better than to resolve the issue in time for the Republican candidate, George Bush, to gain the maximum amount of vote-catching publicity before the Americans went to the polls.

On June 2 Fidel Castro managed to wind up the tension even tighter by issuing a bellicose challenge while addressing a conference of "non-aligned" countries in Havana. Cuba had the means to confront any South African adventure in Angola, and "if they want to fight," he warned, "the enemy can suffer a serious defeat."

Castro then set off on a flight of fancy in which known facts played little part. The recent fighting had totally changed the military balance in southern Angola, he claimed. South Africa wanted to negotiate because of the losses it had suffered at the hands of a Cuban force it had never previously faced. On January 13, February 14, February 25, March 1 and March 25 they had attacked Cuito Cuanavale but had been beaten each time; during the last three attacks the South Africans suffered "a high number of losses. Then South Africa showed fear and began to refuse to fight ... From now on the history of Africa will have to be written before and after Cuito Cuanavale".

It was a bravura performance which must have evoked sniggers among veterans of the Lomba River fighting, but it touched on too serious a matter to be dismissed as mere face-saving for the Cubans' miserable performance on the battlefield. The South Africans took the matter very seriously indeed, not so much in anger at what Magnus Malan called Castro's "aggressive bravado" but because the Cuban president was an unguided missile, determined that his investment of personal prestige in "internationalism" should not be wasted , completely unpredictable in his actions and apparently accountable to nobody, Although diplomats claimed that by agreeing to the September 29 deadline Russia had committed itself to force the Cubans to withdraw, the SADF was already quietly preparing for a mass call-up of its conventional-warfare troops, with commanding officers of units quietly being told to expect a formal mobilisation. On June 8 Jannie Geldenhuys confirmed that mobilisation had started. Just back from a visit to the operational area, he told journalists that the Cubans were still creeping southward and in places were no more than 20km from the border; a few days earlier a Cuban scouting party had actually clashed with a South African group less than 12km

north-west of Ruacana. The hydro-electric scheme had to be protected, he stressed, because of its importance in providing the water supply to drought-ravaged Ovamboland.

In South Africa, messages began to go out to various units of the conventional-warfare formations and mobilisation plans were put into effect to call thousands of Citizen Force soldiers from their workplaces. A surprising number volunteered before being called up, some because of the prospect of fighting, others from anger that they had seen the border war through to its end, only to have the Cubans upset everything. It was a formidable force, virtually every man a seasoned border soldier and many of them veterans of the external operations.

Nevertheless, calling up the CF was a calculated risk for the South African government. Once the men were mobilised it would be difficult to demobilise them and repeat the process later on (although in at least one case a full battle-group had its call-up postponed by a month after its mobilisation procedure was already far advanced).

In addition, their time was limited. In terms of the Defence Act, no CF soldier could be compelled to serve for more than 120 days in every two-year cycle, and a large number of the conventional troops had already spent half of their current cycle on internal-security call-ups. However, there was plainly nothing for it. An estimated 17 000 Cubans now lay within a stone's throw of the border, integrated with about 5 000 Angolans and 2 000-odd Plan members, and they were cockier than they had ever been before, so that by mid-June more and more violations of SWA/Namibian airspace were taking place (the South Africans gritted their teeth and did nothing, having decided that they would not be provoked into retaliation which might wreck hopes of reviving the bogged-down peace talks).

The consensus was now that the Cuban/Angolan presence was essentially for the dual purpose of image-boosting and enabling Plan to deploy into the shallow area, which it had not been able to do for some time. The problem was that nobody could be sure that the Cubans would not take it into their heads to chance their arm and attempt a border violation, which would surely result in full-scale fighting and a summary end to all hopes of peace.

Late in June the peace talks resumed, this time in Cairo. It was a grim affair which threatened to run aground on the question of the Cuban troop withdrawal. The Cuban delegation indulged in what one conference source described as "histrionics", to which Pik Botha replied with characteristic passion, and a threatened breakdown in communication was only prevented when the Soviet Union's Anatoly Adimishin made a surprise intervention and pulled the Cubans into line.

The delegations then jetted home, having agreed to meet again; several days later one of the Angolans present, UK ambassador Elisio de Figueiredo, claimed in London that while only the Soviet intervention had prevented a collapse, the Angolans had saved the day by advancing a set of proposals more reasonable than those of the South Africans, which had been too ludicrous to contemplate. De Figueiredo maintained that the Cuban advance southwards had the backing of his government.

On June 26 the long-expected clash between the South Africans and Cubans took place. It is worth describing the encounter in detail because it was the first time that forces composed mainly of Cubans and South Africans met head-on and not as elements of an Angolan and Unita operation, and also the last time the SADF and SWATF fought in Angola.

At that stage the Cubans' newly arrived 70 Armoured Division had a brigade at Xangongo and a battalion at Techipa, near Calueque. Members of the latter force, which had been reinforced by artillery and six SA-6 high-altitude missile systems, were very aggressive, in word as well as in deed. They patrolled constantly and exhibited great keenness to tackle the South Africans (Commandant Mike Muller, OC 61 Mechanised Battalion at the time, later recalled that the Cubans had been issuing challenges by way of the local population to "the Boers to come and get their arses kicked"). The South Africans, on the other hand, were under orders to be equally aggressive and dominated the area between Techipa and Calueque by means of 101 Battalion and 53 Battalion.

While they did so, South African army engineers worked at making it possible to take tanks over the Cunene River at Calueque. The bridge at the pumping station was not strong enough to support the Olifants' great weight, and another, which ran along the top of the barrage wall, was unuseable because the entry/exit ramps on either side had been left uncompleted in 1975 when the Angolan civil war broke out. So, while the fighting troops patrolled the no man's land by day, the sappers laboured at night to complete the ramps.

It soon became evident that 101 and 53 Battalions, basically armed and equipped for counter-insurgency duties as they were, could not withstand the Cubans (it was not generally known at the time, but Johan Papenfus had been captured during one such clash, in which three Casspir armoured personnel carriers had been knocked out) and were kept constantly on the run. The Cubans would be unstoppable if they decided to move southwards into the Techipa-Ruacana-Calueque no man's land.

In June, therefore, Muller was ordered into the area with a reinforced battle-group comprising 61 Mechanised Battalion; two batteries of G-5s; a battery of 127mm MRLs; a troop of G-2s (the old 5,5-inch guns); a squadron of Olifants; an anti-tank platoon consisting of eight Ratel-90s (Ratels mounting 90mm guns) and two Ratels fitted with guided missiles; and a 120mm mortar group. He was also given one company from 32 Battalion to use for scouting and similar duties.

Muller's original orders were to attack Techipa, but this was cancelled after Major Jan Hougaard of 32 Battalion came within an ace of being shot down by an SA-6 missile while reconnoitring the area in a Bosbok spotter aircraft and the higher headquarters concluded that the Cubans were in the area in brigade rather than battalion strength.

His amended orders required him to protect Calueque and Ruacana by keeping away both the Cubans (whose exact positions were not known, except that they were in the Techipa area) and any Plan insurgents who might be moving down to attack the water scheme. It was not an ideal area to fight - there was very little natural cover because the cold weather had denuded the trees, and the terrain was very flat, barring some higher ground about eight or 10 kilometres from Calueque, and a few low ridges part of the way up the road to Techipa — but Muller had some Reconnaissance Regiment scouts far forward and 32 Battalion in the middle distance to provide early warning.

On June 23 the battle-group was deployed east of the Techipa road when his scouts reported that a substantial Cuban force was advancing down the western side of the road from Techipa to Calueque. The Cubans then halted, probably on sighting the South Africans, and withdrew for 10km towards Techipa. Next day they proceeded to advance again, and by June 25 they were 25km from Techipa and had sent scouting parties to within 15km of the Cunene River.

Up to this stage the battle-group had avoided contact, but on the morning of June 26 it deployed on either side of the road to warn off the newcomers. About 10am the mobile observation posts reported that the Cubans were approaching in three columns to the west of the road, and a little later enemy vehicles were spotted moving east of the road as well.

Slowly, so as not to kick up dust and betray his plans, Muller brought forward his tanks, two mechanised companies and a mixed artillery battery. At this stage he did not know where the Cubans' tanks were and did not take immediate action, relying on the 32 Battalion company - which was spread over an area of 12km forward of him - to provide early warning.

Around 5pm it was clear that the Cubans did not intend to halt their movement southwards; Muller called down missile and artillery fire on the columns and also on the artillery emplaced around Techipa. The Cuban artillery fired back, but (obviously hampered by a lack of spotters) did not do any damage to the South Africans.

To Muller it was evident that the Cubans had decided that his force was in the early stages of an attack, and his forward scouts reported that the SA-6 launchers had been made ready for action, no doubt because it was thought that the SAAF might launch a strafing attack. By means of an ingenious ruse the Cubans were induced to fire six SA-6s. This enabled the South Africans to pinpoint three launcher positions; waiting till near dusk so that it was unlikely the Cuban MiGs would be called in, they eliminated the sites with G-5 fire.

Muller re-appreciated the situation and decided that it was likely the Cubans would resume their advance down the road next morning, so he regrouped his force in order to use it to maximum advantage if the need arose. He ordered his artillery and missiles further back, leaving the tanks and their accompanying infantry in place to protect the MRL battery till it followed the guns to the rear, and deployed another mechanised combat team under Major André Vermeulen to positions east of the road and parallel with it.

About 5am on June 27 one platoon of 32 Battalion scouts became aware that the Cubans were moving down the road again. When they tried to communicate this information to Muller, however, they discovered to their frustration that they had suffered a communications failure. At Muller's headquarters, in the meantime, the Cubans' engine-noises had also been heard, but because there had been no warning from 32 Battalion it was assumed that the sounds in question were being made by the forward elements, which were still moving back.

Daybreak showed Vermeulen that his position, which had been taken up during the night, was not suitable, and he was given permission to shift to a slightly better location. In due course he set off, his Ratel-90s leading, followed by the missile Ratels and then the 81mm mortar Ratels, with the infantry on the flanks and bringing up the rear.

About 8am, as Vermeulen's force was moving along a grassy slope on the reverse side of a low ridge which screened it from the main force, it was fired on by tanks and infantry of the Cubans' forward element.

Almost immediately one Ratel-90 was knocked out, the platoon commander being killed, and another Ratel-90 was immobilised by a shot in the gearbox. At this time the missile Ratels were in the worst possible position to come into action, being at the bottom of the slope, but they managed to destroy a Cuban tank and two BTR-60 armoured personnel carriers.

By this time Vermeulen had radioed back that at least another squadron of tanks was approaching from the north. Muller sent his tanks to Vermeulen's aid, and about 20 minutes later the two forces made contact. In the meantime Vermeulen withdrew slightly and provided supporting fire, having managed to recover the body of his dead officer, although the knocked-out Ratels could not be brought back without endangering more lives.

A sharp exchange took place between the newcomers – in one instance, two of Muller's Olifants fired together at a T-55 on which a platoon of infantry were riding, Russian fashion; both shots hit, destroying both the tank and the riders – and after about half an hour the Cubans broke contact and withdrew northwards.

Muller, who had spotted the dust thrown up by two other approaching Cuban columns, decided on a tactical withdrawal to better positions on the high ground north of Calueque. Keeping the Cubans in sight, he leapfrogged his units southwards while peppering them with accurate G-5 fire directed by his artillery observers. The central Cuban columns halted when a direct G-5 hit set two of its vehicles ablaze, but the westernmost column continued to advance rapidly, obviously intending to cut Muller off.

Muller was now ordered to withdraw to Ruacana. Leaving his tanks and a mechanised combat team to keep an eye on the central column, he deployed another combat team east of Calueque and concentrated his artillery fire on the western column, knocking out eight vehicles and halting its advance.

His intention had been to bring his entire force over the Calueque barrage wall, whose ramps had finally been completed, but in the meantime a Cuban air strike had changed the situation completely.

At 12.30pm, while Muller was still engaged in his withdrawal, eight Cuban MiG-23s had taken off from Lubango, hedge-hopped due south to Ruacana, then turned eastwards to Calueque, maintaining strict radio silence. At Calueque they pulled up to 1 600 feet and four of them left the formation to set up a "combat air patrol" in case of SAAF interference. The other four streaked over Calueque and each dropped two parachute-retarded bombs, then turned left and came in again, dropping another seven bombs. The South Africans opened up on them with 20mm guns and SA-7 manpack missiles; one of the hand-operated 20mm guns scored a near-miraculous hit and damaged a MiG-23 so badly that it suffered a systems failure and crashed near Techipa.

Within minutes the raid was over, but in that brief time the MiGs had struck a grievous blow at the South Africans. Several accurately-aimed bombs had destroyed one of the freshly constructed ramps, while another had missed its target but exploded among a group of soldiers who had just

come up from Ruacana as escorts to an artillery ammunition convoy, killing 12 of them.

Tactically, the raid meant a substantial alteration to Muller's plans. He ordered the G-5s and most of his infantry back to Calueque, then moved the tanks and their attached combat team to Ruacana by an alternative route.

The deaths of the 12 soldiers caused a wave of grief and anger in South Africa, and angry questions were asked about why the SAAF had allowed the MiGs such easy passage. A senior SAAF officer gave the only possible reply: "They maintained radio silence and so achieved surprise. Very few air forces can withstand this sort of attack; under the circumstances you can do little but provide ground air defence ... Their (bombing) accuracy was very good under the circumstances, very accurate."

Oddly, about a month later Fidel Castro told a rally in Havana that the purpose of the raid had been an act of revenge for the earlier ground fighting, saying nothing at all about the fact that it had been a tactical success; no doubt he felt his explanation would have greater emotional appeal, because the ground fighting had been a great blow to Cuban military pride.

The losses on the South African side came to one officer dead, one officer and one other rank slightly wounded, and two Ratel-90s destroyed. Cuban losses in the field and at Techipa, according to the South Africans, amounted to about 300 overall, while three tanks and three BTR-60 armoured personnel carriers had been destroyed and one anti-tank gun damaged, as well as a number of soft-skinned vehicles.

On June 30 the Cubans disputed the South African description of the clash. Only 10 Cuban soldiers had been killed, not several hundred, they said, and no vehicles had been destroyed, although one T-55 tank had been damaged. The South Africans had been "almost annihilated", losing four Ratel fighting vehicles knocked out and one captured.

An SADF spokesman noted in reply that a "factual statement" had been issued on June 28 and its updated version on the following day, and "the facts speak for themselves and are at least open to public scrutiny". Another spokesman, asked if the Cuban body-count had been compiled by making estimations based on the quantity of abandoned weapons and equipment, said that he could not reveal the precise techniques used because of security considerations, but "that's why we were firm on the figure. It's correct to within 10 on either side ... either you believe us or you don't. But I'd like to point out that the other force decided to retire – if they had lost only (10) men they would surely not have turned back."

More than a year later it transpired that Reconnaissance Regiment "operators" had infiltrated the fringes of Techipa itself, not only keeping tally on the Cuban casualties but accurately directing artillery fire on the gun and missile emplacements.

He confirmed that the South Africans were keeping a presence at Calueque in order to protect the water supply to Ovamboland, although reliable sources indicated that the presence had not been enlarged and that there were no plans to fortify Calueque.

On July 3 Cuba's Jorge Risquet, in Lisbon for talks with Portuguese officials about the situation, blasted South Africa for jeopardising the negotiations by keeping troops in Angola, claiming that "the talks would not be at risk if there was no South African intransigence in Angola and if Pretoria respected (the UN resolution) on withdrawing its troops from Angolan territory".

The following day he was more conciliatory. While still claiming that the Cubans had inflicted a heavy defeat on the South Africans at Calueque and now enjoyed air, ground and anti-aircraft superiority in southern Angola, Risquet added that both Angola and Cuba were serious about reaching a settlement at the next round of talks (now scheduled for July 11 and 12 in New York), although he doubted if South Africa had the will to reach agreement. But if agreement could be reached on a set of principles there would be another meeting a month later, he added.

On July 11 the New York talks opened with US officials stating they were feeling hopeful, and that while serious differences remained there was "an amazing amount of common ground". Probably this was not the whole truth, since there were now persistent reports that there had been secret meetings between US and Soviet officials which had left both moving closer to a shared set of viewpoints about the peace talks. The Evening Standard newspaper of London quoted an unnamed White House official as saying: "Gorbachev has reached the conclusion that Angola will probably be an endless drain on resources."

The talks ended on July 13 with much progress made but major differences remaining about the timing of a Cuban withdrawal and implementation of Resolution 435 still staying with Angola and South Africa. Chester Crocker told newsmen that "the core of a settlement" had been reached, but while a "large gap" still remained to be bridged over the timings, the negotiators had agreed that "this was not the time to come to grips with the problem".

The negotiators then returned to their home countries, and on July 20 South Africa, Angola and Cuba announced that they had agreed on a set of principles designed to bring peace in Angola and independence in SWA/Namibia.

The agreement ran to 14 points, and agreed among other things that Angola and South Africa would co-operate with the UN Secretary-General in ensuring "the independence of Namibia through free and fair elections"; redeployment to the north and then the "staged and total withdrawal" of Cuban troops, subject to on-site UN verification; non-interference in one another's affairs and "abstention from the threat and utilisation of force against the territorial integrity and independence of states"; agreement that their territory would not be allowed to be used "for acts of war, aggression or violence against other states"; verification and monitoring of compliance "with the obligations resulting from the agreements that may be established"; and a "commitment to comply in good faith with the obligations undertaken in the agreements that may be established and to resolve the differences via negotiations".

It was a breakthrough, Pik Botha told a press conference in Pretoria, but he warned that future problems "could not be under-estimated". Chester Crocker was equally cautious, describing the agreement as "a first step - not more than that".

Unita, as always, was the ghost at the feast. Its comment on the accord, issued on July 21, praised the agreement but said that attention would eventually have to turn to Angola's internal problems. A comment by Dos Santos the same day was equally unyielding: "For the Angolan people Unita

stands for division, terrorism, suffering, sorrow, pain and treason … It is a stain that must be wiped clean from the history of Angola". That the stain would not disappear easily was made plain that day by a US government statement that there was "no way" in which the Reagan government would stop its aid to Unita unless the Soviet Union cut back on its help to the MPLA.

There is always more to the murky world of diplomacy than meets the eye, however: On August 1, the day before the negotiators (having tied up various details during a July 24 meeting on the Cape Verde Islands) were due to gather in Geneva, a senior Cuban diplomat, described as being connected with the negotiations, was quoted by the New York Times newspaper as saying that Cuba had given the US warning of its push to the border, adding: "The Reagan administration has been fully aware since last March that our strategy was to hit the South Africans hard, on their own turf. Even if we had not talked to them, which we did, it was plain to see." The writer, Angolan and Cuban specialist Pamela Falk, said Crocker "gave an implicit nod to the Cubans six months ago", and a State Department spokeswoman confirmed that Cuba had alerted the Americans about its plans before striking at Calueque in June.

The negotiators met in Geneva on August 2 as scheduled, the South African team led by Neil van Heerden and Jannie Geldenhuys. After almost three days of talks the participants signed what became known as the Protocol of Geneva. The protocol stated that September 1 would be the target date for reaching agreement on a withdrawal schedule "and all related matters"; that the withdrawal of South African forces "shall begin not later than 10 August 1988 and be completed not later than 1 September 1988"; with effect from August 10 no Cuban troops would be deployed south of an imaginary line running through Chitado, Ruacana, Calueque, Naulila, Cuamato and Ongiva; the Angolans would "guarantee measures for the provision of water and power-supply to Namibia" after the South African withdrawal; a "combined military committee" on which the US would be invited to serve would be established to oversee the "period of particular sensitivity" after September 1; and all parties undertook "to adopt the necessary measures of restraint in order to maintain the existing de facto cessation of hostilities … Angola and Cuba shall urge Swapo to proceed likewise as a step prior to the ceasefire … which will be established prior to 1 November 1988. Angola and Cuba shall use their good offices so that, once the total withdrawal of South African troops from Angola is completed, and within the context also of the cessation of hostilities in Namibia, Swapo's forces will be deployed to the north of the 16th parallel".

On August 10 the South Africans began to withdraw as scheduled, the troops leapfrogging southwards while convoys of lorries and flatbed trailers carrying tanks plied between Ruacana, Oshakati and Grootfontein. It was not the end of an era - yet. A date for a Cuban withdrawal had yet to be decided on at a meeting scheduled for August 22; the word was that the South Africans would insist on a total pull-out within seven months, and if no agreement was reached the entire process would be back where it started.

In the meantime the question of Savimbi and Unita continued to haunt the peace process. On August 11, with the South African withdrawal in its earliest stages, Angola's UN ambassador, Manuel

Pacavira, rejected the earlier US demand that a halt in aid to Unita be linked to a similar move by Moscow towards the MPLA. The same day, Angop turned down the Unita demand for direct negotiations, describing the rebels as "puppets" controlled by South Africa and adding that their exclusion was "necessary for the establishment of peace".

On August 22, at a meeting at Ruacana of the newly-established "Joint Military Monitoring Commission", a formal ceasefire document was signed by the GOC SWATF, Major-General Willie Meyer, the commander-in-chief of the Cuban/Angolan forces, Lieutenant-General Leopoldo Cintras Frias of Cuba, and the Angolan presidential secretary for defence and security, Colonel Jose Maria. Next day a South African delegation led by Neil van Heerden and Jannie Geldenhuys flew into Brazzaville for three days of discussion with the Angolans and Cubans. In Pretoria Pik Botha said that if agreement was reached South Africa would allow SWA/Namibia's independence programme to start on November 1, as laid down in the Geneva Protocol. But the starting date, he warned, depended on Cuba and Angola setting a Cuban withdrawal timetable by September 1 which would be "acceptable to both parties".

By August 23, according to conference sources, a breakthrough was in sight: the Cubans appeared willing to compromise on their initial stand that the withdrawal would have to be spread over four years, while the South Africans showed signs of moving away from their requirement of a total withdrawal within 10 months and considering the possibility of SWA/Namibia becoming independent before all the Cubans had gone. The withdrawal, as Van Heerden noted to reporters, was still the "crunch issue".

While the diplomats wrangled suavely in Brazzaville, the border war carried on, albeit at its lowest intensity for many years. Sam Nujoma had declared in mid-August that Swapo would voluntarily comply with the August 5 informal ceasefire, even though his movement was not a party to the agreement, but insurgent activity continued, as did the propaganda war. On August 21 a Swapo spokesman claimed from Lusaka that "large numbers" of SWA/Namibians had been shot and killed by the security forces after having crossed into Angola, and said a major build-up of South African troops had been reported. He did not provide any details and a SWATF spokesman poured scorn on the claims, although he admitted that 14 insurgents had been killed in Ovamboland in eight separate incidents between August 2 and August 15.

By August 25 the negotiators at Brazzaville had still not agreed on a formula for withdrawing the Cuban troops, although conference sources said the talks were still on track. However, when they ended on August 26 the core issues remained unresolved, although there had been steady progress towards a mutually acceptable compromise. Angola and Cuba were now talking about a full withdrawal spread over two years, the US delegates were proposing 18 months and the South Africans 12 months, sources said.

One of the South Africans' main concerns, it appeared, was what would happen during the run-up to the SWA/Namibian election required by Resolution 435. For most of this stage there would be very few SADF troops left in SWA/Namibia, and the South Africans were worried about Cuban and Angolan activities in southern Angola while this was

the case. So far, most of the concessions had been Pretoria's, one diplomat said, and what had been offered by the other side "falls quite a way outside our expectations".

On this note the conference broke up, on the understanding that it would re-convene at Brazzaville in a week's time. Comments by some of the parties indicated that part of the problem concerned Unita. The Angolan armed forces chief of staff, General Antonio dos Santos Franca, told reporters that the withdrawal of the Cubans was directly linked to US aid for Unita and "we're not going to sacrifice our security in return for nothing".

An American diplomat, on the other hand, said that his country's support for Unita could not be "a bargaining chip", and added: "It's absurd to ask us to unilaterally disengage … I don't consider it a condition of our mediation." President Dos Santos, too, was reported as standing firmly by his refusal to be pressured by the US into a power-sharing agreement with Unita, and on August 27 (so it was later claimed by Unita) the rebels had spurned a proposal by Crocker that the withdrawal of the Cubans take place over three years.

The South African withdrawal had been continuing all this time, and on August 30, 36 hours ahead of schedule, the last of Pretoria's troops drove out of Angola and crossed the Kavango River into SWA/Namibia. It was not an impressive sight, partly because there were less than 1 000 troops involved; Kavango's Colonel Deon Ferreira confessed later that "it was an embarrassment that we could show so few troops coming out" to the hordes of journalists who had gathered to witness the historic departure.

"We're out of Angola," the newsmen were told by the Chief of Defence Staff, Lieutenant-General Ian Gleeson. "We've lifted the siege of Cuito Cuanavale and we have no more soldiers inside Angola."

Almost immediately the South Africans began picking up reports that the Cubans were once again pouring men, equipment and weapons into southern Angola, so that troop levels there were creeping up from an estimated 52 000 combatants to somewhere nearer 60 000. Just what the reports meant, if true, were not clear. It might be more Cuban image-building, or it might be indications of another impending offensive against Unita.

The Americans were sceptical; the South Africans insisted. On September 2, just three days after the SADF/SWATF withdrawal from Angola, the Department of Foreign Affairs warned that "merely because South Africa is engaged in a negotiating process does not mean that South Africa will not take whatever steps it deems necessary to ensure the protection of its interests." At Jamba, Savimbi told a party of visiting Americans that the Cubans and Angolans were taking advantage of the South African withdrawal to prepare for another big offensive against Unita.

On September 4 General Magnus Malan repeated earlier statements that South Africa's primary reason for intervening in Angola in 1987 had been "her own security interests" as well as that of SWA/Namibia and the region as a whole, and added: "The build-up of Cuban forces contradicts the spirit and intentions of four-nation negotiations. Prospects for peace could therefore be jeopardised. It is unacceptable that an increased build-up of forces and equipment can take place while negotiations are on-going. This increases the potential for conflict and places a question-mark behind Cuban intentions at the negotiation table.

It also illustrates who the real aggressor is in the region".

But in Luanda Defence Minister Pedro Maria Tonha retorted that Angola was worried by manoeuvres South African units had been carrying out along the border over the past month - although, he added, "we believe there is an environment of trust", which meant that it was possible the Brazzaville talks would "achieve positive results". Tonha added that a start had been made with establishing the 11 border monitoring posts agreed on in Geneva.

Given the Angolan tendency towards inflammatory statements, Tonha's remarks were relatively conciliatory in tone; a possible clue surfaced the following day when, for the first time, details became public of a devastating Unita attack on the Benguela line near Huambo two months earlier. Eleven locomotives had been destroyed and 12 railwaymen and Fapla troops killed, leaving the Angolans with only two serviceable locomotives.

The Benguela railway, formerly a generator of large amounts of foreign revenue, was now totally unserviceable; the only line left operating in southern Angola consisted of a short stretch running northwards from the port, and completely separate from the main line.

Meanwhile preparations for the next round of Brazzaville talks had been finalised. All concerned were acutely aware that unless agreement was reached this time there was little chance of the November 1 date for the start of implementation of Resolution 435 being complied with.

On September 7 the seventh round of talks commenced at Brazzaville in an atmosphere distinctly less optimistic than its predecessor, the alleged Cuban build-up in southern Angola high on the agenda - although South African diplomats were said to be treating the reports cautiously, an Angolan negotiator dismissed them as fantasies based on media stories rather than hard intelligence and the US issued a statement casting doubts on whether it was taking place, saying it had detected the arrival of more equipment but not troops. As one conference source said: "There has been some disinformation going on ... They're going to have to thrash out what is true and what is false about the reported Cuban build-up."

Nevertheless, the issue helped to hamper the negotiations; on September 8 Neil van Heerden, who was leading the South African team, opined that "it's beginning to look quite tough". However, he rejected a suggestion that the point had been reached at which the November 1 deadline would be dropped, and said that there was a possibility of the talks being carried over into an unscheduled third day.

This duly happened, and the meeting broke up before lunch-time after the negotiators had agreed "to resume negotiations as soon as possible at another venue". Just before his departure Van Heerden struck a fairly optimistic note: "We feel that this meeting ... has again significantly advanced the process from the previous meeting here," adding that the parties had agreed to meet again soon.

Van Heerden declined to give further details because all the parties involved had agreed to a news blackout on the proceedings, but stressed that "as far as South Africa is concerned, the date of November 1 is still on the table".

While the Brazzaville talks were in progress, Unita officials had been involved in two days of direct talks at Abidjan, the capital of the Ivory Coast,

with a Cuban delegation led by UN ambassador Oscar Oramas. One result of the talks was that the rebels handed back two Cubans it had captured, one of them the deputy chief of the Cuban air force in Angola, Lieutenant-Colonel Manuel Rojas Garcia, who had been shot down in October of 1987. A Unita spokesman said Rojas had also been given a message to relay to Fidel Castro, dealing with the peace negotiations and "the creation of a climate that could lead to total peace in the region".

He did not elaborate, but it was an encouraging development, since it was the first time Savimbi had been known to make face-to-face contact with the Cubans. A US State Department spokesman commented: "In the end ... only direct talks between the Angolan parties in the conflict can produce a settlement that would bring lasting peace to the Angolan nation."

Total or even partial peace was still a long way away, however, to judge by a September 15 Unita claim that it had bested the Angolans and Cubans in a month-long battle for the much-disputed railway town of Munhango. Eight Fapla brigades backed by Cuban troops and Soviet advisers had attacked Munhango on August 9, the rebels said, adding that for a loss of 18 dead and one missing they had killed 123 Fapla troops, shot down a MiG-23 and destroyed 10 tanks and several logistics vehicles.

By now the South Africans were detecting fresh indications that a new anti-Unita push was being prepared, the Cubans' intention being to isolate Savimbi by interdicting his communications with the north, seal off the border to keep the South Africans away and then move into the central and eastern regions to attack Mavinga and Jamba. After that, if necessary, Zaire could be attacked.

Pretoria was not alone in believing that this was about to happen: Zaire and 10 other African states - Zambia, Kenya, Nigeria, Mali, the Ivory Coast, Senegal, Morocco, Togo, the Central African Republic and Egypt - had become involved in an effort to prevent the offensive, believing with some justification that such a move would bring South Africa back over the border and quite possibly drag various other states into a full-blown conventional war for which they were both ill-equipped and disinclined.

The most perturbed of them was Zaire's Mobuto Sese Seko, who was painfully aware of the fact that about 7 500 Cuban and Angolan troops had been concentrated a mere 400km from his border, while Cuban-piloted MiG-23s were continually violating his airspace. Mobuto was in a particularly vulnerable condition. His country was almost bankrupt, his army unreliable and dispirited, his border long and almost indefensible: he still entertained painful memories of two bloody incursions in 1977 and 1978 of his Shaba (formerly Katanga) province by Angolan-based exiles of the former Katangese Gendarmerie, both beaten off only by hastily summoned Moroccan and French troops.

In addition, he had already received an explicit cautioning from the Cubans. Now for the first time details of his interview with Jorge Risquet a few months earlier were revealed. Risquet had warned him that Castro's overall African policy was unashamedly expansionist and that the Cuban troops would not leave Angola while Unita threatened the MPLA government, and demanded that he desist from aiding the rebels; if the war spread, Zambia and Botswana would also be dragged in. If the reports were true, it could only be construed as a naked threat.

The reports were never confirmed, but it was an all-too-likely scenario, and it was obvious that if it happened there was a distinct possibility of the South Africans heading back into Angola.

Just a little later, in fact, though it was never revealed to the public, a substantial Cuban force suddenly headed directly for the border in a way which bore all the earmarks of an intended crossing. The South Africans reacted by sending a Citizen Force composite battle-group of 71 Motorised Brigade, under Commandant Tony Marriner of the Cape Town Highlanders, straight across country for almost 200km to meet the threat.

In spite of incredibly tough going and equipment which was distinctly jaded from the 1987-1988 fighting, the battle-group arrived at its destination ready for battle and without losing a single vehicle to breakdowns - no small feat in the circumstances. The Cuban force then pulled back from the border. Possibly it had merely been a feint, designed to test the South Africans' state of preparedness; if not the Cubans would have had a hot reception, because as far as it concerned the battle-group's officers and men - most of them seasoned veterans with operational service which often dated back to Operation Savannah - it had been a deadly serious "advance to contact".

It also became known at this time that at a summit conference held in Brazzaville the 11 African leaders had appealed to Dos Santos to negotiate with Unita and get rid of the Cubans, seeing that South Africa had withdrawn from Angola and announced its willingness to allow SWA/Namibia to become independent. Dos Santos had snubbed them with the remark that the MPLA would deal with Unita in its own way, since the war was a domestic and not an international matter.

Not surprisingly, the diplomatic offensive did not show any immediate results. Fighting continued in Angola; on September 18 the MPLA claimed it had recaptured five important towns and regained control of the strategic Cangumbe region. Unita provided confirmation of sorts by announcing that it was mobilising one-third of its total forces to stop the offensive. Three days later Luanda claimed its forces had recaptured Munhango and killed 1 300 Unita in a two-week offensive marked by heavy fighting.

The peace process was now in imminent danger of disintegrating altogether, since the offensive was a clear violation of Article 6 of the Geneva Protocol, which had stated that the Cubans would not take part in offensive operations east of the 17th meridian and south of the 15th parallel.

In spite of all this the seventh round of peace talks was being planned for Brazzaville. On September 23 UN Secretary-General Perez de Cuellar said in an interview, as he was about to leave Pretoria's Air Force Base Waterkloof, after a two-day visit that "Brazzaville is the keyword to Namibia's independence. I can tell you that we have made significant progress". He then departed for Luanda.

Around the same time an Ovambo member of the SWA Police's Koevoet counter-insurgency unit, Inspector Michael Hindengwa, became its only known defector when he took hundreds of rands out of the cash register at Okaeve base's police recreation club, commandeered a Casspir and fled over the border into Angola. Early reports that Hindengwa had been decorated for gallantry and had taken his family with him later proved

inaccurate, and the reasons behind his unscheduled departure have never been released.

On September 26 a South African delegation led by Neil van Heerden arrived in Brazzaville for the eighth round of talks, amid reports that Angolan/Cuban preparations for a new offensive against Unita were far advanced. On the eve of his departure from Pretoria Van Heerden made no bones about the South African attitude - although the withdrawal issue would be the main point of discussion, he said, the alleged anti-Unita push would also be on the agenda, because "if you're talking about peace, it doesn't help the process if one of the parties is preparing for war".

It was clear to all concerned that the forthcoming talks were extremely important, and that if no decision was reached the entire peace process could be wrecked.

As at previous talks, the delegations gathered separately and Chester Crocker's team shuttled back and forth, liaising and generally facilitating. Crocker struck an optimistic note in an interview with the Congolese radio service on September 27. "It's an important and decisive moment," he said. "We're still working and we're on track."

On track, perhaps, but nowhere near an agreement on the core issue, the timetable for a Cuban withdrawal from Angola. Luanda had now come down to a three-year withdrawal schedule, but the South Africans were holding out for a shorter period, in return for a phased withdrawal from SWA/Namibia which would start on November 1, thereby setting in motion a seven-month UN-supervised process which would lead to an election by June of 1989. Unless agreement was reached very soon, they would not be able to abide by their undertaking to start pulling out by that date.

As one US official put it to reporters, "it's a real spider's web; there's been a lot of uphill".

September 28 arrived without an agreement being reached, and the South Africans prepared to leave on the midday flight out of Brazzaville. Then suddenly the talks were extended by one more day in spite of a surprise attack by Cuban spokesman Alcibiades Hidalgo, who accused the South Africans of blocking the chances of agreement by "demanding unrealistic and unacceptable periods (for withdrawal)" and linking it to SWA/Namibian independence. South African insistence on linkage, he warned, could "close the door on an agreement".

The extra day failed to bring results, but the negotiators parted on fairly good terms and with the understanding that they would meet again, informally this time, in New York on October 7. Van Heerden's parting comment was that although South Africa stood by its undertaking regarding November 1, it was becoming more and more difficult to meet it.

Meanwhile, rumours of ceasefires were coming from Angola. On October 3 the Unita news agency Kwacha quoted Savimbi as offering a truce to the Cubans supporting the MPLA, saying they had no further justification for fighting in Angola now that South African troops had left the country. He offered to halt attacks on Cuban forces if they refrained from attacking Unita, and also offered to release Cuban prisoners being held by his movement.

However, Dos Santos had already pre-empted this neat attempt at creating divisions. Speaking to the media immediately after conducting talks with Presidents Omar Bongo of Gabon and Denis Sassou-Nguesso of the Congo, he ruled out any settlement with Unita on the grounds that "the Angolan state is a one-party state and the acceptance of such a political organisation (as Unita) is out of the question". No doubt the on-going fighting (Unita had just claimed it had killed 91 government soldiers in the past week) did nothing towards softening Dos Santos's attitude.

As rumours began to circulate of yet another tripartite meeting, this time in New York, Dos Santos and Savimbi continued to assail each other in print.

A Unita spokesman spurned a new Angolan offer of amnesty and repeated his movement's earlier demands for direct negotiations with Luanda, saying: "Unita categorically rejects and repudiates the policy of clemency and pardon, because the only solution to the Angolan question lies in direct negotiations between Unita and the MPLA." He urged the US, South Africa and other African countries "not to let the Angolan government's subterfuge ruin the current favourable climate for talks".

But in an interview published in the New York Times Dos Santos rejected the demand for direct negotiation and commented that "unless there was a massive intervention of South African forces, Unita cannot last very long". In another interview, published on October 4 - this time in the left-wing Paris newspaper Liberation — he stated that he was prepared to speak to P W Botha face-to-face - but not about ending the war. He was, he said, willing to discuss "problems linked with their war of aggression ... We can also, for example, discuss apartheid with South Africa. But I do not think that it is wise to speak to South Africa about Angola".

Dos Santos stressed his aim was for "a just peace, honourable for everybody", including Unita, but first the "external problems" of "South African aggression", SWA/Namibian independence and South African support for Unita would have to be resolved. What all these fine sentiments amounted to, when boiled down, was that there was no change in attitude on either Luanda's or Savimbi's part.

On October 5 Van Heerden and his deputy, Herbert Beukes, arrived in New York for discussions with the UN secretariat on the implementation of Resolution 435 and preliminary talks with the Angolans and Cubans to prepare for the eighth round of talks, which were due to start the next day.

The talks produced little that was concrete, but some progress was made. One source claimed that "they are still some distance apart (but) negotiations have now narrowed the whole thing down to the bone. The test of Cuban willingness to leave can't be far off now". Specifically, it appeared, the Angolans and Cubans were now willing to allow withdrawal to be spread over 30 months instead of four years, while the South Africans had eased up on their initial demands that it be completed within seven months.

Several aspects important to the South Africans remained unresolved, however. There was no clarity yet on how many Cubans would be left in Angola after SWA/Namibia became independent (an estimated 27 000 was the best bet) and how far north of the border they would be; or on the question of whether Unita would be cut off. Nor were the South Africans prepared to budge from their position that their withdrawal and the Cubans' should be more or less matched for size.

This last was, in all fairness, a legitimate standpoint. By now the Cuban presence alone outnumbered the 45 000-odd troops that the SADF and SWATF could muster. As one top military official told this writer a little later: "There is nothing more that South Africa can contribute. What has

been in our power to do, we have done. It is up to the Cubans and Angolans to come forward with a proposal for a withdrawal which is more or less in balance with ours."

On October 9 the negotiators broke up after agreeing to meet again in the near future. Exactly what had been achieved was difficult to define. One source said they had got "close to final choices", while a US official said that the parties were "more or less agreed" on a 30-month withdrawal period. The Americans still professed to believe that the November 1 implementation date was feasible, but their optimism was unmatched by anyone else. Rumour had it (correctly) that Crocker's team had drawn up compromise proposals envisaging a withdrawal period of 24 to 30 months, with all Cubans being north of the Benguela line by election time.

All observers agreed on one thing, however: that the next get-together (probably at Brazzaville) would be a "crunch" meeting.

One person who obviously believed this was Sam Nujoma; on October 17 he said in Dar es Salaam that he was optimistic about signing a ceasefire with South Africa by November 1. A final round of four-party peace talks would soon be held, he said, and "after that has been agreed upon, the talks will come to an end and Swapo will directly come into the peace process to sign the ceasefire".

By now the new JMMC operation was beginning to fail, and for the same reasons as its predecessor of 1984 had failed: Angola's professed inability to keep Swapo under control. The Geneva Protocol, while a fairly comprehensive document, contained a flaw which nobody recognised till it was far too late: the Angolans and Cubans had not been required to control Swapo, merely to use their "good offices" to keep the insurgents away from SWA/Namibia, which they had no intention of doing. The result was to occasion a burst of bloodshed the following year which came close to wrecking the entire peace process.

The Cuban and Angolan attitude soon became apparent once the JMMC began to operate. By agreement the JMMC elements on the ground would meet every morning at 10am, the South African and Angolan regional commanders would meet every week, and the GOC SWATF and his Angolan equivalent would meet every month. Eleven border monitoring posts were to be set up, from the Epupa Falls in the west to Bagani in Caprivi, which would be manned by equal numbers of South African and Fapla personnel, and they would watch out for any violations, which were defined as South Africans crossing the border from SWA/Namibia, Angolans and Cubans doing the same in the opposite direction, and Plan establishing bases south of the "Quiteve Line", the 16th parallel. If violations occurred and the JMMC could not agree on their nature, they would be referred first to regional level, then to the third tier and finally, if still unsolved, to governmental level.

By mid-October there had been 53 insurgent-related incidents in the operational area since the founding of the JMMC little more than a month earlier, and five definite violations: three insurgents fresh from the Xangongo area - well below the "Quiteve Line" - had been captured since September 1. When the South Africans reported the violations, the Angolan and Cuban members of the JMMC refused to accept the reports. The security forces shot two insurgents who were wearing a mixture of Fapla and Cuban uniforms, reported the violations and invited their JMMC colleagues to visit the contact area and see for themselves. The Angolans and Cubans rejected not only the violation reports but also the offer of a visit to the area.

In terms of the agreement the claimed violations were forwarded to the regional level. No agreement was to be found there and so they were sent to the final tier of appeal, again without success. The claims were then sent even higher, to governmental level, and were raised at one of the later Brazzaville meetings, where they were noted and then conveniently buried under matters of greater moment.

"We find that Fapla are completely dominated by the Cubans in working with us," one senior officer said bitterly. "On occasions the Cubans have just stepped in. The Cubans are very dogmatic and refer everything to their higher headquarters; it's quite obvious that Fapla can't control Swapo, or maybe they don't want to. They say we must accept that they don't have control, Swapo has independence.

"If we point out the Fapla uniforms (worn by the insurgents), they say they must be deserters. They always fall back on the story that Swapo is a liberation movement and that they can't really control them ... We're still finding Swapo with Fapla uniforms. They say it's senseless to insinuate that their men are infiltrating, and it stays there ... They say they try to keep them beyond the 16th parallel, but if (the insurgents) are captured internally (Fapla) say they are internal and they have no control over them."

As in 1984, the monitoring troops were hardly crack soldiers. "Most of them came here straight from Luanda," the officer said. "Everything (about their equipment) is brand new (but) in the Epupa area they gave them maize for 70 days, then gave them Russian and Cuban rations ... they are not seasoned troops."

By this stage South African intelligence had located Swapo forward headquarters at Xangongo, Mongua and Anhanca - all of them in the Angolan shallow area where, according to the Geneva Protocol, none was supposed to be allowed. Statistics for September showed that an upswing in comparison with the same period in the previous two years, probably attributable to the fact that the heavy Cuban presence had freed many insurgents from duties in Fapla units.

There had been no incidents at all during June, July and August. Then in September there had been 39 incidents, compared with 17 in 1987 and 23 in 1986. Mine detonations were up slightly (eight, compared with seven in 1987 and six in 1986). Contacts initiated by the security forces had shown a large increase between mid-August and mid-September - 19 altogether, with 20 insurgents being killed and another five captured.

According to the SADF, the insurgents were avoiding contact and engaging in four distinct types of activity: political activation in the SWA/Namibian shallow area, the theme being that if Swapo did not win the forthcoming election it would go on fighting; a heavy emphasis on abductions, with schoolchildren being taken to a centre north of Ongiva, where they were given training in political indoctrination and the handling of weapons and explosives with the intention of sending them back into Ovamboland; intimidation of civilians, with attempts being made to influence black members of the police and SWATF, the theme being that if they did not defect to Swapo they would be dealt with during the election campaign; and the building up of arms caches in preparation for the rainy season.

It was all rather disheartening, as was the news in mid-October that the Cubans' 50 Division was still in the south, deployed between Cahama and the border; it now appeared that when the South Africans had withdrawn from Angola the Fapla/Cuban forces had filled the vacuum in considerable strength, Geneva Protocol or no Geneva Protocol. Meanwhile, the Angolans and Unita were issuing conflicting claims about their war. None of the claims could be substantiated, but they proved the fighting was still very much in progress.

Almost a week passed without new developments, however, while Crocker and other diplomats worked frantically behind the scenes to stop the intiative from dying away. One of the reasons for the delay was the fact that the Cubans had still not responded to the US compromise proposal, and there was a growing suspicion among the Americans and South Africans that they were set on delaying further talks till after the US presidential election on November 8: if Michael Dukakis was elected, American policy towards both South Africa and Unita would change drastically and in a way which could be exploited in Luanda's and Havana's favour.

Meanwhile reports of ongoing fighting in Angola continued to come in, chiefly from Unita spokesmen. On October 10 the rebels had claimed to have killed 61 Angolan troops in ambushes, including 28 in a fight at Ucua in northern Lunda province in which four armoured vehicles were knocked out, and another 20 during an attack on a convoy in the east of Lunda province. Twelve days later Unita claimed it had killed 76 Fapla troops in skirmishes in the south and on October 24 that 46 government troops had died, for an "own" loss of three, in clashes in four provinces, two being major actions near the Zaire border.

November 1 came and went without agreement; a new target date of January 1 was now being mooted, while the Americans continued to labour at their efforts to restart the negotiations.

Several tense days passed. Then - two days after Unita claimed to have killed 75 of Luanda's troops in a week, captured a barracks and attacked a motorcade, burning 57 cars - the presidential election took place and was won by Ronald Reagan's vice-president, George Bush (although the Democratic Party still dominated both houses of the US Congress, giving notice to Pretoria and Jamba that some bumpy rides still lay ahead).

On November 11, with the election out of the way, the negotiating teams re-assembled at Geneva and talks were soon progressing relatively smoothly after surviving some sharp early differences between South Africa and the Soviet Union. By November 13 Crocker felt optimistic enough to report that the negotiations could be reaching a "decisive point", with a definite indication from all parties that they were willing to reach a settlement, although not at any price.

"It is an objective fact that we have never been closer to an agreement," Crocker said. "But if people decide they cannot go the extra mile, you will see a rapid change of atmosphere." On November 14, with the talks nearing a conclusion, Neil van Heerden - never a man to make rash statements - said the negotiations had now reached the "sprinkle of salt and dash of basil" stage. In Pretoria Pik Botha agreed that the gap had narrowed considerably, but "it is, however, too early to say whether an agreement is within reach".

But it was. The negotiations were extended to November 15, opening with a bluntly businesslike statement by Van Heerden: "We have had very little since we have been here," he reportedly told the other negotiators. "We don't need optimistic characterisations. We need substance; we are ready to deal." Later that day consensus was reached. What finally pushed the envoys the last distance which enabled them to meet one another's requirements is unlikely to be known for a long time, although it was probably combined pressure by the United States and Russia.

It did not matter, any more than the fact that some of the details about implementation had not yet been settled. The mountain and Muhammed had finally come to one another, and the delegates toasted the end of the wearisome process in champagne. The agreement had still to be ratified by their respective governments, but the over-whelming feeling was that the process would not be halted at this stage.

The only croaker was Pik Botha, who knew only too well that much work remained to be done - among other things, no decisions had yet been taken on when the Cuban withdrawal would start and what SWA/Namibia's independence date would be - and he was understandably cautious as he told newsmen from Pretoria that the South African government still had to study the proposals, adding: "There are serious and complicated implications at stake, and at this stage no conclusion can be made as to whether what happened in Geneva will be acceptable".

On November 18 the Cubans and Angolans agreed to the plan. If the South Africans assented, the Cubans would be withdrawn over a period of 27 months ("it seems Cuba grabbed three more months, but initially they wanted it to last for up to two and a half years," according to a diplomat from a non-aligned country).

After the endless rounds of talks it was difficult to accept that middle ground had been found at last, and according to The Scotsman newspaper agreement had only been reached because South Africa had made a secret promise to release African National Congress leader Nelson Mandela. According to the newspaper Mandela's release was "part of a cat's cradle of secret protocols and unwritten agreements attached to the accord", and that the South African government was expected to capitalise on the Geneva agreement by calling an election early in 1989, after which Mandela would be set free. The ANC, including Mandela, would then be urged by Pretoria to enter into talks on the future of South Africa.

A few days later an African-affairs specialist with the Washington-based Centre for Strategic and International Studies, Gillian Gunn, made headlines by reporting that Savimbi had told her in an interview that he was ready to step down as Unita leader and recognise the MPLA regime for a period of four years, after which elections would take place. Gunn said he had sent the same message to Luanda.

Speculation about a possible reconciliation between the MPLA and Unita became widespread. In Washington it became known that Reagan had informed the pro-Unita faction in the US Senate that, at Luanda's request, Angola's neighbours were trying to arrange Dos Santos-Savimbi talks which would "operate in tandem" with the final negotiations on a Cuban troop withdrawal, and at a press conference at Jamba on November 20 the rebel leader told journalists that he had concluded an informal ceasefire with the Cubans - apparently in the Ivory Coast in August, when Unita had repatriated the two captured Cuban pilots.

"We are making an effort not to attack (the Cubans)," he said, "and they are making an effort not to attack us."

This was interesting but hardly conclusive news. The early onset of the rainy season had made semi-conventional or conventional operations of the Russian/Cuban type difficult for the next six months; were the Cubans and Angolans merely sitting out the wet weather before moving against Savimbi? Then again, by April of 1989 Resolution 435 might well be in operation in SWA/Namibia, leaving the South Africans at their most vulnerable.

Observers noted, too, that whereas Savimbi was temporarily burying the hatchet with the Cubans, his war against the MPLA regime was still very much in progress. Just the previous week a major clash had taken place in the south, which reportedly ended with Angolan troops seeking refuge over the border in SWA/Namibia; and at the November 20 press conference Savimbi had predicted that Luanda would renew its attacks on his movement "as soon as the ink was dry" on any formal Cuban troop withdrawal agreement.

On November 22 speculation about Savimbi went on the back burner with the announcement by Pik Botha that the South African government had approved the agreement reached at Geneva. Botha warned, however, that although the "hard nut" of negotiation had been cracked, there still remained "a lot to be done", and at that moment the South African negotiating team was in New York to discuss the procedures for monitoring and verifying the withdrawal of Cubans from Angola; South Africa would not sign any "blank cheques" in this regard.

Noting that Savimbi had visited Pretoria the previous day for discussions with himself, the State President and Magnus Malan, Botha said the Unita leader had "welcomed" the agreement as necessary for peace and stability in Angola, provided that there were adequate procedures for verifying the Cuban withdrawal.

Amid the general uproar of celebration, dismay and renewed speculation, hardly anybody noticed that Dos Santos had changed his tune, as he had done on so many previous occasions, and that his earlier talk about reconciliation with Unita was, for the time being, a dead letter again. Angop made this clear by quoting a government spokesman as saying that Angola would not lay down its arms till the SWA/Namibian independence process had begun and his country's security had been guaranteed. Unita's response, predictably, was a vow to carry on with the insurgency till Luanda was willing to talk. This was followed by reports that hundreds of Angolan refugees were crossing into SWA/Namibia following renewed Angolan/Cuban attacks against Unita bases and sympathisers, and a claim by the rebels that they had killed 81 Fapla troops for a loss of 15.

Meanwhile the negotiations were encountering a new rough patch, the verification procedures to be used in checking that the Cubans were withdrawing as scheduled, once the process started. Nevertheless, on November 28 the final round of talks began at Brazzaville. There was a general expectation that the peace process was now complete; but once again problems set in and on December 2 Pik Botha and Magnus Malan arrived in Brazzaville a day early to take part in the negotiations. In spite of this added muscle no finality was reached, and on December 4 the negotiators packed up and left without signing anything.

Botha, who had managed to squeeze in a visit

to President Mobuto Sese Seko in neighbouring Zaire and a meeting with Soviet Deputy Foreign Minister Anatoly Adamishin, was not unduly downcast. He had not predicted that agreement would be reached, he said, and "I have no reason to believe that the problems cannot be ironed out".

In spite of an official denial by a US State Department spokesman, it was obvious that the problem was the verification procedure, and on December 5 Fidel Castro confirmed this when he told a huge political rally in Havana that he would not tolerate allowing South Africans "almost at the heart of our troops" because this would disclose strategic information, and "if they try to impose inadmissible demands, violations of Cuba's principles, we are ready to stay five more years, 10 more years, 15 more years, 20 more years ... If there is no signed solution yet, it is the fault of South Africa, because of its bad faith, its lack of seriousness".

Pik Botha's response was studiedly casual. He did not know exactly what Castro had said, he commented, but "this very difficult question is receiving the serious attention of ourselves and other governments, and I have reason to believe that it can be resolved". He said that South Africa would return to the peace talks with new suggestions that would solve the problem of verification, which had been the "biggest stumbling-block" at the fruitless Brazzaville talks a few days earlier.

Sam Nujoma took the opposite view. Pretoria's walk-out at Brazzaville, he said, had been "sabotage", adding that Swapo had "no alternative but to carry on with our armed struggle." This did not transpire, however; the fact was that at this stage Plan was not capable of mounting a significant assault on the operational area.

On December 13 the delegations came together at Brazzaville, and at last they agreed on a protocol, Pik Botha signing on behalf of Pretoria with the words: "We want to be accepted by our African brothers. We need each other."

The main points covered by the agreement – which was to be ratified at another meeting in New York on December 22 – were:

- Implementation of Resolution 435 would start on April 1 of 1989.
- Three thousand Cuban troops would leave before April 1.
- By August 1 all Cuban troops would be north of the 15th parallel, an imaginary line running about 300km north of the border.
- By November 1 all Cuban troops would be north of the 13th parallel, about 550km north of the border, by which time 25 000 of them would have been sent home.
- Another 13 000 would be withdrawn by 18 months after April 1.
- All discriminatory legislation would be repealed in SWA/Namibia by mid-May.
- By July 1 South African Defence Force strength would be down to 1 500 men, confined to the Grootfontein and Oshivelo bases, and SWATF would have been disbanded, along with all the part-time area-force units.
- On November 1 SWA/Namibians would elect a constituent assembly which would be required to adopt a constitution by means of a two-thirds majority.
- A "Joint Commission" consisting of Cuban, South African and Angolan officials would be formed on January 22 of 1989 to facilitate the resolution of disputes about the interpretation and implementation of the agreement.

On paper the only parties to suffer from the deal were Unita and the African National Congress. Although it was not publicly stated, it was reported that South Africa and Angola had reached a secret "understanding" that Pretoria would cut its support to Unita if Luanda would withdraw training facilities for the ANC. Of the two, the worst sufferer was undoubtedly the ANC. Savimbi, after all, was very much in place, with further supplies of arms from Zaire guaranteed by the US, at least till Washington's capricious foreign policy darted off on a new tack; the ANC, on the other hand, faced the unpleasant prospect of having to pull back to Tanzania – which in spite of its status as a self-proclaimed a "front-line state" was far distant from South Africa.

Savimbi, who had been predicting the end of South African aid, was not noticeably disheartened. On December 16 he pledged that his forces would not attack Cubans engaged in withdrawing and renewed his call for an immediate ceasefire and direct negotiations with Luanda.

In New York, meanwhile, details of the verification process began to emerge. According to one UN official a symbolic force of about 50 men, known as Unavem, would be stationed in Angola to oversee the Cuban withdrawal, although the actual data to be used for checking the pull-out would be supplied by US surveillance satellites. It was later confirmed that the verification force would consist of a Brazilian general and servicemen from Algeria, the Congo, Spain, India, Yugoslavia and Norway.

On December 19 Chester Crocker confirmed to journalists that South Africa and Angola had discussed the matter of ANC camps and "we have the impression that they are reaching an understanding on this very important question". Discussions on the matter were continuing, although it had not been an explicit part of the overall agreement, he added.

Asked about the fact that Sam Nujoma had resurrected the claim that Walvis Bay was an "inalienable" part of SWA/Namibian territory, Crocker tactfully replied that while this matter had not been discussed at the negotiations either, it was generally understood that the port was part of South Africa, and "what we are saying is that Walvis Bay is a question that can ultimately be resolved only between the government of South Africa and the government of an independent Namibia".

On December 22 the peace treaty was signed in New York as scheduled. In essence it did not deviate from the Brazzaville Protocol, except that Pik Botha confirmed that "a number of tacit understandings" had been reached during the course of the long negotiations, the implication being that there was, as observers had suspected, a secret agenda.

The signing ceremony, held in the UN Economic and Social Council, was preceded by a characteristic burst of Cuban tactlessness. Cuban Foreign Minister Isidor Malmierca Peoli attacked the US for continuing to support Unita and added that the treaty "by no means implies any change in the essence of the South African racist regime, whose policy of apartheid embodies the real destabilising factor in southern Africa".

Pik Botha laid down his prepared speech and responded: "I will say no more to my colleague from Cuba today, other than that I am quite prepared to submit the evidence of African heads of state who would wish the Cuban troops to leave Angola immediately. If needs be I will disclose the names of my African brothers, some of whom have actually asked South Africa not to leave Namibia before the last Cuban soldier has left Angola. I am quite prepared and ready … to enter immediately after this ceremony with you in a public debate on the extent to which fundamental human rights are maintained in Cuba and in South Africa."

Significantly, Russia's Anatoly Adamishin pointedly declined to back up the Cubans and instead praised the South Africans' "realistic approach, which we hope will continue".

It is worth recording a passage from Botha's prepared speech. He noted that "we have reached a peaceful agreement, at least on paper … Unless the good faith of all parties involved prevail to cement observance and implementation, the words of a treaty become meaningless".

They were prophetic words, in the light of what was still to come.

The count-down to independence began almost immediately. Before leaving New York Pik Botha announced that the South West Africa Police's controversial counter-insurgency unit, still popularly known as "Koevoet" in spite of an official name-change, would be disbanded in 1989; and that aid to Savimbi would end, although "I would be telling a lie if I said that we would suddenly end our friendship with Unita. We will remain sympathetic towards that organisation".

At Jamba a sombre Savimbi confirmed that he had been given advance warning of the cut-off by P W Botha "because he wants to observe the spirit and the letter of the New York agreement. The decision is total and categorical from today onwards". Savimbi warned that Fapla was planning another offensive against him, scheduled for April or May of 1989, adding that he regretted the lack of MPLA response to his requests for internal peace negotiations: "The MPLA line has hardened against us. We think they will attempt again a military solution, and only after that will they begin to come to their senses".

The year ended with the participants' minds turning to money - lots of it. Angola formally asked the UN to cover the cost of withdrawing the Cubans, which it put at 800 million US dollars (then about R1,9 billion).

In the Security Council, meanwhile, a more pressing - and fateful - dispute was shaping up: the size of the UN Transitional Assistance Group which was supposed to take over security responsibility for SWA/Namibia as the South African military wind-down began.

Originally a force of seven infantry battalions and 360 policemen - about 7 500 men and women - and 2 000 civilians had been envisaged. The cost for this modest force was estimated at about 800 million US dollars (then about R1,9 billion). Now the five permanent UNSC members were pushing for a reduction in the size and thus the cost of the Untag contingent. But the 15 "non-aligned" UNSC members wanted the full contingent because, they said, they were afraid that South Africa would "interfere".

Swapo UN spokesman Theo-Ben Gurirab argued that more peacekeepers were necessary because the number of South African troops had increased from 45 000 in 1978 to 100 000 (a vast exaggeration: in fact the total SADF presence in late 1988 amounted to about 15 000), while the police had increased from more than 2 000 in 1978 to more than 10 000. SWATF numbered 35 000, he added, while the "paramilitary force" (presumably the home guards) had more than 3 000 members.

Arguments and counter-arguments flew back and forth; the upshot of it was that by December 31 no decision had been taken, and another fateful factor had been added.

In all this the toll of the war was almost overlooked altogether: 36 members of the security forces, 261 insurgents and 53 civilians. And it was still to rise by several hundred before peace actually came to the border.

See: "The Angolan Debacle" — Castro's version on page 255.

1989

On January 9, while delegates wrestled with the size of the Untag force, a mine-protected vehicle of the Department of Water Affairs detonated a landmine in the Oshigambo area near Oshakati, although the occupants were unscathed. SWATF troops following up on three sets of tracks leaving the scene were told by local inhabitants that three unknown men had been in the vicinity before the vehicle had gone over the mine. It was like the bad old days - except that it was the exception now.

On January 17 the Security Council voted unanimously to go ahead with deploying Untag, but called for cuts to hold the cost to between 400 and 500 million dollars (R960m and R1,2 billion). The resolution called on Perez de Cuellar to prepare a report estimating the size and needs of the force, and lay it before the UNSC within two weeks, after which a resolution authorising the creation of the Untag contingent would be taken.

The five permanent members' desire to cut the size of the Untag force was no mere exercise in penny-pinching. To all intents and purposes, peace had returned to the border; since October 30 there had been only three Swapo-related incidents anywhere in SWA/Namibia - the latest being the mine explosion at Oshigambo - instead of 70 to 100, as in previous years, and this in spite of the fact that SADF and SWATF elements had been strictly enjoined from crossing the border.

Late in January a high-level Pretoria source told this writer that a little earlier an aide of the Secretary-General had actually asked a top member of the South African negotiating team whether an Untag military force was, in fact, needed at all, to which the South African had replied "no", since it was not necessary to maintain a peace which had already arrived of its own accord, even though Koevoet had been disbanded and the SWA Police reduced by about a quarter, to 6 000 men. They agreed, however, that an Untag presence would have to be sent, but it need not be as large as originally envisaged.

No doubt this information played a part in the Secretary-General's recommendation on February 10 - which was subsequently adopted by the Security Council - that a total of 4 650 Untag troops would be enough, but that he would ask for more if this number proved inadequate.

At the same time there were disturbing signs that all was not going as envisaged in the Geneva Protocol. The Cuban and Angolan members of the Joint Military Monitoring Commission were still evading the issue of Swapo violations, and by now there had been a significant concentration of insurgents in the shallow area opposite central Ovamboland. There were also reports that small groups of insurgents had been crossing into the operational area and building up arms caches.

Right
South African troops in Buffel mine-protected vehicles, hastily called out after the Plan incursion began on April 1, stand by outside Air Force Base Ondangwa, waiting for the order to go into action

Protests by Pik Botha to Luanda and Havana had achieved nothing. On the other hand, the South Africans apparently were not unduly worried about this, since it seemed inconceivable that either Angola or Cuba would allow the massed insurgents to make any rash moves.

There had also been snags in the process of establishing the 11 border monitoring posts provided for in the Geneva Protocol, and on January 15 a Cuban major named Martino had complained of South African obstructionism which was hampering the Luanda allies' efforts.

This prompted the Chief of the Army, Lieutenant-General A J Liebenberg, to break silence on January 30 with rather a different story. All had gone well, he said, till the seventh post had been set up at Santa Clara, opposite SWA/Namibia's Oshikango border gate. East of Santa Clara was Unita territory, however, and the Angolans had

experienced great difficulty in putting up the eighth at Beacon 54. When they managed to do so they could not establish a supply-line, and by the end of January the Fapla monitoring troops were still being fed from across the border by the SADF.

In spite of the urgings of the SADF, Liebenberg continued, the Angolans had been completely unable to establish the three remaining monitoring posts, "and so we did it ourselves and put our own troops there – that is to say, our component of the monitoring force … till now they have not yet placed their troops there … We have even told them to come through on South West African soil" (eventually the Fapla components had to do just this).

The security situation in southern Angola continued to worsen as Savimbi - determined to impress all sides with his importance as a factor in the peace process - mounted what he described as a major offensive, The Angolans' response was to fall back on their old strategem of blaming the South Africans. On February 9 Defence Minister Pedro Maria Tonha claimed that South African troops had penetrated 40km into Angola two days earlier, and had shelled elements of Fapla in the Caiundo area to cover the flight of Unita forces.

On February 10 Dos Santos repeated the allegations while in Brazzaville visiting President Denis Sassou-Nguesso. The Angolans went even further, handing a formal note of protest to the British ambassador in Luanda with the request that he pass it on to the US, and also sent copies to Havana and Pretoria; by this time the "facts" had grown to include a claim that 40 South African soldiers had been killed in the action.

The claims amounted to accusations of a gross violation of the December agreement, which had expressly forbidden Pretoria to help Unita, and enraged the South Africans, who had gone to great pains to keep their noses clean. An SADF spokesman protested that the South African armed forces were respecting the peace accords "to the letter", while Magnus Malan went on record with a stronger statement, labelling Tonha's and Dos Santos's accusation a "transparent lie" and adding: "The reality of the strength, influence and success of Dr Savimbi's Unita is catching up with them. Instead of talking to Dr Savimbi and Unita about reconciliation, they blamed South Africa - and the SADF in particular - for their inability to hold their own against a motivated and purposeful Unita."

A Department of Foreign Affairs spokesman condemned "in the strongest terms" the "unsubstantiated note received from the Angolan government … Such allegations do not contribute to a

Below
South West Africa Police members dig a mass grave for 41 insurgents who were killed in the bloody fighting which erupted after the mass incursion by Plan from April 1 onwards

climate of confidence during the implementation of the New York agreements." The Angolans did not reply, but in Washington, US State Department spokesman Charles Redman said: "We have no evidence of any South African military incursion in southern Angola. Our information indicates that there has been fighting between MPLA and Unita in the area of Caiundo."

Unmollified, the South Africans made an urgent request for an immediate meeting of the new Joint Security Commission, which was due to gather in Luanda on February 23. The request was not acceded to.

Meanwhile, contradictory claims about what had evidently been a clash of substantial proportions had begun flowing from Luanda and Jamba. According to Unita, 275 Fapla had died in heavy fighting when 4 000 of its men had fought against three Fapla brigades which had been supported by Cuban soldiers, tanks and Swapo units. Fapla, on the other hand, said that in the past few weeks it had defeated the Unita offensive, killing 108 rebels and a white South African soldier, who was not further identified.

As a result, its spokesman added, "the so-called general offensive proved a disaster for Unita as they were forced to announce its suspension almost immediately." Unita retorted that it had called off the offensive following an appeal for peace from the Ivory Coast's President Felix Houphouet-Boigny.

On February 18 senior Angolan official Afonso van Dunem repeated the accusation against South Africa while visiting Harare, although he was careful not to go into specifics but confined himself to claiming that there had been a failure to abide by the December agreement. Five days later a South African team under Neil van Heerden jetted into Luanda to attend the scheduled JSC meeting, primed to discuss the Angolan charges and also raise the issue of what might be called the "Shilongo statement", concerning fresh evidence about the Plan build-up in the supposedly neutral area south of the Quiteve Line.

In February the SADF had acquired a new source of information in the shape of a Swapo deserter named Simon Shilongo, formerly a section leader in the insurgents' "Red Square" Battalion, who had slipped away from his camp at Peu Peu, walked 90km, sneaked over the border and then surrendered to the security forces.

Shilongo said he had deserted because of bad conditions in the Swapo camps, lack of food and clothing and ill-treatment by Swapo and Cuban officers. Swapo leaders were having a good life, he claimed, but not ordinary members, and Cubans regularly visited Swapo bases to trade clothes taken from civilians for food, then abused the women.

All this was interesting enough, but Shilongo's information about Plan dispositions in the neutral area was more pertinent. The Plan operational command headquarters was at Peu Peu, he said, with the "Red Square" Battalion in place to protect it. The Plan western area headquarters was situated north of Peu Peu and the central area headquarters near the operational command headquarters, while the "Katanga" logistics unit was sited north-west of Xangongo.

This was a clear violation of the Geneva Protocol and the December agreement, and Shilongo's statements were raised at an emergency meeting of the JMMC. To the South Africans' chagrin the Angolan and Cuban representatives said there was nothing they could do about the matter because the JMMC's jurisdiction covered only 1km

on either side of the border. Ultimately the best the South Africans could do was to secure approval for the matter to be discussed at the Luanda JSC meeting.

This was done, but what transpired has never been revealed. Presumably the Shilongo statement and detailed other information on Plan strengths and dispositions were flatly denied; as far as the Angolans' charges about an alleged South African incursion are concerned, all that is known is that the Angolans produced "evidence" which they declined to make public, and that Van Heerden immediately proposed on-site JMMC inspection, which the Angolans turned down on the grounds that they wanted an investigation at higher level.

The result, as had been the case with almost every important issue raised at the JMMC so far, was an impasse, and on February 24 Van Heerden emerged to say in regard to the Angolan claims the "matter was settled" and "we agreed to disagree, and we hope it has been resolved as an agenda item". The issue of the Swapo build-up in the shallow area was not mentioned at all.

There were no immediate repercussions, however, and during March the SADF began in earnest with the backloading of men, munitions and equipment, not to mention a vast assortment of related items it had accumulated over 15 years of military operations. From Ondangwa, Rundu, Oshivelo and Grootfontein the impedimenta began to stream back to South Africa. Prefabricated housing was taken down, mobile homes lifted off their foundations and on to their wheels, mess decorations packed.

For many South Africans and their families who had fallen victim to SWA/Namibia's strange allure it was a time of wrenching emotions; for the next-of-kin of the fighting troops and policemen in both countries there was an almost audible sigh of relief that their loved ones were safe at last.

Meanwhile the first members of the attentuated and much-delayed Untag force began to arrive as the count-down began towards what the SADF called "R-Day" – April 1, the first day of the implementation of Resolution 435. It was obvious that the UN troops and policemen would not be anywhere near full strength by R-Day, but, given the unwonted peace along the border, that seemed no reason for concern.

According to the withdrawal schedule, the SADF strength would be scaled down to 12 000 between April 1 and mid-May, while SWATF members would be confined to their bases and their arms would be locked up. If all went well, the next phase, from mid-May to June 7, would see the SADF presence scaled down to 7 000, and by June 31 its troops would be reduced to 1 500, stationed at Grootfontein and Oshivelo. There they would remain till election day on November 1, still on stand-by, and would then be withdrawn.

But the final chapter in the border war had not yet been written.

On the night of March 31/April 1, before the ceasefire had even gone into effect, up to 1 000 of the insurgents who had been lying up in the shallow area, carrying small arms, mortars, SAM-7 anti-aircraft rockets and RPG-7 anti-tank launchers, crossed into Ovamboland at four different places, the extremes 300km apart. One column entered just east of Ruacana and another at Ombalantu. Another, split into two prongs, crossed at Oshikango and then advanced down the road known as "Oom Willie se Pad" towards Oshakati and Ondangwa. Another two-pronged thrust entered west of the Nkongo base, one arm aimed at the white farming area around Namutoni and the other at neighbouring Kavango.

It was not long before they ran into the SWA Police border patrols. The police had been expecting just such a contingency since the build-up in the shallow area had started in January, and had set up the special patrols, manning them with former Koevoet members who had been re-integrated into the mainstream force on the disbandment of their unit.

The first contact started around 6am on April 1, just 105 minutes after the beginning of the ceasefire, when a patrol commanded by Sergeant Piet Cronjé moving around west of Ruacana spoke to local inhabitants, who pointed out fresh tracks indicating that between 40 and 50 men had crossed over from Angola late on March 31.

Although his patrol was lightly armed, Cronjé followed the spoor and later in the morning caught up with the intruders. A fierce firefight followed in which 31 insurgents died, two policemen being killed and two others seriously wounded. In the light of later statements, it is interesting to note Cronjé's comment that the insurgents did not run but stood and fought, and that even those who were captured refused to raise their hands in surrender.

It was not till several other contacts had taken place, however, and captured insurgents had warned of more incursions to come, that the police realised the scope of the violation. A swift escalation of the fighting left them in no further doubt, and by April 2, about 130 insurgents and 10 policemen had died.

By now almost continuous fighting was taking place over a 300km front and civilian refugees were converging on Oshakati and Ongwediva. In one incident, according to police, a patrol consisting of two whites and 20 blacks drove into an ambush manned by about 100 insurgents. The vehicles were knocked out by RPG-7 fire and the occupants scattered into the bush, except for the two whites, who tarried to destroy the vehicles but were both captured. One was then deliberately shot in the head and the other beaten to death with rifle-butts.

In the meantime Malaysian and Pakistani members of Untag had flown to the fighting zone and confirmed that the fighting had been sparked by a Plan incursion; according to one newspaper report, UN officials were "furious at the irresponsible conduct of the guerrillas".

Perez de Cuellar's special representative, Martti Ahtisaari, held consultations with Administrator-General Louis Pienaar, after which both agreed to the recall of certain military units from their bases to back up the police, who by this time had lost a number of armoured vehicles (five in one contact alone, according to reports) and were nearing exhaustion. This decision was confirmed by the Secretary-General.

Ahtisaari was later to be severely criticised for this action, but in all fairness he had little alternative. The Plan incursion was a clear violation of the agreements reached and it was obvious that the small Untag element already in-country - most of it made up of advance-party administrative personnel - was powerless to do anything. At this stage the South Africans held all the cards; if they summarily called a halt to the implementation process he would not be able to prevent it.

The first unit to be mobilised was 101 Battalion; frantic efforts were made to recall its members from leave (eventually there was a turn-out of nearly 100 percent), and soon convoys were heading northwards.

Foreign Minister Pik Botha had telephoned Perez de Cuellar on April 1, and now followed it up with a long and angry letter. Calling on De Cuellar and the Security Council to take a firm stand and thereby enable South Africa to fulfil its commitments, Botha claimed that there were another 4 000 to 5 000 insurgents below the 16th parallel and noted that "this inexplicable action on the part of Swapo constitutes a clear violation of agreements reached between South Africa, Cuba and Angola (and) endorsed by the Security Council".

He added: "We are clearly dealing with a situation where Swapo is flouting those agreements and is defying the Security Council. In addition Swapo has, of course, violated the written undertaking it gave you to cease all hostilities as of April 1, 1989.

"I trust you will agree that this is an intolerable situation. The Republic of South Africa has acted strictly in terms of its commitments and will continue to do so. It is significant, Mr Secretary-General, that at the time of writing no statement has been made by the leadership of Swapo on this cynical disregard of its obligation to you, the SC and the international community at large."

Such a statement, however, was not long in coming; in the next day or two, in fact, Swapo was to make several statements, all contradictory.

The first to break silence was Sam Nujoma, who was in Harare for a West European parliamentarians' conference. In a statement to the Zimbabwean state radio he said he was still studying reports of clashes, "but I must make it clear that this provocation is coming from South Africa", adding that he had received reports that well-organised South African troops had attacked civilians at various places and that SAAF helicopters bombed people who were celebrating, adding it was a well-calculated policy of disrupting the election process.

Later the same day Nujoma expressed his shock and dismay at Ahtisaari's decision to allow a redeployment of troops; Swapo was committed to a ceasefire, he said, and he had signed an agreement to that effect on behalf of the Central Committee and had then strictly enjoined members of Plan to honour it.

In spite of incontrovertible evidence to the contrary, Nujoma denied flatly that there had been an incursion, describing the fighting as a figment of the South Africans' imagination and part of a scheme to halt the transition to independence.

What had actually happened, he said, was that thousands of Swapo supporters who had been returning to Tsumeb from celebrations in Windhoek (why they should have celebrated the ceasefire before it had started he did not explain) had been ambushed by the South Africans, and many were now lying in hospital in Tsumeb and Windhoek. The same thing had happened at many other places in SWA/Namibia.

This was followed by another Swapo statement to the effect that the insurgents had "fired only in self-defence after being hunted down and attacked ... It is the earnest desire of Swapo to scrupulously observe the terms of the ceasefire agreement".

Meanwhile the fighting continued. On April 2 there were 30 contacts - an average of three an hour, according to a spokesman - in which 42 insurgents were killed for a loss of four policemen. As losses continued to mount, the US State Department came out in South Africa's support, saying Swapo was "trying to take advantage" of the SA forces' confinement to base, and "all the information available to us indicates that a major infiltration of northern Namibia by military forces of Swapo is occurring."

That night, as the Security Council began with urgent consultations, a mood of cautious optimism that the fighting would soon stop began to take hold of the South Africans, because there were signs that the insurgents were running short of ammunition.

At this stage Swapo's precise motivation for launching the incursion was still unknown, and when two captured insurgents - infantry section commander Phillipus Mateus and reconnaissance officer Johannes Katumba - were presented to the press on April 3 they could throw little light on the subject. Katumba said that the insurgents' primary objective had been to establish bases and then to declare their presence to Untag. Mateus said there had been no orders to attack the security forces. Asked why the insurgents had brought so many heavy weapons with them, he replied: "We had nowhere to leave them".

The matter became a little clearer on April 4 (at which stage the ongoing fighting had claimed at least 190 lives) when Swapo information secretary Hidipo Hamutenya confirmed in Luanda that the insurgents had been sent into SWA/Namibia with orders to regroup at Okahenge and "wait there for the UN forces". But, he added, many of them had already been in-country for several months.

The same day the African states' UN representatives met for a lengthy private consultation, after which they condemned Ahtisaari for loosing the troops, noted that Untag should have been in place on April 1 and said that the UN "must now explain why Untag was not fully operational on April 1 and is still not (so) today". This was a neat evasion of the facts, since the main reason for the delay in implementing Untag had been their protracted opposition to a reduction in its strength. A UN spokesman pointed out that the world body had had two weeks less than had been needed to get the Untag contingent to SWA/Namibia, but that all its members would be in place by April 30.

That night Pik Botha claimed that joint Cuban/Swapo battalions had been deployed less than a kilometre north of the border in two places, in readiness for possible attack, adding with complete truth that the peace process was in imminent danger of collapse. He repeated his warning in a letter sent to Perez de Cuellar and the Security Council's five permanent members), adding that unless the council took immediate effective action and Swapo came to its senses, South Africa would suspend co-operation with the implementation of Resolution 435 because it could not be expected to implement its undertakings if Swapo continued to act in flagrant violation of the agreements with the acquiescence of the UN.

The UN Under-Secretary for Political Affairs, Marrack Goulding, flew to Luanda for talks with the Swapo military commander, Peter Mueshihange, with the aim of arranging a ceasefire. Meanwhile the fighting continued along the entire 300km front. By day, Casspir armoured personnel carriers and Ratel infantry fighting vehicles stirred up clouds of dust; at night the darkness was broken by shots, flares and artillery fire. Gunship helicopters dashed about at tree-top altitude, just as they had for 23 years.

It was reminiscent of the height of the war in 1982, before the start of Plan's military decline, except that the intensity of the fighting was even

greater than it had been then, and chances of a ceasefire seemed slim. According to a police spokesman, Chief Inspector Derek Brune, "when we come into contact with Swapo we have come under fire every time. This is not a situation when we can engage in negotiation".

The total known death-toll at this stage had reached 193 - 172 insurgents and 21 policemen and soldiers — but the swift escalation of the first three days had levelled off, although the fighting was anything but over: on April 4, 15 Casspirs of 101 Battalion fought several contacts with a 200-strong group near Oshigambo, 20km south of Oshikango.

The Swapo high command's motivation - and responsibility - for the objective became clearer that day from remarks made by Sam Nujoma at a memorial service which was held in Harare for Plan's post-April 1 dead.

"Swapo forces were already given orders by me on March 29 that those who were inside Namibia should regroup and wait to be confined by Untag military components inside Namibia in accordance with Resolution 435," he said. "If you read the resolution carefully, it does not say that guerrilla forces who were found in Namibia on April 1 should be driven out by Untag or by anybody else, to be confined in Angola. That is incorrect. Read the resolution properly." (In fact Nujoma was wrong. As UN officials later pointed out, there was no provision in the independence plan for insurgents already inside SWA/Namibia to be confined in bases).

Nujoma then accused Perez de Cuellar of lying in his report that Swapo was infiltrating troops into SWA/Namibia. The information used for the report was untrue and Untag representatives had failed to do their job properly and could not confine SADF or SWATF forces to base, he said.

At this stage observers and analysts were beginning to form a picture of the reasons behind the incursion. Apparently the Swapo high command had misread the withdrawal timetable and failed to grasp the delay in the Untag deployment, and had assumed that in any case the latter would automatically favour the insurgents, as had always been the case with the UN in the past.

This being the case, the plan had been to send a large force of insurgents into Ovamboland, brushing aside the feeble police presence and establishing bases on SWA/Namibian soil for the first time since 1966. Ahtisaari would condone this gross violation of the agreements and immediately ring the bases with his Untag troops, against whom the 1 500 remaining South Africans and the disbanded SWATF members would be powerless.

The insurgents would then have been able to create the "strongman" image so important in Africa by boasting they had come back in spite of the "boers', and would have been able to indulge in intimidation of a kind not experienced in Ovamboland for at least five years. There was a recent historical precedent for this: in 1979 and 1980 thousands of fully armed insurgents had streamed into Rhodesia from Mozambique and Zambia, claiming victory over the Ian Smith government's forces.

If this was, in fact, the Swapo plan of action, it had obviously been based on a series of misunderstandings. Koevoet members had not been demobilised but, being professional policemen, had simply been re-absorbed into SWAPol; the SWATF had not been disbanded yet, but simply stood down; the SADF would not have been scaled down to 1 500 till June 31; only a small proportion of Untag personnel had arrived by April 1; and Ahtisaari, apart from any personal motivations, had been answerable, through Perez de Cuellar, to the Security Council rather than the General Assembly.

There was a school of thought which, analysing the direction of the Swapo thrusts and such information as was available, hypothesised that the establishment of bases would have been only the first phase of a larger plan; that Nujoma had planned to seize Oshakati, the main military headquarters in the border area, and Ondangwa, the largest airfield, while the easternmost of his columns had been aimed at neutralising the part-time "area force" units in the Namutoni-Tsumeb area and capturing Rundu base, the largest airfield other than Ondangwa.

After this he would proceed to Windhoek, possibly backed by Cuban aircraft sent to Ondangwa in response to a "fraternal" appeal for help, and there raise Swapo's flag. After initial protestations the new regime would then be recognised by the Organisation of African Unity, the UN and finally the rest of the world.

This hypothesis has never been proved, but observers pointed out that in essence it would have been a replay of the 1975 Angolan scenario - when the MPLA seized power by force of arms and avoided an election - and quoted unconfirmed reports from SWA/Namibia that Swapo was far from being as confident about its chances of winning a convincing victory at the polls as many people thought.

Yet it is a viable scenario. If, indeed, this was the second phase, the only thing that stopped it from taking place was the Swapo high command's miscalculation about the forces opposing it.

By April 6 the total known death-toll stood at 179 insurgents, 22 policemen and one soldier. By now Ahtisaari had completed his special report on the incursion and despatched it to New York, although senior UN official Cedric Thornberry said in Windhoek that it was unlikely to be made public and that the UN would not say if it believed Swapo was guilty of breaking the ceasefire, because "it's not our policy to say who is at fault".

It did not prevent further attacks on Ahtisaari. Speaking in his capacity as chairman of the 101-nation Non-Aligned Movement, Zimbabwe's President Robert Mugabe accused Ahtisaari of "monumental errors of judgement and shocking insensitivity to the feelings of Namibians", adding that the special representative's decision to remobilise the troops gave rise to serious doubt about his suitability for the post. Swapo's British representative, Peter Manning, accused Ahtisaari of an unauthorised alteration of the peace plan, which had been violated when South African forces had attacked Swapo units which had been assembling in anticipation of being confined to UN bases.

The British government, on the other hand, stood by its belief that Swapo was the culprit. Mrs Lynda Chalker, Minister of State at the Foreign Office, said bluntly: "What has got to stop is the incursion by Swapo. They have, as they agreed to do, to lay down their arms because it was Swapo who declared the unilateral ceasefire." She accepted that the insurgents might not have had hostile intentions, "but on the other hand you don't bring all that equipment down over a border, particularly when Swapo had accepted the arrangements for restriction to bases in Angola and Zambia".

All this time the fighting continued. Hundreds of fresh insurgents streamed over the border, many of them into eastern Ovamboland; at Ongha, north-east of Oshakati, soldiers and policemen in Casspirs and Ratels engaged an estimated 200 insurgents dug into trenches, and a group of similar size was fighting about 80km from the town. The casualty figures had shot up again: at least 253 insurgents had died by now, and 26 members of the security forces, most of them policemen but some from the six SADF and SWATF units which had been mobilised.

On April 8, as more and more insurgents poured into SWA/Namibia and the death-toll rose to 261, the South African government formally froze the implementation of Resolution 435, reintroduced the abolished dusk-to-dawn curfew in Ovamboland, called in strike aircraft and reactivated area force units in the Tsumeb-Grootfontein-Outjo area. Fears of internal clashes between Swapo and non-Swapo supporters were being mooted.

So far there had been a noticeable lack of success in bringing the situation back to the pre-April 1 condition - the most the UN had been willing to do was propose a form of capitulation in terms of which the invaders would be disarmed and confined to bases inside SWA/Namibia, which was entirely unacceptable to the South Africans.

Then some progress was made. In Lusaka Sam Nujoma finally gave in to intense international pressure and called on his men to withdraw from SWA/Namibia within the next 72 hours. Immediately afterwards an emergency meeting of the South African-Cuban-Angolan joint commission was held at the Mount Etjo game ranch 150km north-east of Windhoek. The South African delegation consisted of Pik Botha, Magnus Malan, Jannie Geldenhuys and Neil van Heerden; the Angolans were led by deputy Defence Minister General Antonio Dos Santos Franca and the Cubans by Communist Party secretary Carlos Aldana. Attending as observers were Chester Crocker and Soviet deputy Foreign Minister Anatoly Adamishin.

A day and a half of intensive talks followed, at the end of which the negotiators issued what became known as the "Mount Etjo Declaration" which amounted to a total victory for the South African-American standpoint. The insurgents remaining in Ovamboland (estimated at 1 500) would be allowed a week's grace to present themselves to nine border assembly points Untag would set up by midday on April 11, where they would be disarmed and returned to camps north of the 16th parallel.

Speaking at Windhoek after his return from Mount Etjo, Pik Botha stressed that if the insurgents did not attack the security forces they would not be attacked. If Swapo ignored the amnesty, however, it would lose its Cuban and Angolan support, and "it will mean the end of this organisation".

Botha said he hoped that implementation of Resolution 435 could now be resumed, and "today is the first day on which we can now say that there is a real, good and realistic prospect that it will be implemented, and, I hope, successfully".

The scheme did not start off well - possibly because the news took time to spread through Ovamboland, possibly also because a radio broadcast by Nujoma calling on the insurgents to return pointedly ignored all mention of the assembly points (according to foreign diplomats in Luanda, Swapo had been enraged by the fact that Angola and Cuba had forced it to comply with the Mount

Etjo agreement; one envoy said: "Swapo feels it is being sold down the river").

South African officers on the scene also believed that many of the insurgents would simply cache their weapons and uniforms and merge into the local population, either as part of a long-term intimidation and propaganda plan or because they were tired of fighting, while there were increasing accusations from various sources that the security forces were maintaining an "intimidatory presence" around the assembly points - although the reasons for such an action were obscure, given Pretoria's ardent desire to get back to the April 1 situation.

Whatever the case, by the end of the week's amnesty only a handful had turned themselves in at the assembly points, although there were signs that others were crossing into Angola under their own steam; meanwhile the South Africans reported that another 13 insurgents had died in previously unreported fighting (Windhoek had clamped down on news reporting from the operational area on April 12).

The amnesty period expired and was extended, and by late April hundreds of insurgents were reported to be arriving in Angola, while in Ovamboland messages from Swapo commanders calling on them to return were being broadcast on the radio service and by loudspeaker from helicopters. From April 25, too, the South African and SWATF troops were confined to their bases for three days to facilitate the process, and the following day 34 captured insurgents were released as a gesture of goodwill. By now the official death-toll for the post-April 1 fighting stood at 289 insurgents and 27 members of the security forces; soon afterwards the known Plan losses rose to 305 when the bodies of 13 other insurgents who had been killed earlier were recovered. By April 29 it was estimated that no more than 200 to 400 insurgents remained in Ovamboland.

Several more insurgents were shot and killed after expiry of the three-day confinement to base. Perez de Cuellar issued a demand that the troops be re-confined immediately, and not on May 13, as had been agreed on at a South African-Cuban-Angolan meeting in Cape Town a few days earlier. The demand was rejected, Pik Botha claiming that 350 insurgents were waiting to launch a new incursion on May 4, the 11th anniversary of the attack on Cassinga, and adding: "If there is further bloodletting it should not be laid at South Africa's door".

May 4 came and went without incident. The war of words continued for another few days, and then, on May 19, a joint South African-Cuban-Angolan statement was issued, stating:

"Both the Administrator-General, Mr Louis Pienaar, and the United Nations special representative, Mr Martti Ahtisaari, confirmed that South African forces were again confined to base and that a de facto cessation of hostilities existed in the northern area of Namibia."

The border war was over at last ... perhaps. Only time would tell if the war-clouds would really disperse as SWA/Namibia resumed its journey down the long and thorny path to full nationhood.

Below
The final chapter begins: gleaming white Untag landrovers lined up at the beginning of the peace-keeping operation — with a few others in olive drab, a visible reminder that the last shots had not necessarily been fired

EPILOGUE

The border war lasted for 22 years (or 23, if the final post-ceasefire outburst of violence is included). If the material losses of all the participants are counted, it cost billions in any reputable currency and destroyed the lives of thousands, especially in southern Angola.

Its total casualties will probably never be established; South African sources give known deaths by November 1 of 1988 as 715 security-force soldiers, 1 087 SWA/Namibian civilians and 11 291 insurgents and Angolan soldiers, and it is quite possible that many more Plan fighters died, given the fact that they did not have recourse to the sophisticated medical backup enjoyed by the security forces.

These figures do not include the thousands of deaths suffered by Unita, the Cubans and the Angolan soldiers and civilians as a result of the civil war which was so intimately connected with the border fighting.

The number of dead and permanently disabled is not, perhaps, very impressive when measured against the ghastly losses suffered in greater wars. By the standards of Southern Africa, however, where countries are vast but populations are small, it is a heavy toll, and particularly Angola will be a long time recovering from the loss of blood and treasure.

An interesting avenue of speculation is this: was it necessary for Swapo to embark on its "armed struggle" in 1962? Might it not have been better advised to fight for an independent Namibia on the national and international political battlefield rather than take up arms in its own backyard?

The answer, possibly, is "no" to the first part and "yes" to the second – but the question should be seen in the context of its times. The 1960s was the era of the "freedom fighter", not the negotiator, and in any case the South African government of the time was little disposed towards negotiations with an openly revolutionary organisation which had links with Moscow.

It could be that a less fervently revolutionary attitude on Swapo's part might have averted the police crack-down on its political agitation of the late 1950s and early 1960s; after all, other SWA/Namibians like Chief Hosea Kutako of the Hereros were openly speaking out against South African rule. And then again, perhaps not. Once more this matter must be seen in the context of the times. Southern Africans of all races are vastly more politically sophisticated in the late 1980s than they were in the 1950s and 1960s. They are certainly less prone to calls of the blood and the appeal of raw ideology.

An intriguing idea some observers play around with in their idle moments is the theory that perhaps the war did not hasten South West Africa's progress towards independence but actually delayed it. True or false? It is difficult to say, for there is no clear answer.

It is true that the war accelerated social and political change in the territory. On the other hand (as I mentioned earlier), it is also true that changing times brought changed attitudes; neither South Africa nor its mandate have stood still, but have responded to greater influences which were not necessarily purely political – both north and south of the Orange River, for example, the strongest impetus for such reforms as desegregation of social facilities and parity of pay came from simple economic imperatives.

It is a fact that by the mid-1980s SWA/Namibian society had changed so much that there was a considerable number of Swapo senior members who believed that the time had arrived for the movement to wind down the "armed struggle" and consider entering the internal domestic arena. By that time the South African government had committed itself so firmly to majority rule and allowing Swapo a free political hand if it eschewed further violence that it could not have reneged, even if it had wanted to.

The likely answers to some other questions, however, are less difficult to work out.

For example, it would appear that when Swapo's founders decided to launch their "armed struggle" they over-estimated the appeal of their cause to a nation of deeply divided people who had never had a national identity; as I mentioned at the beginning of this book, 95 percent of the insurgents who died in action during the war were Ovambos, and a great many of them were killed by fellow Ovambos fighting as hard for the government forces as the insurgents fought for Swapo.

At the same time the Swapo leaders under-estimated the tenacity of their opponents, who were not impatient Westerners or reformed colonialists grown weary of the imperial burden but Africans like themselves, who saw the "armed struggle" as one facet of a greater struggle which involved their very survival and so were willing to undertake the long, hard grind of a counter-insurgency campaign.

They were aided in this because of the generally low intensity of the struggle and the fact that Swapo was never really able to take the war much beyond the geographical extent of its main tribal support. As a result the war never significantly disrupted daily life in either territory and certainly did not damage the South African or SWA/Namibian economy.

Over the years much was made of the fact that South Africa was spending an estimated R2 million a day on fighting the war; but R750 million or so a year was a miniscule amount when measured against the annual defence budget, and the budget itself was kept under such tight control that except for one year overall military spending never went over five per cent of the Gross Domestic Product – well within reasonable limits, by normal international standards – and that one exception was not caused by the war but by the fact that in the late 1970s large sums were being spent on the domestic arms industry in order to counteract the international weapons boycott.

It would probably be fair to say that the border war never dug at South Africa's pocket till its forces' extensive fighting in support of Unita during 1987 and 1988, and most of that dip was due not to losses of equipment or deployment of manpower but to expenditure on fuel, artillery ammunition and other running costs. SWA/Namibia's real cost to South Africa was in the billions spent on non-military items like schools, roads, railways, dams, electricity schemes and the like – much of which, as the responsible mandatory power it saw itself to be, it would have spent anyway.

In some ways the war actually benefited the economy in both territories. In little more than a decade South Africa developed the world's 10th largest arms industry and in terms of money earned the Armaments Corporation became the country's premier exporter. South Africa became a leader in the production of mine-protected vehicles, armoured fighting vehicles and many other items, all of them with the supreme attraction, to buyers from other countries, of having been tested in battle. The internationally renowned G-5 155mm artillery piece – arguably the best gun-howitzer in the world – its self-propelled G-6 version and the 127mm

Valkiri multiple rocket-launcher all appeared as a direct result of Operation Savannah, when South Africa's World War II-vintage artillery proved to be outranged by the Russian-origin weapons used by the MPLA.

Many SWA/Namibians profited from the war, ranging from industrialists in Windhoek to the Ovambos and others who opened substantial businesses in places like Oshakati or operated the 12 000-odd little "cuca shops" scattered over the operational area.

The thousands of inhabitants everywhere in the operational area who joined the army or police prospered because for the first time they were earning regular pay which, by local standards, was munificent. For the chronically economically depressed Damara and the largely neglected Bushmen it was an especial boon.

True, all this prosperity was accidental rather than deliberate, in the sense that the security forces recruited locals because it needed them and not as a deliberate effort to provide work; but it happened all the same, and the Ovambos – a people renowned for their mercantile acumen – made the most of it.

Another interesting question is this: Should the South Africans have fought the insurgents?

The answer is probably that, apart from personal inclinations, they had no alternative, once it had become clear that the insurgency was not a nine days' wonder. To many – possibly most – of their voters they would have been seen as "hands-uppers" or worse, and the result of Operation Savannah sealed the matter. After 1976, when the insurgency became really viable for the first time because Angola's new masters threw their support behind Swapo, there was no turning back. The irony of it was that the seeds of the Swapo movement were sown in the 1940s and 1950s, but did not come to flower till late in the 1960s, when attitudes had changed a good deal and gave promise of changing even more.

Yet another good question is this: Could the war have ended sooner than it did? The answer is "yes" – and, popular mythology to the contrary, the fact that it lasted as long as it did was not simply the result of stonewalling by the South African government.

While the South Africans had their moments of intransigence, there is some evidence that it was not rooted in simple white supremacist feelings, as various observers would have one believe. On the evidence of Andreas Shipanga, Prime Minister John Vorster and President Kenneth Kaunda signed a detente document as long ago as late 1974 which committed South Africa to self-determination for South West Africa, guaranteed Swapo freedom to take part in non-violent politics and urged South West African exiles to return. It is also a fact that they had a powerful motivation to end the war and let SWA/Namibia go its own way, namely, the enormous amount they had to spend on loans and subsidies.

On the other hand, Swapo has also been guilty of acts of intransigence, and here the published record speaks for itself – looking back, there were at least two occasions on which Swapo killed the peace talks stone dead.

Another question: Was the United Nations a help or a hindrance in the whole affair? Well, it was both; sadly, however, a glance at the record shows it did more harm than good, particularly the General Assembly, which never made any effort to hide its bias.

Much of this was pure political grandstanding, of course, but the General Assembly's often stridently partisan antics created a rift that usually managed to overcome the best efforts of the UN Security Council, the body bearing ultimate responsibility.

Dr Kurt Waldheim bears much personal responsibility. His assiduous wooing of the so-called "non-aligned bloc" to secure his election to a second term of office led him frequently to echo the General Assembly's obvious bias, with serious consequences for the prospects for peace on several occasions, as in February of 1979.

How much of the present situation in Angola and SWA/Namibia should be blamed on the superpowers?

A great deal, history teaches us. Angola's disastrous slide into chaos was largely due to the Soviet Union's undermining of the post-Caetano era in Portugal. It might well be that the Russians were not working according to a pre-determined plan but were merely seizing a handy opportunity, but that does not alter Moscow's culpability (and the "opportunity" theory is suspect in any case, when one considers that Moscow, Cuba and the likes of Rosa Coutinho had already started working in 1974 to manoeuvre the MPLA into power).

Then there is the matter of Angola, which is generally cast as the war's (and South Africa's) greatest victim. Yet to a large extent the Angolan government could be said to have brought its troubles on itself.

It created its own worst enemy, Unita, by deliberately raping the Alvor Agreement. Then again, in the post-Operation Savannah days it could have repaired the grievous but not mortal damage the country had suffered by working out a profitable modus vivendi with South Africa, using its control over Calueque as a lever.

Instead it aided and abetted Swapo to the greatest extent possible, thereby inviting – and getting – repeated raids into its territory and ensuring that as a matter of simple military strategy the South Africans would give extensive aid and support to its greatest enemy, Jonas Savimbi.

No doubt this suicidal course of action resulted from post-revolutionary hubris, the urgings of Russia and Cuba and the belief that the South Africans would keep their hands to themselves because they had been whipped. It was a bad miscalculation. The Angolans should have accepted the fact (unpalatable though it might have been) that the South Africans had not been defeated, but had withdrawn intact with a large amount of battlefield experience and a very good idea of what they could get away with.

That made them dangerous people to provoke, and the bottom line is that the men in Luanda should have known that their opposite numbers in Pretoria were not going to take the punishment on the chin without reacting.

Angola's fate is its own fault in another sense as well. The record shows it has been guilty of bad faith on various occasions. The 1984 Joint Monitoring Commission failed primarily because the Angolans did not abide by their repeated promises to keep Swapo out of the Area in Question, and in fact actively helped the insurgents to subvert the proper functioning of the withdrawal process.

In 1988/1989 they acted in exactly the same way, which made it possible for the Plan surge over the border from April 1 of 1989 to take place. No doubt they had their reasons.

Mention should be made of several misconceptions about the war, particularly the earlier stages, none of which hold water on close examination.

One dire prediction often voiced by many commentators, particularly in the early and middle 1970s, was that Angola (and by extension SWA/Namibia) would be South Africa's Vietnam.

It was not. Partly by design and partly by the accident of birth, the South Africans pretty much avoided the mistakes the US made in Vietnam. In the first place, being Africans, they did not suffer from the cultural shock and incomprehension of local conditions that hampered the Americans so much. They made mistakes at first, but learnt fast – and the greatest lesson they learnt was to follow the Chinese strategist Sun Tzu's advice and wage the SWA/Namibian war as far as possible with SWA/Namibians, so that by the latter stages the vast majority of the fighting men were locally recruited, from races other than white.

The generals also went to extraordinary lengths to plan their external operations in such a way as to ensure the absolute minimum of casualties, and succeeded to a remarkable degree. In consequence the involvement in Angola and SWA/Namibia excited the disquiet of many political commentators and gave rise to a conscientious-objection movement which drew strength partly from the government's clumsiness in dealing with it, but the dissenters never formed a significant proportion of the eligible conscript and volunteer manpower pool.

There have been many statements that thousands of young white South Africans left the country to avoid service in SWA/Namibia, but this has not been backed up by any conclusive research, and it seems likely that many of those who left did so because they considered that two years of full-time conscription and 720 days of part-time service were too onerous a burden on their careers and personal lives – which is a different matter altogether.

Angola was certainly not South Africa's Vietnam in the sense that the SADF was bogged down there for any length of time. Till far into the 1980s the South Africans did pretty much as they pleased in southern Angola and scored many victories at little cost to themselves. If Angola was anybody's Vietnam, it was the Cubans'. Losses among the Cuban conscripts who were sent there by their government have never been made public, but in some circles it is thought to number thousands – almost all victims of Unita.

Another popular misconception after Operation Savannah was that it had destroyed the "myth of South African military superiority". This was a handy phrase that rolled readily off the typewriter, but the contrary was true. South African military superiority was anything but a myth, then or later.

Unlike almost every other southern African army, the SADF was a long-established body, forged by six decades of independent development and two bloody world wars into the best-organised, best-trained force in Africa. What Savannah proved was that the SADF was not in good shape after 30 years of peace; its equipment was outdated and there was a good deal of deadwood - both in personnel and in doctrine - that needed to be lopped off. To the South Africans' credit they took this lesson to heart, with the border war supplying a handy training-ground. As a result they emerged with a standard of operational expertise which surpassed that of some of the most famous armed forces in the world - and the self-confidence that went with it.

An alternative claim which was often heard at the time was that Savannah had "destroyed the myth of white superiority". This was also not true, or at least not in the sense meant by those who rattled it out with such facility. What Savannah and the border war did do was help white South Africans to discard a certain chariness about using black soldiers as combatants, a prejudice going back to the colonial wars of the previous century - not simply because of feelings of racial superiority but because of a vestigial survival instinct dating from the frontier days.

Things had already begun to change in the SADF, but the border war accelerated the process, so that in less than two decades the SADF became racially integrated at all levels (the SWATF had never been anything but multi-racial from its inception). As a result many South Africans and SWA/Namibians of all races served cheek by jowl with men lighter or darker than themselves and, in the heat of combat and the shared suffering of bush campaigning, found many of their lifelong preconceptions melting away.

The greatest misconception of all, however, was about the fact that the South Africans had been "taught a lesson" by Operation Savannah. They had been taught a lesson, all right, but not the one cherished by most commentators. Apart from showing them that the SADF needed some working up as regards equipment and doctrine, it taught them that in the prevailing circumstances, given careful preparation, thorough planning and well-trained men, they could ignore various ancient military shibboleths and fight successfully against what seemed to be virtually suicidal odds. It was a lesson they embraced with gusto because they had a long tradition of living by their wits on the battlefield - and because they did not have a great deal of choice in the matter.

Were the South African and SWA/Namibian soldiers better than the Swapo insurgents? The answer is "yes" - but one must understand why it was so. It went not about courage or cowardice but about better organisation, better planning, better utilisation and, above all, better training.

Now, with the guns silent along the border for the first time in more than 20 years, one wonders if the men who fought with courage on either side will have the greater courage to keep the peace and work together for their common future. Perhaps they will - and perhaps not. Time can heal wounds, or it can cover them over and let them fester, to erupt years or decades later. The smallness of the leadership pool indicates that the various factions in the Namibia-to-come should join hands.

Perhaps the most important question of all is this: Who won?

It is a difficult question to answer, since this is written before the general election which is likely to decide the shape of the Namibia that is to come. What can be said, however, is that there is no doubt that the South Africans won the armed struggle; and if the government of the new Namibia is neutral towards Pretoria, the South Africans will have achieved their minimum political requirement as well.

If the war proved anything, it was that although most insurgencies end in political solutions, he who has lost the penultimate military phase has no right to say anything when the armed struggle concluded not with a bang but with the whisper of papers being shuffled at a conference-table.

PART II
THE WAR IN CLOSE-UP

To those who did not know better – and to some who did, but found it more convenient to avoid facing the facts – the border war was a simple confrontation between racist whites and oppressed blacks.

The men and women who fought in it knew better, Probably no other Southern African war has ever featured such a motley, many-tongued array of combatants driven by such a variety of motives: patriotism, political belief, a hunger for vengeance, a desire for money, obedience to the authorities.

For some it satisfied a thirst for adventure, because in a sense the border was a fighting man's conflict, in that most of the action in it was Mark One face-to-face soldiering at whites-of-the-eyes range rather than the impersonal killing of enemies at long distance.

It has been called a "colonial" war, but in at least one important aspect it was not. Where it differed from most such wars was that none of the fighters were foreigners, in the sense of coming

to the battle-zone from distant lands, like the Americans in Vietnam and the British in Malaya. All were Southern Africans of one race or another and did not experience real difficulty in coming to terms with their environment.

In some cases, in fact, the difference between the protagonists was tragically small: for the insurgents on the one hand and the Ovambo soldiers and policemen of 101 Battalion and the South West Africa Police it was nothing more or less than a civil war.

A routine security patrol near Ongiva, during the South African "occupation" of the town after Operation Protea, passes a milestone from the Portuguese days giving the distances to Pereira D'Eca (Ongiva's old name) and Mongua

THE
FIGHTERS
SWAPO

Top Left
A young female insurgent after capture, her face set in an inscrutable mask of what might be fear — or defiance. She is wearing typical East Bloc camouflage; Plan members wore the field uniforms of various countries

Right
An insurgent captured fairly early in the war — uniformed in Cuban olive-green, and properly equipped. In his left hand he holds a mortar night sight

Below
A Swapo propaganda document

Who were the people who spent 23 years waging the border war as members of the People's Liberation Army of Namibia?

For most of the war they were almost all Ovambos — one of Plan's greatest weaknesses, because while it meant that insurgents could always merge easily into the Ovamboland population, inhabitants elsewhere tended to spot them easily and quite often reported them to the security forces; and no doubt this was one of the main reasons why the insurgency never took hold, except sporadically, outside Ovamboland itself.

Some were genuine volunteers, motivated by political reasons or grievances against the system, others were conscripted into Plan's ranks after leaving SWA/Namibia in order to obtain further education. Towards the middle 1980s, when recruits became scarce, many Plan fighters were youngsters who had been born to Ovambo mothers in exile or abducted from schools, then raised as insurgents in special camps.

Militarily, the insurgents had pronounced weak and strong points. The average Plan insurgent was often good at fieldcraft, camouflage and anti-tracking techniques, and capable of extreme feats of physical endurance, even when wounded. From beginning to end, however, the rank-and-file insurgent was never as thoroughly schooled in the fighting skills as he should have been, even at the height of the war, in the early 1980s.

What this meant was that novices had to learn on the job, and for many their first incursion was also their last. But some insurgents were very efficient, particularly after they had survived a season or two of operations, and at least one operator of the late 1970s acquired a well-nigh legendary reputation.

Plan fighters' morale varied according to the circumstances. They were certainly subjected to heavy indoctrination, ranging from doses of pure Marxism-Leninism to warnings that capture meant inevitable torture and death. According to prisoners and deserters, the insurgents were strictly disciplined and cut off from independent news sources, while grumblers or would-be deserters were harshly punished. Some "turned" Plan members claimed to have become dispirited by the bad conditions at their base camps and the privileged lives or cowardice of their officers. Other insurgents, however, remained strongly motivated even after capture.

It is not known how many women served in Plan, but there were substantial numbers. It is said that at least one infiltration was led by a woman and that several were wounded in contacts, and a teenager in full uniform was shot dead during Operation Sceptic in 1980.

On the evidence of deserters and prisoners it would appear that female recruits were given full military training; in the early 1980s a surrendered insurgent claimed that although a few women were used for intelligence and supporting tasks, their roles in the forward static bases were "mainly to please", cook the food and look after equipment.

From Botswana reports reveal that at least 2,500 S.African army defectors have pleaded for political asylum in that country since December 1978. Already hundreds have passed through Botswana and found their way to major Western capitals. They have revealed terrifying horrors in the S.A.D.F. army barracks. Part of a statement given by one of them reads:

"It is wholly a chaotic situation. Soldiers live in constant fear -only prayers after prayers which don't bring relief at all. Though not all of us have seen SWAPO guerrillas, one cannot deny their presence. They are there deep inside the country, at the borders, in the remote areas -- they are everywhere. One expect attack evertime and everywhere; this make us become nervous and frustrated. Under such chaotic conditions one cannot but pull a long puff from one of your self - made "daaga cigars". One loses apetite easily: sleep is very seldom... surely death is unavoidable there".

Boer soldiers lived in constant fear and panic. The entire combat troops of racist South Africa in Namibia are absolutely disorganised and demoralised. They are at present only confined to their bases and camps which in most cases are built in the centre of civilian settlements and in Hospital yards. The Boer soldiers maintain a low profile in initiating battles and this decreases at an alarming rate giving head - scratching worries to Botha and his fascist army generals. While Botha forces maintain a low profile, PLAN combatants gain momentum driving the war deep inside the country with heavy clashes reported in the South, just under the very nose of Maj. General Janie Geldenhuys so-called "Officer Commanding S.W.A. Command".

Above
Female Plan members in training at a camp in Zambia in the mid-1980s

Inset
A SWATF tracker fossicks around in the smoking ruins of a school destroyed in a Swapo attack east of Ondangwa

Right Top
A Plan camp somewhere in Angola, fairly early in the war, with the men wearing a mixture of uniforms and civilian clothes

Right Bottom
Plan insurgents went to great lengths to build strong shelters, carefully camouflaged under trees so that they were almost invisible from the air

Left
A Plan fighter, soon after being wounded and captured. Somewhat to his surprise he was not executed but given treatment, then flown out for interrogation

The Security Forces

Popular belief to the contrary, whites and men of colour have been fighting as allies in Southern Africa for hundreds of years. Never before, however, has the net been cast wider than during the border war.

Soldiers and policemen of all races served on the border and beyond it. In the earlier stages of the war most of the soldiers (although not the policemen) were white national servicemen from South Africa and SWA/Namibia, mostly in their late teens, with a thin sprinkling of professionals of the Permanent Force. From early 1976 onwards, thousands of mainly white part-time soldiers of the Citizen Force and Commando Force were called up for border service for up to three months at a time.

Thousands of other South Africans who served on the border were black, coloured and Indian servicemen who had volunteeered for two years' service in the army or marines, or were members of the Permanent Force; it is not generally known that among them were a battalion of Zulu soldiers, recruited from the green hills that had supplied Chaka's impis.

The ethno-cultural complexity of the border forces increased with recruiting of local inhabitants in the mid-1970s and conscription for SWA/Namibians of all races after the SWATF had been established (although compulsory service was never extended to the actual border tribal homelands, where the reservoir of potential recruits was usually far greater than the military's requirements).

Ultimately the border troops' diversity made a mockery of the catchall Swapo epithet of "boere" for anyone who served in the security forces. The troops ranged from pale-skinned blue-eyed blond to pitch-black. The languages they spoke were as diverse as their complexions: English and Afrikaans, Kwanyama and Ondonga, Masubia and Barotse, Kavango and Nama, Zulu and Portuguese, not to mention several obscure Bushman dialects.

Fortunately most of them had at least a working knowledge of Afrikaans, the SWA/Namibian lingua franca, although some lacked even this at first, and picked it up as they went along.

There can be little doubt that in the South African context the crucible of the border will still produce some interesting socio-political ingots. For the first time in a lifetime, men of various races found themselves sharing common hardship and danger on the most basic level, the traditional barriers of their polarised society discarded, and they came back vastly changed.

As Henry V (by Shakespeare's telling, anyway) said to his troops before the Battle of Agincourt;
We few, we happy few, we band of brothers;;
For he today that sheds his blood with me
Shall be my brother

The South West Africa Territory Force

The SWATF was formed on August 1 of 1980. By the time it was disbanded at the end of the border war it was 30 000 strong, incorporating conscripts and volunteers drawn from every corner of SWA/Namibia and supplying about 75 percent of the border's "bayonets", or fighting troops — almost all black.

Its detractors dismissed it as a "surrogate force", the equivalent of the Cubans in Angola; but that was a simplistic view.

Political factors played a role in its formation. For years the SWA/Namibia issue dominated South Africa's press and politics, often in a form negative, not to say hostile, towards the government.

At the same time military planners knew it was not cost-efficient to fight a protracted war with forces composed, thanks to the SADF's peculiar structure, mainly of conscripts and reservists. Provision also had to be made for a post-independence army, in case Swapo fared badly at the scheduled elections and decided to fight on.

It was a success from Pretoria's point of view. Losses became less of an issue, and in the end SWA/Namibia largely ceased to be a matter of public anguish except when some of the South African troops remaining there were killed or wounded.

Militarily, it was also a success. Familiarity with the local area and folkways, efficient support services and good training and leadership resulted in consistently high Plan losses in the 1980s.

By war's end the SWATF had assumed a definite persona. While still commanded by an SADF general, it had its own uniform, organisation and rank-badges and had developed its own mystique.

Thanks to SADF back-up, the SWATF was remarkably long on teeth and short on tail. In its final form it was organised as follows:

The GOC SWATF was headquartered in Windhoek, and SWA/Namibia was divided into seven "sectors". Each border sector was also responsible for operations in its equivalent north of the Cutline.

The SADF controlled the three border sectors — Sector 10 (Kaokoland and Ovamboland), Sector 20 (Kavango, Bushmanland and Western Caprivi) and Sector 70 (East Caprivi) — even though most of the troops stationed there were SWATF members. The SWA controlled Sector 30 (headquartered at Otjiwarongo), Sector 40 (Windhoek), Sector 50 (Gobabis) and Sector 60 (Keetmanshoop).

A joint South African-SWA/Namibian committee controlled overall planning, liaison and co-operation between the two forces.

The SWATF consisted of three legs, the Reaction Force, the Area Force and various non-attached units.

The Reaction Force was formed by:
● A motorised conventional-warfare brigade made up of three motorised infantry units (911 Battalion, a multi-racial national service battalion, Regiment Erongo and Regiment Namutoni, the latter two manned by the Citizen Force), and a CF armoured car unit, Regiment Windhoek.
● Six full-time light infantry battalions, manned by volunteers locally recruited from specific ethno-cultural groups, with a sprinkling of outsiders to provide needed expertise. Each battalion trained its own men and had a specific area in which it operated, year in and year out. The units were 101 Battalion (Ovamboland); 102 Battalion (Kaokoland); 201 Battalion (Bushmen based in Western Caprivi); 202 Battalion (Kavango); 203 Battalion (Bushmanland); and 701 Battalion (Eastern Caprivi).

The Area Force consisted of 26 part-time units, manned by a mixture of volunteers and reservists of all races fulfilling a non-continuous obligation. Varying in size and structure according to regional requirements, they operated in their home areas.

The SWATF's third leg comprised a varied assortment of specialist and support units: one engineer and one signals unit, a parachute battalion and the SWA Specialist Unit. It also had a species of home-grown air force in the form of 112 Squadron, consisting of civilian light aircraft flown by their owners.

Above
Soldiers of the SWA Territory Force parade in battledress in the early 1980s. At this stage they still carried ex-Portuguese Army G-3 rifles

Top Right
SWATF service dress was grey-green, not shades of khaki like the SADF's. The gemsbok badge indicates headquarters personnel

Right
Recruits in basic training at 41 (later 911) Battalion, the SWATF's first multi-racial unit

HITTING PATROL

The various external operations captured the newspaper headlines because of their size and audacity, but the basic building-block of the counter-insurgency campaign was the patrol.

Uncounted thousands, perhaps even millions, of patrols of one kind or another were carried out during the border war, particularly after the military with its comparatively abundant manpower assets took over responsibility for the border areas from the police in 1974. In the early years, most casualties on either side were suffered in contacts initiated by — or sprung on — patrols; from 1978 onwards it was the "external operations" in Angola that caused the loss-rates to soar.

But the patrols never ceased, from beginning to end. The South Africans had learnt the lessons of earlier insurgencies, and realised from the beginning that if they did not dominate the countryside at all times the insurgents would move in to fill the vacuum.

"Patrol" was a word with a multitude of meanings. A patrol could go out on foot, on horseback or in vehicles. It could be an eight- or 10-man section commanded by a corporal, or it could be much larger. Depending on its task, it could be gone several hours, several days or several weeks — or even longer on some deep-penetration forays.

It could be ordered to patrol a base perimeter; sent out at random, more to show the flag than anything else; told to investigate an incident or an area; given a specific mission such as gathering intelligence or setting up an ambush in a likely spot and there lying in wait for endless boring hours till someone walked into it or it was told to pack and go home. The patrol and its long-suffering practitioners were the maids of all work in the counter-insurgency campaign.

Most of the time a patrol accomplished nothing, as far as the men taking part in it could see; it was just one of those necessary evils. But a patrol was never predictable. It might start off with one set of plans and end up engaged in something else altogether. At any time it might run across an insurgent group, or walk into an ambush; and then things usually went from boring to hectic in a very short time.

The pattern of such encounters varied, but not by much. The initial contact was usually followed immediately by a brisk shootout, after which one side or the other gave way. Usually, but certainly not always, it was the insurgents who ran. What happened then depended on the circumstances: contact could be broken off, or reinforcements called in and a follow-up action launched.

Above
A machine-gunner waits while one of his mates enters an Ovambo kraal during a patrol. His bush-hat is tucked in at the sides to improve his hearing

Top Left
Communicating with base could be difficult in the flat Ovambo terrain

Centre
Some patrols were on foot and others on horseback — and sometimes together

Left
A 32 Battalion patrol moves up cautiously along the remains of a bush-fire inside Angola during Operation Carnation

HITTING PATROL

Foot Patrols

The foot patrol was really basic soldiering. Depending on the time of year, its members shivered, sweated, ate dust or wallowed through the mud the border areas produced in such profligate quantities during the rains.

Wet or dry, however, they carried heavy loads, made heavier by the fact that everyone shared the general burden: food, water, spare radio batteries, personal ammunition, magazines or belts for the automatic weapons, 60mm mortar-bombs, the sparse necessities of daily life.

Naturally the patrollers soon picked up various tricks of the trade, like leaving heavier ration items behind and caring for their feet.

They learnt to know the bush. One city boy came back from Caprivi to relate that the most nerve-wracking thing while lying in ambush was the endless whispering of the palm-trees' leaves as they rubbed together in the night breeze; another told of how his patrol had chased away a prowling lion by slapping their hands on their rifles' magazines.

Horse Patrols

The border war also saw the return of an archaic but very effective figure, the horse soldier. Horses had some distinct advantages. A mounted man could range much further afield than his comrade on foot without becoming exhausted, even in very hot weather, and he had a much better view, especially in Ovamboland, which was as flat as a table-top.

Most of all, the horses were quiet. On one occasion a mounted patrol caught up with the rearguard of a Plan group it had, unbeknown to itself, been following. The resulting firefight caused no casualties, since both sides were equally surprised at running into one another.

The horse soldiers rediscovered something any old time cavalryman or mounted infantryman could have told them: under heavy fire some horses tended to panic and buck off their riders. It is said that by the late 1970s a number of such equine deserters were living peacefully in the Jati Strip.

Vehicle Patrols

An alternative method of patrolling was by vehicle. This was slightly less arduous than patrolling on foot and a great deal more ground could be covered, but vehicles were noisy, made good targets for anti-tank rockets and, being more likely to use roads and tracks than men on foot, were more vulnerable to the landmine threat, particularly in the early days, before the SADF could provide enough mine-protected vehicles. Nevertheless, millions of kilometres were covered by vehicle patrols during the course of the war.

Above
Enemy dead are brought back to Oshakati in body bags for possible identification

Above Right
Foot patrols were not always in the bush: Soldiers reconnoitre part of Ongiva in the early 1980s, amid the ghostly silence of abandoned buildings

Centre Right
A typical foot patrol in the Ovamboland bushveld. In front is the tracker, his eyes glued to the ground

Below
A vehicle patrol in Caprivi — effective, but noisy and vulnerable to landmines and anti-tank rockets

Riverine Patrols

The South African Marines had a unique task in the border war: patrolling the great Zambesi River and its environs around the tip of Eastern Caprivi, where SWA/Namibian territory was bordered, along largely notional land and water boundaries, by four different countries, three of them — Zambia, Zimbabwe and Angola — actively hostile and the fourth, Botswana, neutral.

Operating from their riverside "sandbag frigate", Wenela base (whose gate they decorated with an anchor to emphasise their naval origin) the marines patrolled on both land and water. The riverine patrols operated mainly in "Vredenburgers" — camouflaged and militarised versions of West Cape Coast fishing boats — or small inflatables. The land patrols operated on foot, setting up ambushes and pounding the dust or mud, as the case happened to be. Others spent their time swatting flies and/or mosquitoes on Mpalela Island in the river, watching the ferry operate between Zimbabwe and Zambia.

Above
Although thousands of kilometres from the sea, the South African Marines' base at Wenela had a distinctly nautical flavour

Top Left
Mounted patrol moving at speed across an oshona

Centre Left
Marines in a Vredenburger. The marine nearest the camera wears an able seaman's badge

Centre Right
Marines patrol the Zambesi in one of their small boats

Left
A marine Vredenburger launch, adapted from a West Coast fishing-boat design

HOT PURSUITS & FOLLOW-UPS

If the patrol was the basic building-block of the border war, then the nuts and bolts of it were the follow-up action and hot pursuit.

The follow-up was usually launched as soon as possible after a contact, an incident such as a mass abduction, or a physical or stand-off attack; the South Africans made it a rule to follow up on any such action, if possible while the insurgents were still withdrawing or scattering.

Follow-ups had a patchy success-rate, particularly in the early years, because there were so many imponderables. Then again, a follow-up posed peculiar problems. The pursuing troops had to make up the distance covered by the retreating insurgents in the interval between the original incident and the launching of the pursuit — no simple task, given the average insurgent's high degree of physical stamina.

They had to be able to follow the insurgents' spoor, even in adverse conditions, and they had to do it as quietly as possible, which meant that vehicles were not really suited to the task, although they were used quite successfully at times.

So sometimes the soldiers got to grips with the insurgents and at other times they did not, particularly during the rains, when visibility was bad and the rain washed out the spoor. Even if the pursuers did not lose the spoor, a good head start on the insurgents' part meant that the chase might well continue over the border into Angola, at which stage it became, by definition, a "hot pursuit" operation.

Following up was usually nerve-racking, always arduous and often dangerous. Some ignorant South Africans thought the insurgents cowards because they usually scattered and fled after a contact. In fact it was the only logical tactic to adopt against an enemy who usually had local numerical superiority and could call in ground and air reinforcements.

So he who followed up was never quite sure whether his quarry was actually fleeing or had rendezvoused at an agreed-on point and was now waiting for him to walk into an ambush; and there was always the chance that he would run into an unpleasant surprise, like a POM-Z anti-personnel grenade hidden in a clump of bushes, waiting to be detonated by an almost invisible trip-wire strung across a path.

Even if none of these things happened, a follow-up — successful or unsuccessful — was hard, desperate work. In the dry season, thirst was a constant problem; in the rainy season it was a nightmare of mud and torrential downpours. It only sounded easy to someone sitting back home and reading that "a follow-up was launched..."

Above and Below
Swaspes dog-handlers on the spoor. Dogs had advantages — they could work by night because they did not have to see the spoor — but they tended to become footsore, and in wet weather tracking by scent was often difficult

The SWA Specialist Unit

After the war hotted up in 1976 the SADF soon realised that if follow-ups were to mean anything it would be necessary to create a special force which would be trained and equipped to chase after an insurgent group and catch up with it. Thus was born, in 1977, the SWA Specialist Unit, or "Swaspes", as it was commonly called.

The brain-child of experienced soldiers, the unit was designed to overcome the main problems encountered in follow-ups, and in consequence was unlike any other force to see the light in Southern Africa.

Manned by hand-picked soldiers, Swaspes was a composite unit made up of tracking, mounted and motorcycle wings, members of which followed up on their own at times and in combination with their colleagues at others.

The trackers operated on foot, sometimes with the aid of dogs and sometimes without. The "mounties", naturally, rode horses — Arabians in some cases, or the sturdy "Boerperde" which had evolved in the Southern African backveld over the past two centuries — and the motorcyclists straddled heavily muffled scramblers which proved remarkably effective and also quieter than expected; experience also showed that in thick bush it was difficult to pinpoint their whereabouts. If it came to fighting, however, the mounties and motor-cyclists fought like their tracker colleagues — on foot in the normal infantry style.

Needless to say, great emphasis was laid on tracking. The foot trackers had to attain very high standards and pass stringent physical, intellectual, tactical and fieldcraft tests; the mounted men even learnt to track from horseback, incredible as this feat might seem.

Above
An ever-present hazard for the tracker during a follow-up action: a POM-Z grenade hidden in a bush, its nearly invisible trip-wire awaiting the unwary

Left
Lean, keen-eyed Swaspes trackers at their base in 1979/1980

Below
Foot trackers and mounties follow up on the spoor of a group of insurgents

The "Mounties"

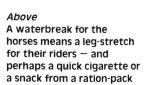

Above
A waterbreak for the horses means a leg-stretch for their riders — and perhaps a quick cigarette or a snack from a ration-pack

Above Right
Although they usually fought on foot, mounties were taught to charge into action if necessary

Centre Right
A figure from another age — but in the vastnesses of the border-war bushveld he made good sense

Centre Left
A mountie doctors his horse's hoof. Horses serving in virtually stoneless Ovamboland were usually not shod

Right
Mounties question a local inhabitant while on a sweep after an insurgent group

The Scramblers

Above
Motorcyclists discard their bikes and take cover. Trained infantrymen, they usually fought on foot

Centre
Motorcyclists advance at speed over rough terrain. As a result of the beating it took, a bushveld bike usually had a fairly short life-span

Below
Motorcyclists speed down a bushveld track. In thick bush insurgents found it difficult to pinpoint the noise of their heavily muffled engines

Left
A motorcyclist waits for orders. His controls are protected by brackets, his R4 rifle clamped in a cradle over the handlebars

One reason why the SADF and SWATF could afford to control vast areas with small groups of men was that in the event of a contact the troops involved could always call for quick reinforcement by means of "reaction force" teams who were on constant stand-by for any such call.

The reaction force units were always crack troops, usually paratroops from one of the SADF's three parachute battalions. They would be helicoptered to the scene of the contact and either join in the fighting or take over the fresh spoor if there was a follow-up to be carried out.

Since the border war provided new opportunities for jumping into action, the "parabats" made a speciality of reaction-force operations, and in various external operations were used in a similar role to be dropped off in the bush to form "stopper groups" behind enemy bases or concentrations which were under attack by the ground forces.

THE REACTION FORCE

Top
Two helicopters scissor out over the endless bushveld of Ovamboland during the dry season, when conditions were ideal for follow-up operations

Centre Left
The hours of waiting over, members of a reaction force group urge their mates into the Puma which will fly them to the fighting

Centre Right
Locked into their thoughts as they tense themselves for action, these soldiers are barely aware of the slipstream battering their faces

Right
Deafened by the whine of the Puma's jet engine, reaction force paratroopers pile in to be flown to the scene of the contact outside Ongiva in Southern Angola

Top
Flying, Ovamboland-style: doors wide open, rifles ready, the ground so near it felt as if you could reach out and touch it

Centre
Reaction-force experts, paratroopers did not jump into action very often during the border war, but they kept their skills polished

Left
Much of Ovamboland was flat, featureless terrain. Pilots soon learnt to cope with navigational problems which were often exacerbated by extremely stressful "contact" situations

Centre Left
Touch-down! Members of the reaction force barrel out through the door and head for cover

101 Battalion

Among the border units 101 Battalion with its rhino-head badge occupied something of a special place as regards both its armament and its duties.

Started in 1974 as a quasi-military auxiliary unit of 40 men to protect key points, it was expanded to 200 men when the war intensified after Operation Savannah and was embodied as 53 Battalion.

The experiment worked and it began to expand, changing its name to 35 Battalion and, on the birth of the SWATF in 1980, to 101 Battalion. Never short of recruits, by the mid-1980s it numbered more than 2 000 men, including about 200 South African and South West African whites.

It could field two "modular" (self-contained) companies of about 250 men each, both deployed in the Oshikango area; an intelligence company — permanently attached to Sector 10 Headquarters — which supplied guides, interpreters and trackers; a civic action company; and four 150-man "Romeo Mike" companies.

The Romeo Mike teams were the primary fighting arm, accounting for an average 40 percent of the battalion's kills. Each team consisted of 30 to 40 men with two officers, mounted in four Casspir light armoured personnel carriers — 101 Battalion was the only army unit to be issued with this highly effective police vehicle. If a Kwêvoël armoured logistics vehicle was attached, the team could operate for 14 days without requiring further supplies or fuel.

Above
A captured insurgent (left) sits on a Casspir's crew compartment with one of his captors. Many insurgents were "turned" and ended up serving in the unit

Above Right
A 101 Battalion patrol about to go out. Their boots are still shiny, but they won't stay that way for long

Centre
Two identified insurgents are brought in after capture by 101 Battalion, blindfolded according to standard practice

Right
Major Willie Snyders of 101 Battalion (left) and some of his men take a rest while on an operation. Clothing was informal in the stifling heat

The Bushmen

When the security forces began casting around in 1977 for a new weapon against the insurgents, they turned to the border area's oldest and most veld-wise inhabitants: the Bushmen.

The senior Bushman unit was 201 Battalion, based at a camp called Omega in the remote and almost unpopulated bushveld of Western Caprivi.

The recruits varied considerably in both culture and appearance. Some were relatively tall, dark men from the Angolan side of the border, others were small yellow men from Western Caprivi itself. Their languages were as different as Swedish and French, and, with the exception of some of the Angolans, their knowledge of 20th-Century life was minimal.

Yet they responded easily and well to modern training. They became machine-gunners, drivers, signallers, medics and mortarmen — but above all they were peerless trackers, trained so that they knew exactly what to look for, and what to expect, when on the spoor of insurgents.

When they had qualified to wear the battalion's strange glengarry-like cap with its badge depicting the white-breasted crow, they were deployed in Ovamboland for varying periods.

Here they put their phenomenal tracking ability to work, finding and following well-nigh invisible spoor as if by magic and at top speed, in spite of the Plan fighters' expertise at counter-tracking. They were tireless, able to exist on the smell of an oil-rag, could conceal themselves in the minimum of cover and seemed to have a built-in sense of direction, so that they never got lost, even in unfamiliar terrain.

They also had an uncanny ability to smell out landmines; and according to one 201 Battalion officer they seemed to have an instinctive understanding of spatial relationships and exterior ballistics, so that they were devastating performers with the 40mm grenade-launchers, although they could never explain exactly why this was.

Many anthropologists were horrified by the Bushmen's crash course on 20th-Century life, but the Bushmen themselves never had any doubts. They were being asked to do a job which was both well-paid and fairly easy by their standards, and 201 Battalion was a haven from persecution.

Their memories of past ill-treatment remained so strong, this writer was told by one officer of another battalion, that on patrols the Bushmen trackers were happy to move in front — as long as they were within sight of a white officer or NCO, because they believed that the blacks regarded them as expendable and would desert them if there was a contact.

Above Left
An officer of 201 (Bushman) Battalion demonstrates the use of the 40mm grenade-launcher. He wears the battalion's glengarry and crow badge. The Bushman on the left is an Angolan, the one on the right a Caprivian

Above Right
Insurgents were not the only danger on operations. Here a soldier scoops up water while a white comrade watches out for crocodiles

Centre
Time out for breakfast during an operation in Ovamboland during the rainy season

Left
A Bushman section heads down the Okavango River during a patrol

THE POLICE

Policemen of various kinds were intimately involved in counter-insurgency operations throughout the border war, although their roles differed considerably and sometimes changed in mid-course to adapt to new circumstances.

When the border war started in 1966, it was handled by the South African Police's small counter-insurgency unit. When the SADF assumed overall responsibility for border protection in 1974, the SAP returned to normal crime-prevention duties, although its counter-insurgency unit stayed in place and continued to operate independently of the military, even after it handed over to the newly-formed South West Africa Police in 1980.

The SWA Police's counter-insurgency wing consisted of three elements: a guard force made up of special constables, an elite COIN unit known as "Koevoet" (and later as "Operation K", although the earlier name stuck), and the SWA Police Task Force, which was responsible for preventing insurgent infiltration across the border from Botswana below the "Red Line" (the lower boundary of the operational area) and also for dealing with urban terrorism.

The South African Railways Police also maintained its own highly secretive special counter-insurgency section till the SARP was absorbed into the SAP in the mid-1980s.

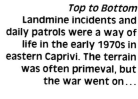

Top to Bottom
Landmine incidents and daily patrols were a way of life in the early 1970s in eastern Caprivi. The terrain was often primeval, but the war went on...

Opposite
Special constables of the guard force undergoing their eight-week training course near Ondangwa. Trained to guard VIPs and key points, many constables were allowed to go on to the full police training course and join the regular SWA Police, while others volunteered to join Koevoet

Inset Top
Policemen soon discovered that survival often meant following a meticulous routine, like periodically checking the base perimeter

Inset Below
A policeman casts an unhappy eye over a landmine crater during the early days in Ovamboland, long before the era of the mine-protected vehicle

Koevoet

Koevoet was founded in June of 1979 with a strength of 10 security policemen, both white and black, and 64 special constables, the aim being a unit which could react without delay to information received (unlike the army, the police never indulged in random patrols) and also interpret insurgent spoor with all possible speed during normal operations.

In early 1980 it acquired its own small fire force as well, and by the end of the year had killed 511 insurgents for a loss of 12. This trend continued to the end of the war, with Koevoet consistently scoring the highest "kills" of any security force unit.

It also acquired a fearsome reputation, its opponents pointing to the various Koevoet members who had been tried for murder and other crimes.

Its standard reply was that it depended to a large extent on information supplied by the local inhabitants, who would surely not have been so forthcoming if it was consistently brutal towards them.

In its final form Koevoet consisted of roughly platoon-sized fighting teams travelling in heavily gunned armoured vehicles, each able to operate on its own for up to a week at a time. Ops K units were stationed in Kaokoland, Ovamboland and Kavango, but teams were not area-bound and went where need took them.

Ops K was manned by a totally multi-racial mixture of regular policemen, police reservists mobilised for short duty tours, volunteer special constables and "turned" insurgents.

Above
Koevoet members loading up belts of machine-gun ammunition before an operation

Top Right
A Koevoet team in its Casspirs preparing to move out on an operation

Centre
An operation in the dry season, when the odds favoured the pursuers

Right
Relentless Koevoet trackers follow up on an ever-freshening insurgent spoor, the Casspirs close behind

Above
Koevoet Casspirs mounted as much heavy firepower as they could find place for, ranging from captured heavy machine-guns to (in one celebrated case) a 20mm cannon from a long-defunct Vampire jet fighter

Above Left
Contact! Koevoet Casspirs swing off the road during a dry-season operation

Centre
A team returns after a contact, the body of a Plan group commander lashed to a mudguard according to invariable Koevoet custom

Left
Koevoet members and a Swaspes tracker question a villager during a follow-up

Following Page
A Russian-supplied GAZ lorry burns in its protective position during one of the external operations, while nearby its more fortunate fellow-vehicles are being readied for an unscheduled trip southwards as booty — some to be evaluated, others to be pressed into service. Captured lorries ended up doing some odd jobs: one Russian vehicle was turned into the personal runabout of the commanding officer at Eenhana base. Soviet trucks like the GAZ-66 fared badly in difficult African terrain; they soon came apart

THE EXTERNALS

The so-called "external operations" were by far the most controversial — and in some ways the most misunderstood — aspect of the border war, not only because they involved crossing an international border but also because the Angolans habitually exaggerated their extent and often camouflaged Unita actions by blaming them on the South Africans, even when this was so unlikely that only a madman would have planned them.

An external operation was almost always a deliberate and often elaborately planned attack, carried out over the border and aimed at pre-empting or interdicting the insurgents' known or suspected action. But each external operation varied according to circumstances. A follow-up could become a hot pursuit, then escalate into an external scheduled to last several days, which would then expand to several weeks.

On the other hand, the security forces might spend months gathering intelligence and planning a sudden swoop on a specific target in an operation involving thousands of men backed by armoured cars, infantry fighting vehicles, ground-attack aircraft and, at times, field artillery.

With one possible exception the externals were not "invasions", the word favoured by Angolan propagandists, since this implies the permanent or semi-permanent occupation of someone else's territory; the possible exception was the period after Operation Protea in 1981, when the South Africans maintained a full-time presence in the Xangongo-Ongiva area till January of 1984.

Even here, however, the occupation was strictly an outgrowth of the SWA/Namibian insurgency and only took place because the Angolans allowed their territory to be used as a launching-pad for infiltrations.

There is also a belief (sedulously fostered by the Angolans) that hundreds of external operations took place. Of the border war's estimated 200-odd formal operations, however, probably less than a dozen — starting with Operation Reindeer in 1978 — were real externals.

The last three — Operations Modular, Hooper and Packer — differed from the rest; although directly rooted in the border war, they saw no fighting against Swapo personnel except by accident.

Most externals were much smaller than is generally realised. It appears no more than about 3 000 men were ever involved in any external, and often much less (the attack on Cassinga, the most daring of all, featured less than 300 men, and Operation Super less than 200).

Military observers agree, in fact, that most externals could have wreaked greater damage if the forces involved had been larger.

The externals all succeeded to a greater or lesser degree, and in fact accounted for most of the casualties the insurgents suffered. The reason was that the South Africans' planning and training was generally good, and — at least till the late 1980s — they enjoyed local air superiority.

Then, too, till late in the war the Angolan/Cuban forces tended to avoid contact and the South Africans were under orders to avoid clashing with them if at all possible. It is interesting to note that the Cubans, in spite of Havana's boasts, never did much either to fight Unita or ward off South African incursions; even the sudden early-1988 build-up took place in the south-west, far from the battle-zones.

All this enabled the South Africans to take calculated risks which, by academic calculations, verged on the foolhardy. The old formulae did not begin to lose their validity till the Angolans and Cubans started deploying mobile tank forces and fighter aircraft from 1984 onwards (although, bad battle-handling made it a cheap lesson).

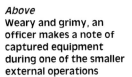

Above
Weary and grimy, an officer makes a note of captured equipment during one of the smaller external operations

Right
Far inside Angola, the bodies of South African troops killed in action are placed in body bags for evacuation to Oshakati

Inset Opposite Left
His "black-is-beautiful" camouflage cream partly sweated off, this officer talks to some of his men

Inset Opposite Right
An intelligence corporal and interpreter question an insurgent captured near Xangongo

1981 Operations Carnation and Protea

While a helicopter screams past in the background, a special forces team prepares to demolish a Soviet-built PT-76 amphibious tank with PE4 *plastique* explosives. The tank became waterlogged and sank alongside one of the banks of the Cunene River near Xangongo during Operation Protea

Above
Captured Russian-origin lorries and an artillery piece at the start of their journey southwards to the border

Inset Right
The bridge at Xangongo, demolished during Operation Protea. The original "White Bridge" at Xangongo was blown up by Unita in 1976

Inset Left
SWATF troops burn sacks of grain they found cached in a Plan camp they had overrun near Xangongo

Right
While boxes of ammunition wait to be loaded, 32 Battalion soldiers board a helicopter to be moved forward to the scene of a new contact

Stiff and sore after a hard day followed by an uncomfortable night, 32 Battalion soldiers await the order to emplane in the early morning

Inset Left
Soldiers uncover and empty a large arms and ammunition cache after a contact — gingerly, because the insurgents often stored explosives incorrectly

Inset Right
Tired, very dirty 32 Battalion officers after searching an Angolan kraal

1981 Operation Daisy

Top
At an open-air "operations room" well inside Angola, Commandant Roland de Vries briefs his officers

Above
At a Plan camp that has been overrun, troops clear a bunker in classic fashion by tossing in some smoke and waiting to see if anyone comes out

Top Right
A Ratel-90 tank-destroyer's supply of 90mm ammunition is replenished

Right
Headlights on in the dusty murk, a Ratel bumps its way over an execrable bushveld track as De Vries's force moves deeper into Angola

Above
Supply Column heads
for the Angola border
with back-up material

Left
The routine was inviolable;
the same precaution each
evening; troops dig in for
the night in case of
a mortar attack

Below
Already deep inside
Angola, the Ratels strike
ever further northwards

Inset
Fully fuelled and
"bombed up", Ratels stand
ready for their crews to
embus when the order to
move northwards into
Angola is given

1982 Operation Vasbyt 5

THE EXTERNALS

One of the many small external operations that never hit the headlines was Vasbyt 5 in 1981, which was designed to disrupt Plan operations in Kaokoland and Western Ovamboland by destroying a base about 4km from the Angolan village of Cuamato. In due course a small South African force pounced on Cuamato and occupied it without firing a shot when its Fapla garrison of several hundred men fled — all but one, who was promptly made prisoner. The invaders dug in and that night hit the Swapo camp. The insurgents fought fiercely; the South Africans withdrew, having lost two dead, and went in again next morning. This time there was no withdrawal: they fought their way through two lines of trenches, killing several score insurgents and scattering the rest, their only casualty being one man who was shot in the arm while searching one of the many underground bunkers. While all this was happening, an Angolan armoured brigade lay just 40km away and did not attempt to interfere. That was how it was in those days; but it was not to be like that for much longer.

Above
A South African on Cuamato's water tower after the bloodless occupation of the town

Top Centre
The Plan base after its capture. It is carefully camouflaged — but the deep, well-constructed trenches are a dead give-away

Centre
Soldiers disembark from their helicopter and immediately dash for cover, because on the way down they saw two insurgents with rocket-launchers near the landing zone. Asked later why they did not fire, they replied that it would have been futile because other helicopters and more soldiers would have arrived to take its place

Right
Men of the assault force pour fire into an outlying position of the Plan camp

Above
A machine-gunner stares down at an insurgent, lying in the muddy trench in which he met his death

Left Top to Bottom
Open ground is bad news when an enemy is waiting, and these troops do not tarry

Smoke bubbles out of a bunker as soldiers stand by to capture any occupant — or kill him if he resists

Soldiers clear part of the trench system — a dirty, hazardous, nerve-racking task

Thoroughly ''blacked up'' South African soldiers after capturing Cuamato

Left
A soldier gets ready to throw a smoke-grenade into a bunker, just in case anyone is hiding inside

1982 Operation Super

Above
A sweaty, stubble-chinned Captain unbuckles after landing

Top Right
A 32 Battalion soldier rolls forward one of the drums of fuel which were dropped off at the temporary helicopter base from which the "choppers" went out to find the Plan camp

Top Left
The way to the Marienfluss valley lay over these rugged mountains — "all straight up and down", as one troopie remarked

Centre
32 Battalion troops disembark to sweep the area after the fighting had ended

Inset
A satisfied Brigadier Rudolph "Witkop" Badenhorst, OC 1 Military Area, with some of the stores and munitions captured after the small but fierce fight which ended Super

Right
Dust billows up from the bleak, stunningly hot temporary base as Pumas prepare to take off

1983/4
Operation
Askari

Above
Its rotor-blades scattering the billows of marker-smoke, a Puma comes down with a load of 32 Battalion soldiers being trooped to a new location in the fighting

Centre Above Left
Captain Bill Good of the SAAF at Cuvelai airfield in January of 1984 after flying in to see if it could be used by Dakotas. He found it suitable — in theory. In practice its surface had been so chewed up by heavy vehicles that take-offs and landings would be too hazardous. So Dakotas never used Cuvelai and the burden fell on the Pumas

Centre Above Right
An Impala fighter takes off from Air Force Base Ondangwa in late December of 1983, bound for Angola to carry out a ground strike

Centre Below Left
A Puma at Mupa. Next to the white building at left are several captured T-55 tanks

Centre Below Right
Bowsers and lorries captured from Fapla parked in Cuvelai town. Most of the vehicles taken were in serviceable condition

Left
A permanent Unita camp somewhere inside what some South Africans jocularly called "Savimbiland" in the Cuando-Cubango province

1987/8
Operations Modular, Hooper and Packer

A G-5 gun-howitzer
fires a 155mm shell at
Cuito Cuanavale late in the
Angolan fighting. The South
Africans used their artillery
to neutralise the base
without laying
a hand on it

THE EXTERNALS

Above
A ragged-edged exit hole just below the commander's cupola of a T-55 knocked out by one APDS (armour-piercing discarding sabot) round from an Olifant tank's 105mm gun during the attack on 59 (Fapla) Brigade on February 14 of 1988

Top Right
A Unita soldier examines the battered nose of the Mi-17. One of the helicopter's rocket-pods can be seen above him

Top Left
3 and 6 Military Regions, where all of the 1987-1988 fighting took place

Centre
Assisted by Unita troops, South Africans recharge a 127mm multiple rocket-launcher during the early Lomba River fighting in 1987

Right
A Russian-origin GAZ-66 lorry burns after being shot up during the Lomba River fighting

Opposite
The Angolans had been claiming for years that the South Africans were using tanks, but it was not till the Lomba River fighting that the SADF actually sent its heavy armour into battle

Above
Major Hannes Nortmann,
SA Armoured Corps, with
wounded neck and hand
immediately after he
recovered three stranded
Ratel-90s, for which he was
later decorated with
the Honoris Crux

Top
Unita troops parade at
Jamba for the benefit of
journalists during a lull in the
Lomba River fighting.
Savimbi's propagandists
have thoughtfully provided
a trilingual slogan on the
huge poster behind them

Centre
Olifants moving through
the dense bush east of Cuito
Cuanavale. Tank-battles
often took place at virtually
point-blank range due to
the poor visibility

Right
Unita troops being briefed
before going into battle.
Savimbi's casualties remain
unknown, but are thought
to number thousands

Top
The mangled remains
of a Ratel attached to 32
Battalion during Operation
Modular. It had been hit by
an Angolan T-55 tank and
was later demolished by
explosives to prevent it
being used by Luanda
for propaganda

Centre
An Olifant grinds along a
track near the Lomba River,
followed by an armoured
bowser and supply lorries.
The SADF encountered
extreme logistic problems;
luckily for them, the
Angolans' problems
were even worse

Left
A Ratel-90 attached to
32 Battalion moves back
over a temporary girder
bridge thrown across
the Cuito River

ONGIVA DEATH OF A TOWN

People speak easily about "the devastation of war", but they do not understand what it means till they have seen it at first hand. After that they tend to speak less about it, because it will haunt their dreams for the rest of their lives.

Once upon a time there was a medium-sized Angolan town called Pereira D'Eca.

D'Eca. It was a neat, rather pretty place, moderately prosperous from its status as a regional capital and the fact that it was a stopping-off point for the unending stream of motorists and truckers travelling to and from the SWA/Namibian border-post at Oshikango.

Then came the civil war, and Pereira D'Eca began to crumble as it changed hands again and again. The MPLA seized it in 1975, were expelled by the South Africans shortly after and then took it back when the SADF withdrew at the end of Operation Savannah. Jonas Savimbi's Unita held it a couple of times for varying periods. In 1981, during Operation Protea, the South Africans took it again after two days of heavy fighting, and stayed there till May of 1985.

By then not much remained of Ongiva. For practical purposes it was a ghost town. A little before the 1985 handover war correspondent Al J Venter visited it while accompanying a hot-pursuit raiding party which passed through the town. He came back to report:

We slept well clear of this city of forgotten ghosts and mangled memories, going in during the daylight hours on recce and patrol, and leaving again well before the town's broad-wing bats emerged from the eaves of blown-up buildings...

Returning to Ongiva after several breaks covering almost two decades was like entering a time-warp. All the buildings — and a few newer ones — remained, some of them barely recognisable in their scarred and blistered shells. Streets and open patches were littered with rotting refuse. In two places, large unexploded shells — the detritus of previous battles — poked their way through the concrete ... Anything that hadn't been nailed or bolted down in the town we found lying in the streets. What hadn't been broken had been scrunched into the ground...

The International Committee of the Red Cross maintains a four-man team there: brave people working in a no man's land. Their role is largely medical and relief, together with one rather beautiful young lady on an identity-search role for people missing during recent years' fighting. Hers is a futile task in a land where a man's life isn't worth the few coins he may be carrying in his pocket...

There wasn't a young man among perhaps a couple of hundred people living within a 10km radius of the town. The women who remained — like the children — were haggard and hollow-eyed. They gave off an aura of having seen it all.

The town was surrounded by about 30km of zig-zag interleading trenches ... There wasn't a building we entered which didn't have huge supplies of communist propaganda lying about ... Posters of Lenin and Marx had been torn down from the walls but their severe presence remained, peeking out here and there. In one sense, what we found in Ongiva was almost apocalyptic.

It was a quality which stunned initially, till you got used to the filth and the stench, and then you just had to accept all of it philosophically. *C'est la guerre. C'est la Afrique.*

Above
Women sweep stacks of forgotten files and discarded propaganda sheets out of a former MPLA headquarters building

Centre
Once this was a cool, comfortable little house. Now it is a roofless shell, filled with rubbish

Right
G-2 5,5-inch guns parked at Ongiva's airfield during the town's long occupation by the South Africans

Opposite Top
The church at Ongiva — more or less intact but for some mortar-bomb damage to the roof. It resisted the ravages of war better than most of the other buildings

Opposite Below
A stencilled wall-painting of the MPLA's Agostinho Neto frowns over a deserted street and looted buildings

THE RECCES

Many elite forces served in the border war, but the most elite combat soldiers of them all were undoubtedly the men of 1 Reconnaissance Commando, which was founded in 1972 and later expanded into several Reconnaissance Regiments (a misnomer, since — like all similar units — Recce outfits have always been large on expertise but small on numbers).

They were also the least known. Official statements seldom identified them as Recces, and on the rare occasions when a Recce was photographed his face was blacked out; about the only exception was the unfortunate Wynand du Toit, who was captured in Cabinda in 1985.

A multi-racial force, the Recces were selected from a variety of volunteers drawn from all the services of the SADF. Some were Permanent Force members, others were national servicemen who had signed up for extra service, still others were Citizen Force men. Several were former Angolans. All had to pass stringent physical tests and a psychological selection process designed to weed out "cowboys" and potential Rambos.

The Recces pulled off some amazing feats, many of which will be secret for some time to come. Although superbly trained as fighting men and sometimes used for that purpose, their actual role was infiltration, observation, land and amphibious sabotage and similar low-profile tasks.

Among other things, they blew up bridges and harbour installations, "took out" Plan bases and collected information under the enemy's very nose; on various occasions they infiltrated far behind the lines to act, for days or weeks, as forward artillery observers; it is said that Recce teams were responsible for the accurate shelling which neutralised Cuito Cuanavale at an early stage of the 1987 fighting in Angola.

Above
"Recces" abseiling down from a hovering helicopter, a standard special-forces technique

Above Right
Reconnaissance Regiment "operators" are taught to use whatever material comes to hand in order to survive

Right
Two heavily camouflaged commandos in an equally heavily camouflaged kayak. One of the Reconnaissance Regiments specialises in amphibious operations

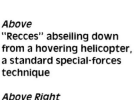

32 BATTALION "THE TERRIFYING ONES"

Although the occasional expatriate foreigner served in the border forces from time to time, the only non-national unit or "foreign legion" was 32 Battalion, commonly known simply as "32" by other soldiers but also known as the "Buffalo battalion" because their unit insignia was a buffalo's head and their base in Kavango was called "Buffalo" ... and "Os Terrivis" (the Terrifying Ones).

The unit — which in fact was at least twice the size of a normal battalion — was recruited from Chipenda-faction FNLA soldiers evacuated from Angola at the end of Operation Savannah in 1976.

From the SADF's point of view it was a happy choice. Most of the recruits were strongly motivated, had previous operational experience which needed only to be polished by SADF-standard training and possessed personal knowledge of southern Angola. In addition they spoke Portuguese, the Angolan official language.

The battalion was not used south of the border; from beginning to end it operated almost exclusively inside Angola, undertaking a variety of tasks according to the requirements of the moment.

Sometimes they acted as conventional infantry, as in Operation Super. At other times they attacked Swapo bases, mounted deep-penetration operations to gather intelligence or locate targets, carried out "area operations" on the outskirts of ground battle zones. One way or another, they saw action almost all the year round.

Now and then they would go into battle in armoured vehicles, but when they moved operationally it was usually by helicopter or on their own feet. Their feats of endurance were legendary. For the 32 Battalion men it was nothing to slog for days on end through ankle-deep mud, wearing normal patrol equipment and also civilian-style hikers' backpacks made especially for them, their only contact with the outside an occasional helicopter bringing fresh supplies.

Like Koevoet, they were the target of an intermittent campaign of accusations about their alleged brutality. Their reply to such accusations was similar to Koevoet's: operating in isolation far into enemy territory and often beyond reach of immediate support, they could not afford to antagonise the locals, otherwise the latter would soon betray them.

In early 1989 — by which time many of the troops were the sons of the founder-members — 32 Battalion was pulled out of SWA/Namibia and relocated in a disused mining village at Pomfret in the northern Cape province. Where it would be operating in the future the SADF would not say. That it would be operating somewhere was not in doubt.

Above
Lieutenant Fred Turner at the Cuvelai headquarters of the Joint Monitoring Commission in 1984 after being wounded in a clash with a Plan group. He is wearing the unit's distinctive camouflage beret and buffalo-head badge

Centre Right
Two 32 Battalion soldiers on an anti-Swapo sweep in the Angolan "shallow area" during the early 1980s

Centre Left
Two 32 Battalion soldiers with the stacks of weapons and ammunition captured during Operation Super

Left
32 Battalion soldiers inside Angola. They are wearing "dayglo" panels on their hats so that SAAF aircraft will know they are "friendlies"

Inset
The roots of 32 Battalion: The stateless expatriates of the Chipenda-faction FNLA contingent who came from Angola in 1976

THE CITIZEN AND COMMANDO FORCES

The Citizen and Commando Forces became involved at an early stage, when the first units were called up in January of 1976 for Operation Savannah, and served on till the very end.

When the insurgency escalated after Savannah, they were the SADF's only source of plentiful trained military manpower, and they were used to the full, often in a series of three-month call-ups.

They served in an almost infinite variety of ways — particularly the Citizen Force, which does not consist only of fighting men but also deploys a myriad of support-services personnel, from engineers and mechanics to doctors and signallers and clerks.

At first CCF units manned border battalion areas. Later many served in the "skeleton battalions" permanent organisations whose strength was expanded or contracted according to requirements.

Others served at headquarters, helping to man operations rooms, intelligence offices, personnel sections and many other essential base operations.

They often puzzled the full-timers. Usually very regimentally orientated, they delighted in strange customs and sporting a variety of distinctive headgear and badges. Junior officers would perform senior tasks, often because they had the experience but had been prevented by call-ups from going on courses, a chronic problem.

Frequently they used their civilian skills in un-orthodox fashion to get things done, and were not above ditching the rule-book, as when one company commander whose supplies were cut during Operation Savannah sent a raiding party down to Ruacana and hijacked a lorry-load of rations.

Many ended up as skilled as the regulars, and some were so from the beginning — most paratroops at Cassinga were Citizen Force, and so was one of the SAAF's ace ground-attack fighter pilots.

Their numbers dwindled as the SWATF expanded in the mid-1980s, but CF soldiers performed valuable service during the 1987-1988 fighting in Angola, and at the very end, in late 1988, the Citizen Force was back in strength during the tense stand-off that preceded Resolution 435's implementation.

Above
The Citizen Force held the line during the 1976 withdrawal. At the Cunene bridge Commandant Willie Kotze of the Permanent Force chats to Commandant J C Bosch of the South African Irish

Centre Right
Piper Mike Wheatley of the Cape Town Highlanders hands out a bit of culture-shock during Operation Savannah

Centre Left
Citizen-soldiers like Lieutenant Eric Wright of the Cape Flats Commando, trained in staff procedures, did yeoman service in running operations rooms for the chronically under-manned full-time units

Right
The regimental sergeant-major marches off parade near Ruacana in March of 1976

Opposite Top
Olifant tanks of the Regiment President Steyn rumble over the Okavango into Angola during Operation Hooper

Opposite Bottom
A Commando Force sergeant watches the land border with Zambia at Wenela.

ZULUS IN ACTION

One of the best-kept secrets of the border war was the fact that the participants included the most famous South African tribal warriors of antiquity: the Zulus. In fact Zulus had been involved in the war from its inception, as individual members of the police contingents, but in the 1980s for the first time the descendants of Chaka's impis saw action as fighting soldiers. Needless to say, they acquitted themselves well of their task, for the Zulus have never relinquished or forgotten their military traditions; it is the soldier's spirit that counts, whether he is equipped with machine-gun and mortar or the stabbing-assegai and oxhide shield.

Above Right
Zulu troops settle into a Puma for the short flight that will take them to their area of operations near Ongiva

Above Left
The Zulus fan out through the Angolan bush in classic counter-insurgency style

Centre Right
Zulus pass the water tower at Ongiva, which still bears a sign advertising the once-ubiquitous Cuca beer

Centre Left
Near a sign bearing long-vanished names from the colonial era, patrol leaders confer while their men hold an all-round defence position

Right
A light machine-gunner and a rifleman, fingers on triggers, during a halt while reconnoitring a deserted but potentially dangerous street in Ongiva

MINES ARE THE MESSE OF DEATH

Found to have an armed anti-lifting device, the mine is detonated by the sweeping team

The landmine occupies an honoured place in any insurgent's inventory. It is economical of effort, since it can be laid without making contact with the security forces, and the disproportionate amount of havoc it wreaks, damages the morale of both the local population and the government soldiery, and casts doubts on the latter's ability to dominate the area.

In a territory like northern SWA/Namibia, where most of the roads are untarred, landmines were a prime terrorist weapon, and Plan made heavy use of them almost from the start. Most of the mines Plan laid were of Russian origin but some were British-made Mark 7s, obtained, no doubt, from Commonwealth countries like Zambia or Tanzania.

One of the most common anti-vehicle mines was the olive-green TM-57, and another which was frequently seen was what the troops called the "cheesemine", the pale brown TMA-3 with its three protruding detonators. The insurgents also deployed a variety of anti-personnel mines, from the PP-MI-SR jumping mine, which did not detonate till it was in the air, to the old pineapple-style POM-Z, detonated by a trip-wire, which insurgents who had "bombshelled" often set up to incapacitate or delay pursuers.

In the beginning the landmine was the weapon soldiers and policemen feared the most, just like the Portuguese before them; it would not be an exaggeration to say that the landmine played a distinct role in creating conditions for the 1974 coup.

Unlike the Portuguese, however, the South Africans had the money and technical resources to fight the landmine — and win. The first mine-protected vehicles started appearing in the early 1970s; the post-Savannah escalation caused some delay in re-equipping, but by 1978 the Unimog lorries packed with sandbags and conveyor-belting had been replaced by the ungainly but effective Buffel.

In the years that followed, various other vehicles appeared, so that in the end the SADF and SWATF were probably the most mine-proofed — and mine-conscious — armies in the world. Plan techniques were analysed, troops taught "mine awareness" and frequently-used roads were swept regularly by engineers. As a result, related deaths and serious wounds declined steeply, and the landmine ceased to be a military factor.

But the civilians suffered grievously. Ovambos in particular use many private vehicles, and the landmines exacted a ghastly toll. Of the 1 087 civilians who died between 1981 and 1988 (the 1966-1980 statistics are not available) the majority were killed by mines Plan had laid.

The official Swapo line was that the "boere" mined roads near civilian population concentrations in order to blame the insurgents; the large numbers of mines found in Plan caches gave the lie to such assertions.

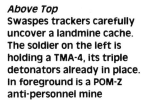

Above Top
Swaspes trackers carefully uncover a landmine cache. The soldier on the left is holding a TMA-4, its triple detonators already in place. In foreground is a POM-Z anti-personnel mine

Above Bottom
An SADF Kwêvoël, one of the world's only armoured and mine-protected civilian logistics vehicles

Top Right
With a muted roar a demolition charge blows up in a booby-trapped vehicle in a spectacular bloom of flame and smoke.

Centre Left
Mine-lifting teams of the South African Engineer Corps went everywhere. This group accompanied security forces on Operation Daisy

Centre Right
A landmine laid by Plan members who penetrated the Tsumeb white farming area destroyed this car, killing the owner

Right
A mine-sweeping team squats behind its front man as he carefully brushes away the sand around a mine outside Eenhana camp

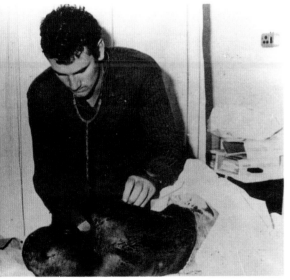

Above
By the end of the war a whole family of light and heavy mine-protected vehicles were in service, like this Ribbok heavy transporter

Below
A Buffel after being recovered, the wheel and housing blown off and the windscreen shattered by the blast. Not one of the 11 occupants was seriously injured

Top Left
A Koevoet Casspir hunches over a mine-crater after losing a wheel to a TMA-3 "cheese mine"

Centre Left
A military doctor examines an Ovambo boy who was badly wounded when a Plan landmine blew up the vehicle in which he was travelling

Centre Right
A Hippo troop carrier leads a convoy through an Ovambo village in the late 1970s. By this time the Buffel was being developed

Left
A Sapper detonates a landmine *in situ* after it had been discovered along *Oom Willie se pad*

THE BACKBONE BOYS

In the classic military lexicon there are the "teeth arms" — the artillery, infantry and armour — and the "support arms", consisting of all the rest. It was a distinction which tended to become blurred in the border war.

Virtually everyone who served north of the "Red Line" was liable to come under fire at some stage, even if only from an inaccurate stand-off mortar bombardment; and during operations, particularly the incursions deep into Angola, the support arms were in the thick of it.

"Tiffies" of the Technical Service Corps performed prodigies in the thick of battle, medical orderlies risked their lives to save others, signallers served their sets within the sound of the guns, the "socks and jam merchants" of the Ordnance Service Corps braved everything from bullets and mines to mud and mosquitoes as they provided food and ammunition and spare tyres and all the other sinews of war.

Then there were the engineers. Wherever the teeth arms went, the sappers went as well, building bridges (sometimes under fire), blowing up obstacles, laying mines and lifting them. In between they also carried out a multitude of less lethal but equally important tasks like providing large quantities of drinkable water.

The teeth arms got most of the medals and most of the publicity. But each fighting soldier, no matter how loud his braggadocio, knew in his heart of hearts that he would not have accomplished anything — might not even have survived, in fact — without the efforts of the boys who made up the backbone of any operation.

1. A signals Buffel in the depths of Angola during Operation Daisy

2. A storeman cleans an R4 rifle at a permanent border base

3. One of the small but important bushveld luxuries: long-life milk with a supply of water in plastic bags

4. Bush repairs to the Puma squadron in the Operational Area

5. Maintenance unit members set up at a helicopter administrative area deep inside Angola

6. A cook about to bake bread — a welcome change from ration "dog-biscuits"

7. Sappers prepare a captured T-34 tank for demolition

8. Sappers purify bilharzia-laden water so that it can be safely drunk

9. Mechanised infantrymen await their turn at a fuel bowser in the field

10. Cooks at a south Angola base during Operation Savannah

11. Watched by a very dirty soldier, a tiffie fills up a Ratel's water tank

12. TSC welders repair some of the ravages of bundu-bashing

13. Sophisticated repairs at a field base in the Operational Area

14. Ammunition storage bunkers at M'pacha in Caprivi

15. At a temporary base in the bush, tiffies lower a turret into an Eland-90

16. TSC tiffies exchange a Ratel's defective engine during Operation Modular

17. A Ratel prepares to tow away an immobilised water bowser during Operation Daisy

18. SAAF mechanics start up a Dakota with a rope around the propeller-boss

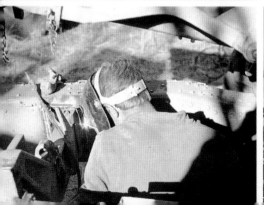

THE WAR IN THE AIR

The South African Air Force was involved in the border war from its very beginning. Years before the rest of the South African Defence Force took over responsibility for border security in 1974, SAAF helicopters were assisting the police in combating the early Plan infiltrations, and in fact one of the first Honoris Crux decorations was awarded to a helicopter pilot who was involved in a skirmish in the early 1970s.

It was a scenario which was to be repeated time and again in the two decades, because the workhorses of the border war were the ageing, unarmoured transport helicopters which SAAF pilots pressed into all sorts of roles, some of them undreamt-of by the men who designed them.

Helicopters were used for everything from ferrying troops to and from battles, speeding the wounded back to base hospitals, carrying supplies, lifting out captured equipment and acting as gunships when necessary; on one occasion, during Operation Super, a helicopter pilot named Captain Neall Ellis found himself commanding a ground battle in between dodging insurgent bullets and missiles.

Ellis's good friend and fellow Alouette pilot, Captain Arthur Walker, became the most highly decorated serviceman of the war when he was decorated with the Honoris Crux (Gold) and bar for his exploits.

Virtually every type of SAAF aircraft was involved in the war at some stage or another. Mirage fighters carried out many ground strikes and shot down two Cuban/Angolan MiG-21s in aerial combat, the smaller, slower Impalas specialised in ground attacks and aerial reconnaissance, the venerable Canberras carried out bombing raids and photographic reconnaissance, the big Buccaneer strike fighters were involved in countless raids.

Backing them up — and the entire security force — were the C-130, C-160 and Dakota transports. That old and much-loved vehicle, "Louie the Min-Dae Train", was largely supplanted by "Flossie, the Min-Dae Aeroplane". The light aircraft, the Cessnas and later the Bosbokke and Kudus, did everything from lines-of-communication flying to hazardous artillery spotting, and sometimes paid the penalty for their daring.

And long after the war had ended and the last SAAF aircraft had left the border area, a few Air Force men got out of their uniforms and into civilian clothes — at the request of the United Nations — to control air traffic in the operational area.

Above
An Alouette comes in to land near sundown

Centre Right
Commandant Tinkie Jones gives his passengers the standard SAAF pre-take-off briefing: Don't smoke when you're not supposed to, don't use the toilet unless you have to because it doesn't work very well, and if you puke on the floor you have to clean it up yourself

Centre Left
A rare sight in a war where ground attacks were the rule: a kill marking on Major Chris Rankin's Mirage

Alongside Left to Right
Death of a MiG: Major Chris Rankin's gun-camera captures the classic sequence of events after he opened fire on the Cuban-piloted fighter in December of 1982

Above
Mirage F-1s on the runway. The SAAF's high-technology fighter, its approaching obsolescence at war's end was compensated for by the high calibre of its pilots

Inset Left
Part of Air Force Base Ondangwa, with Mirages and Impalas parked at the edge of the runway. At centre is the transit building through which thousands of inward- and outward-bound troops passed

Inset Right
Impala rockets churn up an objective somewhere in southern Angola

Centre Left
Impala fighters saw constant action, flying aerial reconnaissance and carrying out ground attacks, often far north of the border

Centre Right
Caught short of mobile air defences, an SADF stopgap was the "Ystervark", a 20mm gun on a modified Buffel. During 1987-1988 at least one and possibly three MiG-21s were shot down by Ystervark crews with their unsophisticated weapons

THE WAR IN THE AIR

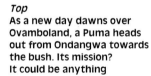

Top
As a new day dawns over Ovamboland, a Puma heads out from Ondangwa towards the bush. Its mission? It could be anything

Above
The SAAF took its small, ageing Alouette transports, turned them into gunships and flew them like Spitfires into the thick of the action

Top Right
A blast of dust, a scream of jet engines, a stink of paraffin — familiar sensations to every border troopie who flew in choppers

Centre
Gunner's-eye view from an Alouette travelling flat out at zero feet across the Ovamboland landscape. The existence of such gunships was the most closely guarded open secret of the border war

Right
Pumas, seen here on the apron at Ondangwa, were used for anything from trooping to casevacs to gunship missions

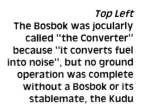

Top Left
The Bosbok was jocularly called "the Converter" because "it converts fuel into noise", but no ground operation was complete without a Bosbok or its stablemate, the Kudu

Above
The "Fighting 42". During Operation Protea, no fewer than five Bosbok pilots of 42 Squadron SAAF were decorated for gallantry

Centre Top
This Dakota was flying a party of generals and Cabinet ministers from a border base to Ondangwa in 1986 when a Plan SAM-7 missile blew off most of its tailfin. The pilot, Captain Colin Green, nursed the Dak to Ondangwa and made an almost perfect landing. The narrow escape shocked the SADF so much that it suppressed news of the incident for more than two years

Left Middle
The famous Tinkie Jones, virtuoso of the heavy transports. Behind him is a C-160 Transall

Left Below
"Flossie, the Min-Dae transporter" opens her cavernous maw to absorb a mountain of kit belonging to homeward-bound border troops

Right Top
Cactus anti-aircraft missiles. Cactuses guarded Ondangwa and other air bases throughout the border war

Right Below
Troops heading for home exhibit the old soldier's trick of sleeping anywhere, even in the juddering, draughty, ear-splittingly noisy cargo hold of a C-130

CASEVAC

The border soldier's most comforting knowledge was that even if the Army made him go cold, wet and hungry at times, it would move mountains to speed him back to hospital if he was wounded, no matter how deep inside the remote bush he might be. Usually this meant despatching a helicopter - into the thick of battle, if need be - with a medical orderly or doctor riding inside it.

In 1982 John Rubython, then chief photographer of the Cape Times, had the rare opportunity of going on such a "casevac", and this is his story, accompanied by his unique series of photographs depicting what he later called "one of the great battles of war ... the struggle to save a man's life":

I saw the war in a nameless little clearing in the northern SWA/Namibian bush last week. I saw a young man dead - and another snatched from death by SADF medics as our helicopter raced back to the base hospital at Oshakati 120km away.

Above
The casevac helicopter whines over the thick Ovamboland bush, heading for the rendezvous radioed to it earlier

Top Right
The slipstream buffets the soldiers who will secure the casevac scene from possible attack while the helicopters are on the ground. They ignore it: they have done this before, and they have no time now to think of anything except the fighting which might be awaiting them

Centre
The medic sprints over to where the wounded officer is kneeling in agony, while in the background the protective element fans out to protect the landing zone

Right
The medic tends to the seriously wounded soldier, ignoring the officer. His eyes vacant with shock, the officer does not realise that he is sitting on the body of a dead soldier

I had been called out of a press conference at an Air Force base in the operational area on Wednesday. With three other newsmen I was bundled into a camouflaged troop-carrying helicopter, its rotor blades whirling in the heated mid-morning air. Then with a scream of engines we were away, banking into a right-hand turn before heading almost due east over the tree-tops.

Riding with us were a "stick" of soldiers from the air base's reaction force. All veterans of many such trips, they crouched inside their harness of webbing, their faces expressionless, fingers curled around their assault rifles while the wind from the open doors tore at their hair and clothing.

No one spoke. There was little to say - and the racket of the engines made conversation almost impossible.

At the time we knew only that there had been a contact. Later, Brigadier "Witkop" Badenhorst of the South African Army, who is in overall command

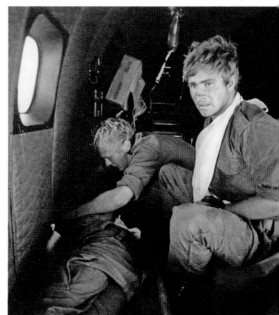

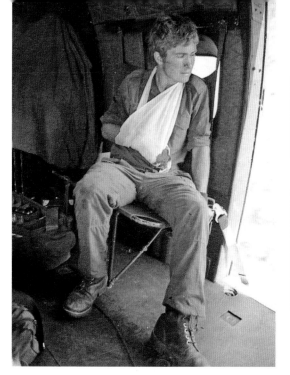

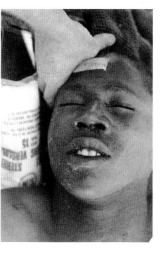

of this part of the operational area, told us that a platoon-strength patrol, consisting of black soldiers led by a white officer and three white non-commissioned officers, had been covering a 10 square kilometre area in eastern Ovamboland about 15km from the border.

On Wednesday morning, they had left their temporary base and soon afterwards crossed a bush road. As one section crossed the road they came under fire from machine-guns, 60mm mortars and AK-47 rifles from an estimated 40 Swapo lying in ambush. As the other two sections, covering the road, fired back, the insurgents withdrew, leaving a white corporal dead and the officer and three black soldiers wounded, two of them seriously.

Brigadier Badenhorst said an estimated three Swapo had been killed in the firefight and a follow-up operation was in progress.

When news of the contact reached operational headquarters, two sticks of the reaction force were sent to the scene in two helicopters. I was in one.

After 30 minutes' fast flying we came down in long grass at the scene of the contact, guided in by orange smoke from a smoke grenade. Members of the patrol lay in a circle around the landing zone, facing outwards to repel any threat to the precious helicopters. At the edge of the landing zone a group of men stood with the wounded.

As soon as our wheels touched the ground the reaction force swarmed out to reinforce the landing zone's defences. The waiting men rushed to our helicopters and loaded in the wounded. Immediately the pilots took off. Our helicopter was barely off the ground when our medical orderly began tending to one of our wounded, a black soldier in a serious condition. Using an intravenous drip and a disposable syringe, he set about stopping the bleeding from his body wound.

We flew west for 10 or 15 minutes. Midway through the journey the medic tapped me on the shoulder with a blood-stained hand and shouted: "Help me!"

I put my camera down and knelt beside him, squeezing the soldier's arm to make a vein bulge so that another intravenous needle could be put in.

I realised then that one of the great battles of war is the struggle to save a man's life.

Minutes later, we landed at a small earth-walled fort built at a short airstrip. Waiting doctors and medical orderlies lifted the soldier out. They laid him on the tarmac next to the helicopter and started working on him. The helicopter's engines had whined into silence and the only sounds were the doctor's orders to his team and their reassurances to their groaning patient.

"You'll be okay, you'll be okay," they told him, over and over.

About 20 minutes later the doctor finished his stitching. The patient was now in a stable condition, he told us. He could be flown to the hospital at Oshakati. He would go along, in case the man's condition worsened.

The two helicopters landed almost simultaneously on the helipad at Oshakati. Waiting ambulances took the wounded to the hospital near by.

Then we flew back to our base.

Footnote: At the time the border war was at its height and the report was censored for sensitive information. The helicopter was a Puma, the patrol concerned was from 101 Battalion, and border veterans will recognise the "small earth-walled fort built at a short landing-strip" as Eenhana base.

Above
Far gone from shock and loss of blood, the seriously wounded soldier probably does not even understand that the medic is steadying his head against the helicopter's vibrations

Top
Moved to the door, the officer stares out at the bushveld flashing past below the helicopter, perhaps reliving the fear and excitement of the contact — and the grief and pain which followed

Centre
At Eenhana, a waiting medical team gives the seriously wounded soldier further treatment before evacuating him to Oshakati

Left
Unnoticed by the medics tending to the seriously wounded man, three soldiers lift the dead man out of the other side of the helicopter and carry him to a waiting ambulance

THE "PEOPLE TIFFIES"

Border troops liked to refer to the doctors, nurses and orderlies of the South African Medical Service as "the people tiffies", which included "teeth tiffies" (dentists) and associated persons like "tears tiffies" (welfare officers) and "soul tiffies" (chaplains).

Behind the jokes, however, lurked the certain knowledge that if you were sick or wounded the medics would do almost anything to save your life. In operations and out, they formed a chain along which a patient passed as soon as possible after he was wounded or fell ill.

At the lowest level was the so-called "ops medic", an infantryman who had been given enough training to render the immediate aid which often spelt the difference between life and death. Above him in the chain were the SAMS orderlies and doctors who manned armoured ambulances and medical aid posts, or flew into the thick of battle in helicopters (for a graphic account of such an operation, see CASEVAC! in this section). Further back were the surgeons, either in the field or at the base hospitals.

Whatever its other shortcomings, the SADF spared no trouble or expense to save lives. In one case a C-130 transport flew to Pretoria with only one passenger in its cavernous cargo hold: a critically wounded soldier who was being sent to 1 Military Hospital at Voortrekkerhoogte for the most advanced treatment. He died en route, but not for the lack of trying.

In a famous display of cold courage in 1983, Major Cornelius Meyer de Villiers and two Citizen Force colleagues, Captain Frikkie Eloff and a Captain Reynecke, risked their lives to remove an armed and extremely sensitive rifle-grenade from the chest of a 32 Battalion soldier.

The medics' secondary role was to help out in the military "civic action" programme. To this end SAMS teams and individual members served in all parts of the operational area, providing the full range of services — general medical practitioners, anaesthetists, dentists, pharmacists, health officers, welfare officers, nurses and veterinarians. Apart from such organised services, many field units' medical officers were in the habit of holding daily clinics for the local population.

Hundreds, if not thousands, of civilians were flown to hospitals by helicopter or other aircraft. In 1982 alone 182 Ovambos — mostly victims of road accidents or landmine explosions — were evacuated like this, at a total cost of R720 000, while medics at 26 bushveld clinics treated about 180 000 civilians for everything from stomach-aches and cooking-fire burns to venereal disease, opthalmia and pre-natal complications.

Some of the medics were Permanent Force members, others national servicemen, still others Citizen Force surgeons and similar specialists taking time off from their civilian practices to lend their skills to friend, enemy and civilian alike.

Through the years the anti-conscription lobby in South Africa made sporadic attempts to prove that SAMS doctors could be forced to torture or neglect prisoners: the Surgeon-General's reply was that no doctor was allowed to serve in the SAMS if he did not subscribe to the Hippocratic Oath, and by regulation could not be ordered to carry out any act which conflicted with the oath. As a result, a wounded insurgent invariably had a better chance of survival if he was captured. It was just another of the border war's many ironies.

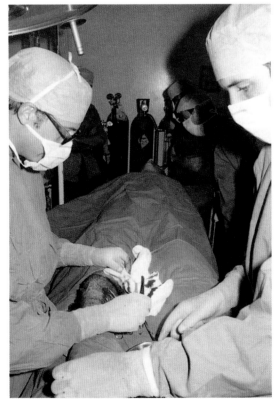

Above
An ops medic conducts an impromptu open-air "clinic" for minor ailments at Eenhana base

Centre
For the inhabitants of the operational area like this Caprivian woman, the SADF's intensive "civic action" programme brought unparalleled care and attention — medical, agricultural and otherwise

Left
Wherever the fighting troops went, the medics went too. Doctors André Heyns and Marius Pretorius deep inside Angola with Battle-Group Foxbat during Operation Savannah in 1975

Right
At the base hospital at Oshakati, surgeons prepare to operate on a soldier who was shot through the leg in a contact

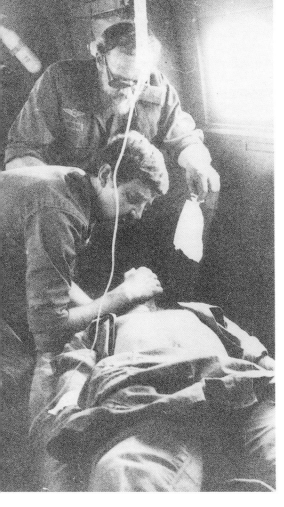

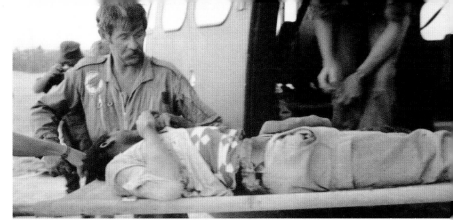

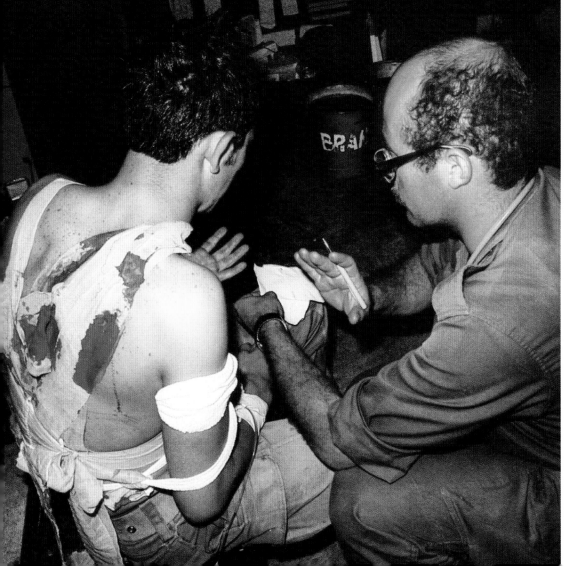

Top
A wounded insurgent is loaded into a helicopter for transport back to a base hospital. Since Plan groups had no medical back-up, being taken prisoner means he will survive

Above
Ops medics give immediate aid to a wounded soldier, preparatory to evacuating him. At left centre can be seen the standard field medical pannier. The bearded officer is famed cartoonist Len Lindeque

Top Left
Lindeque and another medic resuscitate the wounded soldier as the helicopter which has just picked him up speeds to the base hospital at Oshakati

Left
Shortly after the first battle of Cuamato in 1981 the wounded were brought into the primitive headquarters building in the town. Two men died in this attack and Al Venter, who covered the fighting, was injured the next day

TOO MUCH OF EVERYTHING

Eventually winter would turn into spring, then summer. By September it was very hot; by October even the locals kept out of the sun. Troops unfortunate enough to be involved in operations would drink almost anything as long as it was wet — water contaminated by fuel, the juice out of tins of preserved vegetables, even condensed milk.

Then, sometime in late October or early November, the rains would start falling ... and the cycle would begin again.

Top
While border troops squelched through the Ovamboland mud, their mates sweated among the arid dunes of Walvis Bay

Above
Precious water is scooped up from a reservoir made from a ground-sheet

Top Right
Swaspes trackers resort to an old trick and make water by condensation

Centre
When the heavens opened, miniature lakes covered every low-lying area

Right
Far too much moisture everywhere: the Okavango, the rain — and the sweat inside each man's non-porous raincoat

When it came to the climate, the operational area and its Angolan equivalent usually had too much of everything at any given time.

First and always there were the rains.

The short rainy season was in the last two months of the year, and the long one started in January and went on till roughly the end of April — and it is one of the war's greatest ironies that the traditional bringers of life also became the signal for death, because the course of the war was dictated to a great extent by their arrival and departure.

Near the end of the year, as the short rainy season arrived, the insurgents in their Angolan camps would begin to prepare for infiltration southwards across the border, a tiresome and dangerous business because the camps were located far from the border to protect them from lightning pre-emptive attacks and the infiltrators might have to dodge various enemies, ranging from the Unita rebels to the SADF and SWATF patrols.

If there were no pre-emptive attacks the main infiltration would start with the long rains. The guerrillas would move south to the "shallow area" just north of the border, restock from hidden caches if necessary, and start to filter over the Cutline in small groups.

Conditions would be at their most favourable, the grass tall and the bush thick, providing maximum cover; the "oshonas" or flood-plains would have become large shallow lakes, providing drinking water, while the heavy rain would slow down SADF and SWATF follow-ups, make tracking difficult and curtail air activity.

Around the end of April the rainy season would peter out and insurgent activity would die down as the Plan fighters went to ground or headed back over the border again.

For a while the weather would be balmy. Then winter would arrive. Troops who had recently spent all day in a bath of sweat would find themselves shivering through savagely cold nights. Oshonas and roads would be dry, throwing up clouds of pale dust that penetrated everywhere. Noses dried out, lips cracked, eyes went bloodshot.

But now the advantage was with the security forces. Although they eventually became adept at operating in wet-weather conditions, it is no coincidence that most external operations took place in the dry season.

Top
"Blougat" border troops soon learnt to dig rain-trenches — and "score" a few metres of plastic latrine sheeting to supplement their ground-sheets

Above
Winter brought dust — and pity the fellows at the tail-end of the convoy

Left Top to Bottom
Hard slogging along a sandy track — especially on the "middelmannetjie"

Recipe for bogging down: drive down an Angolan wet-weather track which has just been churned up by a few 10-ton artillery tractors

Come midday, jackets and jerseys will be too warm ... for a few hours

Right Top to Bottom
Come the rains, yesterday's dirt track turned into today's mud-wallow

Early border troops had a sublime faith in their Unimogs' go-anywhere ability — but sometimes even the agile "Mogs" came to grief

For airmen tired of rainy-season Ovamboland, there was always the Namib

Left
Winter in Ovamboland meant dust, cracked lips and bone-biting cold

HOME IS WHERE THE HEART IS

e it ever so humble, the old saying goes, there's no place like home. As far as the border soldier was concerned, "home" had a multitude of meanings. It could be a big, long-established place like Oshakati or Ondangwa, with barrack huts, canteens, a steakhouse and other "mod cons", or a permanent tented border base on the very edge of the Cutline, like Eenhana, or a comfortable regimental bushveld base like Buffalo in Kavango or Omega in Western Caprivi. It could also be a waterproof (more or less) shelter made out of whatever materials came to hand, such as a square of groundsheet, a length of "liberated" latrine screen and the odd bit of corrugated iron, usually lashed together with lengths of tough green "ropes utility". The requirements of the construction depended on the time of year. And finally there was the most basic home of all, a shallow trench in a suitable clump of bushes — a group of which was dignified in official despatches with the appellation of "temporary base". Whatever his circumstances, he made the most of it; so he ate and drank and slept as well as he could and enjoyed the small civilised amenities like a clean pair of socks or a letter from home. Echoing a saying which must have originated with Julius Caesar's legions, he would proclaim: "Any fool can be uncomfortable."

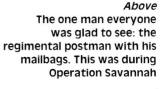

Above
The one man everyone was glad to see: the regimental postman with his mailbags. This was during Operation Savannah

Top Right
One of the several 24-hour ration-packs

Top Left
A rifleman lays aside his R4 and reads his little issue New Testament

Centre Right
A visiting cat "inspects" trenches at Eenhana

Centre Left Top
An officers' mess in Caprivi: the "tablecloth" is a purloined bedsheet

Centre Left Below
Racial segregation had no place in a contact — or in the showers

Left
Volleyball had a strong off-duty following

Opposite
Out of action, the soldier's best friend was his battered, smoke-blackened "firebucket", or canteen cup

KAVANGO BORDER-DUTY AUG?:?

DON'T DIE FOR YOUR COUNTRY, LET THE ENEMY DIE FOR IT

DUNNOT FAR 2000 KM

SAAF CITY

1. A typical border permanent base: endless rows of olive-drab tents — and a suitably fierce exhortatory sign

2. The traditional military pastime of carving helped to pass the time for many a border soldier

3. The dartboard has seen better days, but it's good enough to pass the time with

4. Airmen's humour at a border base: a fake telephone and a cheerfully depressing sign

5. Eenhana base on the border. The circular construction is an 81mm mortar position

6,7 and 8. Regular scenes, seen a thousand times each day in the operational area adjacent to Angola

9. The SAAF officers' pub near Katima Mulilo. The traffic light was ... ahem ... obtained from a street in Pretoria and put to new use: when it was green the ice-cold beer was flowing. When it turned red, however, it meant that the tap had been turned off

10. Be it ever so humble ... lots of air-conditioning, and plenty of running water — particularly if your shelter springs a leak when it's raining

11. Christmas on the border. This was Rundu, Christmas lunch 1977. Troops out in the bush had their Christmas dinner when they got back, days or weeks later

THE "PBs"

In official parlance, a locally resident civilian of any given area was known as "a member of the local population" in English and "'n lid van die plaaslike bevolking" in Afrikaans. The border soldier, regardless of what language he was speaking, sometimes referred to them as "the povo", Portuguese for "the people" (specifically civilians on the Angolan side of the border), but more often usually settled for "PBs".

In the beginning a "PB" was usually a black civilian in the operational area; eventually the term came to be jocularly applied to non-military people of all races, including workers and soldiers' dependents at the larger bases.

"PB" could imply many things. For some, like the expatriate South Africans, being a PB meant the adoption of a way of life that stole into the heart, so that when the war ended many made silent and not-so-silent vows to return after independence.

To the real PBs, the permanent residents, it meant a lifelong submersion in the changeless march of the seasons and a feeling of belonging, or the chance to prosper from the injection of money and required skills resulting from the military presence. But all too often it also meant living with the constant danger of death — by landmine or "hard" intimidation, or in crossfire — and the necessity for a balancing act in which every day could bring a new peril.

1. Caprivian fishermen with their canoes, hollowed out of tree-trunks

2. The women of South West Africa/Namibia are among the most colourful anywhere in Africa

3. An Ovahimba girl, still locked into her tribe's traditional folkway in spite of the war, Swapo and the SADF

4. An expatriate South African wife in the operational area

5. Ovambo member of the Koevoet Counter-insurgency unit

6. Beer time in Caprivi

7. Farmers near the operational area quickly evolved security systems of their own. Radio communication was essential

8. Commandant (now Major-General) and Mrs Minnaar Fourie at a cocktail party for the press in Caprivi in 1974

9. A farmer's son opens a gate for his father

10. The milk-run Dakota which daily ferried mail, freight and passengers to various parts of Ovamboland

11. Ovambo civilians, wearing the carefully blank look they often adopted towards strangers — at first, anyway

12. A farmer with his home-converted armoured bakkie. This was strictly an interim measure early on in the war

13. A young 1975-vintage Angolan refugee

THE SAVIMBI CONNECTION

If there is one term which describes Dr Jonas Savimbi better than any other, it is "survival expert". Of the major leaders who were active at the start of the war, only he and Swapo president Sam Nujoma were still active by the end of it; all the others were dead, defeated or deposed.

In Savimbi's case it meant a victory against incredible odds. His tiny 1960s-vintage band of insurgents grew into a mighty military-political movement which ended up controlling and operating in a great swathe of Angolan territory, and he became a major political figure who was accorded virtual head-of-state treatment in many foreign capitals.

He managed all this in the face of a world climate of opinion which varied from hostile to apathetic, relying on the more or less clandestine support of a few nations of which the most visible was South Africa.

His enemies portrayed him as a mere surrogate for Pretoria, which of course he was, in the sense that his operations benefited the struggle against Swapo. But Savimbi never saw the alliance as anything more than a short-term confluence of interests, and from the late 1970s onwards his dependence progressively lessened as his war effort commenced to grow.

His remarks to Fred Bridgland in 1983 best sum up his attitude: "The moral case is clear. Unita is fighting for a free and independent Angola. We are fighting the Cubans and Soviets who would deny us our nation.

"Yes, Unita receives aid from the Republic of South Africa, but it is hypocritical of the Soviets to claim that this means we somehow endorse the Pretoria government. We oppose apartheid. Fortunately, it is a dead ideology. It cannot be exported...

"Do not suppose that Zaire, Zambia, Botswana and Namibia will remain committed to the West when faced with an unopposed (Soviet) base in Angola. They will be forced to make their political accommodations with the Soviets just as most of Eastern Europe fell under Nazi political domination in 1938 without a shot being fired.

"That is why I say that Unita is the key to Angola, Angola is the key to Africa, and Africa is the key to the west.

"I am not alone in this assessment. The Soviets agree."

In the end Savimbi's war and Pretoria's became so intertwined that the one could not be separated from the other. To observers it was patently obvious that there could not be a lasting peace in the one theatre of operations if fighting continued in the other. Finally, as this book was going to press, what appeared to be serious moves towards a rapprochement finally started. So Jonas Savimbi might yet prove the vital factor in the emergence of a peaceful and independent Namibia.

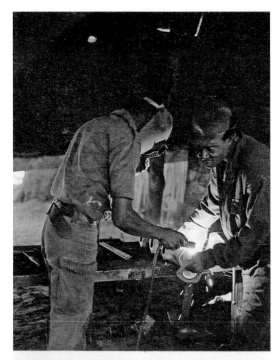

Above
A reconditioned AK-47 rifle being fitted with a new buttstock and forearm at one of Savimbi's bushveld workshops at Jamba

Top
The great survivor in the full flow of his eloquence

Centre Top
Journalists visiting Jamba were surprised to find Savimbi's mechanics carrying out fairly advanced repairs

Centre Below
A Unita officer shows off the flying helmet of a Cuban aviator shot down by Savimbi's men

Right
Savimbi's personal aircraft parked on the airstrip at Omega base in Caprivi in 1983 for repairs to one of its engines